WALTER BENJAMIN

A BIOGRAPHY

WALTER BENJAMIN

A BIOGRAPHY

Momme Brodersen

Translated by Malcolm R. Green and Ingrida Ligers
Edited by Martina Derviş

VERSO

London • New York

This book has been published with financial support from
Inter Nationes, Bonn

First published by Verso 1996
This edition © Verso 1996
Translation © Malcolm R. Green and Ingrida Ligers 1996
First published as Spinne im eigenen Netz. Walter Benjamin – Leben und
Werk
© Elster Verlag GmbH & Co. KG 1990
All rights reserved

Verso
UK: 6 Meard Street, London W1V 3HR
USA: 180 Varick Street, New York NY 10014–4606

Verso is the imprint of New Left Books

ISBN 1–85984–967–9

British Library Cataloguing in Publication Data
A catalogue record for the book is available from the British Library

Library of Congress Cataloging-in-Publication Data
A catalog record for this book is available from the Library of Congress

Typeset by Keystroke, Jacaranda Lodge, Wolverhampton
Printed by Biddles Ltd, King's Lynn and Guildford

To P. v. H.

Contents

Author's note

This book has been revised and extended for the English edition. The bibliography at the end, which has now been tailored to an English-speaking audience, has been compiled by Reinhard Markner in Berlin. This replaces my original bibliographical notes, which have partly been superseded by more recent publications.

A lengthy work of this kind is not possible without the help of a great number of friends and colleagues, as well as the staff of a great variety of institutions. It is the least that I can do here to name them all personally as an expression of my sincere thanks.

For conversations, tips, access to unpublished manuscripts, translations and so on, I would like to thank Philippe Balsiger, Manford Belmore, Kurt Bergel, Margot von Brentano, Wilhelm Emrich, Michel Espagne, Gisèle Freund, Elisabeth Freundlich, Klaus Garber, Wil van Gerwen, Albrecht Götz von Olenhusen, Jacques Grandjonc, Peter von Haselberg, M. Gräfin Hatzfeld, Wolfgang Fritz Haug, Ulrich Herrmann, Eduard Heußen, Lorenz Jäger, Chryssoula Kambas, Manfred Kleinschneider, Lotte Köhler, Werner Kraft, Wolfgang Kraushaar, Sonja Kurella, Götz Langkau, Arthur Lehning, Carl Linfert, Kurt Mautz, Claudia Mertz-Rychner, Volker Michels, Pierre Missac, Winfried Mogge, Marga Noeggerath, Ernst Osterkamp, Gerda Panofsky, Richard Plant, Sandor Radnoti, Hans Sahl, Giulio Schiavoni, Gerhard Seidel, Gary Smith, Kitty Steinschneider-Marx, Marie-Louise Steinschneider, Guy Stern, Reinhard Tgahrt, Erla Uhlig, Francesco Vergara, Marret Westphal, Bernd Witte, Erdmut Wizisla, Timm Zenner and Liselotte Zoff.

I would also like to thank the staff of the following institutions for their help in searching for and obtaining the great diversity of material and documents that were looked at while researching this book:

- Internationaal Instituut voor Sociale Geschiedenis in Amsterdam;
- Literature Archive of the Akademie der Künste, the Akademie der Wissenschaften Berlin, Document Centre,

Pädagogisches Zentrum, Staatsbibliothek Preußischer Kulturbesitz, the registry offices in Berlin I, Tiergarten and Wilmersdorf in Berlin;
- Paul-Klee-Stiftung, Kunstmuseum Berne;
- University Library in Bonn;
- Bremen municipal and university libraries;
- Börsenverein des Deutschen Buchhandels, Deutsches Exilarchiv in the Deutsche Bibliothek, Max-Horkheimer-Archiv, municipal und university libraries, and the publishers Suhrkamp in Frankfurt am Main;
- Albert Ludwig University in Freiburg im Breisgau;
- the publishers Rowohlt in Reinbek;
- Jewish National and University Library in Jerusalem;
- Bundesarchiv in Coblenz;
- the publishers Gustav Kiepenheuer in Leipzig;
- Warburg Institute in London;
- Josef Stocker's bookstore in Lucerne;
- Deutsches Literaturarchiv in Marbach am Neckar;
- Bayerische Staatsbibliothek, Ludwig-Maximilians Universität, Stadtbibliothek, and the publishers R. Piper in Munich;
- Institut für Publizistik in Münster;
- Leo Baeck Institute in New York;
- Bibliothèque Nationale in Paris;
- University of Pittsburgh Libraries in Pittsburgh;
- Städtische Kunsthalle in Recklinghausen;
- Gemeinde-Archiv in Schermbeck;
- Institut für Auslandsbeziehungen in Stuttgart;
- University Library in Tübingen;
- Library of Congress in Washington;
- Stadt- und Landesbibliothek in Wien;
- the Archiv der deutschen Jugendbewegung, Burg Ludwigstein, in Witzenhausen.

By contrast, my work received no support whatsoever from the trustees of the Benjamin estate in Frankfurt. My numerous requests for information and access to certain documents were all flatly refused, and the door was closed in my face when I attempted to enter the hallowed sanctuary of the Adorno archive.

Momme Brodersen

Editor's note

For this first English-language edition, Momme Brodersen's original book has, with his collaboration, been expanded to include information that may be helpful to non-German readers, examination of relevant material that has come to light since its first publication, and more extended extracts from Walter Benjamin's own writings. Existing English translations of some material in the text, referenced in the footnotes, have been revised where necessary.

Reinhard Markner has given expert and invaluable assistance with almost every stage of this work. Translation of some additional texts by Benjamin and others were provided by Dafydd R. Roberts, Pierre Imhof and Martin Chalmers. The book's commissioning editor, Malcolm Imrie, gave advice and practical help throughout.

I would also like to thank a number of others for their assistance with research: Alexandra Grüebler, Benedikt Hüttel, Chiara Levrini and Michael Neumann. Much of the keyboarding of revisions was skilfully done by Sandra von Haselberg. We discovered that the 'P. v. H.' to whom the book is dedicated is her grandfather, Benjamin's contemporary, Peter von Haselberg.

Martina Derviş
August 1996

Chronology

1892	Born on 15 July in Berlin
1905/06	Attends the Haubinda boarding school; pupil of Gustav Wyneken
1910	First publications
1912	School finals; commencement of university studies at Freiburg im Breisgau; travels to Italy; first contact with Zionism; continuation of studies in Berlin
1913	Second and last semesters at Freiburg University; first Paris trip; publications in the magazine *Der Anfang*; participation in the First Free German Youth Congress; studies at Berlin (until summer semester 1915)
1914	Outbreak of the First World War; Benjamin's friend Fritz Heinle commits suicide
1915	Break with Wyneken; becomes acquainted with Gerhard (later Gershom) Scholem and Werner Kraft; 'The Life of Students'; student in Munich; friendship with Felix Noeggerath, Rainer Maria Rilke and Erich Gutkind
1917	Marriage with Dora Sophie Kellner; break with his friend Herbert Blumenthal; continuation of his studies at Berne
1918	Birth of his son Stefan Rafael
1919	Receipt of his doctorate under Richard Herbertz for his thesis on the 'Concept of Art Criticism in German Romanticism'
1920	Return to Berlin
1921	Work on his periodical *Angelus Novus*, which was never to be produced
1922	Friendship with Gottfried Salomon-Delatour

1923	Friendship with Siegfried Kracauer and Theodor Wiesengrund (Adorno); translation of Charles Baudelaire's *Tableaux parisiens*
1924	Appearance of the first section of his essay 'Goethe's Elective Affinities' in Hugo von Hofmannsthal's journal *Neue Deutsche Beiträge* (the second part appears in January 1925); several-month stay on Capri; first meeting with Asja Lacis; beginning of his interest in Marxism; death of Florens Christian Rang
1925	Withdrawal of his application for *Habilitation* at the University of Frankfurt am Main; first publication in the *Frankfurter Zeitung* as well as the *Literarische Welt*; journey to Spain, Italy and Lithuania
1925/26	Several-month stay in Moscow
1927	Radio debut with a talk entitled 'Young Russian Poets'; six-month stay in Paris; begins work on the 'Arcades' project; appearance of the first volume of Proust in the translation by Benjamin and Franz Hessel (*A l'ombre des jeunes filles en fleurs*); first experiments with drugs
1928	Publication of *One-Way Street* and *The Origin of German Tragic Drama* (Ernst Rowohlt, Berlin)
1929	Start of regular work with the broadcasting companies Südwestdeutscher Rundfunk in Frankfurt am Main, and Funkstunde in Berlin; death of Hofmannsthal; becomes acquainted with Bertolt Brecht
1930	Divorce; journey to Norway; publication of the second Proust translation by Benjamin and Hessel (*Le côté de Guermantes*)
1930/1	'The Politicization of Intelligence', 'The Crisis of the Novel', 'Theories of German Fascism' and 'Left-Wing Melancholy': all printed in *Die Gesellschaft*
1932	First stay on Ibiza; work on 'A Berlin Chronicle' and 'Berlin Childhood around 1900'; gives last radio talks for the Funkstunde in Berlin; Adorno

holds a seminar in Frankfurt on *The Origin of German Tragic Drama*

1933   Gives last talks for the Südwestdeutscher Rundfunk; leaves Germany; second and last stay on Ibiza; illness (malaria); numerous publications in the *Vossische Zeitung*; beginning of exile in Paris

1934   First publication in the *Zeitschrift für Sozialforschung* ('On the Current Social Situation of the French Writer'); visit to Brecht in Denmark; 'Franz Kafka. An Appraisal' published in the *Jüdische Rundschau*

1934/5   Visit to his ex-wife, Dora Sophie Kellner, in San Remo

1935   Last publication in the *Frankfurter Zeitung*

1936   Appearance of 'The Work of Art in the Age of Mechanical Reproduction' in a French translation; *German Men* published by Vita Nova Verlag, Lucerne; the Moscow magazine *Das Wort* publishes his first 'Paris Letter'

1937   'Eduard Fuchs, the Historian and Collector'; Paris literary correspondent for the *Zeitschrift für Sozialforschung*

1938   Last visit to Brecht

1939   Expatriation; 'Some Motifs in Baudelaire'; outbreak of the Second World War and temporary internment in a camp near Nevers

1940   Accepted into the Exile PEN Club; last publications during his life in the periodical edited by Adrienne Monnier, *La Gazette des amis des livres*; writes his theses 'On the Concept of History'; flight to Lourdes; flight across the border from France to Spain; suicide

1942   Posthumous publication of 'On the Concept of History' in the volume *Walter Benjamin zum Gedächtnis*, published by the Institute for Social Research

1947   First posthumous publication in France

1949	First posthumous publication of major essays in East and West Germany
1950	'Berlin Childhood around 1900' published by Suhrkamp
1955	Publication of Benjamin's *Schriften* [Writings] in two volumes
1960	'The Work of Art in the Epoch of Mechanical Reproduction', first translation of a major essay into English
1968	During a student occupation, the Institute for German Studies at the University of Frankfurt is renamed temporarily the 'Walter-Benjamin-Institut'
1969	Appearance of the first of fifteen volumes in the Japanese edition of Benjamin's writings
1972	Beginning of the complete edition of Benjamin's writings in German (*Gesammelte Schriften*). Completed in 1989
1982	Beginning of the complete edition in Italian
1994	Inauguration of Dani Karavan's Portbou monument, 'Passages'.

One of the traditions of Berlin is to be oblivious to its own past.[1]

Walter Benjamin was born on 15 July 1892 in Berlin, at a time – halfway between the founding of the Empire and the First World War – when the capital of the new German Empire was developing into a metropolis whose appearance scarcely recalled the dignified propriety and austere beauty of the old seat of the Prussian kings. In the closing years of the nineteenth century, economic expansion and technical innovation were transforming virtually every major city in Europe, physically and socially. In Berlin these changes were so radical and came at such breathtaking speed that residents, like visitors, hardly knew whether they were coming or going.

A Berlin childhood and youth around 1900

In the decades around 1900 the city rose new from the ground, a city on such a scale and of such diversity that its history and its past were almost completely obliterated. The destruction of historical Berlin was visible in the tremendously wide and virtually identical streets that cleared broad corridors through the fabric of the city.[2] With these thoroughfares based on Haussmann's Parisian avenues and boulevards, the new created a space for itself and gradually buried the old beneath. Just how bad an effect this 'infiltration' had on Berlin's appearance could be seen in the juxtapositions and jarring mixtures of genuine and fantastical architectural styles. Neo-Gothic and German Baroque, Florentine Renaissance and the Classicism of Frederick the Great, and even Moorish elements, held stylistic orgies on the façades along the splendid new boulevards, the whole being crowned by Berlin's characteristic brand of pomp that gave all too obtrusive testimony to the spirit of the new time.

Contemporaries regarded Berlin as the most modern metropolis of its day, and in many respects they were correct. Where only yesterday the streets had been dominated by horse-drawn vehicles, they now bore witness to the latest technical revolutions. In place of the trundling spoked wheels that created that inimitable grating sound of sand between steel and stone, so that travellers felt every metre that they drove in the innermost

Berlin, a city at the height of its times

'The breakneck speed at which the city is being remodelled allows neither inhabitants nor visitors enough time to catch their breath.'[1] (Alexanderplatz, Berlin)

fibres of their bodies, the pace of life was now set by new, noisy and pestilential means of transport: the steaming, snarling monsters of the Ringbahn and Stadtbahn; then the electric trams, whose poles and overhead conductors spread a lattice of wires and iron over the city; and finally the car whose triumphant progress could not be halted by even the most wishful nostalgia for the old days of magnificent horses and steadfast cabbies immortalized in Hans Fallada's novel *Der eiserne Gustav*. Calm and contemplation – needed to register and digest these changes – had no more place in a world in which nothing and no one looked back, and everything pointed to the future.[3] In the centre of Alexanderplatz there once had been a green hillock with bushes and benches that had invited the passer-by to dally. But redevelopment put an end even to this oasis of peace and tranquility in the heart of the city. Encircled and 'imprisoned' by the emporia of the new business world, this little park had become an obstacle to the scurrying hordes of customers – and so the hillock was levelled. (At the turn of the century its place was taken by the much ridiculed figure of a newly invented goddess of Berlin: Berolina, a monumental beauty devised by Emil Hundrieser.)

In another respect the modern age was anything but a newcomer to this city, whose population had more than doubled in the two decades between 1871 and 1892 and was now about to pass the two million mark (which it reached in 1905). Berlin was already honeycombed by the notorious tenement blocks into which the majority of the population – primarily the office and factory workers who by now represented more than half of the city's inhabitants – were penned. Here, in a world of misery hidden in the dwellings surrounding the endless courtyards, the capital demonstrated its less dazzling, if equally modern side. Here the entire 'egotism, short-sightedness and arrogance'[4] of the times was palpably present.

As an eyewitness to the almost eruptive development and reshaping of Berlin, Benjamin was truly destined to analyse his relationship to his home city. And he did not shirk the task. What this city meant to him, the experiences he had in it and the whole extent to which they coloured the way he lived and thought, would be captured in a large number and variety of his writings: in early and later essays, in finished texts and fragments (the 'Arcades' project), in aphorisms ('One-Way Street'),[5] in reports ('Paris Diary'),[6] in critiques and reviews ('Die Wiederkehr des Flaneurs' ['The Return of the Flâneur]),[7] in his townscapes[8] (it is no coincidence that Benjamin opened his portrait of Moscow with the words: 'More quickly than [the

'The hiddenmost aspect of the cities: this historical object of the new metropolis, with its uniform streets and interminable rows of houses, has realized the architectural dream of the ancients: the labyrinth.'[2] (Berlin tenement blocks, circa 1890: 'Looking from outside down the perspective of the courtyards is like peering down a tunnel.'[3])

Russian capital] itself, one gets to know Berlin through Moscow')[9] – but above all in his reminiscences of his childhood and youth in turn-of-the-century Berlin. He began them in his late thirties, and they have come down to us in the various versions of *Berliner Chronik* [A Berlin Chronicle] and *Berliner Kindheit um Neunzehnhundert* [Berlin Childhood around 1900].[10] His life's work, to use a term that somewhat mis-leadingly suggests the idea of an unbroken continuity, is basic-ally a constant reflection on his own city origins. It amounts to a meditation on the experience of the individual's altering needs and possibilities within the labyrinth of constantly and rapidly changing impressions, and on whether he can still perceive or grasp his historical and social environment in some sort of context, or indeed make any kind of picture of it. In a nutshell: how to cope, how to find one's way around.

Dates in the city's political history (or in his own biography) play a very minor part in these reminiscences of his Berlin days, although they are not completely absent. 'A year without Sedan Day'[11] – without the annual military parades to celebrate the victory in the Franco-German war of 1870/71 – would have been quite inconceivable for a child of the Wilhelmine era. And naturally the outbreak of the First World War just as surely left

Pharus map of Berlin.

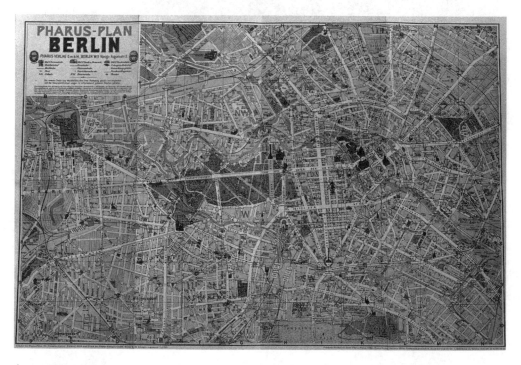

its mark on Benjamin's life. But apart from these, the thread that runs through Benjamin's retrospective observations is not the chronology of world political events, or even of his personal experiences. Only in the early drafts were they intended as 'A Berlin Chronicle' being later revised to form a 'Berlin Childhood around 1900' in which years, months and days lead a somewhat shadowy existence. But it is precisely in this that these observations reflect an experience that is intimately linked with this city. Their modernity, their 'eternal nowness', as it was finally referred to in the 'Arcades' project, simply escapes the '"historical" approach'.[12] Thus the images that Benjamin recalls from the first two decades of his life are not structured through numbers or similar abstractions. Rather they are connected to places and things – to streets, railway stations and squares, rooms and flats, to everyday objects – which make his depiction far more vivid. Hence the individual texts included in 'Berlin Childhood around 1900' bear such titles as 'Zoological Gardens', 'Victory Column', 'Corner of Steglitzer and Genthiner Straße', 'Blumeshof 12', 'Telephone', 'The Stocking' and 'Needlework Box'. This is certainly not the stuff of normal memoirs. This is a particular kind of recollection, in the original sense of the German word *Erinnerung**: observations of the interior – of one's own self and its surroundings, of the city as world and landscape, of time as space. The accounts could be termed a biography of society, or, better still, the topography of a metropolis as a world of life and experience, in which even the most out-of-the-way corner is illuminated. And by giving an unspectacular yet faithful account of these monuments of his childhood, they topple the lying tales in the school history books from their thrones. But anyone who hopes to gain a comprehensive picture of the appearance and life of the city on the Spree has expectations of the wrong book. The finger that traces the stations of this childhood on the Pharus Map of Berlin will scarcely stray to the north, south or east of the city, where the huge industrial plants were situated and the smoke from their chimneys coated the surrounding districts with a grey residue that matched their architecture all too well. When it does not actually leave the boundaries of the city, it circles constantly within the bounds of the (at first) old, then later the new, west side of Berlin.

---

* Translators' note: The German word *Erinnerung* can be construed as 'retrieval from within'.

Berlin's move to the west

Benjamin's birthplace at Magdeburger Platz 4 was in the 'old' west of Berlin, a district inhabited by the genteel and well-to-do. Opposite stood the recently built market hall from whose interior the young child soon gained a first vivid impression of the times into which he had been born: 'Behind us lay the forecourt, with its dangerous, heavy swing doors on their whip-lash springs, and we had now set foot on the flagstones, slippery with fish water or swill, on which you could so easily slip on carrots or lettuce leaves.'[13] These treacherous slopes to the new world, as they are captured by these allegoric reminiscences of a place from his childhood, were accompanied by anonymity and estrangement: the stalls inside the market hall were separated from one another by wire mesh, and each was marked with a mere number (something quite unusual at the time); the visitors and shoppers formed a slowly flowing 'stream of silent customers'.[14]

'Behind us lay the forecourt, with its dangerous, heavy swing doors on their whiplash springs, and we had now set foot on the flagstones, slippery with fish water or swill, on which you could so easily slip on carrots or lettuce leaves.'[4] (Berlin market in the 1920s, possibly the one in Magdeburger Platz)

Towards the end of the nineteenth century, Berlin began its 'move to the west'. The cramped city centre was no longer able to accommodate the rapidly expanding business world. Increasing numbers of shops and firms moved away. The entertainment and shopping district around Friedrichstraße and Leipziger Straße extended into Potsdamer Straße. From there the showy shops, cafés and bars extended into Bülow- and Kleiststraße and on to Tauentzienstraße, then finally to meet

the glittering Kurfürstendamm which had just been built. The physiognomy of the old western Berlin – formerly an upper middle-class reserve – gradually changed, losing in the process its aura of seemingly indestructible romance. Residential buildings gave way to offices, and from now on the rhythm of life was determined by shoppers, office workers and officials.

Those who could afford it fled this cold, noisy world of commerce which 'had no longer anything habitable or hospitable' about it, 'emanating forlornness between the shopfronts and even danger at the crossings'.[15] The Benjamin family also moved

'The "old West" had also lost that certain something, as one says of beauties who have gone out of fashion. It was not done to live in the old West. By the turn of the century, well-to-do families were moving to the Kurfürstendamm district and later further on to Westend or to Dahlem, assuming they had not managed to acquire a villa in the Grunewald.'[5] (Present day view of the Benjamins' house in Carmerstraße)

home several times at short intervals, and this was not only the result of their growing demand for domestic comfort. In the mid 1890s they were already living in Kurfürstenstraße, near Magdeburger Platz, and a few years later in Nettelbeckstraße. They then moved further west to Carmerstraße, which was already outside the city boundaries in Charlottenburg. With this move they had crossed, as it were, the demarcation line between the past and the present, swapped the city's old historic part for the new west of Berlin. Beyond this was nothing but forest, the vast expanse of the Grunewald. Eventually in 1912, Benjamin's father bought a 'castle-like'[16] villa on the edge of the old royal hunting grounds, in Delbrückstraße, in those days unimaginably remote. The family inhabited the more stylish first floor of the villa – the *bel étage* complete with conservatory – and rented out

7

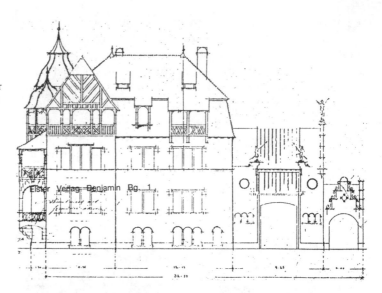

Architect's plan of the Benjamins' villa. The remoteness of Delbrückstraße is underlined by the fact that a special omnibus for bank staff ran for a while between Grunewald and the Berlin stock exchange: 'Speedy Moses', as it was termed in the Berlin vernacular.

the rest. (As it happens, the house was almost next door to that of Maximilian Harden,[17] the publisher of the journal *Die Zukunft*, who as a close supporter of the toppled Bismarck became one of the greatest opponents of Wilhelm II.) If Werner Hegemann's book (*Das steinerne Berlin*, 1930) is to be believed, the merchant Emil Benjamin obtained his villa in the country-side virtually for free. By moving to Charlottenburg, which lay outside the municipal boundaries of Berlin, he was only required to pay a fraction of the taxes demanded of those who lived in the city. The differences in the taxation of his income must have been enormous. As the 'possessor of a certain wealth', he saved so much money within so short a time that it was no great feat to buy 'a villa worth several hundred thousand marks':[18] tax evasion of a totally legal kind – but immoral in wishing to enjoy the benefits of the city which lay before the front door without wishing to carry any of its burdens.

A silver spoon

At the turn of the century the Grunewald was both home and Eldorado for land speculators. 'Just about everyone' speculated here, a contemporary observer remarked. Businessmen, factory owners, engineers, architects, artisans, doctors, artists, academics and civil servants of 'different ranks', and even a few clergymen did not disdain to buy land so as 'in an effective manner to lighten their cares for the future'.[19] Not that these people ever saw themselves as 'speculators'. Such an insult, in their view, could only come from the petty-minded, or by those who had failed to establish themselves. And indeed their transactions rarely involved much risk. So when they did not insist on using 'proper' professional designations (Benjamin's father referred to himself as a merchant for the whole of his life), they were rentiers – the usual term at that time for those who lived on the proceeds of their investments. The term also had the advantage – protagonists of German literature, from Goethe's *Elective Affinities* to Fontane's *Effi Briest*, provide sufficient evidence of this – of having a quite positive ring to it. People who not only placed their money in government stocks, but also in shares, land, options and the like, were seen as truly progressive. This attitude still coloured Benjamin's portrait of his father. For all his distance from him – the result of a tension in their relationship that developed very early on – Benjamin wrote in his recollections: 'My father possessed at base, along with a number of inhibitions stemming not only from his decency but also from a certain civic worthiness, the entrepreneurial nature of a big businessman'.[20]

After an apprenticeship as a bank clerk – one would now say – Emil Benjamin Benjamin[21] (1856–1926) left his home town of Cologne while still a young man to spend several years in Paris. Towards the end of the 1880s he then moved to Berlin where he met Pauline Elise Schoenflies, thirteen years his junior, whom he married in 1891. They had three children: Walter, Georg (1895–1942) and Dora (1901–1946).

While a partner in Lepke's in Kochstraße, a flourishing firm of auctioneers dealing in art and antiques, Emil Benjamin still had a 'proper' profession: that of auctioneer. His son, however, knew him as such only through early childhood imagination: what impressed him most on looking at the gavel that lay on the writing desk was 'to imagine the gavel blows with which [his] father accompanied the auction'.[22] When Emil Benjamin's interest in the firm was bought out by the other shareholders, 'he concerned himself increasingly with speculative investments of his capital'. He bought shares in numerous firms and consortia, including a medical suppliers, a building firm and the 'Central Wine Distributors', as well as the 'Ice Palace' skating rink built in 1910.[23]

His family saw Emil Benjamin 'as a particularly nice and sociable person'[24] whose 'outward manner' was 'always courteous and pliable', only occasionally, especially in business and trade, demonstrating the 'bearing and decisiveness' that must have 'corresponded to his sometimes great wealth'.[25] Outwardly, he seems to have fitted this picture to the full, at least so far as

Marriage certificate of Emil Benjamin and Pauline Elise Schoenflies.

Advertisement for the Berlin Ice Palace skating rink.

one can tell from contemporary photographs. Of average
height, with a well-groomed appearance and a slight tendency to
corpulence, his entire bearing reveals a certain self-composure
and bourgeois distinction that is further underlined by his
facial features: from his high forehead suggesting intelligence,
his serious yet melancholy eyes, the hint of mockery about
his lips and his huge moustache. Although this moustache was
a concession to contemporary taste, it does in fact express a touch
of independence and unstudied assurance, for it had no great

10

Emil Benjamin and family (his wife and his two sons, Walter and Georg).

similarity to the 'Wilhelm II' which the court hairdressers had in those days begun to promote – a moustache that sprouted upwards at right angles conveying no more than a pushy 'I'm really somebody' or 'I've made it'. But it was not these traits that were to remain in his son's memory. Clearer in his mind was his father's intolerable inclination to submit almost every decision in daily life to the logic of trade and business. It reached the point that even the 'family's amusements' were brought 'into the harmony with his business enterprises that he had been able to establish for all its other needs'. He may have been unaware of just how far this led him to intervene in the lives of other family members, especially as his wife had a disposition that matched his own. Through her the children discovered little more of

Contemporary advertisement for court hairdresser Haby's special tonic. You, too, can have an upright moustache just like the Kaiser's.

11

'I grew totally perplexed when people demanded that I should look like myself. This was how it was at the photographer's. Wherever I looked, I was surrounded by canvas screens, cushions, dados, which hungered for my image as the shades of Hades lusted after the blood of the sacrificial beast. Finally, a crudely daubed backdrop of the Alps was brought for me. I stand there, bare-headed, with a torturous smile on my lips, my right hand clasping a walking stick.'[6]
(Benjamin around 1900)

their home town, this melting-pot of new and unsuspected impressions and experiences, than the 'caverns of commodities' into which they were dragged to be forced into new suits, to stand there with their 'hands peeping from the sleeves like dirty price tags'.[26]

Pauline Elise Schoenflies (1869–1930) must have been a very resolute woman, practical in thought and deed, for whom everything in life clearly had its own obvious, incontestable order. Her husband could not have been the only one who did 'not always find life easy' with her[27] – her children must have been even more aware of her determination which they were scarcely able to resist unless through protests which generally met with swift punishment. It is not surprising then that in Benjamin's autobiographical writings, accounts of dissent between him and his mother outweigh the moments of tenderness. Later he was to hold her responsible for all kinds of personal inadequacies: for his (supposed) unworldliness as well as his cluelessness about everyday matters. The claim that he was still unable 'to make a cup of coffee' at the age of 40 may well be an exaggeration, but makes it clear what it was that he was rebelling against: a world in which all thought and action, all behaviour and every kind of support were measured solely in terms of the needs of practical life. This was also the reason for Benjamin's 'dreamy recalcitrance' on shopping trips with his mother to the city centre, for 'the pedantic care' with which he 'always kept half a step behind her'.[28]

His family's 'flight' ever further west meant that the young Benjamin scarcely came into contact with other social worlds. There were no 'street kids' in his neighbourhood, and when he did encounter them elsewhere an ever-present nanny knew how to prevent these undesirable contacts that were out of keeping with his station. That was the negative side of the sheltered surroundings in which he grew up. He spent his childhood as 'a prisoner of the old and new west', as he wrote in his reminiscences, and the remark points clearly to a poverty of experience which seemed to him to be the characteristic feature of his environment and an unmistakable blemish on his upbringing. 'My clan', he continued, 'lived in these two districts with an attitude that combined doggedness and self-satisfaction, making them into a ghetto, which it regarded as its fief. I remained shut off in this wealthy district without knowing anything else.'[29] Doubtless Benjamin gave a somewhat selective description of his situation so as to emphasize the point. No one could have seriously prevented him from making up for his shortage of experience off his own bat – by going to the next bus or tram stop, for instance, and setting out on an expedition to the north, south or east of the city. (The memoirs of other former inhabitants of Berlin who grew up in similar milieux are full of descriptions of the tricks they used in their younger years to escape from their surroundings.)[30] And naturally the nanny was simply fulfilling her obligations by keeping him from 'bad company'. That was a normal part of child-rearing among the better-off, for they thought it important to prepare their children for life in 'higher circles'. And to do this it was also essential to make them aware, from an early age, and over and over again, of the fact that they belonged to the upper echelons of society. The 40-year-old Benjamin could scarcely have forgotten any of this. But at that age he found little consolation in the mere recollection of the conveniences and advantages that might earlier have made up for his being prevented from doing or learning about this or that. By the time he wrote his reminiscences, such splendours were long gone.

Apart from the large domestic staff, which ranged from the lowly kitchen maids to the 'French governess',[31] another taken-for-granted feature of the boy's day-to-day life were the frequent lengthy journeys with the whole family: to the North Sea and the Baltic, to the high peaks of the Riesengebirge between Bohemia and Silesia, to Freudenstadt in the Black Forest, and to Switzerland. Holiday homes not far from Berlin (first in Babelsberg, then in Potsdam) and pre-school private tuition were just as much the visible signs of an economically secure, indeed completely carefree existence as the wholly material trappings of immense wealth which the child occasionally saw at the soirées held by his parents: when his mother put on her jewellery, whose centre-piece was a collection of dazzling gems that sparkled 'in many hues – green, blue, yellow, pink, purple' – and which seemed to the child to be so large and heavy 'that one wouldn't be able to wear it on one's breast'; or when on special occasions the household's gold and silver treasures that were normally stored safely away, the fine china and splendid crystal glassware, the 'champagne glasses spangled with filigree' were brought out, and all the valuable 'implements' for lobsters and oysters, for sherry and port – that 'honoured' (?!) him – passed through his hands too while he laid the table.[32] Presumably for Benjamin those 'high trumps' of 'ancestry' which his mother was never tired of pointing out were far more tangible here than in all her tales of the 'career' of this or that ancestor, his 'grandfather's maxims' or whatever else she was able to tell him of his forebears[33] with the intention of making him precociously aware of his special position in society. At that time he would not have questioned more of this world of visible material possession than its subjectively constricting and contradictory aspects, which he had ample opportunity to experience in his 'ghetto'.

Walter Bendix Schoenflies[34] Benjamin: the full name, of which its bearer made such a secret throughout his life,[35] leads directly to the history of what he himself called the 'clan'. In keeping with best tradition, the name referred to both of his parental families. Bendix went back to his paternal grandfather Bendix Benjamin (1818–85), who was born in Schermbeck in Westphalia, while Schoenflies came from his mother's family, whose forebears and relatives came largely from Bad Schönfließ in the New Mark, the present-day Trzcińsko Zdrój in Poland. The Benjamins and Schoenflieses did not, then, belong to the 'natives'[36] of the town, but were newcomers. (That applied, incidentally, to the vast majority of 'Berliners' at the time.) They were attracted to the capital primarily by the promise of the economic boom in the up-and-coming metropolis. In some respects this is quite understandable, for they were all business-men and merchants, bankers and factory owners – people who had a strong business sense and only showed a secondary interest in other things, such as the arts. This point in common would have smoothed over all the differences between the two families which their differing geographical origins, for instance, would have produced. It was left to their sons (and daughters?) to perceive, in pursuing their own interests, the contradictions in the unifying aspects of respectable bourgeois life – the clay-footed underpinnings of their circumstances and the ques-tionability of their lifestyle. The result was that they tried to distance themselves from all that they felt to be representative of their parental homes and which impeded their personal development.

If one searches Benjamin's family tree for relatives who injected a dash of *esprit* into the world of commerce and calcula-tion, one comes across on the paternal side the name of Heinrich Heine. Benjamin's grandmother Brunella, née Mayer (1827–1919), Bendix Benjamin's wife, was related to him at some (not very great) distance. According to the family saga, which even the grandson enjoyed relating, the great poet had lived long enough to rock her on his knees. But that exhausted Benjamin's 'relationship' to his illustrious predecessor. Throughout his life he felt little attachment to the man's writing. He only knew

Heine's works superficially,[37] and of the little he read only his political material was 'at all assimilable', but not his 'poetic material'.[38] Perhaps it was simply because Benjamin's grandmother was a less than ideal person to mediate the world of this combative writer, whose biography, for all its literary merits, was flawed in the eyes of orthodox Jews by his baptism. And in her heart of hearts, Brunella Mayer must have been a rather conservative woman who was still largely attached to the old traditions. She was apparently the last guardian of kosher customs and mores in a family that, in Walter Benjamin's day, was already more or less assimilated, especially on the Schoenflies side. In her home, 'the Jewish festivals and Friday evenings' continued to be observed and 'celebrated' accordingly.[39] She only receives a passing mention in Benjamin's reminiscences: as the already elderly mother of his father who lived across the road from his undoubtedly preferred maternal grandmother, so that this bit of the old western part of Berlin became for him 'an elysium, a shady realm of the immortal yet departed grandmothers'.[40]

'Like a considerable number of Jews of our generation before Hitler, we [Scholem and Benjamin] did not feel close to Heinrich Heine, and I cannot remember ever discussing Heine's writings with him [Benjamin].'[7] (Heinrich Heine, in a portrait by Moritz Oppenheim, 1831)

A much larger role in his personal and intellectual development must have been played by Brunella Mayer's daughter, his father's only sister Friederike (1854–1916), a Joseephi by marriage. She was the complete antithesis to Benjamin's father, and had a broad range of interests as well as contacts in the world of science, art and literature. Her closer friends and acquaintances included Lily Braun, Else Lasker-Schüler and Doris Davidsohn (the mother of the expressionist poet Jakob van Hoddis). As a former pupil of Jules Crépieux-Jamin, whom Benjamin was also to meet personally,[41] she initiated him early into the mysteries of graphology.[42] (Her nephew was able to make use of his knowledge, at least for a while: in the 1920s he wrote graphological reports[43] in order to top up his household resources, and he also instructed young girls from Grunewald in the subject for '30 marks an item').[44] Friederike Joseephi committed suicide in 1916 during a fit of depression. Until her death, she clearly maintained an intimate relationship with her nephew, which had developed during the summer vacations her family spent with her sister-in-law's family in Schreiberhau, Silesia.[45] She always acted as the mediator in the frequent arguments between Emil Benjamin and his son.

'There was no bell that gave a friendlier ring. Beyond the threshold of this flat I was even more safe and secure than at my parents. It was incidentally not called Blumes-Hof, but Blume-zof'.[46] The tender affection apparent in these lines was

15

'In Muri he [Benjamin] told of a dream he had had at Seehaupt in the spring of 1916, three days before the suicide of his favorite aunt, Friderike Joseephy [sic]. He said this dream had greatly excited him, and he had spent hours in a futile quest to interpret it. "I was lying in a bed, my aunt and another person also lay there, but we did not mingle. People walking by outside were looking in through a window." He said he did not realize until later that this had been a symbolic announcement of his aunt's death. I do not recall whether he explicitly stated that one of the persons who looked in through the window was his aunt herself; that would have made his story plausible.'[8] (Friederike Joseephi)

directed to his maternal grandmother, Hedwig Schoenflies, née Hirschfeld (1844–1908). During the part of his childhood that he could recall, she was already widowed. Her husband, Georg Schoenflies (1841–94), three years older and a well-to-do tobacco and cigarette manufacturer born in Schwerin an der Warthe, died in 1894. Her obviously immense wealth allowed her a standard of living that may well have surpassed that of her daughter's family. She took 'long sea voyages or even trips into the desert organized by "Stangen's Travel Agency"' which said as much about her circumstances as her 'Manorially Furnished Ten-Room Apartment' (as portrayed by her grandson in *One-Way Street*) in whose setting 'misery' definitely had 'no place'. Benjamin felt that he had inherited her love of giving presents, a gift that became obvious to all on Christmas Eve, when every branch of the family gathered together to celebrate at Blumeshof. Only then did it become apparent 'why in fact [so many] rooms had been constructed': in order to accommodate the 'long tables' which 'were needed for present-giving', and which were 'heavily laden on account of the large number of recipients'. The grandmother also showed her generosity to her grandson on a more everyday level, such as when she took his theatre visits 'under her wing', for instance, which made the occasion an incomparably great event, especially given the select locations (either Schinkel's Playhouse, or Knobelsdorff's Royal Prussian State Opera), the 'dazzling programme' and the 'imposing circle seats' from which they took in the performances.[47] Such details already indicate that the Schoenflies branch of the family far more visibly represented the realms of the spirit and of enlightened thought. This was one of the reasons why Benjamin would on the whole feel closer to his mother's side of the family where he probably received the stimulation and confirmation of his own interests and inclinations that he needed.

The bourgeois interior of the 1860s to the 1890s, 'with its gigantic sideboards distended with carvings, the sunless corners' and the 'soulless luxuriance of the furnishings',[9] as Benjamin came to know it in his grandmother's house.

Her brother, Gustav Hirschfeld (1847–95), had been one of the first in the family to pursue an academic career. After converting to Christianity (a price that Jews almost always had

17

to pay at that time if they did not wish to remain unwaged *Privatdozenten*)*, he became professor of classical archaeology at Königsberg. In particular he made his name through his excavations at Olympia during the middle and late 1870s.[48] Arthur Moritz Schoenflies (1853–1928), the younger brother of Benjamin's grandfather Georg, also taught at the university as a professor of mathematics. He later was among the founder members of Frankfurt University, and was even its rector in 1920/1.[49] A final proof of their close relationship can be found in a short note that Benjamin wrote in 1928 on the occasion of his great-uncle's burial. Among other things, he wrote that Arthur Moritz Schoenflies personified within the family that particular 'kind of Jew with a strong Germano-Christian leaning', which his nephew had never felt 'to be even remotely so winning in anyone' else. Benjamin also thought well of the way he treated younger people: a 'relationship' that was free of any 'calculation' or 'strategy . . . because the older man's interest was based almost entirely on kindliness'.[50]

The last person who deserves mention here is his cousin Gertrud Chodziesner (1894–1943), who was his junior by two years. He remained in contact with her, the daughter of his aunt Elise Schoenflies (1872–1930), until he went into exile. The two were linked by their literary interests. Under the pseudonym Gertrud Kolmar, Gertrud Chodziesner achieved early acclaim as a poetess. A first volume of poems was published in Berlin in 1917 by Egon Fleischel. During the 1920s (she was by now working as an interpreter and teacher of deaf children)[51] she saw only a few of her poems published, but they all appeared in highly reputed periodicals. Benjamin assisted her attempts to find an audience with practical help and advice; he was able to place several poems from the cycle 'Preußische Wappen' [Prussian Coat-of-Arms] in the *Neue Schweizer Rundschau* edited by Max Rychner (1897–1965);[52] and in 1928 he actually wrote an introduction to her 'Two Poems' in the *Literarische Welt*: 'less in order' to recall her 'earlier works' than with the intention of introducing readers to a poetic tone that, in his opinion, had 'not been heard in women's writing since Annette von Droste'.[53] The importance Gertrud Chodziesner attached to her cousin's advice and judgement can be seen by the fact that after the publication of 'Preußische Wappen'

'My mother's uncle, the mathematician Schoenflies, has died. I have seen him often in the past few years and have gotten along really well with him. As you may know, I also lived with him while the Frankfurt business was going on.'[10] (Arthur Moritz Schoenflies)

* Translators' note: A *Privatdozent* is a university teacher who has gained the post-doctoral qualification of *Habilitation* but has not been appointed as a professor.

(1934), she was unable to envisage a more qualified reviewer than him. 'Naturally I would be delighted', she wrote in her letter to him, 'if you were to write the review, although you – who knows? – might be a harsher critic' than some impartial 'reviewer; but I am sure that your interest would be quite different, far deeper than that [of an] outsider'.[54] (Her wish remained unfulfilled due to the historical circumstances.) In 1938 another, last book of Gertrud Kolmar's poems *(Die Frau und die Tiere [The Woman and the Animals])* was published by Erwin Loewe, which had, however, to be withdrawn and pulped shortly after its appearance. Her life ended after years of privation and forced labour in Berlin factories, in 1943, probably in Auschwitz.

In school I never copied; that was not conscience, but rather intelligence, short-sightedness (nature).[1]

Kaiser Friedrich School

Benjamin received his first instruction in reading, writing and arithmetic from private tutors,[2] as befitted his social position. Only when he was nearly nine, at Easter 1901, was he sent to school. His parents sent him to a grammar school, the Kaiser Friedrich School in Charlottenburg – not the most distinguished establishment in Berlin, but certainly one of the better ones, as can be seen from its pupils' social backgrounds. They came almost entirely from the families of wealthy merchants, people of private means, bankers, factory and estate owners, high-ranking officers, health inspectors, pharmacists, university professors, headmasters, government and legal officials, ministers and members of parliament. The names of these sons of wealthy homes were no less illustrious. The names Delbrück, Simmel, Heck and Meyer were already famous far beyond the city's limits.[3] Others, such as (Kurt) Badt, (Willy) Wolfradt (two art historians later to achieve renown) and (Albert) Salomon (who was to become a lecturer at the German College for Politics in Berlin and editor of the social democratic periodical *Die Gesellschaft*),[4] were to become famous later. It is also possible that this high school was one of those preferred by the Berlin Jewry. At any rate the annual reports show that before the First World War, Jewish children always made up more than one-third of the pupils. In accordance with the spirit of the times, the headmaster presented this circumstance to the school authorities as regrettable, but, 'in view of the economic situation and the intellectual interests of the circles' from which these boys came, he chose not to regard the situation as actually deplorable!'[5]

Little can be ascertained about the majority of Benjamin's school- and class-mates, not even those with whom he did his *Abitur* [school finals]. Herbert Blumenthal who later changed his name to Belmore (1893–1978) and Franz Sachs (born 1894) were among his close childhood friends, as is shown by the letters from their once lively correspondence that have survived and been published. During their last years at school and early college days they and Benjamin, together with Fritz Strauß, were linked by their involvement in the German Youth Movement. Alfred Cohn's (1892–1954) contact with Benjamin

Nr.	Name	Geboren am	Geboren zu	Religion bzw. Konfession	Stand und Wohnort des Vaters	Jahre auf der Schule	Jahre in Prima	Jahre in Ober-Prima	Gewählter Beruf
					b) zum Ostertermin:				
79	Benjamin, Walter	15. 7. 92	Berlin	mos.	Kaufmann in Grunewald	5	2	1	Literatur, Philosophie.
80	Böninger, Theodor	3. 3. 93	Kolmar i. E.	ev.	Regierungsrat in Charlottenburg	10½	2	1	Jura.
81	Brauer, Alfred	9. 4. 94	Charlottenburg	mos.	Kaufmann in Charlottenburg	11½	2	1	Maschinenbau.
82	Bröseke, Friedrich	20. 11. 92	Charlottenburg	kat.	Baumeister in Charlottenbg.	13	2	1	Chemie.
83	Buschmann, Bernhard	7. 7. 92	Schöneberg	kat.	Direktor in Charlottenburg	11½	2	1	Jura.
84	Faeke, Alfred	11. 3. 93	Berlin	ev.	Kgl. Eisenbahn - Rechnungs-revisor in Wilmersdorf	2½	2	1	Landmesser.
85	Fraustädter, Werner	7. 6. 94	Leipzig	mos.	Kaufmann in Charlottenburg	12	2	1	Volkswirtschaft.
86	Katz, Erich	28. 4. 93	Marienburg	mos.	Justizrat in Charlottenburg	11	2	1	Jura.
87	Kranz, Walter	8. 3. 94	Gr.-Lichterfelde	ev.	Rechnungsrat in Charlottenburg	9	2	1	Medizin.
88	Marcus, Ernst	8. 6. 93	Berlin	mos.	Landgerichtsrat in Berlin, Geheimer Justizrat	9	2	1	Zoologie.
89	Nerger, Lothar	4. 7. 92	Liegnitz	ev.	Fortbildungsschullehrer in Charlottenburg	10	2	1	Theologie.
90	Sachs, Franz	17. 1. 94	Berlin	mos.	Kaufmann in Charlottenburg	12	2	1	Jura.
91	Salomon, Richard	25. 6. 94	Charlottenburg	mos.	Kaufmann in Charlottenburg	11½	2	1	Jura.
92	Schöen, Max	7. 11. 93	Charlottenburg	ev.	Professor an der Technischen Hochschule zu Charlottenburg	9	2	1	Jura.
93	Simon, Franz	2. 7. 93	Berlin	mos.	Rentner in Wilmersdorf	12½	3	1	Mathematik.
94	Steinfeld, Alfred	4. 6. 93	Berlin	mos.	Kaufmann in Charlottenburg	12¼	2	1	Jura.
95	Strauß, Fritz	5. 9. 94	Berlin	mos.	Kaufmann in Wilmersdorf	11½	2	1	Geschichte.

Brauer, Faeke, Sachs, Salomon, Strauß unter Befreiung von der mündlichen Prüfung.

Benjamin's class during his last year at school.

was never completely severed. Theodor Böninger's family was so closely acquainted with the Benjamins that they once even spent a holiday together in Switzerland.[6] Erich Katz, Franz Simon, Alfred Steinfeld and Hans-Albrecht Korschel also appear now and then in Benjamin's letters and diary entries. Alfred Brauer later made a name for himself as a natural scientist, and emigrated during the Nazi period to America, where he continued to teach into the 1970s at Princeton and other universities. There are no traces of the rest, however, from shortly after they left school.

An unhappy memory

Walter Benjamin was not one to look back wistfully on his schooldays. Far from it. By the age of 40 he scarcely once recalled those times with anything but horror, hopelessness and revulsion. Of course, a degree of over-sensitivity played a part in this. Even after so many years, he remembered the 'compulsion incessantly to remove my cap . . . when another of the teachers passed' as degrading, and 'the school discipline in the lower forms – caning, change of seats or detention' – as humiliating; he had hated the 'excursions to the country' and games on the fields at Tempelhof or on 'a drill ground in the vicinity of the Lehrter Station'.[7] Movement and discipline,

'The architect of the Kaiser Friedrich School must have had something of the order of Brandenburg brick Gothic in mind. At any rate, it is constructed in red brick-work and displays a preference of motifs commonly found at Stendal or Tangermünde. The whole, however, gives a narrow-chested, high-shouldered impression. Rising close by the precincts of the municipal railway, the building exudes a sad, spinsterish primness. Even more than to the experiences I had within, it is probably to this exterior that I should attribute the fact that I have not retained a single cheerful memory of it.'[11] (Present view of the Kaiser Friedrich School, built in 1900)

physical training and an almost militaristic drill were the order of the day in the Wilhelmine era. The extent of this general glorification of military virtues and of their effect on day-to-day life in even the royal Prussian schools can be seen from such 'uplifting' contemporary German essays as 'The Benefit of Universal Conscription' or 'If I Rest I Rust', and in the war games that the boys 'from the lower forms' went to play in the Grunewald. This disastrous mentality could even be felt in the seemingly innocuous new regulations for the school breaks: 'Walking in double time in place of breathing exercises has proved beneficial during the breaks; each day, and at the end of every break, the pupils are to walk for five minutes in double time to the beat of a drum.'[8]

When Benjamin started in the early 1930s to write down his reminiscences of his years in Berlin, he evidently planned to include a chapter on his former teachers. At any rate his notes for this work contain a sketch with a long list of their names: 'Hagemann (history of Karageorgievitch), Wehner (Latin master; democrat), Fiedler (short-sighted, piping voice), Timpe, Tonndorf, Lucas, Zernecke, Wilke, Mackensen, Mehwaldt, Hunger, Herrfarth, Paarmann, Schütze (moustache, killed in the war), Steinmann'.[9] It is impossible to reconstruct what he had in mind, for this part of the 'Berlin Chronicle' was never written.

But perhaps it was what Albert Salomon once described as one of the everyday phenomena at Prussian secondary schools that had yet to be scrutinized: 'Among the teachers: the role of the reserve officer in competition with academic training. No one has studied just what social influence is exerted by the social prestige of the reserve officer, an invention of the last Kaiser.'[10] The last teacher to embody both of these roles at the Kaiser Friedrich School was the headmaster and Greek teacher, Alfred Zernecke.

During his younger years, Benjamin 'was often sick', as was always noted meticulously in his reports. One of them, or so we are told in *Berlin Childhood around 1900*, records that he missed 'one hundred and seventy-three lessons' in one year. These absences from school, which often lasted weeks, were not necessarily unwelcome to the growing boy, for his bouts of measles, chicken pox and frequently recurring fever allowed him to escape the oppressiveness of daily school life. Greek, maths and PT were grey and monotonous for him. He only experienced real feelings of warmth and security at home: when his mother joined him and told him stories about his ancestors.[11] It was also thanks to his illnesses that Benjamin was granted a long break from his martyrdom at the Berlin school – and underwent the decisive experience of his childhood. His parents removed him from the school in 1904 for health reasons. Then, after he had been without tuition for months on end, they finally sent him to a country boarding school in Haubinda, Thuringia. The two years he spent there were among his dearest and most precious possessions in the treasure chest of memories.

The seeds of a later life

Haubinda is so small that it is seldom found on maps, yet it was of the greatest importance to Benjamin's personal and intellectual development. Here he grew up, as he wrote in a later account (of a dream); in Haubinda 'the seeds' of his 'later life were sown'.[12]

For all the ups and downs in its history, the former Haubinda boarding school is still remembered for its links with some of the better-known names in the history of German thought. Theodor Lessing, the university professor and journalist who was later murdered by the Nazis, taught here until he was dismissed in 1903 as a consequence of the 'Haubinda Jewish Dispute'; the educational reformer Gustav Wyneken (1875–1964) taught here from 1903 to 1906 before he, too, had an altercation with

'On one of the very gentle elevations is a house. The house is Haubinda, where school pupils live. It is called a half-timbered house, its impassive height, which yields no view over the woods covering the plain, is the throne. Behind it, then (and this one is never allowed to forget) is the forest. Behind that are villages with names which come from the end of the world.'[12]

August Halm: 'He was a funny little chap with an unforgettable look in his solemn eyes, and the shiniest bald patch I ever saw, surrounded by a semicircular wreath of dark, tightly curled locks.[13]

the school's founder, Hermann Lietz,[13] and went his own way, finally founding the Wickersdorf Free School Community with his colleague Paul Geheeb. Also worthy of mention are the musicologist August Halm (1869–1929), Wyneken's brother-in-law, to whom Benjamin was to dedicate an almost tender reminiscence well over two decades later, and Martin Luserke, who became particularly well-known for his work in the theatre and as the headmaster, for a time, of the Wickersdorf Free School Community and later the 'School by the Sea' on the island of Juist in the North Sea. Pupils also included the writers Bruno Frank, Erich von Mendelssohn and Wilhelm Speyer (1887–1952). Thanks to these two last, we know a number of details about daily life at the school, which Benjamin so rarely gives in his numerous reminiscences of the years at Haubinda. In 1914 Mendelssohn wrote an autobiographical novel under the title *Nacht und Tag [Night and Day]*, published posthumously with an introduction by Thomas Mann; Wilhelm Speyer had two novels published (*Schwermut der Jahreszeiten* and *Der Kampf der Tertia [The Melancholy of the Seasons; The Struggle of the Fourth-Formers]*, in 1922 and 1928 respectively) in which the school and its neighbourhood provide an unmistakable background to the story. All three novels were among the most successful books of their years of publication. *The Struggle of the Fourth-Formers* was even made into a film shortly after its appearance (Benjamin wrote an article on it in the periodical *Die literarische Welt*),[14] and it has remained a bestseller for young people to this day.

Haubinda was founded in 1901 as the second of Lietz's country boarding schools. (The first had been established in 1898 in Ilsenburg in the Harz mountains, and a third was added several years later in Bieberstein.) Thomas Mann described the school, which was based on English models, as a 'modern Thuringian educational establishment'.[15] Decades later, looking at the rampant idealism and chauvinism of Lietz's programme which was soon joined by a scarcely concealed anti-Semitism, we might not necessarily agree. But however disastrous such a mixture has proved to be in German history, this kind of school did represent a real alternative to the cane-swinging pedagogics prevalent in Prussia's state schools. Pupil representation which conveyed at least a feeling of collective responsibility, an enlargement of the curriculum that went beyond purely intellectual education through the encouragement of musical gifts and the inclusion of practical activities (handicrafts): this and more had a beneficial effect on the young adults' developing personalities.

The 'catastrophic encounters' which otherwise seemed to dog Benjamin's schooldays only manifested themselves on the first day of his stay at Haubinda. Amid the inevitably alien and 'threatening circumstances' of this new situation, 'a tall hostile-seeming lout' asked him whether his '"old man" had already left'. Benjamin was quite 'unfamiliar' with this 'piece of school-boy parlance'; 'an abyss opened up before' him, which he 'sought to bridge with a laconic protest'.[16] The actual nature of the reply is, however, passed over in silence by the author of 'A Berlin Chronicle'. Nor should the remark lead to the assumption that in Haubinda the sons of wealthy parents came to mix with the *hoi-polloi*, for the boarding school scarcely differed from the ghetto of old and new western Berlin in terms of the pupils' social profiles. However much Lietz's country boarding schools, or at least their programme, emphasized the social aspect of education and called for the elimination or at least 'reduction of class differences which tear apart our population and endanger its unity',[17] the annual tuition fees of 'between 1400 and 2000 gold marks'[18] undermined such high-minded intentions from the very start. Here in Haubinda, the children of industrialists, wealthy merchants, professors, Prussian gentry and officers were among their own kind.

On paper, the daily routine and curriculum in Lietz's country boarding schools appear strictly regulated. Nevertheless, they must have allowed the pupils sufficient opportunity to develop in their own way, even if their 'self-fulfilment' had always to be

Excerpt from the German curriculum at the Haubinda country boarding school

Tageswerkplan
der L. E. He.

Im Sommerhalbjahr.

	Ilsenburg	Haubinda	Bieberstein
Aufstehen	6:40	6:00	5:40
Dauerlauf	7:00	6:20	6:00
1. Unterrichtsstunde	7:15—8:00	6:45—7:30	6:15—7:00
Frühstück	8:00	7:30	7:00
2. Unterrichtsstunde	8:30—9:15	8:00—8:45	7:30—8:15
3. Unterrichtsstunde	9:30—10:15	9:00—9:45	8:30—9:15
4. Unterrichtsstunde	10:30—11:15	10:00—10:45	9:30—10:15
5. Unterrichtsstunde	11:30—12:10	11:00—11:45	10:30—11:15
Turnen, Singen			11:20—12:00
Mittagspause	12:15—2:00	12:00—2:00	12:00—2:00
Praktische Arbeit*) Zeichnen, Musikübung	2:00—3:30	2:00—3:30	2:00—3:30
Vesperpause	3:30—4:00	3:30—4:00	3:30—3:45
Spiel, Turnen, Gesang		4:00—4:45	3:45—4:30 (3mal)
Wiss. Arbeitsstunden	5:00—6:40	5:00—7:30	4:30—7:30
Abendmahlzeit	6:45—7:10	7:30—8:00	7:30—8:00
Kapelle	7:15	8:00	8:00
Zu Bett	8:00	9:00	9:00

Freie Nachmittage: Mittwoch und Sonnabend bis 5 Uhr.
Familienabende: Mittwoch.
Sonntags früh Kapelle um 8 Uhr, frei von 9 Uhr früh bis 7 Uhr abends.

Daily timetable for Lietz's country boarding schools Ilsenburg, Haubinda, and Bieberstein.

attained under guidance. But the farm work, the long rambles through the local contryside,[19] the musical and literary discussion group (the 'Chapel'), a less anxiety-ridden learning situation and a generally more scientific form of tuition left their mark on Benjamin. It is no accident that his scattered reminiscences of this period refer to precisely these things. Even the central pedagogical ideas behind his 'Programme for a Proletarian Children's Theatre' (presumably written in 1928/9) are scarcely anything but a distillation of his adolescent experiences at Haubinda.

The encounter which undoubtedly had the greatest consequences for Benjamin was that with Gustav Wyneken, who taught, among other subjects, German and philosophy. A remark in a *curriculum vitae* written by Benjamin in 1911 mentions both him and his lessons. According to this, the special importance that Benjamin attached to his stay in Thuringia lay 'above all in the stimulus' he received during German lessons, which later guided his 'aspirations' and 'interests'. His 'liking for literature', which until then had solely been 'satisfied by unsystematic reading', was deepened by Wyneken and directed

along certain paths by the 'critical aesthetic norms' he imparted. In addition, 'this tuition awoke' Benjamin's 'interest in philosophy'.[20] It was Wyneken's particular way of teaching these subjects that impressed his pupil, and determined the way he would approach art and literature in the future. Benjamin was taught to work independently. He learnt that essays should not be misconstrued as the products of pedantry and industry, but be constructed with method. Nor was the formulation of aesthetic questions treated as a confession of personal attitudes. And the 'basis of [his] philosophical tuition' was the view that the 'world is my ideation', as was formulated in a number of Wyneken's thoughts on the reform of German boarding schools. The fact that his ideas were aimed primarily at promoting especially gifted pupils, at an 'elite school', and moreover one cluttered with all manner of fashionable nonsense (such as 'the canon of the saints' and the 'cult of genius'),[21] becomes clear if one looks by way of comparison at the regular (state) schools. The tendency there was to demand *too little* rather than too much of the pupils. Their inadequately trained teachers were unable to show their pupils how to study, or even how to assimilate factual information.

Where is Walter Benjamin sitting or standing – fourth from the left? Teachers and pupils at the Haubinda boarding school, Easter 1906. Seated in the middle is Gustav Wyneken; behind him, with a cane in his hand, is August Halm.

On returning to his native city, Benjamin was enrolled once again at the Kaiser Friedrich School near the Savignyplatz S-Bahn station at Easter 1907, and initially admitted to the fifth form 'for a trial period'. After all, his stay in Thuringia had cost him two whole years, although the loss was none too painful for him, for he had left Haubinda full of initiative. In Berlin, as we can read once more in his *curriculum vitae* of 1911, he now 'developed above all aesthetic interests' out of a 'natural synthesis of his general philosophical and literary interests'. These led to a deep 'interest in dramatic theory', which found its first expression in his close reading of the

great plays of Shakespeare, Hebbel and Ibsen in particular, in the meticulous study of Hamlet and [Goethe's] Tasso, as well as in a profound engagement with Hölderlin. Indeed, these interests expressed themselves in the endeavour to form a personal opinion about literature.[22]

Just how unfavourable the school was to the development of personal powers of aesthetic judgement can be seen in the manner in which literary matters were treated. A pot-pourri of pronouncements by the Berlin German masters that Benjamin compiled immediately after leaving school in an essay on 'Unterricht und Wertung' [Tuition and Evaluation], gives a keen insight into just how off-putting this tuition must have been to the interested pupil. The teachers did not wish to go 'any further than Kleist', not even with their fifth-form students. 'Modern writers are never read' for the simple reason that ' "these people depict [nothing but] the ugly side of life. Ibsen – one look at that monkey face of his is enough!" ' No, instruction of this kind did anything but sensitize the pupils to the questions of modern art and literature, for they could gain 'no serious relationship to works of art' from this form of tuition. Works were analysed 'to the point of exhaustion in terms of content and perhaps form, but it never came to a fruitful, i.e. comparative, examination because the necessary criteria' for that were missing.[23]

The pupils had to develop their own criteria for art and literary criticism. Benjamin and a group of his friends met one evening a week in order to read and discuss the plays of Friedrich Hebbel, Arno Holz, Gerhart Hauptmann, Hermann Sudermann and Frank Wedekind, as well as German translations of the Greek tragedies, Shakespeare, Molière, Ibsen, Maeterlinck and Strindberg. Among the participants in this youthful 'reading circle',[24] who were presumably spurred on to penetrate the unknown modern spirit by their teachers' lack of understanding for modern currents in art and literature, were Herbert Blumenthal, Alfred Steinfeld, Franz Sachs and Willy Wolfradt. Already then they were producing their first critical work – reviews which the youngsters wrote after theatre visits and which one of the participants (Franz Sachs) even half a century later still considered to be 'worthy of publication'[25] (although they were never actually published).

It does not require much imagination to guess that the initiative for these literary meetings came from Benjamin. From his enthusiasm for the Swiss author Carl Spitteler, who was widely read at the time, and his 'recommendation' of the compositions of Anton Bruckner (even though he scarcely understood a thing about music), to the way the afternoons and evenings they spent together were organized, almost every trail leads back to Haubinda: to his teacher there, Wyneken, who had a boundless admiration for Spitteler; to his music teacher August Halm, who wrote a monograph on *The Symphonies of Anton Bruckner* (published in Munich, 1914); and finally to the 'Chapel' meetings, which presumably were run on much the same lines as the discussions held by the friends. The only difference was the content. Modern literature now replaced pedagogical writing and books for the young. In a number of basic respects, these regular discussions also anticipated an institution that came into being a few years later in the German Youth Movement, and to which many were to be indebted for their intellectual socialization: the *Sprechsaal* or debating chamber.

'Ardor'

Benjamin's trial period in the fifth form proved to be quite superfluous, and he completed his remaining years at school without any further interruptions or delays. At Easter 1909 he passed the 'one-year exam',[26] which reduced to just one year the three years of military service that young adults normally performed on the completion of their school studies. (This was in fact of no further significance to Benjamin, for he never had to 'serve'.) Benjamin received a fairly good mark ('two minus') for his German essay on the topic 'The Calling of the Bell' (with reference to Schiller's 'Song of the Bell').This matched his marks at school.

The following year saw Benjamin's first attempts as an author. Several of his poems ('Der Dichter', 'Sturm', 'Des Frühlings Versteck' [The Poet; Storm; Spring's Hiding Place])

Regular attendance and
commendable behaviour
– Benjamin's
school-leaving certificate.

Zeugnis

über die

wissenschaftliche Befähigung für den einjährig-freiwilligen Dienst.

Walter Benjamin

geboren am *15* ten *Juli* 18*92* zu *Berlin*

Kreis   Reg.-Bezirk

Bundesstaat *Preußen*, *mos.* Konfession, Sohn des *Kaufmanns Emil Benjamin* zu *Charlottenburg*

hat die hiesige Anstalt von der Klasse *S. O. III* an besucht und der Sekunda *1* Jahre angehört. Er hat in den von ihm besuchten Klassen an allen Unterrichts-Gegenständen teilgenommen.

1. Schulbesuch: *regelmäßig* Betragen: *lobenswert*

2. Aufmerksamkeit und Fleiss: *gut*

3. Mass der erreichten Kenntnisse: *genügend, z. T. gut*

Der Besuch der Unter–Sekunda ist erfolgreich gewesen.

Er war dispensiert vom ——

Charlottenburg, den *24* ten *März* 19*09*

Direktor und Lehrerkollegium der Kaiser-Friedrich-Schule.

Zernsdts,   *Wehner*

Direktor.   Oberlehrer.

Page one of Benjamin's
final year exam paper in
German.

and prose texts ('In der Nacht: Gedanken zu einem Schumann'schen Stück', 'Die drei Religionssucher' [In the Night: Thoughts while Listening to a Piece by Schumann; The Three Seekers of Religion])[27] were printed in the school magazine *Der Anfang [The Beginning]* under a pseudonym, to avoid his being expelled from the school for forbidden activities. *Der Anfang*, which appeared at that time in a tiny print-run of just 150 hectographed copies, was distributed among students and school pupils. The name of the editor was given as that of a Berlin high-school pupil, Georges Barbizon. The magazine was produced with great enthusiasm, and its first series ran to a total of 23 issues; its title reflected the beginnings of what was to become the German Youth Movement.

For his earliest works, Benjamin also had a Latin pen-name, Ardor, chosen with equal care, for it was aimed at giving a clear impression of its bearer's commitment to the concerns of youth. And the noun's numerous meanings, which vary with context (e.g. passion, zeal, fierce heat, effulgence and love), leave the reader spoilt for choice among all the associations that the word awakens. The young high-school pupil's earliest publications were evidence of and reflections on his recently awoken awareness of the need for a new form of school and education. The poems are not formally accomplished, and the prose texts have yet to assume 'theoretical' positions, having instead an untamed character, at times a distinct rhetorical pathos, characteristic of a generation that was attempting to change its world from above – from the head, from the school and the university, from art and literature – and which would pay dearly for its illusions just a few years later in Langemarck.

Youth is a Sleeping Beauty which slumbers unaware that a Prince is approaching to free her. And that Youth may awake, that it may participate in the struggle that is being waged about it, this is what the magazine tries to contribute to as best it can. This understanding, which informs our magazine, is already firmly established in the works of the greatest men of literature.[28]

These remarks are taken from an essay written by Benjamin in 1911 entitled 'Das Dornröschen' [Sleeping Beauty]. The magazine mentioned here is once again *Der Anfang*, which had now found a publisher in Niederschönhausen near Berlin, and appeared in proper printed format with a new subtitle (the *Magazine for Future Art and Literature* had become a *United Magazine of Youth*). The opening and closing sentences of the essay, these lines also mark the limitations of their project. Understanding of society could be simply read off from literature; the heroes of the works of Shakespeare, Schiller, Goethe, Ibsen and Spitteler could be instrumental in the struggle for better education and training. The idealism of these notions speaks for itself. It would be some time before Benjamin attained a less naive understanding of the workings and logic of political conflicts. His gradual break with the School Reform Movement at the beginning of the First World War, when the Youth Movement began to split into the most diverse groups – national, social-democratic, communist, anarcho-religious, anthroposophical and denominational – was an important step in this direction.

In December 1911, Benjamin formally applied to take the *Abitur* at Kaiser Friedrich, which he then passed after a succession of oral and written examinations (in February/early March 1912). The idea that he might not have passed these exams, as suggested by a remark in 'A Berlin Chronicle',[29] need not be taken at face value. It is true that his Greek paper – a translation

The new consciousness

'The solution to the 1st problem has not been found; the 2nd and 3rd problems have been answered correctly, as has the majority of the 4th; only the construction of the coordinates of the point of intersection contains 2 mistakes. Satisfactory. Marks attained in class are also adequate.' (Mathematics homework)

'The essay shows a deep understanding of both plays. He generally expresses himself elegantly, and always in a straightforward manner. Note: Very Good. Marks achieved in class are also very good.' (German essay)

from Plato's *Euthyphron* – was a complete disaster, so that he did fail in the most important subject at a school specializing in classical languages (the sixth form received eight Greek lessons a

Handwriting: inadequate – Benjamin's final-year certificate.

week), and worse still in a subject marked by the headmaster, but he had no problem in making up for this during the oral. And the remaining written examinations showed steady progress: 'satisfactory' for maths, 'good' in Latin, and 'very good' for his German essay (on 'Can it be said of Grillparzer's "Sappho" that the author "ploughed the field with Goethe's calf"?')[30], which the senior master Lucas praised for its deep understanding and elegant style. All in all his marks were pretty average, except for an 'inadequate' in handwriting (a judgement with which anyone who has ever attempted to decipher Benjamin's writing would sympathize).

Only gradually did Benjamin manage to adjust to his new life. Months after leaving school, he noted in his diary:

Never perhaps since finishing my exams has it struck me so strongly as it has now just how incredible it is that I am no longer a pupil, that I no longer have to give answers, that my mornings are not controlled by someone else and that my thoughts no longer find composure and satisfaction in writing essays.

But he was nevertheless determined to leave these largely unloved experiences and memories behind him. 'The old consciousness', he continues in his diary, 'rose up once more against the new, which must at last establish itself'.[31]

Travelling and writing

The fact that Benjamin was even permitted to pass his *Abitur* was largely thanks to his aunt Friederike Joseephi. She overcame her brother Emil's resistance to his son doing higher school examinations.[32] His father seems, though, to have shown his more generous side once the exams had been passed. At Whitsun 1912, Benjamin set off on a journey to Italy, which took him to Milan, Verona, Vicenza, Padua and Venice, among other places. In those days, lengthy journeys abroad were uncommon, even for the upper middle class. It was Benjamin's first long journey without his close family. In their place he was accompanied by his former classmates Erich Katz, Franz Simon and Franz Sachs. The latter left the party at Lucerne, to continue his own travels with two youngsters named (Ernst?) Joël and Börnstein.[33]

'Of the three greatest wishes in my life', writes Benjamin in 'A Berlin Chronicle', 'the first I recognized was for distant, but above all lengthy journeys.' He had inherited his longing for distant parts, as he said, from Hedwig Hirschfeld, his maternal grandmother and a 'decidedly enterprising lady'. With her

From Benjamin's
'Wengen Diary' (1911).

greetings from Tabarz in Thuringia, from Brindisi and
Madonna di Campiglio, she laid the foundations of the carefully
guarded postcard collection 'that kindled my love of travel' in a
way that 'none of my boy's adventure books' could do.[34] His
passion for travel had always been combined with that for
writing as can be seen from his diaries[35] of his journeys to the
Riesengebirge (1902), Franconian Switzerland (1906), the
Thuringian Forest and Switzerland in 1911, and finally to Italy
in 1912. Later it was not so much in his diaries that he gave
written expression to this passion, as in the notes on his visits
to Naples, Moscow, Ibiza and Marseilles. Writing as the reworking of experiences gathered during travel: that exhausts the

similarities between the earlier and later journeys. There is a great chasm between the attitude of the youngster going on educational trips and that of the more mature man seeking 'refuge' in travel – between, as it were, Benjamin's 'earlier' and 'later' faculties of observation, powers of perception, and above all degree of openness to anything new or different. Two remarks from the travel diaries illustrate this quite well. 'Travelling is an international cultural action', he wrote as late as 1912.[36] Twenty years on, this became: 'For is not travel the overcoming or cleansing of age-old passions that are rooted in our customary surroundings, and thus a chance to develop new ones, which is doubtless a kind of transformation?'[37]

'An Italian Journey is in the making'.[38] The sentence comes from a letter that Benjamin wrote in June 1912 to his friend Herbert Blumenthal, and its context becomes clear from the diary entries that introduce his Whitsun journey to Italy: 'The journey will only properly come into being with the diary that I shall write. In it I wish to allow the development of its essence, the silent, self-explanatory synthesis required by a journey undertaken for personal development which characterizes it as such.' Benjamin, vying with a great model from the past, wished to write down his impressions and experiences of an 'Italian Journey'.[39] The finished work was to be passed round among his friends, then later perhaps to be published. With Goethe's shade looming perceptibly in the background he continues, somewhat stiltedly:

'One should not wear one's worst suit when travelling, because travelling is an international cultural action: one steps out of the private realm into public life.'[14] (Benjamin around 1912)

This is all the more incontrovertible to me in that not one single experience possessed the power to colour my overall impression of the journey. Nature and art culminated equally and in all places in what Goethe termed 'solidity'. And no adventure, none of the soul's desire for adventure, presented an effective or alluring backdrop.[40]

Hardly any of this, it should be added, is to be found in his notes. There is a discrepancy between the reality and the pretensions which makes these early attempts appear awkward and unsuccessful. And, more than that, his perceptions and descriptions of the social reality of Italy are superficial, to put it mildly. Between banal observations on da Vinci's 'Last Supper' or the Santa Maria Gloriosa dei Frari in Venice, he makes disparaging comments about the country and its people. He repeatedly turns up his nose at the nasty smells that issue from every corner, and makes numerous disdainful remarks about the rarely well-mannered Italians who are are loud, grimy, plebeian and constantly spit, smoke bad tobacco, swindle, beg and idle away their time. The 'interviu' about the Italian-Turkish war that Benjamin did with Venetian workers in order 'to inform himself of the mood among "the lower classes" ' – a failure, but not as a result of barriers of language – fits this picture all too well. The person speaking or writing here is not merely someone on an educational journey, travelling about with all sorts of preconceived ideas while looking out for some Arcadia, and having little more than derogatory and dismissive remarks for everything that does not fit into his picture. For Benjamin in certain respects bears an unfortunate resemblance to those educational philistines whom he was attacking so vehemently at the same time in his articles on schools and education. These notes show a rather spoilt, reactionary, narrow-minded, exceedingly *German* youth, whose arrogance goes so far as to delight in the brawl he instigated among several down-at-heel children by deliberately leaving behind a lit cigarette.[41] He remained silent, though, when it came to the reasons for their ragged state. They had yet to find a place in his world-picture. Naturally there is much youthful uncertainty, awkwardness, immaturity and lack of reflection behind Benjamin's defensive attitude. So it is no great surprise when the 20-year-old's return from the country where life was not *la dolce vita* for all should, in the end, take the form of a flight. Back in Freiburg, though, the 'revulsion' he had felt gave way to a 'longing'[42] for southern Europe.

Freiburg im Breisgau: Benjamin enrolled here as a philology student in April 1912 at the time-honoured Albert Ludwig University, which was then dominated by the philosopher Heinrich Rickert (1863–1936) and the historian Friedrich Meinecke (1862–1954). He was accompanied by his friends Fritz Strauß and Franz Sachs (with whom he lived at the same address at 7^{II} Konradstraße).[1] His wish to escape the control and influence of the parental home must have been an important factor in his decision to exchange the cosmopolitan atmosphere of Berlin for the provincialism of distant Freiburg. But he was unable to gain much from the town and its university (to which he returned for a second and last semester in summer 1913), as is shown by the sometimes melancholy, sometimes derogatory, remarks in his letters.

Student years in Freiburg and Berlin

The new student plunged into his studies with verve. His end-of-semester report for 1912 shows that he attended more lectures than he ever would at other universities, whether in Berlin, Munich or Berne. But on the whole the performance of high officers, professors and humble *Privatdozenten* appears to have made very little impression on him. For them there was nothing but scathing irony, if not outright scorn and derision. The '"fille de Sophie" (i.e. daughter of wisdom) exerts her demoralizing influence on men', as he wrote in a letter to his childhood friend Herbert Blumenthal in May that year. 'They regain – like true lovers – consciousness only in the evening' in cafés. While wrangling and discussing, one comes 'to realize that there are many valuable things but proportionately few valuable people.'

If that's philosophy . . .

Dear Herbert:
Science is a cow
I listen to
I sit in the lecture hall
While it goes: moo!
(It is a fact that in Freiburg I am able to think independently

Freiburg University certificate for studies and morals.

about scholarly matters only about one-tenth as often as in Berlin.)[2]

The narrowness and stuffiness of the Freiburg atmosphere may have inspired Martin Heidegger, who sat in Rickert's lectures alongside Benjamin; but the university, as he became acquainted with it here, made a rather poor impression on the Berlin Jew with his upper middle-class background. The fact that he was anything but alone in his disappointment over such unimaginative academic scholarship – which was remote from its own times and allowed little room for the students' own ideas – can be seen in the example of his later friend, Albert Salomon. After several decades, all he could find to say about his experiences as a student at Freiburg (several semesters before Benjamin) was: 'Freiburg: Rickert: if that's philosophy . . .'[3] His friends in Berlin pitied him as 'a victim of academia', and that is also how Benjamin saw himself. If this did not too greatly demoralize him, it was because he dedicated himself with far more élan to questions that interested him in his role as a 'hero of school reform'.[4]

'The Free Students are also here and, in absolute terms, the city must be called a university town. Yet only in small part is it situated in a world that is imaginable; for the most part it lies in a world that is unimaginable. This can be proved primarily by the peculiar consistency of Freiburg time. It is not enough that it is not Central European . . . It is strangely fleeting in nature. But the proximity of the local philosophical faculty absolutely forces it to assume its true being . . .'[15] (Rickert on epistemology and metaphysics: a page from Benjamin's course book, summer semester 1912)

'Sunday 5 May arrived at Freiburg 11.45 a.m., Hotel Salmer, then met up with Benjamin, Sachs, Papmeyer, Strauß – remained together at Luisenhöhe till 10 p.m.'[5] Gustav Wyneken's terse diary entries on a journey to Freiburg in 1912 read like the notes in an appointment book. It is not the only section in which Benjamin's name appears, for between 1912 and 1914 the two met as regularly as was allowed by the busy lecturing programme that Wyneken took on after leaving the Wickersdorf Free School Community. On one occasion (13 March 1913) the great school reformer was even a guest at Delbrückstraße.[6] Later on, Benjamin described his encounter with Wyneken as the 'decisive intellectual event' of his early years. (This comment appears in a letter from October 1912 to a fellow student in Freiburg, the writer Ludwig Strauß.) Nor was he exaggerating. Already during Benjamin's last school years, Wyneken had assumed a guiding role in all his thoughts and actions. One or two years after his time in Thuringia, Benjamin began to study Wyneken's thought in greater depth. During this period he came to be 'so moved' by the promises in Wyneken's 'Programmatic Writings' that from then on he devoted himself wholeheartedly to the 'Wickersdorf idea' (a phrase that he used for his ideas on school and educational reform).[7] What had begun in the fairly relaxed atmosphere of a 'circle of friends' – fellow pupils from the Kaiser Friedrich School, whom, as has already been mentioned, he gathered around him – shortly afterward assumed

Luisenhöhe

'The most frequently used route, particularly during the warm season, is the shady forest road, which was built under the auspices of the town of Freiburg and which runs from Rebhaus via the woods at Kreuzkopf and Illenberg, right to Luisenhöhe. The hotel of the same name is particularly popular with ramblers and people taking advantage of the therapeutic properties of its healthy altitude and its glorious view.'[16] (Hotel Luisenhöhe in Horben near Freiburg around the turn of the century)

a more binding form. Benjamin also began to publicize his convictions through articles in the magazines *Der Anfang* and *Die freie Schulgemeinde [The Free School Community]*, edited by Wyneken. Then during his years at college he was to become active in various organizations and institutions: in the committee of the Berlin branch of the Free Students' Union, in the *Sprechsäle* and above all in the Detachments for School Reform. This last institution was the main reason for Wyneken's visit to Freiburg in spring 1912. Some six months earlier he had coupled the publication of an article on students and school reform with a call to German universities to form Detachments for School Reform within the already existing Free Students' Unions, so as to go beyond mere propaganda and pave the way for a broad, fundamental reform of the education system.[8] 'A large number of copies of that issue' of *Die freie Schulgemeinde* containing Wyneken's programmatic article 'were sent to the German universities, but except for Freiburg without any visible result'.[9] To these words of the philosophy student Christian Papmeyer (1889–1972), one should append 'at first', for within a very short time other universities followed Freiburg's example.

A Detachment for School Reform was set up at the Albert Ludwig University almost directly after Wyneken's call. The 'first group' to act 'completely in accord with Wyneken's ideas' began work there under Papmeyer's leadership.[10] Another reason for Benjamin's departure from Berlin may well have been the vanguard role played by Freiburg. The town had become a centre for a number of the most active among Wyneken's followers who had chosen their place of study solely on the basis of the needs, as they saw it, of the 'political' struggle being waged around the college and school system. In some ways Freiburg was an apprenticeship for Benjamin, during which he gained a first-hand insight into the workings of a Detachment for School Reform.

What was the actual activity of this institution upon which Wyneken, in particular, placed such great hopes for the dissemination of his ideas, and with which he managed to get a foot inside the portals of the university – the place where future teachers received their training? First, there were weekly training courses and evening discussions on the problems of school reform. These included, for instance, magic lantern shows on country boarding schools and talks on such topics as 'Friedrich Nietzsche and the school of the future'. In addition the students conducted an 'inquiry instigated by Wyneken into their schools and schooldays',[11] although their eagerly collected data would seem never to have been analyzed.[12] Finally, the youngsters who were active in

Gustav Wyneken, 1914.

the Freiburg Detachment for School Reform were the initiators of a series of lectures put on by the Free Students' Union in the summer semester of 1912. A number of speakers, including Ludwig Gurlitt, Johannes Langermann and Gustav Wyneken, came to talk on such topics as 'School and Culture', 'State Education' and 'Schools and Youth Culture' (Wyneken on 27 June). The talks were published a little later in an anthology entitled *Students and School Reform*, which also contained articles by Benjamin ('School Reform, a Cultural Movement'), Papmeyer and Wilhelm Ostwald. This pamphlet, printed in an edition of 10,000 (!), was distributed free of charge around all the universities of Germany. The aim was to generate enthusiasm elsewhere for the creation of an institutionalized forum in which the need for and the issues involved in a comprehensive reform of the school and educational system could be discussed.

Benjamin's short article on school reform as a cultural movement now seems fairly insubstantial. It contains a great deal of pathos and rhetoric ('youth, a new school, culture – that is the *circulus egregius* which we must go through again and again in all directions'), as well as a socio-political idealism which gives an insight into the range (or paucity) of the author's experience:

In short: the school reform movement expresses clear and pressing needs of our time which, like all of its major afflictions, lie in the fields of ethics and culture. School reform is no less important than our social and religious problems – but perhaps slightly clearer.[13]

There is a lot of political naivety in Benjamin's earliest writings in which he readily equates the appalling state of the schools with the wretchedness of social conditions, and attributes the origins of social inequality above all to atrophied ethics and weakened morals. It should be remembered, however, that these young people were carrying a lot of dead weight in their intellectual baggage, in the form of out-dated traditions that were reinforced daily by their schools and homes, and which merely encouraged the ideologization of the real situation in society. In addition, the sons and daughters of the wealthy bourgeoisie had never received the object lessons that were necessary to counter this short-sighted view of the world. The knowledge 'of any other' (as even 'A Berlin Chronicle' puts it vaguely), of the working world, social misery and class struggle, was simply missing:

The poor – for rich children of his generation they lived in the country. And if at this early age he could picture the poor, it was, without his knowing either name or origin, in the image of the sponger who is actually a rich person, though without money, since he stands – far removed from the process of production and the exploitation not yet abstracted from it – in the same contemplative relation to his destitution as the rich man to his wealth.[14]

The possibility of Zionism

It was not only his studies and his work for the school reform movement that preyed on Benjamin's mind during these months and years. In addition, demands were made on his conscience during a holiday in Stolpmünde on the Baltic (now Ustka, in Poland). Here 'for the first time', according to a letter written in August 1912, 'Zionism and Zionist activity' entered his mind 'as a possibility and hence perhaps as a duty'.[15] During this holiday, Benjamin's companion, Franz Sachs, introduced him to a young student named Kurt Tuchler who presented the ideas of Zionism to him in 'daily, one might even say hourly' conversations[16] – with the intention of winning him over. It was the first time that Benjamin was seriously confronted with the question of his Jewish origins, but it was not to be the last. In the 1920s his personal and economic circumstances even led him to consider emigrating to Palestine. His reasons for not taking this step were already evident in this early confrontation with his Judaism.

It is important to note that it seems always to have been outside elements which prompted him to achieve clarity in this matter. These were either personal encounters, changes in his situation and practical circumstances, or the effects of major historical upheavals, such as the seizure of power by the Nazis in 1933. During the years 1912/13, two of Benjamin's acquaintances urged him to reflect upon his Jewish roots: Kurt Tuchler, with whom he continued to exchange ideas after their meeting in Stolpmünde (at first by letter, and then on a joint trip to Paris in May 1913), and Ludwig Strauß, a fellow student in Freiburg. Benjamin's correspondence with Tuchler appears to have been lost, but his letters to Strauß survived intact and provide some interesting insights into the culture of the time. Benjamin's attitudes towards his Hebraic origins were probably shared by a large proportion of the 'old-established' Jewry in Germany, especially in Berlin.

Benjamin's family were part of the group of 'German citizens of Jewish origin' whom radical Zionists at the time disparagingly called 'Christmas Jews'. The expression alluded to the general deterioration of customs and traditions, which was demonstrated very clearly by the fact that many 'Sons of Israel' celebrated not only the important Jewish festivals, but also Christmas – in the same way as their Christian neighbours: as a 'national festival',[17] complete with carols and gifts under the Christmas tree. What was seen by orthodox Jews and Zionists at the very least as the crude bad taste of those around them, was of course the norm for Benjamin. Throughout his life he failed to gain a deeper relationship with his Jewish roots, least of all during these early years. He had enjoyed, as he wrote in a letter to Strauß, 'a liberal upbringing'. He had gained his 'key intellectual experience before Judaism ever became important or problematic' to him. 'All that' he 'really knew of it' was 'simply anti-Semitism and a vague piety. As a religion it was remote [to him], as a national aspiration unknown.'[18] Even during the religious instruction that he received at school from the Rabbis Kroner and Galliner, he was taught nothing more than the 'conciliatory religious standpoint' which stressed 'affiliation to a cultural community rather than to a people'. The Kaiser Friedrich School was no

The 'New Synagogue' in Oranienburger Straße, 1932.

fertile ground for Zionism. Just as slight was the consideration shown towards what the headmaster of the school called the 'exaggerated demands of the parents' that the 'religious holidays and Sabbaths' should be respected.[19] Benjamin was simply not brought up as a Jew. The few aspects of his roots that did manifest themselves tended to be rejected by him during his childhood and adolescence. His memoirs are full of remarks that express a quite passionate dislike of religious services. He attended them in the large 'New Synagogue' in Oranienburger Straße – the pride and symbol of the city's rising liberal Jewish bourgeoisie – in a spirit that verged on 'blasphemous indifference'.[20]

At first sight, this reflection of the situation seems to contradict Benjamin's assertion that traditional and liberal approaches to Judaism still competed in his parental home. His mother, 'on grounds of a family tradition', sympathized with the Jewish Reform Community, while his father's 'upbringing inclined him more to the orthodox rite'.[21] Naturally, the mother was the main influence in questions of the children's faith, and the significance of this can be illustrated in a brief look at Jewish Reform Communities.

Jewish Reform Communities came into being all over the German Empire during the latter half of the nineteenth century. Their innovative efforts[22] were aimed primarily at modernizing the synagogue service. On closer inspection it becomes apparent, however, that these innovations depended greatly on the communities' readiness to assimilate themselves to their German surroundings, even in ritual acts of worship. A Berlin group of the Jewish Reform Community took these changes particularly far. Almost everything was new: the temple itself; bare-headed visits to the synagogue (now on *Sundays*, instead of Fridays); the liturgy (accompanied by the organ and chorales composed by the eminent former musical director of the Berlin Opera House, Giacomo Meyerbeer); and prayers and sermon in the *German* language. The services were virtually interchangeable with those of the Protestant church, and the political aspects of the reforms, which were only marginally less radical and extensive in the other liberal Jewish communities in Berlin, were quite evident. In many respects these changes simply reflected the new requirements of the members of the community. Too many among them no longer had sufficient grasp of the language of their forefathers to understand more than the bare substance of the ancient Hebraic invocations to Yahveh in the prayers and sermons. The changes also paid due attention to contemporary aesthetic tastes, as well as to the new ideas about

'Nor do I want to say anything about Zionism. I have not found principals such as yours in the Jewish work of any Zionist I have hitherto met. I did not feel that the Zionists led their lives in a Jewish fashion or had more than vague notions regarding the Jewish spirit. Jewishness was for them a question of instinct, Zionism a matter of political organization. Their personalities were not inwardly determined to any degree by Jewishness: they propagate Palestine but booze just like Germans. Perhaps they are necessary: but they are the last people who should talk of the Jewish experience. They are neither here nor there. Have they ever reflected upon about schools, literature, inner life, the state in a Jewish way?'[17] (Benjamin to Ludwig Strauß) form. Did not music and song intensify the general rapture? And was it not high time to put an end to the 'lack of culture' in the synagogues: that unholy confusion of the voices and the people within (all the many individuals who turned to their God in prayer), which was alluded to in the vernacular in the scornful expression 'as noisy as a Jewish school' (meaning a synagogue)? In their entirety, these reforms amounted to something that stirred the foundations of a particular concept of Jewishness. A final example shows how far the implementation of anti-traditionalism, conducted most energetically by the radical Berlin Reform Community, simultaneously undermined the characteristic, historically evolved identity of the Jews. Among the 'innovations' came a small revision of the prayer books: gradually the rather too literal references to the Jews returning (or being led back) to the Promised Land were removed. 'Zion', the holy mountain of Jerusalem, became the victim of general ethical declarations: once understood as the concrete geographical destination of the Jews upon redemption, it was now reduced to a mere symbol, and thus, 'the messianic idea was abstracted to a notion of salvation applying to mankind in general'.[23]

Anyone, like Benjamin, who had grown up within *this* tradition of Judaism would have had great difficulty in finding an identity in their origins alone. This helps to explain why there was never an open swing towards Jewishness in any of his thought or work, even after the seizure of power by the Nazis. It also explains his harsh, dry rejection of Zionism, which was diametrically opposed to his own cosmopolitan notions. As he wrote in another letter to his friend Ludwig Strauß,

if you . . . say: school, the question of the woman, socialism: none of these have anything to do with Judaism, these are human questions; then I would say that a nationalism that does not examine everything – above all the most human and important questions – is quite worthless, is nothing more than a dangerous force of sloth.

Consequently, it seemed to him that 'everything Jewish that goes beyond the self-evident Jewishness in me is dangerous', and he felt unable to make Zionism his personal 'political persuasion'. Indeed, he even felt the need to fight it with 'radical politics'. Benjamin felt his only link was to a 'fruitful cultural Judaism' which had firstly to develop its own concepts. But he wished to 'keep a principled distance' from activities concerning 'practical Zionism'. The most he could imagine himself doing was to contribute to work on a periodical that Strauß was planning at the time. In addition, he had no wish to break from his 'firm four-year commitment' to the Wickersdorf idea.[24] (And his most active period in the school reform movement was still to come.)

The Youth Movement

'Nothing negative whatsoever has been noted regarding his conduct at the university.' (Benjamin's leaving certificate from the Royal Friedrich Wilhelm University, Berlin, from 11 April 1913)

Benjamin spent the winter of 1912/13 back in the city of his home, where he enrolled in October as a student of philosophy at the Royal Friedrich Wilhelm University. During his first semester in Berlin he took the opportunity to attend lectures by Georg Simmel. (Shortly afterwards Simmel left Berlin for Strasbourg – then German – where he finally received the professorship that he, as a Jew, had always been denied in the foremost university of the Reich.)[25] A complete picture of Benjamin's views on Simmel cannot be gleaned from any of his letters, diaries or literary portraits. But numerous, both incidental and detailed references to and remarks about Simmel as well as direct citations in conversations, autobiographical works and other writings indicate that Benjamin saw him as one of the more positive figures of his academic career.[26] Seen as a whole, they permit the conclusion that Benjamin had a silent admiration for the man, though not without certain reservations. Benjamin the student was fascinated by Simmel's absolute precision in speech and writings, the diversity of topics in his lectures, his eye for detail, his references to marginal cultural and historical phenomena, his inquiring scepticism: in short by his ability to promote independent thought and a growing awareness rather than to induce numb astonishment at the monuments of the history of philosophy. His admiration was shared by distinguished figures such as Stefan George, Charles du Bos, Ernst Bloch, Georg Lukács, Gertrud Kantorowics, Margarete Susman, Ludwig Marcuse, and Gershom Scholem. Simmel was, as Albert Salomon once put it, 'a genuinely philosophical spirit',[27] beside whom most other university lecturers paled by comparison. So it is doubtless no accident that the other professors whose lectures Benjamin attended during his five semesters in Berlin (the philosophers Ernst Cassirer and Benno Erdmann, the art historian Adolf Goldschmidt, the Germanists Max Hermann and Gustav Roethe)[28] are scarcely mentioned in his writings, except in ironic or polemical allusions. It should be noted, however, that what Simmel deemed to be an exemplary attitude towards the manifestation of cultural history only came to play a part later on in Benjamin's intellectual development. For the time being his inclinations and activities remained firmly with the Youth Movement.

Just how much of his time he devoted to the movement can be seen from the numerous initiatives in which he was involved. Benjamin was one of the founder-members of the 'Detachment for School Reform'[29] which was established at the Friedrich Wilhelm University at the beginning of the winter semester. In addition he was elected (in 1912/13) on to the committee of the Free Students' Union.[30] Outside the university he worked for the Berlin group of the 'League for Free School Communities', taking his turn at chairing meetings and occasionally giving talks to members and guests.[31] Finally, his resources must have been further taxed by his frequent meetings with Wyneken [32] which were by no means restricted to planning and revising various lecture and discussion evenings (such as the one in November at Benjamin's former school).[33] For Wyneken also read to his star pupil, in private, from his own works,[34] which clearly demonstrates the depth of their mutual trust at the time.

School Reform, Free Students' Union, Free School Communities and Wyneken: if one adds to these the words *Sprechsaal* and *Anfang* (the youth magazine), one has more or less outlined the field within which Benjamin's concept of the 'Youth Movement' existed. It was doubtless a somewhat restricted view of the general awakening of the youth, given the large number of groups and initiatives that came into being all over Germany during the two to three decades around 1900, or so it might seem. Naturally, pedagogic reform was by no means all that the Youth Movement publically encompassed. A great diversity of groups and societies, some peripheral some with more lasting influence, participated in the movement. The spectrum ranges from protest movements in the stricter sense (the early 'Wandervogel' and the School Reform Movement) to the movements for healthy living (anti-alcohol campaigners, vegetarians, naturists), from artists' colonies (Worpswede and Dachau) to the People's Theatre Movement and consumer and housing co-ops (the Workers' Movement, the Zionists, the country commune 'Eden' near Oranienburg), and from the Garden Town Movement of the Kampffmeyer brothers to the 'New Communities' (Monte Verità in Ascona, the Berlin community run by the Hart brothers). If the Wyneken followers viewed themselves as being at the heart of the Youth Movement, it was with the self-confidence of young people who had assumed the most advanced position in the struggle over the contents of a new, more modern education and way of life. They

'My main interests were philosophy, German literature and art history. Consequently I mainly attended lectures by the professors Cassirer, Erdmann, Goldschmidt, Hermann and Simmel in Berlin.'[18] (Georg Simmel, Max Hermann)

Gustav Roethe.

47

formed an avant-garde which was quite uncompromising in the way that it constantly defended its convictions, and this not only brought them frequent censure from their parents and teachers, but also from the other (state) authorities and guardians of public order (e.g. parliament, the police and the courts): 'people were relegated from schools and universities, forbidden to assemble or enter the country; there were house searches, orders from the police to disband, preliminary hearings at court'.[35] Indeed, several representatives of the (Bavarian) people showed their concern about the proponents of 'Youth Culture' by means of anxious questions and debates in parliament. In numerical terms – one of their former advocates Siegfried Bernfeld, later to be a professor of psychology, estimated their number at around 3,000 in the year 1914[36] – the Wyneken followers constituted a minority, and their influence on the Youth Movement was correspondingly small. Consequently, they were always the underdogs in the factional struggles, generally the losers at the ballot meetings, and normally came away empty-handed from the nominations for the more important positions in the various organizations. But they were scarcely put off by this, for they did not measure the success of their work by such formal and quantitative criteria. Benjamin's 'We are always very few' but 'we really don't care about that'[37] clearly expresses their attitude.

The pupils and students around Wyneken defined themselves as a movement for youth culture. In keeping with their teacher or (intellectual) 'leader', they did not see 'the education problem' as being purely restricted to school (and university) reform, but rather as a question of an overall view on the world.

We are living in a dark interlude, a period of transition. Anyone who wishes to take only these times into account and to feel at home in them must say: 'Après nous le déluge.' But we want to say: 'Après nous la jeunesse!' We must find the way through these times. That, at present, is the great task of education, one that will have consequences for world history. Right now, when it is no longer simply a matter of passing on received traditions but rather of paving the way for a new culture, the entire onus of our responsibility to culture and world history lies in education. Through education we must shape the future and tap the springs of a better age – in a new mentality that will be utterly alien to the present generation.

The adherents were fully aware of what 'extreme and radical idealism'[38] lay at the core of this world-view. A similar pathos filled Benjamin, who regarded himself at the time as a 'strict and fanatical adept of G. Wyneken'.[39] In the previously mentioned essay 'School Reform, a Cultural Movement', we find sentences that have a very similar ring to them:

We are growing beyond the bounds of our present time. Not merely because we think sub specie aeternitatis, *but because by educating we both think and operate* sub specie aeternitatis. *What we want is ... the* nurturing *of the natural upward development of humanity:* culture. *The expression of this, our wish, is: education.*[40]

This determined desire for culture formed the background even for work which seemed entirely practical.

When, in the years before the Great War, the first criticisms began to be levelled at the parental home and the conservative school tradition, this was always done with positive reference to the boarding school. The initial demands that this kind of school be universally acknowledged were made with the Lietzian model in mind. Later this model was replaced by Wyneken's Wickersdorf School Community. Wynekenians scarcely stated explicitly that they wished to establish the 'Free School Community' as the standard. They did not see themselves primarily as just school reformers. An essay by Benjamin on this topic begins, by no means by accident, with the following remarks: 'The FSC [Free School Community] has not arisen from the need for partial reforms; its central aims are not: "Less Greek, more sport", or: "No corporal punishment, but rather a teacher–pupil relationship based on mutual respect".' After this comment aimed at Lietz's boarding-school system, which he knew from first-hand experience, he continues:

Even if its programme contains many of the demands of modern pedagogics, even if one of its self-evident premises is above all an open intercourse between teachers and pupils that is not ruled by official authority, the essence of its establishment lies far beyond pedagogics in the strict sense, for it is centred rather on a philosophical, a metaphysical idea – albeit one that is 'free from the cosmological metaphysics of this or that party'.[41]

The Freiburg faction

Now, in the course of this magnificent summer, I have achieved peace and quiet: and when I look out of my window at the church square, the old well, a single very tall poplar in the sun and behind it houses that look like they belong in Goethe's Weimar (very small) – I can hardly imagine the appalling fact

*that I almost (if I had been elected by the Free Students' Union)
remained in Berlin.*[42]

Benjamin is describing here the view from the window of his
'digs' in 49[1] Kirchstraße, Freiburg. He had not returned there
completely of his own free will. Contrary to expectations, he
had not been re-elected to the committee of the Berlin Free
Students Union, so now he could assume other responsibilities
for Wyneken and his fellow campaigners.

After Christian Papmeyer, one of the most active of
Wyneken's followers, had departed from Freiburg, the political
activity of the School Reform Movement at the university
had come to a virtual standstill. Doubtless this was in part a
consequence of the fact that they had cast themselves, somewhat hastily and with exaggerated expectations, into the arms
of the Free Students' Union. Wyneken's call at the time to form
Detachments for School Reform within the existing unaffiliated
students' organizations made good sense, as such. By entering
an existing institution he could expect his ideas to have a
broader impact, and the Free Students' Union, a body repre-
senting the interests of those students who were not members
of the fraternities, might be turned into a powerful vehicle for
the fight for fundamental changes in education and training.
But he does not seem to have allowed for the sluggishness of an
apparatus that was too often controlled by people who, even if
they were agreeably different from the drinking-and-duelling
fraternity corps, were also quite rigidly traditional and not keen
on radical reform. They attached more importance to the
administration, prestige and solemn evocation of handed-down
educational ideals, than to justified demands for long-overdue
political reforms in (university) education. In any case they
rejected the radical nature of these reforms because it shook
their conservative world-view.

Perhaps because the Free Students at the Albert Ludwig
University mirrored the outside image of their organization too
closely, or because they were represented here by young people
singularly lacking in initiative, it was a fact that the Freiburg
Union existed in name only from the beginning of the summer
semester in 1913. 'There are no announcements to be seen on
the bulletin board', Benjamin wrote indignantly in a letter
shortly after his arrival, 'no organized groups – no lectures.' The
letter dated 30 April 1913 was to Carla Seligson (1893–1956),
a close friend in Berlin and fellow campaigner in the Cultural
Youth Movement. He went on to write that, having left Berlin,

he was beginning gradually to get a clearer picture of the Free Students' Union of its attitude to the Youth Movement in general and the School Reform Movement in particular.[43] Benjamin finally received confirmation of his momentary suspicion over a year later, at the 14th Free Students' congress in Weimar, to which we shall turn shortly.

According to Benjamin's autobiographical accounts of the time, his return to Freiburg was prompted not only by his defeat at the ballot in Berlin, but also by 'a friend's letter'[44] and by Wyneken's request that he take over the Detachment for School Reform in Freiburg. Understandably, Wyneken very much wished to see this institution continue to function as an efficient body, for it was in Freiburg that his movement had first entered university, and consequently the credibility of his work and ideas and the proof of their tenability were reflected in this detachment. The detachment that Benjamin found on his arrival consisted of a small circle of literary-minded friends, no more than ten male and female students in all, who met each Tuesday in the 'Akademikerheim' at 29 Friedrichstraße, also the meeting place of the Free Students' Union,[45] for joint readings and discussions. Among the members was the Expressionist writer (and medical student) Philipp Keller,[46] whom Benjamin already knew from the summer semester of 1912, and who at the time was writing a novel which was to be published that year by Rowohlt, *Gemischte Gefühle [Mixed Feelings]*, later described by Benjamin as 'one of the most readable books of 1913'.[47] Other members included Christoph Friedrich Heinle (1894–1914), Gertrud Kraker, Otto (Harald Alfred) Manning and Georg Englert. With the exception of Heinle, with whom Benjamin remained close friends until the former's early death, he shared little more than a feeling of camaraderie with these people. The fact that they adhered to the formal address of *Sie*, customary among students at the time, shows the limits of their intimacy. A definite distance was certainly produced by the presence of intellectual antagonisms, above all in Benjamin's relationship with Keller.[48]

It is difficult to see from the documents and reports available what innovations Benjamin actually brought to the re-established Freiburg group. It is possible that their discussions adopted a new, more impassioned tone, which their leader knew how to use to good effect.[49] It is also possible that they were more zealous in gaining new subscribers to *Der Anfang*, which devoted more space to the writings of Spitteler and Wyneken. But apart from this, things seemed to remain as they

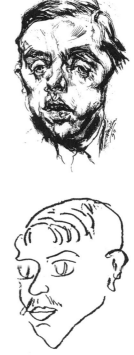

'The kind of people I associate with! [. . .] There's Keller, with the beginning of a new important novel and with a beautiful girlfriend whom I often see. There's Heinle, a good fellow. "Drinks, eats a lot, and writes poems." [. . .] An eternal dreamer and very German. Not very well dressed. Englert – he dresses even worse. Also has a girlfriend. His childishness is of immense proportions. He worships Keller as a god and values me as a demon. Note that all the people with whom I associate here are Christians, and tell me what this means.'[19] (Ludwig Meidner: portrait of P. Keller; portrait of C. F. Heinle)

51

were. Even the list of members scarcely differed from that of the literary circle previously led by Keller.

A lecture by Jonas Cohn on 'The Aims of Education and Instruction' was closely linked with Benjamin's school reform activities. However, of all the lectures and seminars that he attended at the Albert Ludwig University during the summer semester in 1913, the only one that struck him as noteworthy was evidently Rickert's lecture on logic, with its 'as yet unpublished system which is not even known to his personal students'. The 'philosophy of values' propounded by the neo-Kantian philosopher enriched the classical areas of logic, aesthetics, ethics and religious philosophy by introducing a 'completely new discipline': "the axiology of the perfected life". It is within the context of the "perfected life" that the "principle of the feminine" gains its meaning. Benjamin found the conclusions that Rickert drew from his views 'on woman and the relationship between the sexes' unacceptable because they declared 'woman as in principle incapable of the highest moral perfection'. The issue in itself affected him because questions about the relationship between the sexes, Eros, prostitution ('What is the moral meaning of a prostitute's life?') and 'women's culture'[50] in general were among the subjects most hotly debated by the 'Youth Culture' wing of the Youth Movement.[51]

'Cohn's Seminar on the "Critique of Judgement" and Schiller's aesthetics has been chemically purified of ideas. The only thing you get out of it is that you read the texts. Later I'll give them some thought. I also just sit and pursue my own thoughts in Rickert's seminar . . . All of literary Freiburg now attends his lectures; as an introduction to his logic, he is presenting an outline of his system which lays the foundation for a completely new philosophical discipline: philosophy of the perfect life. (Woman as its representative.) As interesting as it is problematical.'[20] (Arch-Ducal Baden Albert Ludwig University: Walter Benjamin's course list for the summer semester of 1913)

Arch-Ducal Baden Albert Ludwig University: Walter Benjamin's course list for the summer semester of 1913

At Whitsun, Benjamin travelled for the first time to Paris. He was accompanied by two fairly longstanding acquaintances, both Zionists: Kurt Tuchler and Siegfried Lehmann, Benjamin's childhood playmate who was later to run the Jewish people's home in the *Scheunenviertel* district of Berlin near Alexanderplatz.[52]

From Benjamin's
postcard collection: Paris.

The decision to take the trip came like a 'stroke of fortune',[53] as Benjamin wrote in a letter to his friend Blumenthal. At the time he probably had no idea how firmly he was establishing his future relationship with the city. Although he only got to know Paris properly in the 1920s, his intimate relationship with the city was founded in these two short weeks, which later seemed to him like 'three whole months'. During his first visit to Paris, on the *grands boulevards* and at the Louvre, in whose galleries he came to 'understand art' without actively taking part in it, he already felt almost 'more at home' than in Berlin. In its streets, whose 'houses [seemed] made, not to be lived in, but to be stone stage sets' for the *flâneur*,[54] he absorbed something that appeared to be totally lacking in his home city: tradition and history, in all the facets of its evolution. 'Paris, the city in the mirror', as he later entitled a declaration of love to this 'capital of the world':[55] a mirror of its times.

The little green magazine

The first issue of *Der Anfang*, or more correctly the first issue in its 'official jacket', appeared in May 1913. A distinguished publisher in Jena, Eugen Diederichs, had been approached, but he did not like the idea of a periodical for young people, so the little green magazine was eventually printed by Franz Pfemfert's Expressionist publishing house Die Aktion.[56] Wyneken was legally responsible for its contents under the terms of the press laws. (The imprint also named one Fritz Telmann as responsible for Austro-Hungary – the magazine appeared simultaneously in Berlin and Vienna.) It is obvious that Wyneken had as little to do with the editorial work as his Austrian colleague. The work was in fact done by two young people: Georges Barbizon in the German capital, and Siegfried Bernfeld in the two capitals of the Habsburg Empire. A form of *Der Anfang* had already existed since 1908. It had been founded by adolescent school pupils with the aim of creating a forum in which young people could talk openly about their problems, without being denied their say by their parents or schools. At that time the periodical had been 'edited in Berlin, Vienna, Zurich, Paris, London and once again in Berlin'.[57] These were the various stations in the life of Georges Barbizon, to whom the magazine largely owed its existence. His real name was Georg Gretor, and his pseudonym came from the French town of Barbizon, where he was born on 25 July 1892, the son of an art dealer. For all the antagonism that developed in their relationship during the period around 1913/14, initially the biographies of Benjamin and Barbizon show more parallels than contrasts. Both came from well-to-do families, and both had the same man to thank for the pivotal experiences of their adolescence: Gustav Wyneken. Barbizon did not encounter him, as Benjamin had, at Haubinda (where the school reformer was still subject to numerous constraints regarding his notions on teaching and intellectual breeding), but first met him in Wickersdorf.[58] But here he became an ardent admirer of his teacher and a fanatical defender of his ideas for a free school community, which, in Barbizon's view, were not even compromised by

'. . . under the present cultural conditions, the only platform where school pupils can express themselves without being patronised.'

Advertisement from Franz Pfemfert's magazine *Die Aktion*.

Wyneken's questionable attitudes at the outbreak of the World War. Early on Barbizon, in collaboration with Siegfried Bernfeld, developed an explicitly political and to some extent socialist interpretation of these ideas. This was finally to separate him from Benjamin, who at that point was neither willing nor able to construe Wyneken's ideas in this way. Their paths had first crossed in Berlin, where Barbizon lived for a while with the family of Käthe Kollwitz, with whose son, Hans, Benjamin was also acquainted. With the outbreak of the war, Barbizon moved to Switzerland: first to St Gallen, then to Zurich (where he was an active journalist, promoting a slightly modified and extended Wickersdorf idea) and finally to Basle. Despite the bitterness of their previous disputes – the two of them had come to blows in connection with an attempt by Heinle and Simon Ghuttmann to take over the editorship of the *Anfang* by means of a kind of *coup de main* – they still maintained 'superficial contact' with one another in Switzerland (Benjamin first arrived in the middle of 1917).[59]

Siegfried Bernfeld (during his student days).

The first *Anfang* was subtitled a *Magazine for Future Art and Literature.* But this did not necessarily reflect the ideas of the editors and contributors. Rather, the periodical attempted from the start to tackle 'adolescent problems' in the broadest sense and in a highly provocative manner. Almost inevitably this led to conflicts with the adult world, with teachers and parents who felt that their authority was being undermined. Their threats and protests forced the young journalists to 'content themselves for a while with literary allures',[60] which is to say: to devote themselves to purely literary topics. This camouflage did have the advantage of drawing wider circles of school pupils to the magazine: young adults who first found the publication genuinely attractive after reading its literary contributions. May 1913 saw the publication of the first issue of the third and last series of the *Anfang*.[61] Benjamin had played a considerable role in its production. The subtitle was changed to *A United Magazine for Youth*, and it was indeed a magazine for young people, produced by young people. The contributions came exclusively from students and school pupils, except on one occasion, in June 1913, when the editors felt justified in publishing an article entitled 'Find Yourself' by Wilhelm Ostwald.[62] However, the rest of those working on the magazine responded at once with harsh protests at such high-handedness.[63] The 'Ostwald case' remained the only instance in which the periodical opened its pages to 'adults'. Their only opportunity to contribute to the *Anfang* was in the 'readers' letters' section. (Among the better-known writers who availed themselves of this possibility were Gustav Wyneken, the critic Alfred Kerr and the philosopher Paul Natorp.)

With the publication of the *Anfang*, 'the resolute Youth Movement entered the public arena'.[64] This entry was however quite limited, as is evident from the magazine's circulation: just over one thousand copies were distributed amongst school pupils and students. The above recollection by the chief editor in Berlin was not intended to glorify his work in retrospect as being of broad political impact. The *Anfang* never had such an impact, as was agreed by all who were responsible for its production. During the bare eighteen months of its existence (the last issue appeared in July 1914), sixteen issues were compiled. The contributors were pupils and students from the whole of Germany and Austro-Hungary. The majority had their articles published under the cloak of total anonymity, signed them with just their initials, or chose evocative pseudonyms: Fritz R. (the brother of Grete Radt, Benjamin's fiancée at the time) signed alongside H.S. and E.R.M., a (Greek) 'Ado' ('I sing') and a Latin 'Numquam Idem' ('never the same'), the deity Hyperion and 'Agathon' ('the virtuous one'),[65] 'a female student' and a certain '(M.G.) Grünling' (the appellation chosen by Martin Gumpert). Only a few placed their whole names at the foot of their articles, such as Herbert Blumenthal, Hans Kollwitz, Alfred Kurella, Grete Radt and Hans Reichenbach.

Martin Gumpert.

Puberty cannot be assuaged by poetry

Right from the start, the anonymity of the attacks in the *Anfang* on schools and the parental home was a thorn in the side of the country's conservatives. Without the authors' names, the threatening gestures and sanctions with which they were accustomed to intimidating or even silencing critics of their educational precepts were of no avail. The 'cry of outrage'[66] that passed through the adult world upon publication of the first issues led to sustained fire at the magazine from the printed media, and even parliament was eventually involved in the consequences. Among the first to become acquainted with the narrowmindedness of the reactionary circles of Wilhelmine society – teachers' associations and philological societies, former and active members of student fraternities, officers and politicians from the right – was Benjamin's friend, Herbert Blumenthal. One of his essays appeared under the heading 'Eroticism and Youth', and the title alone provoked a scream of indignation. For the newspaper journalists of the *Frankfurter Oderzeitung*, the *Essener Volks-Zeitung*, the *Tägliche Rundschau*

'Particularly urgent and vivid is an article, "Youthful eroticism", contributed by Herbert Blumenthal, a truly disturbing expression of the distress of a boy suffering the torments of adolescence.'
(From the *Frankfurter Oderzeitung*, 3 October 1913)

(Berlin) and the reactionary protestant *Neue Preußische Zeitung*, Blumenthal's expositions on prevailing double standards revealed nothing but 'abysms of mental and moral confusion' which could only have a 'devastating effect on unformed minds'. The publication of such articles was considered 'a crime against youth', and demands were made to the 'proper authorities to consider what should be done'.[67] Naturally, threats of this sort were not reserved solely for the students and pupils who wrote for the magazine. Others were also intimidated: above all Wyneken, who was constantly denounced by these circles as a kind of 'Pied Piper of Hamelin'. He was not only accused of editing the *Anfang* (some adult participation was legally required), but also of influencing the content of individual contributions. After Wyneken, the chief target of this hostility was the leftist publisher Franz Pfemfert. These circumstances were quite clear to those affected and they repudiated the charges as slander. They also prompted the young editorial board of the *Anfang* repeatedly to issue statements emphasizing the journal's non-political standpoint.

Benjamin was actively involved from the very start, and contributed to the first issue with an article entitled 'Teaching and Evaluation', criticizing the school system.[68] In the June 1913 issue, under the title 'Romanticism', he published a 'speech to school pupils that was never given'. This was his first presentation of a real example of a 'young people's philosophy of life, to prove to opponents and ignoramuses that such a thing exists, and to provide friends with something to read and reflect upon'[69]. It was a hymn to the 'romanticism of truth', which was meant to grasp the 'intellectual connections, the history of work', and allow 'this understanding to become an experience

The first issue of *Der Anfang*, May 1913.

so as to act thereupon in a highly sober, unromantic manner'.[70] The author was no doubt unperturbed when the editors of the right-wing *Kreuz-Zeitung* (as the *Neue Preußische Zeitung* was nicknamed by its critics) found his article 'incredibly unclear'.[71] A response to his article that appeared in the pages of the *Anfang* itself he took more seriously.[72] Benjamin claimed that this 'sermon', as he called it, allowed nothing but the kind of dark, mysterious and reactionary romanticism whose 'sounds, rising from dark, ghostly realms, make us shudder and fill us with holy terror'.[73] He responded with the terse comment that 'art should not be morphine for the human will, suffering under the painful present'. Committed youth, maintained Benjamin, holds 'art too high' for that, apart from which 'puberty cannot be assuaged by poetry'.[74]

Benjamin completed his period of study at Albert Ludwig University on 1 August 1913, after which he took a trip with his parents, his brother and his sister to Freudenstadt for a few days. He then travelled with his mother and an aunt to (South) Tyrol for several weeks, 'presumably', as he confided to his former schoolfriend Ernst Schoen, not without a trace of self-irony, so as to 'bring some order into [his] life and to stabilize a six-month period of inactivity, May to September'.[75] Finally he returned to Berlin at the beginning of September, earlier than originally planned. During the following weeks, Wyneken, Benjamin, and his friends Sachs, Blumenthal, Barbizon and Heinle devoted themselves entirely to their joint preparations for the next major events of the German Youth Movement, which were staged during the first two weeks of October 1913.

The League for School Reform had held its Third German Congress for Young People's Education and Youth Research under the title 'The Sexes and Young People's Education' in Breslau on 4 October. Professor of psychology William Stern (1871–1938),[76] Gertrud Bäumer and Benjamin's former teacher at Freiburg, Jonas Cohn, gave the principal lectures[77] before 'almost five hundred leading personalities from the circles of school reformers and three hundred men and women from all walks of life who are involved in the work of the School Reform Movement'.[78] This congress was followed by the 'First Student Pedagogic Conference', organized by the Pedagogic Group at the University of Breslau. Benjamin gave a lecture on the 'Goal and the Direction of the Student Pedagogic Groups at the Universities of the German Reich'.[79] This conference, attended by well over 100 participants,[80] saw the first open confrontation

'You may have heard about the pedagogical student congress that will take place in Breslau on 7 October. I recently learned that I will be giving a talk there; besides me, [Siegfried] Bernfeld, head of the Academic Committee for School Reform in Vienna, will also give a talk. A third speaker is a Mr [Alfred] Mann, who is a member of an opposition group. Both orientations represented by the student movement, the one associated with Wyneken and the other with Prof. Stern (my cousin), will confront each other for the first time at this congress. In Breslau we will also for the first time get an overview of our troops (as I believe they can be called), our wider circle of friends.'[21]

between the two prevailing factions within the student pedagogic movement: the so-called 'Breslau faction', represented by William Stern and his students, and the 'Freiburg faction', represented by Gustav Wyneken and his adherents. One of the aims of the conference was to amalgamate the various pedagogic reform groups: this was not successful. The differences that emerged during the talks by Wyneken, Stern and Benjamin, as well as during the joint discussions, proved irreconcilable. The 'Breslau faction' was more interested in practical work, whereas the Freiburg group had a decidedly intellectual orientation. In the end, they simply agreed on a mutual information policy.

Young voices

Benjamin travelled from Breslau to Kassel to participate in the First Free German Youth Congress which was held between 10 and 12 October on the ('High') Meißner[81] and at Castle Hanstein. The conference had been convened by several of the most active groups within the Youth Movement (including various Wandervogel Leagues, school communities and academic groupings). The meeting was generally seen as the climactic event of the Youth and Wandervogel movements, and was celebrated with according enthusiasm. And before the conference had even ended, Franz Pfemfert published a hymn in *Die Aktion* dedicated to these young people, who had at last found their own voice:

Die deutsche Jugend steht an einem geschichtlichen Wendepunkt. Die Jugend, bisher aus dem öffentlichen Leben der Nation ausgeschaltet und angewiesen auf eine passive Rolle des Lernens, auf eine spielerisch-nichtige Geselligkeit und nur ein Anhängsel der älteren Generation, beginnt sich auf sich selbst zu besinnen. Sie versucht, unabhängig von den trägen Gewohnheiten der Alten und von den Geboten einer häßlichen Konvention sich selbst ihr Leben zu gestalten. Sie strebt nach einer Lebensführung, die jugendlichem Wesen entspricht, die es ihr aber zugleich auch ermöglicht, sich selbst und ihr Tun ernst zu nehmen und sich als einen besonderen Faktor in die allgemeine Kulturarbeit einzugliedern. Sie möchte das, was in ihr an reiner Begeisterung für höchste Menschheitsaufgaben, an ungebrochenem Glauben und Mut zu einem adligen Dasein lebt, als einen erfrischenden, verjüngenden Strom dem Geistesleben des Volkes zuführen, und sie glaubt, daß nichts heute unserm Volke nötiger ist, als solche Geistesverjüngung. Sie, die im Notfall jederzeit bereit ist, für die Rechte ihres Volkes mit dem Leben einzutreten, möchte auch in Kampf und Frieden des Werktags ihr frisches reines Blut dem Vaterlande weihen. ¶ Sie wendet sich aber von jenem billigen Patriotismus ab, der sich die Heldentaten der Väter in großen Worten aneignet, ohne sich zu eigenen Taten verpflichtet zu fühlen, dem vaterländische Gesinnung sich erschöpft in der Zustimmung zu bestimmten politischen Formeln, in der Bekundung des Willens zu äußerer Machterweiterung und in der Zerreißung der Nation durch die politische Verhetzung. ¶ Die unterzeichneten Verbände haben, jeder von seiner Seite her, den Versuch gemacht, den neuen Ernst für Jugend in Arbeit und Tat umzusetzen; sei es, daß sie den Befreiungskampf gegen den Alkohol aufnahmen, sei es, daß sie eine Veredlung der Geselligkeit oder eine Neugestaltung der akademischen Lebensformen versuchten, sei es, daß sie der städtischen Jugend das freie Wandern und damit ein inniges Verhältnis zu Natur und Volkstum wiedergaben und ihr einen eigenen Lebensstil schufen, sei es, daß sie den Typus einer neuen Schule als des Heims und Ursprungs einer neugearteten Jugend ausgestalteten. Aber sie alle empfinden ihre Einzelarbeit als den besonderen Ausdruck eines ihnen allen gemeinsamen Gefühls vom Wesen, Wert und Willen der Jugend, das sich wohl leichter in Taten umsetzen als auf Formeln bringen läßt. Diesen neuen, hier und da aufflammenden Jugendgeist haben sie als den ihnen allen gemeinsamen er

'German youth stands at a historic turning-point!'

An invitation to the 'Centenary Celebration on the High Meißner'.

Youth speaks. For the first time young people are speaking about their wishes, their needs, their yearnings, without questioning whether people will listen. But they will force themselves to be heard if they are indeed the young people we hope for. Youth is speaking, the future.[82]

But anyone who took a look behind the scenes would have noticed that for all their demonstrations of 'strength' (i.e. in purely quantitative terms), the movement had in fact very little unity. All attempts to form a powerful, non-aligned oppositional force within Wilhelmine society were foiled both by those participants who were all too willing to make compromises, and by a general fear of any intimate contact with politics. In the end, this meeting on the Meißner failed to ring in the new era in which young people between the ages of 15 and 25 would have their say in the shaping of society's future. Rather it was the beginning of an end, although only a minority of the participants realized this at the time.

The event was nevertheless a bone of contention for the country's conservative forces. For them, the fact that an itinerant youth wearing 'strange Gypsy-like costumes' dared 'to place themselves next to the student fraternities', as an indignant contemporary wrote in the *Casseler Tageblatt*,[83] seemed outrageous. What the author of this article (an unremitting tirade of hatred for youth culture, Wyneken and the *Anfang*)[84] simply (or deliberately?) overlooked in his agitation, was the fact that the young people who congregated on the Meißner did not *compare* themselves with the student fraternities but opposed them and all of their compulsory duels of honour, obligatory fencing matches and similar nonsense, and thus also opposed the presiding authorities of the German Reich. (Wilhelm II referred to himself as the 'first' fraternity student in the country.)

In contrast to Wyneken, Benjamin did not pay much attention to the denunciations published in the right-wing press, and the only indication that he had even noticed them was an ironic dedication to the *Tägliche Rundschau* in his own article on the Meißner conference. Apart from this, the article reads more as a reply to Pfemfert. Under the heading 'The Youth Remained Silent' (which was in itself explicit enough), his article was above all a damper for any over-hasty storms of enthusiasm. His message was that the youth should not allow themselves to be dazzled by the event: although they were experiencing a 'new reality', demonstrated by the large number of participants, this was 'nothing more than a confirmation of the spirit of the youth. Going on hikes, wearing ceremonial attire and doing folk dances

Gustav Wyneken holding his talk on the High Meißner.

are inconclusive activities and, in 1913, still have nothing to do with the intellectual spirit'. Besides which, this gathering proved that 'few' as yet 'had grasped the meaning of the word "youth"'. The idea that it alone radiates 'a new intellectual spirit, *the* intellectual spirit', cannot be recognized in these attempts to seek 'age-old, rational pretexts for self-discovery' or to achieve 'racial hygiene or land reform or abstinence'. This was the reason why those 'addicted to power' continued to have the real say. They had 'sullied the festival of youth with party jargon'. And for Benjamin 'the worst thing' was that the young people had put up with Ferdinand Avenarius's[85] 'jovial bonhomie'. This 'blitheness' simply 'robbed' the young people of 'the holy gravity' with which they gathered there. 'Distance' should be promoted, not 'smiling conviviality'. 'These young people', as Benjamin concluded, had 'not yet found their enemy, the one born for them to hate'. The 'protest against the family and school' was absent, and that was precisely where their intrinsic *youthfulness* – 'their indignation' – should have revealed itself. But the young people had remained silent in this respect. 'That powerful ideology: experience – maturity – authority – reason – the goodwill of adults – it was neither perceived nor eradicated at the youth conference'.[86] Benjamin suffers no illusions about ideological complexities and is fully aware of the coming balance of power when he describes the symptoms of the failure of the Youth Movement, and above all of its core: the Free German Youth. While previously it had been able to develop more or less unhindered and untouched by the world of the adults and their problems, as soon as it risked the first step into the public realm it was wooed and subsumed by the whole range of political parties and the most diverse groups, and above all by a large number of greater and lesser utopians, each of whom was their own self-anointed messiah. Consequently the Youth Movement gradually disintegrated after the Meißner conference, principally because it split into a large number of mutually competitive and at times antagonistic groups. Each created its own set organizational form, introduced membership rolls, furnished itself with statutes and formed editorial committees, and the favoured means for combating dissent became the expulsion of the members and factions concerned.

The first signs of decay were soon to become noticeable in Benjamin's immediate spheres of activity and personal life. The beginning was marked by events at a literary evening organized by the Berlin Free Students in December 1913. Benjamin wanted to read a critique of the majority's politics, but was prevented from doing so by the decision of a jury.[87] Just what 'reasons of principle' made them stop him stepping on to the stage can no longer be determined, as the relevant documents are missing. Perhaps it was the uncompromising blatancy of Bnejamin's statements, for his speech, at least in its printed form, begins by saying that it is necessary to unmask the apathy, intellectual vacuity and 'inadequacy' that resides in 'student society'. But perhaps it was the wilful way in which a philippic was to be delivered through the medium of art, so to speak. For it was quite clear in Benjamin's mind that the 'betrayal' of the youth issue also, indeed primarily, manifested itself in aesthetic ideas. Or was it simply his openly elitist demand for 'an even stricter process of selection for the genuine leaders' among the avant-garde of the Youth Movement?[88]

The movement's steady decline continued during the opening months of 1914: in the *Sprechsaal* and on the editorial board of the *Anfang*. In February Wyneken intimated that he wished to withdraw from his position as editor, thus triggering a heated debate over who was to be his successor. One person who pushed his way to the front of this struggle was the writer Wilhelm Simon Ghuttmann, who was closely linked to a group who called themselves the 'Neopatheticians'. The 'Neopatheticians' stemmed from the 'New Club' founded in 1909 by Kurt Hiller and seven of his friends. This literary club, which promoted a heady mixture of late symbolism, arrogant intellectualism and youthful iconoclasm, was the foundation stone of literary expressionism, and could boast such members as Georg Heym, Jakob van Hoddis and Mynona (Salomo Friedlaender), who were among the foremost writers of the movement.

Together with Heinle, Ghuttmann stopped at little in his attempt to seize the magazine's editorship. It is unclear just what part Benjamin played in this attempt, which was finally foiled by the resistance of Barbizon and Pfemfert. At any rate, Ghuttmann intended that Benjamin and Heinle should replace the editorial team of Barbizon/Bernfeld and set the magazine on an 'intellectual–literary' course. This would have concurred far more with Benjamin's ideas than the increasingly sharp political tone favoured by Barbizon and Bernfeld, whose own conceptions were drifting closer and closer towards the notion of a class struggle staged by the youth. In the middle of February, Benjamin, Barbizon 'and about six others' discussed 'the future of the *Anfang*' together. The fruit of these negotiations was the idea that one of the coming issues should be 'completely un-political, perhaps with poems by Hölderlin on the title page'.[89]

But this was never to materialize. The internal struggles were already sufficient reason for Benjamin to distance himself from the magazine. From then on he cloaked himself in what he considered to be a meaningful silence.[90] (It should be noted that his last article in the *Anfang* had in any case appeared some four months previously.) Later he toyed with the idea of publishing a 'lead article' in the magazine entitled 'My Farewell', in which he wanted to make those responsible 'ashamed of this publication and ask that it be allowed to disappear'.[91] But this also proved to be no more than empty words.

Benjamin's work with the Free Students' Union remained for the time being untouched by this wrangling. Despite suffering several nasty defeats, he continued 'sincerely' with his work during the summer months[92] even though his belief that his efforts might be crowned by some tangible success was lost in the process. In February 1914 he was elected to the committee of the Free Students' Union (for the summer semester of 1914), along with Heinle, Ferdinand Cohrs, Suse Behrendt and Alice Heymann. Benjamin credited himself with having done something towards raising the 'standards' of the Free Students' Union during his period of office by inviting a number of prominent speakers to its gatherings,[93] including Martin Buber (for a discussion on his book *Daniel*, published in 1913), David Baumgardt, Kurt Breysig and Ludwig Klages (who spoke on 'The Duality of the Personality and the Essential Differences between Mind and Spirit').[94] Upon considering this list of speakers, none of whom could be said to have been on the left, one might be tempted to draw conclusions about Benjamin's own political affiliations. But in fact at this time he placed himself 'somewhat to the left', somewhere between 'left-wing liberalism' and social democracy.[95]

One of the key events in the history of the Cultural Youth Movement although less significantly of the Free Students' Union itself – was the 14th Free Student Congress which began on 4 June in Weimar. It had been 'reserved' as the setting for the 'final statement' on the Youth Movement by the Free Students' Union,[96] and consequently fundamental discussions and fierce debates took place, which ended in a fiasco for the Wynekenians. Almost all of their motions were defeated by overwhelming majorities, above all one forwarded jointly by students from Munich and Berlin, for a more open stance towards the Youth Movement. The wording of the motion was diplomatic enough: 'The Free Students' Union will speak up for those young people, who have not yet acquired the requisite age

'We, the undersigned committee, would like humbly to inform your magnificence that the committee will defer as ever to the decisions of the authorities in questions of the regulation of the order of discussions.' (Letter to Max Planck after the re-election of the committee of the Berlin Free Students' Union)

Freie Studentenschaft
der Universität Berlin
Geschäftsstelle: Dorotheenstraße 6

Berlin, den _25 April_ 19_14_

[handwritten letter in German, Walter Benjamin]

'Might I ask you for the opportunity to talk with you in my capacity as representative of the Berlin Free Students' Union?' (From an unpublished letter to Martin Buber on 25 April 1914)

'A pupil of Gustav Wyneken, Walter Benjamin, spoke about the new university. It was wonderful to see how he, who has made his own way in the spirit of his teacher, directed his ideas towards one pole, towards the pinnacle of education. The only thing that detracted from this was that he – with the quite arrogant manner typical of these young Wickersdorf supporters – totally questioned the university, science and the culture of the past. In their own newly gained awareness of life these youth forget that all enduring cultural manifestations realize an awareness of life which is of the same strength and depth as theirs, and demands no less respect than the respect that this new youth wishes to command.'[22] (Walther A. Berendsohn)

for admission to university, whenever attempts are made to curtail their right to hold their own personal convictions'.[97] Nevertheless the motion was defeated by seventeen votes to five.[98] The responsibility for this rebuff lies in two areas: first Benjamin's utopian ideas of a reformed, even revolutionized university syllabus, which he presented from his position as the Berlin representative in a talk on 'The New University'; and second, the 'cold, politicizing element'[99] which Hermann Kranold from Munich introduced into the discussion, with his demand that 'the academic groups of the Meißner movement' be amalgamated into a 'working unity, a "bloc of the academic left" '.[100] This was slightly too much for the proud upholders of a 'German academic educational ideal'.[101] How could these traditionalists, who agreed with the country's conservatives in their conviction that what 'youth' demanded 'was not complete liberty and independence, but rather authority', show any understanding for ideas that 'totally questioned universities, scholarship and the culture of the past'?[102] They were interested in the 'fulfilment of old [!] dreams', as it was phrased by one of their protagonists, Walther A. Berendsohn (who after the Second World War became a noted expert in German exile literature).[103]

Benjamin was so embittered by the events in Weimar that he and his fellow campaigners from Berlin resolved not to be caught out a second time, at least not in their own territory. The next major events on the calendar included the new elections for the committee of the Free Students' Union. Clearly Benjamin and his colleagues were not completely certain of being re-elected, so this time they did not wish to leave anything to chance. The greatest threat was from the group that had already managed in Weimar to divert the Free Students' educational policies in a conservative direction: Berendsohn in particular had become active in a number of ways which the Berlin group felt compelled to counter decisively. They too began to master the art of political strategies and tactics, as is demonstrated by their efforts to influence the outcome of the election in advance. Benjamin turned to his friend Fritz Salomon, who was studying in Breslau, with the request that he help by sending a telegram – not the only one the pre-election committee was to ask of its party members, as can be seen from the wording of the letter that arrived in Breslau on 22 July:

Dear Fritz Salomon, please would you be so kind as to send a telegraph expressing sympathy, signed by the organization or yourself, to 'The Free Students' Union, Restaurant Tiergartenhof, Berlinerstr. 1', tomorrow, Wednesday, so that it arrives at around 10 a.m. Berendsohn will be there. Other org. will send telegraphs as well. It will create an impression. Our re-election is at stake.[104]

The sole purpose of Berendsohn's presence in the German capital was to spread propaganda about the political direction he represented among the non-fraternity students in Berlin, in order to win over a majority within the Free Students' Union.[105] Harsh confrontations took place during the election campaign, as can be read in the first memo circulated by the old committee when it was re-elected after all. The memo is concerned almost entirely with the events prior to the ballot and during the electoral meeting.[106]

Not a spark of martial fervour

A few days after this memo was drafted, the World War broke out. The event was greeted everywhere and in all strata of society with inconceivable raptures of joy. Politicians and intellectuals of every hue vied with one another in spoken and written words, and their deeds, to further augment the madness of this battle amongst nations. Benjamin took no part in such 'indecent

Berliner Freie Studen-
tenschaft.

Eingegangen 26.7.1914.

Berlin, den 25. Juli 1914.

Rundschreiben der Berliner Organisation.
- -

Wir fordern zu reger Beteiligung an der Hellerauer Woche auf.
Der Plan dieser Woche geht von Berliner Freistudenten aus, in der
Absicht, uns mit unseren Freunden und den uns Entgegenkommenden,
überhaupt mit allen, die sich aussprechen wollen, über die wesentlichen neu sich ergebenden Aufgaben, innere Fühlung zu finden, die
in Weimar, wo es sich um politische Kämpfe handelte, nicht immer
ermöglicht wurde. Wir wollen hier versuchen, in reinen und sach-
lichen Gesprächen die neue Form zu finden, die uns für die Ge -
staltung des Studententums notwendig erscheint.

Nach diesen Gesichtspunkten haben wir schon im vergangenen
Semester hier in Berlin gearbeitet, soweit es in einem kurzen
S/S möglich ist, nichts schien also selbstverständlicher, als
durch Wiederwahl des Präsidiums Benjamin das, was nur angebahnt
werden konnte, erst einmal auszubauen und wirken zu lassen. So
wollte es auch der Beirat; er schlug deshalb der A.V. Wiederwahl
vor. Doch dies zu verhindern, eilt Herr Dr.Berendsohn von sei -
ner Agitationsreise für das Deutsch - Akad. Bildungsideal nach
Berlin. Er verbündet sich mit allen, die allein der fanatische
Wunsch eint, das Präsidium zu stürzen.

Er verschmäht nicht :

einen Kandidaten zu unterstützen, der freistudentische
Arbeit noch nicht geleistet hat, der aus dem freistudentischen
Ideenkreis, dessen Kenntnis er vorgab, nur die Forderung des
Gegensatzes zwischen Korporierten und Nichtkorporiertem als we-

sentlich erfasst hatte, und der damit bewies, wie unwesentlich
ihm freistudentische Bildungsarbeit erscheint.

Er verschmäht nicht:

den durch seine Nichtentlastung sattsam bekannten Herrn
Kurt W u l f f für die Dringlichkeit eines Vertrauensvotums
für die Vorortsleitung sprechen zu lassen, Herr Wulff, der in
der Gründungsversammlung für den Berliner stud.Ausschuss zu den
Korporationen gewandt erklärte, dass er wohl über den Verdacht
erhaben sei, mit der "anrüchigen Freien Studentenschaft" etwas
zu tun zu haben ! Für die Zeitung des Herrn Wulff, die jeder
Berliner Ehrenbeamte meidet, weil Herr W. sie durch skrupellose
Ausnutzung rechtlicher Vorteile der Freien Studentenschaft aus
den Händen gewunden hatte, liefert Herr Dr.B. Beiträge !

Nicht genug damit. In dem Moment, wo er erkennen musste,
dass sein Spiel für dies Mal verloren war, fordert er seine
Freunde auf, die Versammlung zu verlassen und an den Weiterbera-
tungen nicht mehr teilzunehmen.

Er, der Leiter des Vororts macht den Versuch die Berliner
Freie Studentenschaft zu sprengen !

Trotz dieser Kämpfe erwarten wir vom nächsten Semester eine
stetige Fortentwicklung und gedeihliche Arbeit. Wir glauben,
dass das Präsidium durch Hinzutreten neuer Kräfte an Aktions -
fähigkeit und Elan gewonnen hat.

Getreu dem Beschluss der Hauptversammlung wird das Präsi -
dium in Fortführung seiner bisherigen Tätigkeit seine Kraft
dafür einsetzen, dass die Berliner Freie Studentenschaft in der
Deutschen Freien Studentenschaft verbleibt. Wir haben den Willen
zur Erhaltung der Deutschen Freien Studentenschaft allen zentri-
fugalen Kräften entgegen zu wirken.

Das Präsidium der Berliner Freien Studentenschaft
für das Winter/Semester 1914/15
Walter Benjamin I.Vorsitzender.   Bernh.Reichenbach,II.Vorsitz.
C.F.Heinle, I.Schriftführer   Dorothea Johannsen.II.Schriftf.
Suse Behrendt,Kassenwart   Joachim Kaiser.
Hans Kollwitz

---

public exposure'. Surrounded by overzealous enthusiasm, he chose to remain silent. Not a word, not a line has been recorded of his opinion at the time, either for or against the war. Nonetheless, Benjamin's attitude towards this – as he later termed it[107] – imperialist war and its ideological justification

The circular letter of the committee of the Berlin Free Students Union, 25 July 1914.

'In the years 1912 and 1913, Georg Heym's poems anticipated the then inconceivable mental state of the masses that appeared in 1914, in his disconcerting descriptions of hitherto unseen collective groups: of suicide cases, prisoners, invalids, seafarers or madmen. In his verse the earth prepared itself to be covered by the red deluge.'[23] (August 1914.) German troops on a 'trip to Paris'.

67

was entirely clear. It is sufficient to recall the short article on the Free German Youth Congress of October 1913, in which he denounces above all the militant speech given by the Austrian Ernst Keil. On the other hand, his experiences at this gathering on the Meißner must have convinced him of the utter futility of raising his voice when others were wallowing in irrational emotions. Chauvinism and sabre-rattling received considerably more applause than all of the appeals and entreaties to the young people not to yield to vague, obscure instincts.

According to the 'Berlin Chronicle', Benjamin spent the first days of August sitting with friends and acquaintances in the old Café des Westens, in those days 'the headquarters' of the Berlin bohemians; he and his comrades-in-arms from the Youth Movement had, however, little in common with them. Their mutual relationships never extended beyond fleeting contact,[108] even though they obviously knew each other, and not simply from evenings spent together in the café. The editor of *Die Aktion*, Franz Pfemfert, was not merely a patron of the modern literary movement, but also the publisher of the *Anfang*. Simon Ghuttman had become a perhaps somewhat unloved acquaintance of the students and school pupils since his unsuccessful attempt to gain influence over the publication of the *Magazine for Youth*. Wieland Herzfelde, on the other hand, for whom Benjamin felt a certain warmth because he had paid him several compliments at their first meeting (he 'told me a lot of profound things about myself'),[109] was amongst the intellectual antagonists of Franz Sachs and Herbert Blumenthal in the *Sprechsaal*.[110] But otherwise these two groups were worlds apart, less perhaps in their underlying political and aesthetic views than in their general dispositions. On the one side were the serious, industrious disciples of Wyneken – constantly immersed in 'feverish concentration' on their work, which was induced by their 'concern about the large number of rival campaigns' – and on the other the 'sated, self-assured' representatives of literary modernism and their entourage, whose demonstrative naturalness Benjamin observed with a mixture of incomprehension and indignation.

But the discussions held between Benjamin and his friends at the outbreak of the war were far removed from conversations about the latest literary fashions and the best strategies for promoting school reform. Rather they were busy agreeing on the regiment or the barracks for which they should 'volunteer' so that, given the inevitability of their being called up, they would at least remain 'among friends'. They decided on the

'Then, one day in Switzerland, I read that the Café des Westens had been closed. I had never been much at home in it. At that time I did not yet possess that passion for waiting without which one cannot thoroughly appreciate the charm of a café.'[24]

cavalry in Belle-Alliance-Straße, which permits certain conclusions about the social make-up of this circle. Benjamin duly appeared there 'on one of the following days', without the slightest 'spark of martial fervour in [his] breast'.[111] But he was fortunate. His physical condition was so remote from the Prussian notion of the able-bodied soldier that a superficial glance sufficed for the doctors to dismiss him for the present as unfit for service. Bernhard Reichenbach was at the local office of the Free Students' Union when Benjamin returned from the physical:

He said with that ironic smile of his, and repeating the appropriate gesture: 'I simply held out my hands to the doctor'. The backs of his hands had been severely swollen since birth; that gave him his dispensation, also at later recruitment inspections.[112]

Since Walter was unfit for service, his place was taken by the next in line in the Benjamin family, his 19-year-old brother Georg, who at that time still felt impelled to take arms by an 'untamable lust for adventure', coupled with the professed 'duty to fight barbarism'. He was 'taken on as a cuirassier', as he telegraphed back home proudly, a few days after his inspection.[113]

For his older brother, people and occurrences had slipped into the distance long before. 'On 8 August came the event that was to banish for long after both the city and the war from my mind.'[114] In the 'home', which was simultaneously the premises of the *Sprechsaal* as well as the 'Bureau for Social Work of the Berlin Free Students' Union', Fritz Heinle and his fiancée Rika Seligson had turned on the gas tap and departed from life: out of the heartache of their love, as the newspapers wrote – because of the war, as Wolf Heinle and his brother's friends and acquaintances realized.

There is something deeper than logical clarity, which is the spirit that descends from heaven. Whatever I shall do, I shall do it for the sake of this spirit. I live in the present which strides on invisibly and turns into memory in the past. Farewell, for this was my departure. And I shall also carry out my task.[115]

These words were written by Wolf Heinle on 28 August 1914 as he was about to follow his older brother's example. They show the extent of the confusion that war and death created in these young people's minds. And just how reasonable suicide seemed

'I cannot say that we had close relations to the literary Bohemia whose days, or nights, were spent there; [. . .] the world of our "movement" was different from that of the emancipated people around us [. . .] A mediator between the two sides for a period was Franz Pfemfert, editor of *Die Aktion* [. . .] Else Lasker-Schüler once drew me to her table; Wieland Herzfelde [. . .] was to be seen there, and Simon Ghuttmann [. . .] but the list here reaches the boundaries of our narrower world. I believe we were alien to the café.'[25] (Ernst Ludwig Kirchner, 'Head of Ghuttmann before a round table and figures', 1912; Else Lasker-Schüler)

69

Georg Benjamin, volunteer.

'Wolf Heinle, who has recently become very close to his brother, wishes to kill himself out of despair over the war and because he foresees the general collapse of the spiritual realm; and in addition "everything is love, and the source of love has been stolen from him by the death of his brother".[26] (Sketch of Wolf Heinle)

to many of them – as a response to the events that, with one fell swoop, had made them all aware of the meaninglessness of everything that they had done until then – is also shown by the behaviour of Wolf Heinle's closest friends. Hardly a single one of them, not Rika Seligson's sister, Traute, nor Suse Behrendt, Wilhelm Caro, nor Benjamin, was at first able to see the futility of such a gesture, let alone try to prevent Heinle from carrying it out. Rather they felt that they had at last attained the 'insight' that they 'could not assume the responsibility' of 'hindering [Heinle] in his "final task"'. A veritable 'cult' grew up around him, as Loewenson (who provides this unique source of information about the time) described the mood in these circles. 'Those close to him had adopted the same gesture, the same smile (of being over and above everything) and the same physical movements as he.'[116] There can hardly be a more heart-wrenching example of the devastating effect of the events that descended on these young people during the opening weeks of August.

At first Benjamin was plunged into complete inactivity by the occurrence. That July he had been elected onto the committee of the Free Students' Union for a further six months, but he no longer wished to perform his duties and functions as the first chairman during the 1914/15 winter semester.[117] And just how little he was now capable of gaining even from his studies can be seen from the lengthy description of the desolation of Berlin University, in a letter to Ernst Schoen in October 1914:

The only salient point . . . is that this university is capable even of poisoning our turn to the spirit. On the other hand, this is the only salient point: that I made the decision to run the gauntlet of the course of lectures . . . and saw the shrill brutality with which scholars display themselves before hundreds of people; how they do not shy away from each other, but envy each other; and how ultimately they ingeniously and pedantically corrupt the self-respect of those who are in the process of becoming, by turning their self-respect into fear of those who have already become something, of those who have matured early, and of those who are already spoiled. The naked accounting I made of my shyness, fear, ambition, and more important of my indifference, coldness, and lack of education, terrified and horrified me. Not a single one of them distinguishes himself by tolerating the community of the others. I know only one scholar [Kurt Breysig] in the entire university, and he is vindicated (perhaps) only for having come so far by his utter seclusion and contempt for such things. No one is equal to this situation, and I understand the total inevitability of your decision; you must eliminate from your own life any possibility of having to face this situation, because the sight of such vulgarity is unspeakably humiliating.

Benjamin's elegy concludes, as an expression of his unabating consternation at the death of his friend, with a sentence from the diary of Fritz Heinle, for whom he felt called to intercede from that point on: 'Oh, if only all of them were great men and I could address them as familiarly; it is becoming difficult for me to learn from others.'[118] One can only speculate why Benjamin expressly excluded the historian (and friend of Stefan George) Kurt Breysig (1866–1940) from his general critique. His seminar on the 'German Spirit', which was devoted to the interpretation of selected 'documents, letters and curiosities relating to the life histories of important Germans of the seventeenth, eighteenth and nineteenth centuries',[119] and which he began in the summer semester of 1914 (and continued over the war years), may have contributed to Benjamin's ripening conviction that the 'break with the spirit' can only be countered by a certain stance that at first sight appears anachronistic. Even without knowing more about the content of discussions at this seminar, it is conceivable that the young student received his first impulses here for his later 'Theorie der Verpackung' [Theory of Packaging][120] and 'Theorie der Rettung' [Theory of Rescue], which are already contained in essence in his essay on 'The Life of Students' from the years 1914/15, the clearest example of which can be found in his late anthology of letters, *Deutsche Menschen [German Men]*. (It is not by chance that these testimonies to a secret yet truly humanistic Germany consist of the most confidential remarks made by major personalities, ranging from Lichtenberg to Gottfried Keller.)

'The Free Students have some good evenings coming up, such as today's discussion with Buber about his *Daniel*, and at a later time lectures by Ludwig Klages and Prof. Breysig.'[27] (Kurt Breysig)

Regardless of what one might think nowadays of all the pathos in the words and gestures with which Benjamin and his friends conveyed their rejection of the war, their attitude towered above that of the people who jumped at the possibility of showing their naivety and political opportunism. In contrast to large parts of the German intelligentsia, these youngsters did not lose sight of either the causes or the foreseeable consequences of the events of August 1914. This is particularly evident from the dispute that arose with their teacher, Gustav Wyneken, following his speech in Munich on 'War and Youth' in November 1914.

Disgrace and degradation: the break with Wyneken

'Are we to reach the point where it will merely be necessary to call certain words to you: Germany, national, in order to hear your applause and cheers?'[121] Wyneken had finished his address to the German youth at the Meißner with these words of reproach, only to succumb himself, just one year later, to the ideology that the fatherland was being threatened from all sides. A number of his pupils, above all in Benjamin's circle, were not willing to accompany him in this volte-face. Restrained criticism came from the circle around Franz Sachs, who said it would have been better not to have given the speech.[122] The reactions of Ernst Joël and Hans Reichenbach were fiercer. The latter wrote an open letter[123] to Wyneken in February 1915, which lacked nothing in directness.

Initially Reichenbach had also felt 'that silence [would have been] a better expression of one's opinion in these times than all this discussion'.[124] But then he delivered a philippic which represents one of the few testimonies to an utterly uncompromising opposition to the war *from the very outset*. In his opinion, the 'political unity of the parties is a very superficial bond' which merely clouds rather than harmonizes 'healthy and upward-moving contradictions'. The 'parties of the big landowners and capitalists' are the first to benefit from the unity, because it merely consolidates the existing relationships of power and control. The fateful 'spirit of the bourgeois family' with all its petty bourgeois 'companions' was celebrating 'one triumph after another'. Reichenbach's accusations finally culminate in the words:

You, the older generation who we have to thank for this wretched catastrophe, how can you still dare to speak to us of ethics and set us goals for our lives? You who, even in your own cultural community, have failed to guarantee the right to personal safety from the predatory urges of his fellow human beings, you have forfeited the right to be our leaders. We despise you and your magnificent epoch.

Wyneken's response to the author of this letter proved to be simultaneously evasive and palliative, helpless and outrageous:

The rulers and exploiters are in the habit of making war; the exploited do not want it. Youth sits in both camps. And it is highly probable that the older generation (or let us say the rulers) of our nation are quite innocent in bringing about the war – because in fact this struggle for power is insisted upon, for example, by Russia.

The conclusion is an accusation of defeatism: 'So should everyone fight, with just the exception of you? I simply consider your attitude to this question a deficiency.' Reichenbach dismissed this all as empty words, for neither did the reply contain a proper answer to his accusations nor did it express any 'contempt' for the circumstances. His lack of compromise towards his former teacher prompted Wyneken to make a final rejoinder, arrogantly believing that he could single-handedly end the controversy:

I want, indeed I would like, to render honour to you and our comradeship and conclude by saying, quite candidly, that I now expect you to admit without reservation that I am right and to openly and proudly return to my camp. (May we see this happen, for once!)

These impertinent threats were not the first thing to prompt Benjamin to sever his links with his teacher, for the first dissonances in their relationship had already become clear in the early summer of 1914. His letter of March 1915, in which he disassociated himself from Wyneken 'completely and without reservation',[125] only touches on Wyneken's Munich speech in passing. All that had needed to be said about it had been stated by Reichenbach and Joël (who had also written to his teacher). Apart from this, Benjamin considered, as he told Reichenbach, that merely reading the speech would make him 'party to Gustav Wyneken's betrayal of his self'. He could 'not see the slightest possibility of raising any thoughts or arguments against the text, not on account of the text itself, but because of the fact that Gustav Wyneken had written and spoken it'. It was 'unparalleled disgrace and degradation'. Regardless of all the factors that already divided them, he felt that to express this to Wyneken would constitute the last possible evidence of loyalty. For him the 'image and character' of this school reformer had long been 'damaged' beyond repair.[126]

The First World War clearly marked an intellectual and personal turning point in Benjamin's life. It led him to estrange himself more or less completely from all of the people who had previously determined his interests and activities, not least because he was no longer in direct contact with the majority of his closer friends and acquaintances. Blumenthal had been surprised by the outbreak of war while studying in England; Sachs was on the battlefield, like the majority of the former school- and classmates with whom he had felt closely bonded through the Free Students' Union, *Sprechsaal* and *Anfang*; and

'Robert Jentzsch went by, [Georg] Heym's friend whom I know slightly. I said hello to him and he spoke two words about books I have to lend him. He is a most polite and reticent person [. . .] He seems highly educated. He conducts himself in a refined and sympathetic manner. You sense he is a precise thinker. I know he is studying mathematics. He is by nature absolutely fastidious about matters of form. I have rarely spoken alone with him. He spends a lot of time with Heinle.'[28] (Robert Jentzsch)

since Heinle's suicide, death had reaped a grim harvest amongst those close to him: the death in October of Peter Kollwitz, son of the artist Käthe Kollwitz and brother of Benjamin's colleague in the School Reform Movement, Hans Kollwitz, was the first in a long list of mortalities, which seemed to conclude with the death of Robert Jentzsch (in March 1918), but which was probably longer still. The disruption of his personal relationships, which was caused by external circumstances, accelerated Benjamin's renunciation of all that had linked him *visibly* with the Youth Movement. He was to study in Berlin for two more semesters before moving to Munich and putting a distance between himself and his past. Events accompanying the outbreak of the war had brought on months of complete inactivity, but he eventually found the energy, at the turn of the year 1914/15, to write his 'first substantial work':[127] an 'aesthetic commentary' on Hölderlin's poems 'Dichtermut' and 'Blödigkeit'[128] ['Poet's Courage' and 'Timidity' – two different versions of the same poem]. The essay was dedicated to Fritz Heinle. Benjamin did not submit it for printing, but merely allowed a copy to circulate among friends.[129] Writing in 1930, Benjamin stated that in his entire life he had not had the chance to build on the splendid foundations of this early essay.[130] This fact in no way diminishes the outstanding importance that it had with regard to the development of his perspectives, his methodology, and his personal style. One would certainly refrain from using superlatives when describing the paper as a whole (at the time one of the very first to be concerned with just a single work by Hölderlin).[131] The wording seems wooden in places, the work is difficult to understand as a whole, and the commentary is not logically formulated on a conceptual level. But all this underlines the fact that the essay was largely an attempt at coming to terms with his intellectual self. Benjamin does not tackle Hölderlin's poetic works with preconceived opinions or an existing philosophical theory. Rather, a number of constituent parts of his theory are first unravelled in the process of commentary. Basically, the essay is nothing more than a preliminary attempt to extract the concepts of a personal theory and method from the subject matter. This intention is expressed in the somewhat convoluted methodological remarks at the beginning of the essay:

The inner form, or what Goethe termed content [Gehalt], *will be shown in these poems. The poetic task is to be established as a prerequisite for assessing a poem. The assessment cannot be based on how the poet solved his task, but rather the seriousness and magnitude of the task itself determines the assessment. For this task is discerned from the poem itself. It is also to be understood as a prerequisite for understanding the poem, being the intellectual–physical structure of the world to which the poem bears witness. This task, this prerequisite is not to be understood here as some ultimate reason that is accessible to analysis. Nothing of the process of poetic creation will be determined, nothing of personality and world view of the creator but rather the particular and unique sphere in which the poem's task and prerequisites lie. This sphere is both the product and the subject of the study.*[132]

Benjamin's intention is nothing less than to demonstrate Hölderlin's modernity, and his affinity to the present is certainly not difficult to discern in such lines as:

Of the living are not many well-known to you?
On the truth don't you walk as they would on rugs?
Boldly, therefore my genius,
Step right into the thick of life!

All that happens there be welcome, a boon to you!
Be disposed to feel joy, or is there anything
That could harm you there, heart, that
Could affront you, where you must go?[133]

Do not these emphatic words already contain a – possible – answer to the question of how to react to the schizophrenia of one's personal historical and political present, indeed, how personal strokes of fate, such as Benjamin had experienced particularly through Heinle's death, can be mastered in a productive sense?

Benjamin's last year at university in Berlin was fairly uneventful. He received an invitation from his former antagonist in the Free Students' Union, Ernst Joël (1893–1929) to contribute to a magazine he was editing, *Der Aufbruch. Monthly Magazine of the Youth Movement* (a kind of successor to the *Anfang*). During the four months of its existence,[134] the magazine became one of the few forums of German pacifism. Yet Benjamin declined Joël's invitation. Presumably he was unwilling to identify himself with a form of opposition to the war that, with all of its 'moral' distinctions between defensive and offensive war, was ultimately just beating about the bush. For even if this balanced approach was adopted simply because of rigid military censorship, in

75

The 'Joël Petition'.

effect it amounted to a deception and a helplessness to which no one was willing to admit. Benjamin's refusal did not prevent him, however, from signing a petition supporting Joël when, on top of everything else (the magazine had been long since banned), he was expelled from the university. The authorities wanted to make an example of Joël,[135] so even an opponent of his could not refuse to express solidarity with him. This explains why he was one of the signatories on a petition that placed him in unpleasant company, for it was also signed by Julius Bab, Thomas Mann and Gustav Wyneken, people whose approval of the war was somewhat contradictory to their support for the pacifist Ernst Joël.

The last occurrence during this period worth mentioning is a lecture held in Berlin in June 1915 by Kurt Hiller. His topic was 'The Nature of the Historical Process', and it consisted of a 'vehement denunciation of history as a power opposed to the intellect and life', as one of the audience, the barely 18-year-old Gerhard Scholem, noted in his diary. 'History? Nonsense! We live without history, what has all the rubbish of the millenia to do with us? We live with the generation that was born with us!'[136] Such theses did not go unchallenged, as the ensuing discussion demonstrated. It took place a week later in the *Siedlungsheim* in Charlottenburg. Hiller did not attend the evening in person, but he was represented by his friend Rudolf Kayser – before an audience that included Paul and Werner

Verein Siedlungsheim Charlottenburg E. V.
Sophie=Charlotte=Straße 80¹·
Fernsprecher: Amt Wilhelm (7114)

Kraft, Hans Blüher and Dora Sophie Pollak, née Kellner (later Benjamin's wife). According to Werner Kraft, after a certain amount of general debate, Benjamin began a speech which simply 'glowed with an inner fire. He spoke on the life of students.'[137] By and large he drew on remarks that he had made either at his inaugural speech as chairman of the Berlin Free Students' Union (in May 1914), or a month later at the Weimar Student Congress. Even without knowing all the details of how this speech was adapted to become the article on 'The Life of Students' published in 1915, it is possible to imagine which parts of it were formulated for the first time for this occasion.

The printed version begins:

There is a conception of history that, trusting in the infinitude of time, distinguishes only the tempo of men and epochs which roll forward quickly or slowly on the paths of progress. To this corresponds the lack of context, want of precision, and strictness of demand, which this conception places on the present. In contrast, the following observations consider a definite condition in which history rests as if gathered together into a focal point, as it has long been in the utopian images of the thinkers. The elements of the final condition are not evident as a formless tendency towards progress, but rather are deeply embedded in each present as the most endangered, most disparaged and derided creations and thoughts. The historical task is to purify the immanent condition of perfection to the absolute condition, to make it visible and dominant in the present. This condition cannot be delineated through a pragmatic depiction of particulars (institutions, customs, etc.), which on the contrary it evades. It can only be grasped in its metaphysical structure, like the Messianic Kingdom or the idea of the French Revolution. The current historical significance of students and the university, the form of their existence in the present, thus deserves to be described only as a parable, as the reflection of an ultimate metaphysical situation of history. Only in this way is their significance understandable and possible. Such a depiction is neither a summons nor a manifesto, both of which have remained ineffectual; but it exhibits the crisis that, residing in the essence of things, leads to the decision by which cowards are overcome and to which the brave subordinate themselves. The only way to deal with the historical place of studenthood and of the university is through the system. As long as certain conditions for this are lacking, all that remains is to knowingly free the future from its misshaped form in the present. Critique serves this alone.[138]

'Walter Benjamin – admittedly I included him in the first volume of ZIEL, 1916, but not because I "recognized his genius" (I have still not recognized it), but rather because I wished to encourage a student whose ideologies were close to my own and who was in his early twenties (I was 30) and thus with a little effort I tolerantly overlooked the rather banal and irrelevant aspects of his essay which did indeed show some talent.'[29] (Kurt Hiller)

Hiller does not seem to have perceived the scarcely concealed digs[139] at his ahistorical and atheoretical rationalism,[140] whose 'utter quixotism' in the political arena Benjamin only really took to task in later years.[141] On the contrary, Hiller felt that he had found a new follower in this young student, and included the essay, already published in 1915, in Efraim Frisch's *Neuer Merkur*, in the first of the *Ziel* yearbooks he was editing (published in 1916).

It was at the Charlottenburg meeting that Benjamin became acquainted with Scholem,[142] who had also 'stood up to protest

Gerhard Scholem, 1913.

– albeit rather clumsily – against Hiller's concept of history'.[143] The two of them met again several days later at the university library, and an invitation from Benjamin during this chance encounter led to the start of a deep, lifelong friendship.

Nothing distinguishes genuine productivity from absent or false productivity as clearly as the question: has the man learned in good time – in the years between 15 and 25 – what makes him keep his mouth closed, what makes him taciturn, knowing and thoughtful, and what are the experiences that he will always vouch for, never to betray or divulge their secrets.[1]

4
(1915–1919)

After being exempted from service for another year on account of his severe shortsightedness,[2] in the autumn of 1915 Benjamin followed his friends Suse Behrendt, Grete Radt and Jula Cohn to Munich to continue his philosophy studies at Ludwig Maximilian University.[3] His departure from Berlin was more or less an escape: he wanted to move on and away from the empty and oppressive atmosphere of his home town to distant Bavaria, so that he could return to himself and to concentrated work. He was to leave the Bavarian capital after just over eighteen months, 'feeling purified and transformed'.

Munich and Berne

Benjamin's reports at the beginning of his time in Munich, about the city, its atmosphere, social life, and university are very similar to the outspoken remarks he once made to his friends about Freiburg. It seems that hardly anything appealed to him. But it was almost always that way for him, whenever he embarked on a new period in his life. At first he saw only the negative side of things. At the same time, however, he would use this approach to gain an approximate idea of how and where he would proceed, in order to assert his own activities.

Initially he was disappointed to find that there was absolutely nowhere in Munich that had, as he saw it, a 'cosmopolitan atmosphere'. He was unable to sense any trace of elegance and exclusivity in the city's bars, cafés and restaurants – as he wrote to his closest friend at the time, Fritz Radt. Even a visit to the theatre reminded him of Munich's inferiority: the scenery, like the audience, seemed 'shabby'.[4] On just one occasion, and quite by chance, he found a place where he could breathe the thoroughly open-minded, modern, refined air he sought: at a reading by Heinrich Mann to which he took his fiancée Grete Radt (who was dressed in an elegant Persian lamb coat). The reading was held in an art gallery, and judging by his descriptions this was evidently the Hans Goltz Art Salon, whose owner is known to have organized regular 'Evenings for New

Berlin, a Mount Olympus by comparison

Literature' on his premises from the following year onwards.[5] Heinrich Mann read excerpts from his newly published *Zola* before a select audience. 'There were beautiful women and even more beautiful clothes', as Benjamin wrote in a description of an evening at which everyone and everything – the audience, the setting, the occasion, the topic of the lecture, the speaker's diction – seemed to harmonize. 'Mann sat', the description continues, 'on the platform beneath a colourful, pleasantly-sized Futurist painting' and read the excerpt 'Erdengedicht' [Poem of the Earth] 'in a very spiritual, sonorous, low voice [. . .] The intent with which he tackled the present war by turning to the last one, the way this was done and the way he raised his voice at one point, modestly but unmistakably' struck Benjamin as quite 'magnificent and passionate' in a 'political sense'. Summing up his impressions, Benjamin wrote that Mann had 'great, fertile ideas', above all when it came to spheres transcendental to art. He had left his listeners with the thought-provoking sentence that there are 'just two kinds of people: those who want happiness (for humanity), and those who want power'.

In view of his excessive moralism, which was demonstrated in essays on the Youth Movement written not so long before, Benjamin's capacity to be seduced by a *mondanité* which reduced even the most serious occasion to a 'social' event, must surely be one of the more confusing aspects of his personality. This impression is reinforced by a remark he made directly after his description of the reading, in which he says that he and his fiancée had finished the evening in the 'manner which befitted it', drinking 'French champagne in an exclusive bar'.[6]

A similar snobbishness can be discerned in his descriptions of university life in Munich. For Benjamin, it was nothing but an uncultured morass. The 'intellectual standards' of the students there, even of those 'of the better social classes' were, as he announced after his very first encounters, so 'low' that Berlin seemed like 'Mount Olympus by comparison'.[7] Nor did he find the professors much better. His hope to find a 'teacher' at Munich University[8] – a Wyneken substitute as it were – remained unfulfilled. His intended choice, Heinrich Wölfflin (1864–1945), whose *Klassische Kunst* he had once viewed as 'one of the most useful books about concrete art',[9] proved a total disappointment. This man had the 'most disastrous influence' that he had 'ever encountered at a German university'. He had no real 'relationship to art', but tried nevertheless to approach it with 'all his personal energy and resources', and

Benjamin's residence documents from the University of Munich.

VERZEICHNIS

759

von Herrn *Walter Benjamin*

phil geb. zu *Berlin am 15 Juli 1892* Heimatsstaat: *Preussen* belegten Vorlesungen.

Namen der Dozenten in alphabetischer Reihenfolge	Bezeichnung der Vorlesungen	Zahl der wöchentlichen Stunden	Einbezahlter Honorarbeitrag einschl. Dienergeld, Prakt.-Beitrag und Inst.-Gebühr	
Adam, Prof	*Geschichte der altkirchlichen Busse*	2	—	/
Geiger, Prof	*Übungen zur Psychologie des Gefühls*	1	—	/
Geiger, Privatdoz	*Übungen über Descartes Leibniz u. Unterschiede*	1	—	/
K. Escherich, Prof	*Einführung in die allgemeine Naturkunde u. Biologie*	2	—	/
v. d. Leyen, Prof	*Die schöne Dichtung im Überblick (u. d. Anfängen bis zu Goethe)*	4	16 V	/
Zink, Prof	*Das Grenzwesen i. Abschnitt in d. Geschichte d. 19. Jahrh.*	1	—	—
Wölfflin, Prof	*Übungen: Denkmäler mittelalterlicher Zeichnung*	2	V 50	
			16. 50.	

'The literary historians and critics are also useless. Not to mention the young Mr Strich, whom Grete remembered far too positively, and I don't get on much better with the famous von der Leyen, so I shall wait a couple of days to see whether I shall even continue to attend his course (history of German literature). And he is above average compared with his colleagues. It still remains to be seen how Geiger's seminars will develop.'[30] (Geiger on the psychology of the emotions: from Benjamin's course book in Munich, winter semester 1915/16)

above all with those aspects of his abilities that were of 'absolutely no relevance'. Lacking a theory that touched the 'essence of the work of art, his only access to it' remained 'exaltation' and a 'moral sense of duty'. According to Benjamin, he did not see the work of art in reality, but merely felt 'obliged to see it', demanding 'that others see it', and considering 'his theory a moral act'. Even Wölfflin's 'concept of noble-mindedness and distance', which was to be maintained towards the object, could not conceal his 'lack of receptive genius'. The classes that were held by the renowned scholar, who had just published his *Principles of Art History* evinced no more than an average 'cultural awareness'. Hence the 23-year-old student soon allowed the great professor and his 'seminar [on] early mediaeval miniatures' (which was in any case more of a lecture than a proper forum for discussion as a result of Wölfflin's constant monologues) to carry on without him.[10] Since he was unable to gain much more from the other luminaries at the Munich Alma Mater (Friedrich von der Leyen and Moritz Geiger), Benjamin fled (not least because of the fortunate experiences he had had in similar situations in Berlin) to the more 'second-rate' courses. Here everything that the city and university was otherwise unable to provide was offered in an at least rudimentary form: a 'public lecture on the history of atonement in the orthodox church', held by the theologian Karl Adam, which he attended in the company of just 'three or four monks',[11] as well as a practical course given by the ethnologist Walter Lehmann (1878–1939), at whose classes he became one of the most faithful participants in Munich. Lehmann's seminars (more of a social event than an academic exercise) decisively furthered Benjamin's 'interests in the philosophy of language', the foundations of which had been laid by Ernst Lewy, a *Privatdozent* in Berlin.[12] The first coherent expression of these interests finally appeared in an essay 'On Language as Such and on the Language of Man',[13] which he wrote while still in Munich in November 1916.

The concept of a central theme, that runs through all the disconnected and inconsistent remarks in Benjamin's accounts of Munich, is most likely to be found in his comments on the topic of 'reception'. This is particularly noticeable in his criticisms of Wölfflin, which should not, however, be seen as too significant, as they fail to do justice to the man's scholarly achievements. Benjamin's central interests at this point become increasingly directed at questions of how documents from the past should be tackled, the spirit in which this should be done, and the preconditions that should be met and respected.

The universal genius

For all his disappointment about the standards at the university and its lack of any cosmopolitan atmosphere, Benjamin at least had his stay in Munich to thank for a few agreeable acquaintances. Among the people whom he met here and who exerted a certain influence on his intellectual development was Rainer Maria Rilke (1875–1926), with whom he attended a series of exclusive tutorials that Lehmann held for a select group of students.[14] He also had the opportunity to become better acquainted with him in an even more intimate circle, a working group consisting of just four students, who discussed Kant's *Critique of Judgement* in connection with a relevant class held by Moritz Geiger. Benjamin had always numbered among Rilke's admirers. He found many of his own thoughts and feelings of that time already formed and 'wonderfully' expressed in Rilke's poems.[15] After their first brief meeting (Rilke had to leave to report for military service in Austria at the beginning of January 1916),[16] their paths were to cross again in the mid-1920s in matters concerning translation.

Another acquaintance in Munich whom Benjamin mentioned in particular was the writer Max Pulver, who was his elder by three years and was also interested in philosophy. However problematic he found the dignity of his philosophical views as

Rainer Maria Rilke, drawn by Emil Orlik.

a whole,[17] Pulver certainly constituted a learned and above all stimulating conversation partner. And it was through this friendship that he was introduced to the work of a writer whose intellectual biography demonstrated in its total contradict-oriness, its discontinuity and fragmentariness – in the 'sudden swerves which constantly precipitate him into new intellectual landscapes', and in a thoroughly 'eccentric turn of mind', as Benjamin was later to put it[18] – a number of similarities with his own life: the philosopher Franz von Baader (1765–1841). Pulver had come across Baader in the course of his studies for his thesis[19] (he had obtained his doctorship in Freiburg, 1911, with a dissertation on 'Romantic Irony and Romantic Comedy'), as well as in connection with anthroposophical research. In 1917 Benjamin finally managed to acquire the sixteen-volume edition of Baader's collected works he had 'long sought after',[20] but his studies of Baader were just the prelude to a far-reaching and intensive appraisal of German romanticism.[21] The provisional conclusion of these studies was his own dissertation, which shows clear traces of the initial intellectual impulses that he received from Pulver.[22] Benjamin returned to Baader some twelve or thirteen years later, this time to write a friendly review in the *Frankfurter Zeitung* of the *Habilitation* thesis 'Franz von Baader and Philosophical Romanticism' (Halle 1927) by David Baumgardt, who had been one of Benjamin's closer friends during his time as chairman of the Berlin Free Students' Union. A final point of contact with Baader was during a rather tragic episode in Benjamin's life. In 1934 he was forced to part with his Baader edition. The £16 that he received for it from Jerusalem University library helped him to temporarily bridge a period of poverty. Apart from literature and philosophy, Benjamin's and Pulver's intellectual interests also converged in a discipline that had little more than a Cinderella existence among the philological sciences: graphology. Pulver even made this interest his livelihood in later years when he became a lecturer in graphology and anthropology at the Zurich Institute of Applied Psychology. Graphology was also more than a fleeting passion for Benjamin, as can be seen from a number of texts he wrote in his later years.[23] So it is easy to imagine the scintillant conversa-tion between the two of them: on the one side Benjamin, versed above all in the theories of Ludwig Klages, on the other Pulver, evoking Freud's notion of the unconscious.

The acquaintance in Munich who made the most lasting impression on Benjamin is only referred to in his letters as 'the genius' (or the 'universal genius'), and occasionally as 'the

Max Pulver.

Alte und neue Graphologie /

Zum Vortrag von Dr. W. Benjamin am Sonntag, den 23. November

Die wissenschaftliche Graphologie ist heute gute dreißig Jahre alt. Sie kann, mit gewissen Vorbehalten, durchaus als eine deutsche Schöpfung und 1897, da die deutsche graphologische Gesellschaft in München gegründet wurde, als ihr Geburtsjahr bezeichnet werden. Auffallend genug, daß die akademische Wissenschaft dieser Technik, die nun schon drei Jahrzehnte lang Beweise von der Echtheit ihrer Prinzipien gegeben hat, immer noch abwartend gegenüber steht. An keiner deutschen Universität gibt es bis heute einen Lehrstuhl für Handschriftendeutung. Da verdient es festgehalten zu werden, daß nunmehr eine der freien Hochschulen — die Lessing-Hochschule in Berlin — dazu geschritten ist, ein Zentralinstitut für wissenschaftliche Graphologie (unter der Leitung von Anja Mendelssohn) sich anzugliedern. Offenbar hat man diese Tatsache auch im Ausland als einen Markstein in der Geschichte der Graphologie erkannt. Jedenfalls hat der älteste noch lebende Vertreter dieser Wissenschaft, J. Crepieux-Jamin, aus Rouen auf den Weg gemacht, um der Eröffnung des Instituts beizuwohnen. Man lernte einen alten, etwas weltfremden Herrn in ihm kennen, der einem auf den ersten Blick ganz gut als Mediziner erscheinen konnte. Und zwar aber als ein bedeutender Prak-

tiker, denn als bahnbrechender Gelehrter. Damit wäre denn in der Tat auch die Stellung Crepieux-Jamins und seiner Schüler in der Graphologie umschrieben. Er übernahm das Erbe seines Lehrers Michon, der 1872 sein „Geheimnis der Handschrift" veröffentlicht hatte, in dem der Begriff Graphologie zum erstenmal auftauchte. Was beide, Lehrer und Schüler, gemein haben, ist der scharfe Blick für Handschriften und eine große Dosis gesunden Menschenverstand im Verein mit kombinierendem Scharfsinn. All das hat sich vorbildlich in ihren Analysen niedergeschlagen, die freilich den Anforderungen des praktischen Lebens eher als denen einer wissenschaftlichen Charakterologie entsprechen. Deren Forderungen sind zuerst von Ludwig Klages in seinen grundlegenden Werken „Prinzipien der Charakterkunde" und „Handschrift und Charakter" erhoben worden. Klages wendet sich gegen die sogenannte „Zeichenlehre" der französischen Schule, die Charaktereigenschaften an ganz bestimmte Schriftzeichen bindet, die sie als Schablone ihrer Deutung zugrunde legt. Demgegenüber deutet Klages die Handschrift grundsätzlich als Ganze, die Ausdrucksbewegung. Bei ihm ist nirgends von bestimmten Zeichen die Rede, sondern nur von allgemeinen Merkmalen der Schrift, die nicht auf irgend eine bestimmte Form gewisser Buchstaben beschränkt sind. Eine besondere Rolle spielt dabei die Analyse des sogenannten „Formniveaus" — eine Betrachtungsweise, in deren Zusammenhang alle Charakteristika ihrer Schrift grundsätzlich doppeldeutig

— positiv oder negativ — auswertbar sind, wobei erst die Niveauhöhe der Schrift darüber Aufschluß erteilt, welche von den beiden Deutungen jeweils stattfinden müsse. Die Geschichte der neuesten deutschen Graphologie wird im wesentlichen durch die Auseinandersetzung mit den Theorien von Klages bestimmt. Sie hat an zwei Punkten eingesetzt. Robert Saudek kritisierte die mangelnde Exaktheit der schreibphysiologischen Befunde bei Klages sowie seine willkürliche Beschränkung auf den deutschen Duktus. Er strebte eine differenzierte Graphologie der verschiedenen nationalen Handschriften auf der Grundlage exakter meßender Festellungen über die Schriftbewegung an. Während bei Saudek die charakterologischen Probleme zurücktreten, stehen sie für eine zweite Richtung, die sich grade jetzt mit Klages auseinanderzusetzen sucht, im Mittelpunkt. Von ihr wird die Definition der Handschrift als Ausdrucksbewegung beanstandet. Max Pulver und Anja Mendelssohn, die ihre führenden Vertreter sind, suchen dem Weg zu einer „ideographischen" Schriftdeutung freizumachen, d. h. einer Graphologie, welche die Schrift auf die unbewußten zeichnerischen Elemente, die unbewußten Bildphantasien hin deutet, die sie enthält. Wenn im Hintergrunde der Graphologie von Klages die Lebensphilosophie der Georgeschen Schule, im Hintergrunde der Saudekschen die der Wundtschen Psychophysik steht, so ist in den Bemühungen Pulvers der Einfluß der Freudschen Lehre vom Unbewußtsein nicht zu verkennen. W. B.

Schriftprobe des Dichters Rainer Maria Rilke.

Schriftprobe des Massenmörders Haarmann.

An excerpt from Benjamin's radio talk on 'Old and New Graphology', 1930; the handwriting samples are from Rilke and Hermann Haarmann, a mass murderer who was executed in 1925.

gentleman', an 'older, highly important colleague'[24] or 'a Kantian (Marburg)',[25] without ever being referred to by his real name: Felix Noeggerath (1885–1960). This doctor's son had acquired the reputation of all-embracing scholar through a highly adventurous academic career. As a student for more than ten years in Munich, Marburg, Jena, Berlin, Erlangen and Bonn, he had studied, or at least experienced a taste of, more or less every subject taught at universities at the time. History and philosophy, theology and psychology, indology, American studies, even maths: there was scarcely an area in which he would not have felt 'at home', nothing that would have restrained his intellectual curiosity. Consequently the endless list of his teachers reads like a page from some almanac of German university professors, and included such names as Benno Erdmann, Ernst Cassirer, Georg Simmel, Hermann Cohen, Wilhelm Pfänder and Moritz Geiger (to name just those with whom Benjamin also had some connection either through reading their books or taking their courses). Noeggerath's almost universal knowledge and his ability to divide his attention between the most varied problems and topics made an enormous impression on Benjamin at first. He was 'quite stunned', as he noted, that 'the genius' was able, more or less simultaneously, to devise a complete philosophical system and review the whole of 'mythology from the Orient to America', while dedicating himself to intensive philological studies and also trying to find a 'proof for Fermat's theorem' (a problem from number theory which was only solved in 1993).[26] Benjamin's curiosity was further awoken by the numerous, in some cases close, relationships that Noeggerath had with people he knew more than just by name: with Hermann Cohen, for example, and with Norbert von Hellingrath, who was admired by Benjamin, and with Alfred Schuler; but above all with the Stefan George circle:[27] with Friedrich Gundolf and the 'great master' himself, as well as with Karl Wolfskehl with whom he became acquainted through this new friendship. Along with Jula Cohn (who was the sister of his former schoolmate Alfred Cohn and the girlfriend of the George-pupil Robert Böhringer, and who had an atelier in Munich), the 'genius' provided Benjamin with deeper insights into the life and atmosphere of a literary circle to whose 'priestly science of poetry'[28] he was far more receptive than this rather reserved comment from a later date might suggest.

Benjamin had the opportunity almost every day to admire Noeggerath's 'most phenomenal knowledge of mathematics, linguistics, religious philosophy and in fact of every imaginable subject',[29] which had won him the respect of the leading figures in Munich's cultural life. Thus he could plumb his intellectual depths 'inch by inch': in Moritz Geiger's seminars, where he first encountered Noeggerath; in the Kant working group mentioned earlier, in which Benjamin constituted the fourth cloverleaf, as it were (the third being Rilke's friend Erwein Carl Freiherr von Aretin); in Walter Lehmann's classes,[30] during which Noeggerath would demonstrate the weight of his entire personality by occasionally puffing 'incredibly thick smoke rings' grandly into the air before the speakers; and finally during the hours they spent together in Munich's various cafés, reviewing the discussions from the Mexican studies' seminar and taking the opportunity (as was so common among students in those days) to test the theoretical ground in more depth. Their conversations were concerned mainly with mythological problems, and Benjamin appeared in them as the 'purely theoretical spirit', so much so that he would at the same time derive future personal 'tasks and goals' from them. 'Comparative mythology', as a subject in itself, seemed to open up completely new perspectives for him at the time. Being in itself a very new, in some ways unspoilt discipline, he viewed it in the context of his thoughts and debates on epistemology and the history of science as the very essence 'of an up and coming realm of scholarship'.[31]

Benjamin's high regard for a subject that presented, perhaps

'If the smoke from the tip of my cigarette and the ink from the nib of my pen flowed with equal ease, I should be in the Arcadia of my writing.'[31] (Felix Noeggerath)

for the first time, a truly fitting field for his metaphysical genius to work and experiment, was qualified not least by his overall efforts to apply his mind to new areas and find other forms of expression for his productive work. In Munich he began 'to devote his attention to the laws of productivity in general', and especially to those regarding scholarship. 'Theory' became the new magic formula for his analytic creativity. The power of conceptual thought promised ultimately to give him a certain order over all the unconnected and disparate elements of his mental landscape:

It is theory that actually constitutes the burgeoning fruitfulness of our production, its health in the highest sense. The relationship between productivity and life is organized and maintained by theory. The life of the creative person is fulfilled rhythmically by means of production, in keeping with theory. Theory guarantees the purity of the production, because it constantly illuminates with a clear, steady fire the images of the initial, most basic ideas to which productivity must constantly return if it is to develop and grow. The light of theory is infinite, being brilliance per se, *however limited the objects might be.*[32]

Naturally, this leap into the deep end of abstraction was also, indeed primarily, the expression of concrete experiences of an academia whose fruitlessness and lack of reflection was making a remorseless return to the lecture halls and publications of the day. Faced with a totally atheoretical, positivist approach to research, Benjamin made a recourse to the philosophy of German idealism and asserted the right to speculative thought. The fact that he also did this with systematic intentions is characteristic of his philosophical sketches of this time, but remained without any far-reaching consequences for his work in general, particularly since much of it, such as his 'Metaphysik der Jugend' [Metaphysics of Youth][33] which he worked on from early 1914, remained in fragmentary form.

The concepts behind and the content of his writing under-went an appreciable change at the very latest during his time in Munich. However, his underlying intention always remained the same: to establish relationships between the subject matter of art and literature, ethics and morals, history and law, with life.[34] By this he did not mean 'real' life, perceived through the senses, but rather one belonging to a 'pure reality', or to put it another way, using a term that from now on was to be of great importance in his work, that of its *idea*. Consequently this is not to be sought in the manifestations of our everyday actions, but rather in those of our thoughts. This 'life' must, as he wrote in a letter to Blumenthal, 'be sought in the spirit by means of all names, words and signs'.[35]

Writing with an effect

Anyone who, like Benjamin, was so committed to a metaphysical view of life, must have felt that the call to adopt a more active stand on current momentous events and political problems, was almost a provocation. As a result he more or less categorically refused all invitations from editors and publishers to make any such contributions to their periodicals. The case of Ernst Joël and his *Aufbruch* has already been mentioned, and Martin Buber, whom Benjamin knew from Berlin, had a similar experience when in 1915 he invited the former chairman of the Free Students' Union to express his opinions 'on the question of Judaism'[36] in an article for his magazine *Der Jude* [The Jew]. He received a fairly curt refusal,[37] and it is worth taking a deeper look at the reasons why Benjamin responded in this way.

The fact that Buber turned to a student who was barely 23 years old shows the extent of the reputation Benjamin had already gained from his articles in the *Anfang*, the *Freie Schulgemeinde*, the *Aktion* and the *Tat*.[38] In certain circles, which admittedly must have been fairly small, both he and his profound manner of thinking were evidently held in high regard – although the image that the people in these esoteric circles had of the young author and his writings does not always seem to have corresponded with the latest stage of his intellectual development. Or that at least is how Benjamin perceived the situation. At a time when he had long since bidden farewell to all concrete links with day-to-day 'politics' – less to discover the divine heights than the chthonic depths of human existence – his readers appear to have viewed him as still standing with both feet placed firmly on the ground. (Obviously their judgement of Benjamin's intellectual development could only be based on its manifestations, which were at the time merely the articles that had been published before the war.) This was quite unjust, according to Benjamin, because: 'I am just as incapable of understanding writing designed to have an effect as I am of composing it'.[39] Of course this comment betrays a good deal of self-stylization, especially in its suggestion that this had always been the case. What else had his earliest writings, whose petitioning tone simply leaps up from the page, been aimed at than influencing and convincing the reader and achieving a more or less immediate effect? But Benjamin wished now to have nothing more to do with the kind of writing that succumbs to the illusion that a written or spoken entreaty is capable of affecting or changing a notion, or of having a decisive influence on the reader's or listener's thoughts and actions. His experiences from August 1914 alone made him opposed to this; all the shameful appeals, pledges of solidarity and other spoken and written testimonies by the guardians of morals, ethics and general humanity had shown one thing above all: how little their own teachings and confessions, their lectures and writings had influenced their own selves. Even Benjamin's teacher and 'master' in intellectual matters, Gustav Wyneken, had succumbed to the fever of war. Thus this sentence should be read less as an accurate description of his productive work to date, and more as a declaration of his intentions.

At first Benjamin was totally unwilling to distinguish himself with any of his own works. In his opinion, they would simply be (mis)understood either as a continuation of his past writings (for he no longer wished to be thought of as a 'specialist in these student matters'),[40] or as partisanship (and he was equally loath to being harnessed to the cause of Zionism). Thus he gave priority over every public expression of his opinions to reflections on the principles of writing, with the intention of dispelling the speechless state in which the shock from the events of August 1914 had left him. And the arguments in his letter of refusal to Buber concentrated on just such problems. The widespread opinion that it is possible to influence the moral behaviour of people through writing, in as far as this writing invites action, is based, according to Benjamin, on a notion of language that is too restricted. It views language and writing merely as a means to a deed, a deed whose impulses are not inherent but are to be found in 'some kind of utterable and expressible motives'.[41] (Later he was to denounce these as 'demagogic'.)[42] In the dialectic of mutually contradictory motives, the deed would prove to be the product of 'an arithmetic process' that was 'tested from all sides'. The fact that this relationship between word and deed was consistently gaining acceptance 'as a mechanism for the realization of the true absolute' seemed disastrous to Benjamin. He saw it as important to fight this kind of certainty. (Years later he said that it is essential to unmask the barren pretension to integral solutions as ideology.)

From now on, as Benjamin continued in his letter to Buber, he could only conceive poetic, factual or prophetic writing, in terms of 'its effect' as 'magical, that is as un-mediated: every salutary effect of writing, indeed every effect not inherently devastating', resides, in his opinion, 'in its (the word's, language's) mystery. In however many forms language may prove to be effective, it will not do so through the transmission of content, but rather through the purest disclosure of its dignity and its nature.' At first this emphatic definition of the nature of the spoken and written word conveys a scarcely veiled element of deep resignation which is quite alien to Benjamin's positively belligerent tone in his publications prior to 1914. It is accompanied by the reinterpretation of everything that is generally associated with the terms 'politics' and 'effect'. He goes on:

My concept of objective and, at the same time, highly political style and writing is this: to awaken interest in what was denied to the word; only where this sphere of speechlessness reveals itself in unutterably pure power can the magic spark leap between the word and the motivating deed, where the unity of these two equally real entities resides. Only the intensive aiming of words into the core of intrinsic silence is effective. I do not believe that there is any place where the word would be more distant from the divine than in 'real' action. Thus, too, it is incapable of leading into the divine in any way other than through itself and its own purity. Understood as an instrument, it proliferates.[43]

A few years later Benjamin formulated this synergy of word and deed into the concept of determined knowledge:

This knowledge that determines action assuredly exists. Yet it is not determinant as 'motive' but rather by virtue of its linguistic structure . . . It is clear that this knowledge, that determines action, leads to silence. For this reason it cannot be taught as such.[44]

Silence as an expression of inner protest at contemporary events: little doubt was cast on the legitimacy of such a stance at the time. The withdrawal into one's own innermost self, into subjective tranquility or the realm of metaphysics, had yet to be regarded as political opportunism, as a comfortable retreat from a criminal reality. And quite rightly so, when one considers Benjamin's political biography. Yet the confusion this led to in the meanings imparted to the central concepts of our normal understanding of political action and thought, is clearly illustrated by his own example. One would even be willing to agree with his criticism of an all too optimistic assessment of the power and influence of words and writing in everyday political life. But his conclusions, which divert the whole problem into a theological realm, are far less convincing.

Politically motivated thought and action simply cannot avoid using language in a somewhat coarse manner (as Benjamin viewed it) by debasing it to a mere means of communication. After all, the chief concern is no less to initiate something in any form 'divine' (one could also term this humanitarian), than it is to put some kind of stop to unremitting misery and misfortune. However impotent they may be, attempts of this kind will always be *protests*. And it is precisely this aspect that is ignored in Benjamin's concluding remarks on the equidistance of both the word and 'real' action from the 'divine'. Nevertheless, a few words should be added here in Benjamin's defence: he deserves the credit for having turned our gaze to the question of how an absolute connection between word and deed can even be *conceived* without being broken by the depressing experiences that were rife at that time.

Scholem's view that Benjamin's refusal to collaborate on Buber's magazine was also, if not primarily, an expression of his complex inner struggle with Judaism,[45] is fairly implausible. Why should a person, who has broken so radically and visibly with particular traditions of thought, seek refuge in the security of tradition (in this case of Judaism)? There could be no going back from this standpoint, only a 'progression' towards something undefined that had yet to possess any contours and whose lines had still to be drawn. In the question of defining this concept, there are either no answers or an infinite number of them, all of which fail to make one any the wiser. The ultimate answer to all questions of humanity, the wisdom of some supernatural being, truth: these do not exist as something that can be physically grasped and seen with mortal eyes. At the very most, truth can be perceived acoustically. Yet for all the theological notions that appear in these few short lines, Benjamin was actually concerned with something quite different. The problem that he addresses by means of these notions – however vaguely – is that of a form of creative production which refuses, in its very nature and conditions, any kind of instrumentalization, whether ideological or theoretical.

A number of the ideas cited here appear almost word for word in an essay that touches on the most primal aspect of thought and writing: language. The essay is the previously mentioned 'On Language as Such and on the Language of Man' which Benjamin wrote over a period of just seven days, whilst

'In the spring Insel catalogue, I saw the following entry: Buber, Martin: "Die Lehre, die Rede und das Lied" [The teaching, the talk and the song]. This is precisely the linguistic classification of modes of expression I made in a letter to him to which he did not respond. Might his response be concealed behind the title? Perhaps an indication of his approval? Perhaps without indicating the person to whom this approval is addressed?'[32] (Martin Buber)

still in Munich. This text seems to reach the outermost limits of what is still linguistically and logically comprehensible to mere mortals. But this also applies to the majority of the texts and notes that Benjamin wrote during this period, which, as initial attempts to formulate his ideas, were only intended for circulation and discussion among his friends and acquaintances, and did not need to meet the criterion of general comprehensibility. His thoughts were aimed at an attempt to gain clarity about the 'nature of language'.[46] The importance of this question came, for Benjamin, from the conviction that 'questions about the essence of knowledge, justice and art are related to the question about the origin of all human intellectual utterances in the essence of language'.[47] What is language? What does it communicate? Is there such a thing as linguistic disobedience? And if so, what constitutes it? Can the intellectual nature of the world be expressed? These and similar questions were the objects of his reflections. He took it for granted that language is not merely a means of communication, but far more: the communication of intellectual substance.

Language is the principle directed at the communication of intellectual substance in a given linguistic situation, be this technical, artistic, judicial or religious. All communication of intellectual substance is language, and communication in words is only one example of language, the human example and the example which gives rise to, or is the basis of language (e.g. of judicial or poetic language). The existence of language, however, does not only embrace all areas of human intellectual expression, to which language is always in some way inherent, but it embraces absolutely everything. There is no event or object, either in animate or inanimate nature, that does not in some way partake of language, for it is in the nature of all things to communicate their intellectual substance.[48]

Although the intellectual essence of the world is conveyed *in* language, in Benjamin's opinion the two are not identical. Thus he distinguishes between an intellectual and a linguistic essence of language. The intellectual essence of man is not conveyed *through* language but *in* it. Hence a part is omitted because the intellectual essence can only ever be communicated to a limited extent. Language is 'the "medium"' of this 'communication'.[49]

Benjamin's early linguistic theory, as set down in this short text (it was in fact the first of a number of projected parts[50] of a systematic exploration which, in fact, never developed beyond the 'Series of Notes on the Work on Language'),[51] remained in substance consistent, right into his late works. There is a more or less unbroken line of thought stretching from this work, via the 'Epistemo-Critical Prologue' to his *Origin of German Tragic Drama*,[52] to his later texts, written in the 1930s, on the 'Doctrine of the Similar',[53] and the lengthy review essay on the 'Problems of Linguistic Sociology'[54] that appeared in 1935 in the *Zeitschrift für Sozialforschung* [Journal of Social Research]. The only change was in the perspective from which he studied the issue. While the emphasis of his earlier ideas was placed on the question of the origins of human speech, his 'Problems of Linguistic Sociology' shifted the emphasis to its changes over the course of history.

Almost unwillingly Benjamin returned to Berlin in 1916 during the holiday between the winter and summer semesters. The prospect of once more being subjected to the oppressive atmosphere of his parental home made him anything but glad. Prior to his visit he let it be known that 'Given all that we hear from Berlin, it is not good to be there'.

The simplest everyday chores appear to be accompanied by appalling difficulties and feelings of oppression, at least for those who lead a family life. But we must put up with this for the length of our stay in Berlin. It is important to keep it as short as we can, and to ensure that as little of its duration as possible is spent at home. Even though our health has not benefitted during these weeks, we have gained the greatest longing for and receptiveness to improve our wellbeing, which makes the above behaviour imperative.[55]

Admittedly Benjamin had important matters to attend to: he came to Berlin with the intention of asking Grete Radt's father for her hand. A number of allusions and references in his autobiographical writings of the time suggest that this decision was based not least on his wish to escape the influence of his parental home. For all the resolution with which he and his fiancée announced their desire to tie the knot, they seem to have been very uncertain about the step they were taking.

Thus it was probably no great surprise to their close friends – above all to Fritz Radt, Benjamin's 'highly esteemed brother-in-law'[56] – when the two of them did not in the end get married. Whether this was simply because of Grete Radt's doubts about her decision, which she experienced at the last moment,[57] or because Benjamin's 'heart', as he wrote in the 'Berlin Chronicle', was already lost to another,[58] cannot be ascertained from the documents we have. But no great importance should be attached to this question because their split did not lead to a final break in their personal relationship. (In 1921 Grete Radt married a friend from Benjamin's youth, Alfred Cohn, with whom he remained in contact well into the 1930s.)

Judging by letters written at the time, the summer semester appears to have been fairly uneventful. Benjamin attended his lectures at the university and, as is revealed by a few brief notes made during these months, also at last found time for some reflection and writing. He paid several more visits to Berlin in early and late autumn 1916, during which he was re-examined for military service. The last of these examinations for the time being, which he underwent around Christmas time, resulted in him being reclassified, which understandably made him very agitated.[59] He was pronounced 'fit for light field duty', and although this did not mean that he would have to take up arms immediately, it was now inevitable that he would receive his call-up. Indeed, it arrived shortly afterwards, on 8 January 1917. However, a number of very sudden and severe 'attacks of sciatica' prevented him from becoming any more closely acquainted with Prussian military drill. Apparently the symptoms were brought on by hypnosis, 'to which Benjamin was very susceptible',[60] and they seemed so genuine that even a doctors' committee, which was brought to Delbrückstraße, was convinced by them. For several months Benjamin made an impressive show of his affliction to the world around him.

He returned to Munich in mid-April. There he renewed, 'after more than a year', his friendship with Noeggerath,[61] who in the meantime had received his doctorate, supervised by Paul Hensel, in Erlangen, with a thesis on 'Synthesis and the Concept of System in Philosophy: A Contribution to the Critique of Antirationalism'. Although Benjamin only ever became familiar with a small section of the 'genius's' (still unpublished) thesis, he felt 'quite plainly' that it was 'extremely significant'.[62] Even though one should not overrate such emphatic judgements, there were certainly a number of points in Noeggerath's thesis that touched on Benjamin's own interests: the subject of work and the questions that it raised (the attempt to follow the changes in Kant's concept of synthesis, performed on the basis of two of his major works, the *Critique of Pure Reason* and the *Critique of Judgement*), and the intentions and prospects that this opened up (the salvation of Kant by the creation of a new doctrine or system of categories). Benjamin was to undertake something similar when, scarcely six months later, he made a renewed attempt at clarifying not only the importance of Kant for his own thinking, but also for the philosophy of the *future*, no less. His essay 'Programme of the Coming Philosophy', written in November 1917 and completed with an addendum in March 1918, set itself the express aim of rescinding Kant's distinction between (pure) knowledge and experience while preserving what was '*essential* of [his] thought'.[63]

In his essay, Benjamin states that 'the primary challenge' that has 'to be faced by contemporary philosophy . . . is, according to the typology of Kantian thought, to undertake the epistemological foundation of a higher concept of experience'.[64] The rest of the essay, to summarize it very briefly, then turns to the philosophy of history as a means to attempt to rescue metaphysics, or rather metaphysical experience. As such, this programmatic text merely follows on from and elaborates on ideas contained in his previous works. In his article 'Erfahrung' [Experience], dated 1913, he talked of a 'different experience' which was the 'most beautiful, most untouchable' and above all 'most immediate' known to youth.[65] And in his critical and theoretical reflections on language written slightly later, it is conspicuous how often he investigates the realms of that which cannot be conveyed in or through language. Now, in the 'Programme of the Coming Philosophy', Benjamin sought to summarize these ideas, to a certain extent, to form a philosophical system, which at the time he still considered possible. (Only when he had experienced at first hand the incredulity of philosophies developed solely by the intellect, did he begin to doubt the dependability and tenability of closed models for explaining the world, which aimed essentially at totality.) However, this systematic attempt remained by and large an invocation, and was unable really to indicate how one can formulate 'on the basis of the Kantian system a concept of knowledge to which a concept of experience corresponds, of which the knowledge is the doctrine'. [66] Above all, this text fails to convince because it merely maintains the existence of a 'higher experience' without showing how one could 'gain access to it'.

Although Benjamin was registered as a student in accordance with the rules at Munich University up to and including the summer semester of 1917, presumably he only attended the four-hour long metaphysics seminar held by one Matthias Mayer so that he could carry on using the university library. Apart from this, he had already excused himself from all of his courses by November 1916. From 10 May onwards he stayed in Dachau, north of Munich, ostensibly to take advantage of the mud baths in order to cure his chronic sciatica, but in fact to prepare his 'flight' from there to take refuge in neutral Switzerland. 'Finally something decisive is to be done for the paralysis and the pain that have sapped my strength completely in recent days', he wrote in June to his friend Scholem. His explanation went on: 'The doctor insisted on a month's stay at a spa in Switzerland.'[67] He achieved his goal two or three weeks later, and was able to leave the country quite legally.

We have been here for a week; I found this spot – I may say – after years of struggle, and finally set foot here after my last relationship, which obscurely entrapped me with things from the past, had died away in Zurich. I hope to have absorbed the two years before the war like a seed and everything since then has purified them in my spirit. When we see each other again, we'll talk about the Youth Movement, whose being has experienced such a total and disastrous decline. Everything was in decline, except for the little that let me live my life, and here I find salvation in more than one sense: not in the leisure, the security, the maturity of the life here, but in having escaped from the demonic and ghostly influences, which are prevalent wherever we turn, and from the raw anarchy, the lawlessness of suffering.[68]

Everything was in decline: Benjamin's Swiss 'exile'

Benjamin's relief at escaping the war – with all of its unendurable concomitants which even made themselves apparent in everyday life – can clearly be sensed in these lines written on 30 July 1917 in St Moritz.

'We' were he and his newly wedded wife Dora Sophie, née Kellner (1890–1964). The daughter of the Viennese professor of English Leon Kellner (once a close friend and adviser of Theodor Herzl), Dora had previously been married to the journalist Max Pollak. Benjamin had got to know them both in the months prior to the war. While he was chair of the Berlin Free Students' Union, the philosophy student Max Pollak was running the Detachment for School Reform and University Pedagogy together with Fritz Strauß. His wife Dora had also keenly taken part in the activities of these Berlin students, especially in the programme of the *Sprechsaal*. She viewed Benjamin as the most outstanding thinker in the group, and did not fail to show him her admiration. After his inaugural speech as the newly elected chairman of the Free Students' Union (on 4 May 1914), she spontaneously presented Benjamin with roses, a gesture whose charm instantly captivated him: 'flowers had never made me as happy as these', he wrote to Blumenthal.[69] During the following weeks and months, Benjamin frequently met up with the Pollaks. The apparent reasons for these meetings varied from discussions about projects for the *Sprechsaal*, to group readings of books (such as the *Wege zur Musik [Paths to Music]* by Benjamin's former teacher at Haubinda, August Halm, which was published in 1913). But gradually these meetings must have assumed a more intimate character; and inspired by Dora Pollak's musicality, Benjamin even began to learn to play the piano, although he never advanced beyond 'charming thirds and octaves',[70] and could not read music. The outbreak of the war brought Dora to Seehaupt in Bavaria. From here she accompanied Benjamin on a trip to Geneva to visit their mutual friend Herbert Blumenthal in spring 1915.

During his subsequent period as a student in Munich, Benjamin was a frequent guest at the Villa Pollak by Lake Starnberg. Then, after a length of time spent apart, Dora and Walter finally decided to live their lives together, and married on 17 April in Berlin. In retrospect, Dora Kellner viewed it as a 'marriage of mutual interests'. Benjamin had needed someone who would prevent him from committing suicide, and she had found in him someone who gave meaning to her life.[71]

Although she was a highly successful translator, (thriller) writer and journalist (she worked during the 1920s on the influential *Literarische Welt* [Literary World], and the Ullstein magazine *Die Dame* [The Lady] and was editor of *Die Praktische Berlinerin* [The Practical Berlin Woman]), Dora Sophie Kellner did not exert a profound influence on her husband's thinking and creative output. She may have provided the impetus on one or two occasions for some of Benjamin's articles,[72] and it was certainly thanks to her that several of his texts were actually published,[73] but that was all. Nor was she to play any significant role as his intellectual antagonist. On the contrary, she devoted

Dora Sophie Kellner, 'was very beautiful' (Werner Kraft), and had 'striking looks which alone gave her a "presence". But there was more to her than that. A blonde Jewess with slightly protruding eyes, a heart-shaped mouth with full red lips, she exuded vitality and *joie de vivre*.'[33]

herself completely to protecting her husband from the adversities of daily life and above all to providing him with assistance in practical matters.[74] What this actually amounted to can be gathered from the fact that for years on end she was almost completely responsible for sustaining the family financially, not to mention for raising their son Stefan Rafael, born on 11 April 1918.

The few portraits of her personality we have, from her husband and his friends and acquaintances, depict Dora as an engaging, socially confident, intellectual, musically talented, and exceptionally beautiful woman. The only exception to the general admiration she received came from Blumenthal, to whom Benjamin was referring in a letter to Schoen when he spoke of the 'last relationship' which still 'obscurely entrapped him with things from the past', and with which he had now made a clean break. Blumenthal (who had by then changed his name to Belmore) hardly had a good word to say about Benjamin in his memoirs of their early years in Berlin, their schooldays and their involvement in the Youth Culture Movement; and even less so about his wife. In his opinion she was nothing but an 'ambitious goose' who had already thrown herself at her first husband simply because he was the 'cleverest and richest man in [their] circle'. And when Benjamin appeared on the horizon as 'the coming man', she left Max Pollak without giving the matter a second thought.[75] These are bitter, indeed cruel, words which seem to be a belated revenge for the breech of a friendship, for which Blumenthal would appear primarily to blame Dora Benjamin.[76] And in his letter to Schoen Benjamin certainly chose a curiously impersonal way to mention a man who had, after all, once been his closest friend.

The actual cause of their split cannot be determined with certainty from either Benjamin's or Blumenthal's autobiographical writings. Not only geographical distance – the result of Blumenthal's stay in London where he was doing further training as a graphic artist – but also the outbreak of war, must have contributed to their mutual estrangement, for a year was to pass before they met again. In view of the personal consequences of the tumultous events going on in the world, which were particularly severe for Benjamin, that year was almost an eternity. In addition, the differences in their opinions as to how the Youth Movement was now to be rated, may have played a part. Where Benjamin made a radical break with his past, Blumenthal hesitated. 'I thought about our youth in Berlin', he wrote in his personal notes of this period,

'Walter's words are great and divine, his thoughts and works important, his feelings small and cramped, and his deeds reflect all of this. But a lot will change when he at last comes to love.'[34] (Benjamin, 1917)

and how strongly it was imbued with the desire to serve, to dedicate ourselves with the full weight of our responsibility. The present desire to assert oneself and prevail over one's surroundings and the whole world is no less strong than our yearning at that time to devote ourselves to a higher cause – to serve it with all our energy, which we knew to be strong, and become one with it. I believe that the aspirations of the past constitute the willpower of the present. We found nothing to which we could have dedicated our pure willpower without sinking into a lesser reality. The demand for pure energy was non-existent, and there was scarcely anywhere where it was even tolerated. There was no community, no belief, no divine worship, no work: that's how we experienced the world. All that remained for us was to survive in the face of the cruelty it showed us. Wasting our energies on illusory values would have amounted to betrayal. The highest reality – and for our generation of young people the most distant – was our own existence. This was where our energies crystallized, became hard and barbed. But the old aspirations live on inside us and torment us. Our weakness and our better judgement prevent us from meaninglessly squandering our most valuable personal qualities; but our strength and unknowing, banished to within, continue to call us.[77]

Finally, there are a number of negative traits in Benjamin's personality that might have played a part. The document from Blumenthal quoted here mentions 'evil instincts' to which Benjamin yielded within himself; Scholem and Dora Benjamin asserted much the same.[78] And when one recalls what was undoubtedly a similar situation involving Alfred Cohn (for a period he also simply ceased to exist for Benjamin), this assertion seems to be confirmed. Cohn was at the time intending to become a primary school teacher. With this absolutely 'disreputable' – 'totally weird and drastic – plan'[79] he took his life in 'a direction' that, as Benjamin saw it, removed 'him dramatically from the ideas and goals which, I won't say he shared with me, but he sympathized with in me'.[80] The collapse of his long-term friendship with Herbert Blumenthal also reveals Benjamin's inability to make lasting relationships. The list of alliances in his life which had once begun to develop, only to break off later on more or less abruptly or to be left buried for years on end, is a long one. It stretches from the dissolution of his engagement to Grete Radt to his failed marriage with Dora Sophie Kellner, and from the numerous grave interruptions in his friendship with

Werner Kraft to his sometimes highly precarious acquaintance with Siegfried Kracauer.

Benjamin's 'flight' to Switzerland was doubtless partly a conscious escape from Wilhelmine Germany, from its unceasing jingoistic patriotism, from its orderly, disciplined mentality, from militarism, from the undisguised imperialistic character of its politics, from the repression within, and above all from censorship, (which, as revealed in a number of curious notes in his correspondence, still intimidated him, even in Switzerland).[81] But not even the safety of exile could induce him to return to the public eye and produce articles and written appeals. The events of the day were too vain, they offered no foundation where historical (self)-knowledge could be anchored. Ernst Bloch expressed this in truly lapidary style in his *Geist der Utopie* when he said that 'there is no longer any point in talking about it'.[82] Benjamin must have felt much the same, and he accepted the radical consequences of this. From now on 'light', as he wrote in one of his first letters from Switzerland, made him 'circumspect in the spirit of the past years'.[83]

It is hardly surprising, then, that he failed to maintain any contact with the political opposition during these years of 'exile', such as with the Society of German Republicans in Switzerland which was established in 1916, and which set up its mouthpiece, the *Freie Zeitung. Organ für demokratische Politik*, the following year. Indeed, in some respects Benjamin developed a fear of contact. Whenever he stumbled across this circle, he made his escape as quickly as possible. And although he came to know a number of its outstanding personalities (for a while he lived next door to the Dadaist Hugo Ball in Berne),[84] these encounters had (for the time being) no personal consequences. This even applied to his acquaintance with Ernst Bloch. Although Bloch was the first to seriously challenge Benjamin's steadfast 'rejection of every current political trend',[85] there are no traces of this in his writings of the time. Bloch's name appeared for the first time in a 'political' context in his later writings: in the mid-1920s, when Benjamin began to devote himself to Marxist philosophy.

Bloch was the only acquaintance from Switzerland who was of importance to Benjamin. In addition to his personal liking for Bloch, Benjamin's esteem for him was founded primarily on his admiration of the work *Der Geist der Utopie*, published in 1918. Despite its 'enormous deficiencies' in the detail, Benjamin

The light of the past

Hugo Ball and Emmy Hennings, with whom the Benjamins 'socialized in Berne'.[35]

acclaimed it as one of the 'few truly contemporaneous' of 'contemporary works'.

Because: the author stands alone and philosophically stands up for his cause, while almost all philosophical thought we read nowadays on contemporaneity is derivative and adulterated. You can never get a grip on its moral centre and, at the most, it leads you to the origin of the evil that it itself represents.[86]

'Benjamin was rather whimsical and eccentric, but in a very fruitful way. He had not written much as yet, but we spent long nights immersed in conversation.'[36] (Ernst Bloch around 1920)

The aspects that Benjamin underlines here as the work's strengths – its relevance to the present day and its sense of responsibility[87] – were to become central features in his own work.

According to Bloch, Benjamin led a very 'secluded' life, keeping himself – as 'his wife Dora said – up to his ears in books'.[88] Basically, the same can be said for all of his years in Switzerland. Already by the end of 1917, Dora lamented to Scholem that, although on the whole they were 'doing splendidly', the one thing they lacked was 'company',[89] lively discussions which would relieve their daily life of its monotony. There was the occasional visit to the theatre, or to a piano recital featuring Ferruccio Busoni, which represented one of the few opportunities to make a social appearance, 'very elegantly dressed and bowing in all directions'.[90] But that was nothing compared to the sociable lifestyle in Berlin. The visitors to their home in Berne and later in Muri were also few and far between. Their first guest was Scholem, who visited after he too had moved to Switzerland in May 1918; then in November of that year Werner Kraft lived with the Benjamins for a while; and finally there was Wolf Heinle, who came in spring 1919 and was more or less the last in their 'string' of guests. Benjamin did not use his university contacts to develop a new circle of friends. As ever, he found everyone and everything there tedious, and his time in Switzerland was thus largely devoted to intense study. In his correspondence from this period he talks of hardly anything other than his involvement with the problems of Judaism, his interest in Nietzsche's writings, a deep examination of Kant's philosophy and his studies towards the dissertation that he was shortly to begin.

After having originally set his sights on Basle and Zurich as suitable places for his study, Benjamin finally enrolled for the 1917/18 winter semester at the University of Berne. The choice of university was in any case fairly irrelevant to him, for he was simply interested at that point in finishing his doctorate as quickly as possible, so that he could dedicate himself to 'real research'.[91] During the first of his four semesters in Switzerland, he attended courses such as an 'Introduction to Logic', one of several taught by Richard Herbertz (1878–1959), who was later to become his doctoral supervisor, a course on elementary psychology, and also a seminar on the 'Psychology of Suggestive, Hypnotic and Occult Phenomena' by Paul Häberlin (1878–1960), and the 'Outline of Philosophy' presented by Anna Esther Tumarkin, the first female member of the teaching staff at this university. During the following semesters he also attended Herbertz's lectures on the history of philosophy and epistemology, Häberlin's psychology seminars, and seminars held by the germanist Harry Maync (including one on the 'History of German Romanticism').[92] But according to his personal notes, he was not greatly impressed by any of these courses. He found the 'situation of the contemporary university entirely hopeless' in Berne as well, and he felt that he was wasting his time writing papers 'on Schleiermacher's psychology',[93] on Bergson, Hegel ('an intellectual brute')[94] and Freud.

Nevertheless, these semesters in Berne did leave their mark on Benjamin's intellectual development.[95] He began to study Freud's works as a result of Häberlin's seminars, and in fact his psychology studies in Berne seem to have provided the impetus for him to reflect on the problems of perception, which were to play such a major part in his later writings, above all in the 'Arcades' project.

Shortly after enrolling at the university, he began to think about a subject for his doctoral thesis. At first he wanted to write 'on Kant and history',[96] but he soon rejected this topic on account of the intrinsic difficulties that it posed. In the end he embarked on a thesis 'on the philosophical foundations of romantic art criticism',[97] and had already finished his first draft by April 1919. The result had real substance, as even he realized: 'It has turned out as that which it was meant to be: a pointer to the true nature of romanticism, of which the secondary literature is quite ignorant.' Although he was compelled to make a number of compromises in order to satisfy the conventions regarding academic works, he nevertheless hoped that while respecting the 'expected' learned tone, his allusions to the existence of something that was intrinsically different and genuine in his work were not completely lost: 'I hope to have achieved the following in this work: to deduce this state of affairs from the inside out.'[98]

The question arises: how did Benjamin hit upon the idea of

Romanticism? Was it merely the impulses that he received from others, or was there something else, something more, behind his choice? It is noticeable that his central interests and choice of reading matter during these years lay in quite different areas. His letters, at any rate, were concerned (before he began his thesis) with just about everything: with linguistic philosophy, with the Jewish theology of revelation, with Plato, Kant and Nietzsche, with the Marburg neo-Kantians and Husserl, but not with German Romanticism. Judging by his personal notes, his choice of topic was little more than a spontaneous idea that arose incidentally from his work on Kant. As he wrote to Scholem in March 1918, he hit upon the topic whilst waiting for a suggestion from his professor in Berne:

Only since Romanticism has the following view become predominant: that a work *of art in and of itself, and without reference to theory or morality, can be understood in contemplation alone, and that the person contemplating it can do it justice. The relative autonomy of the* work *of art* vis-à-vis *art, or better, its exclusively transcendental dependence on art, has become the prerequisite of romantic art criticism.*[99]

The prospect of finding in Romanticism a belated justification for his rejection of Wölfflin must also have held a certain attraction for Benjamin. The 'schooling' that he underwent during his doctoral studies consisted of gaining for the first time a keener 'insight into the relationship of a truth to history'.[100]

Although the thesis could not yet give an exhaustive answer to the accompanying question of how 'the relationship of works of art' (as manifestations of this truth) were connected 'to historical life',[101] it did clarify many of the prerequisites for presenting this problem. In addition – and this was more decisive in terms of the development of his thought and creative production – while tackling Romanticism he arrived at a notion of critique which, with a few minor modifications, was to become an integral part of his own work: 'The modern concept of criticism has developed from the romantic concept; [and] in terms of art, it encapsulates the best insights of contemporary and later poets, a new concept of art that, in many respects, is our concept of art.'[102]

Benjamin's thesis concludes with 'an esoteric epilogue',[103] which he hoped would identify it to his closest friends as his work. Specifically, this refers to the chapter on 'The Early Romantic Theory of Art and Goethe',[104] in which he included some of what was occupying his emotions at the time. For all of its conventionality – with which he satisfied the requisites of academic treatises – his thesis was also a first systematic attempt to work out a theory of criticism which 'not only' differed (as he wrote in the advertisement for his thesis upon its publication) 'from the current corrupt and directionless practice of art criticism by virtue of its high standards, but also by its methodical approach. This allows . . . perfectly clear criteria for authentic criticism to be established'.[105] What exactly these criteria of authenticity consisted of, however, cannot be gleaned either from his advertisement or from the treatise itself; only the esoteric conclusion contains some few indications:

For him [Friedrich Schlegel], the elevation of the created work to the absolute, the critical process, was of supreme importance. It may be conveyed by means of an image, as the creation of radiance in a work. This radiance – the sober light – extinguishes the multiplicity of the work. It is the idea.[106]

Benjamin's thesis appeared in 1920. It was printed in Berlin by Arthur Scholem (the father of his friend), and published by Francke in Berne.[107] It does not seem to have found a particularly large readership. The larger part of its in any case modest print run (probably little more than 1,000 to 1,200 copies)[108] was destroyed by a fire at the publisher's.[109] The meagre remainder was only put on sale in the mid-1930s. (Other copies collected dust in the cellars of Berne University for an even longer period of time.)[110] The book's low sales were reflected in the critical response. Only three reviews have been discovered.[111] It is scarcely worth mentioning what these critics had to say on the contents of the thesis even though one of them, Rudolf Unger, was a noted literary historian. If not the brevity of the reviews, then certainly the commonplaces they included, such as a 'work that at times makes exceptionally deep and fine distinctions',[112] make it clear that the reviewers tended to consider *The Concept of Art Criticism in German Romanticism* a fairly unproblematic academic treatise. The only person who took the trouble to analyse Benjamin's first book publication in more detail, albeit in the form of a personal rather than an open letter, was his paternal friend Florens Christian Rang (1864–1924). Some of the comments in this long letter of August 1920, which used a scarcely comprehensible logic and language, and which lent more precision to certain aspects of the work while also in part asserting itself against it, came to be

'For the rest, *libelli mei* are beginning to experience *sua fata*. A short time ago I heard that all the printed copies of my dissertation that remained in Berne were destroyed in a fire. I will therefore give you an invaluable tip by letting you in on the fact that there are still thirty-seven copies in stock. If you were to get hold of them, you would be assured of a regal position in the second-hand book trade.'[37] (Benjamin's doctoral thesis) adopted by Benjamin. Traces of Rang's expositions on academic methodology as the 'most circuitous means for the mind',[113] to reach the object of its studies, are to be found *mutatis mutandis* in the 'Epistemo-Critical Prologue' to *The Origin of German Tragic Drama*. And thanks to his friend's objections, Benjamin was never again to formulate the distinction between Goethe's and the Romantic position, on questions of art criticism in such a pronounced form.

All that remained for him during the last weeks of his final semester was simply to 'study in the most methodical way'.[114] His application for entry to the doctoral examination under the jurisdiction of the council of the philosophy faculty was accepted on 23 June 1919,[115] and four days later he defended his work before the examination commission. He managed magnificently to clear this last hurdle on the way to the academic title that he felt he owed his family.[116] Chaired by the deacon, Otto Schulthess, the professors Herbertz, Häberlin, Maync and Jacques Louis Crelier gave him a 'first' in this oral in philosophy, psychology and modern German literature. Apart from the 'second' he received for philosophy as a main subject, he was able to endorse the marks he received for his written examinations, and he came away with the highest distinction possible.

Only a view that acknowledges downfall as the sole reason for the present situation can advance beyond enervating amazement at what is daily repeated, and perceive the phenomena of decline as stability itself and rescue alone as extraordinary, verging on the marvellous and incomprehensible.[1]

A few days after receiving his doctorate, Benjamin left Berne for Iseltwald by Lake Brienz[2] to recuperate for several weeks with his wife and child. He even delayed informing his relatives and acquaintances about the successful conclusion of his studies – less as a result of his otherwise strong liking for 'mystery-mongering',[3] than in order to grant himself a little rest 'before the great storm broke out'. Benjamin knew all too well that the successful completion of his studies would rekindle a conflict that had merely been suspended by the war years and his physical distance from Berlin. And the storm, in the form of new altercations with his parents, came far sooner than he had expected.

A tour of German inflation

Despite all Benjamin's precautions, his parents, Pauline and Emil, quickly found out about his doctorate and appeared, quite unexpectedly, at his retreat in August.[4] It was a flying visit which brought him little joy, for he realized that instead of celebrating his success together, they would merely argue about money and his future profession. Benjamin's parents felt that the moment had come for their oldest child to face the 'serious side of life', or rather, to take control of his life and (financially speaking) that of his family. And given the family tradition, who could blame them for thinking in terms of a business profession? They knew all too well that economic security, indeed the possession of *more* than adequate financial means, was a basic requirement if a Jew was to receive social recognition. But their son was certainly not without reservations. He was less than enamoured by the prospect of spending his life in some stuffy office or behind the counter of a bank. Furthermore, he agreed with many Jews of his generation that the process of acculturation, i.e. of assimilation with their German surroundings, was not merely to be accomplished by means of money, but rather required a certain rounding-off on 'higher planes'. Emil Benjamin, on the other hand, was quite averse to such notions. He had only ever learnt to measure the achievements in his everyday life in terms of, quite literally, financial successes. As a result, he was incapable

Family conflicts

of showing any understanding whatsoever for the 'unremunera-tive occupation' of a *Privatdozent* (or, worse still, of an *homme de lettres*). As far as he was concerned, the course had already been set for his oldest son's future profession. The way had been paved by their ancestors, and if Walter was not even ready to bow to *their* authority, it was his duty as father to persuade him, for example, by threatening to withdraw his allowance.[5]

Just how unwilling Benjamin was to share his parents' views on life is finally evinced by a short text entitled 'Analogie und Verwandtschaft' [Analogy and Kinship] which he wrote in Iseltwald. This essay, which is concerned primarily with epistemological questions, contains a passage which reads like a philosophical commentary on his quarrels with his parents:

The view of kinship as a principle of analogy is the unique element in a modern notion of authority and family fellowship. This notion expects to find analogies between the kindred, and views conformity as a goal of upbringing, whose responsibility is that of authority. True authority is, however, a directly emotional relationship that does not reach its object via the analogies of conduct, choice of profession and obedience, but is only able, at the utmost, to manifest itself in them.[6]

It is highly unlikely that Emil Benjamin ever set eyes on these lines. And presumably he would also have rejected the tacit criticism of his 'pettiness and need for control',[7] merely dismiss-ing it as the product of youthful over-sensitivity. At any rate he did not allow anyone, least of all his own son, to intervene when it came to money matters – which are, generally speaking, the most effective means of asserting personal authority. This attitude played no small part in the general breakdown of their relationship during the first years after the war.

This break with his parental home also explains Benjamin's extreme restlessness during these years. Torn 'between having to earn a living at any cost and a *Privatdozentur*',[8] he travelled back and forth, his thoughts jumped from one project to the next, and he considered one occupation after another as a means to earn a living. His efforts to ensure a more or less stable income remained fairly half-hearted, and thus it was almost inevitable that his attempts to work as a book dealer or a reader in a publishing house came to nothing. Finally he even toyed with the idea of emigrating to Palestine. But although he claimed that, 'under certain, not entirely unlikely, conditions', he was 'determined' to emigrate,[9] basically he seems to have felt no great calling 'to carry stones to the road to Jerushalajim' (Theodor Lessing).[10]

Before leaving Switzerland for good, Benjamin spent a few weeks in Lugano. At the beginning of November 1919 he left Berne (where he made a farewell visit to Richard Herbertz) and went first to his parents-in-law in Vienna. From there he travelled with his wife to nearby Breitenstein, where they stayed until February 1920, in a guest-house owned by his wife's aunt.[11] After three years of Swiss 'exile',[12] he finally returned to Berlin with his wife and son in March. In view of the 'categorical orders' that his parents sent to him in Austria, that he was to live from then on with his family in Delbrückstraße, he did 'not happily look forward' to his forthcoming stay in Berlin.[13] And the events of

> Sanatorium
> und Erholungsheim
> in Breitenstein
> am Semmering.
> ⊲⊳⊲
> Interurb. Telephon Nr. 1.
> ⊲⊳

WALTER BENJAMIN   Berlin-Grunewald,...
                                   Delbrückstr. 23.

---

the ensuing weeks confirmed his gloomy prognosis. After just a short while he and his parents had 'split totally'. Consequently, he and his wife fled to the 'wonderful patriarchal hospitality' that was extended to them by Erich and Lucie Gutkind in the South Eastern garden suburb Grünau-Falkenberg.[14] Within their four walls, he experienced a solidarity that could only have been the result of a 'very similar situation'.[15] Gutkind,[16] fifteen years his senior (and who also came from the 'better circles' of the Berlin Jewry: his father was a wealthy textile manufacturer), had problems similar to Benjamin's. He too was a frustrated *homme de lettres* for want of a suitably generous parental apanage. His quite unbefitting sympathies, as his parents saw them, for social democracy had endowed upon him his penniless state. This precarious financial situation forced Gutkind to work from time to time 'as a travelling salesman dealing in margarine.'[17] In Benjamin's view, this fate was a vivid illustration of the appalling living conditions forced upon creative production. 'Hunger', as he wrote in one of his letters, without the slightest trace of irony, 'poses a most serious threat to anyone seriously engaged in intellectual pursuits in Germany.'[18]

Benjamin's most confidential writings (above all his letters and diaries, but also his preliminary notes which he never intended for publication) are full of similar remarks which strike the reader as very obstinate – to put it mildly – generalizations of personal impressions and experiences. And in addition, they give the impression that someone is leisurely recording their observations on the political and social situation from the *bel étage* of his villa in Grunewald. This feeling appears to be confirmed on reading a text that constitutes a kind of systematic inventory of the conditions in Germany. The text in question is Benjamin's 'Thoughts about an Analysis of the Conditions in Central Europe', a text that he later included under the title 'Imperial Panorama' in his collection of aphorisms, *One-Way Street*.

In all probability he began these notes shortly after his return from Switzerland, for they draw on impressions and experiences that he gained during his travels across Germany, as well as from conversations with friends and acquaintances. The picture he presents is one of a truly German depression. During his 'Tour of German Inflation' (the final subtitle of the piece), he was confronted from all sides by hardship and misery, stupidity and conceit, helplessness and ruin, degeneration and sickness. But if one looks at the individual statements he makes in the light of what is generally considered to be known about the history of the early years of the Weimar Republic, they appear largely to be an unwarranted projection of personal experiences, which also possess a rather 'superior' tone (not to mention his occasional outrageous 'case' studies). He talks of a 'complete demise of distance', as is 'especially apparent in the arrogance shown by people who perform the most menial tasks to which they are obliged'. Or the general decline of social relationships is demonstrated in the decline of the 'art of cookery'.[19] Admittedly these weaknesses were largely eliminated during the various revisions, abbreviations and extensions that the 'Imperial Panorama' underwent from its first notes to its final publication in 1928. The result is that the image cast by his projections comes across as far less vague and more appropriate for its object. Naturally

'By the way, at the moment Berlin in particular is totally unbearable; its people are as bitter as they are helpless and, in the last few days, both their bitterness and helplessness have increased because of a widespread and sudden shortage of bread.'[38] (Germany 1923: butter sales under police supervision)

Benjamin does not try to develop any kind of social theory with these observations; he is attempting rather to create a phenomenology of everyday life.

Benjamin would have required training in political thought before he could produce a systematic social theory, and he had yet to embark on this. And his teachers included people whose philosophies and ideas about life could not have been more different. Viewed figuratively, the conservative Florens Christian Rang stood opposite the communist Asja Lacis, the Marxist theorist Georg Lukács opposite the Germanophobe anti-Semites Léon Daudet and Charles Maurras, and finally his sympathies for the various philosophical, political, aesthetic and other sects competed with those he held for the Communist Party. Furthermore it should be remembered that Benjamin conducted his political sallies within the literary field. The beginning of these was a controversy about a 'school' to which Benjamin still felt very close at the time: that of Stefan George. It occurred in a rather inconspicuous manner: as a controversy about the theory and practice of the translation of poetry.

In opposition to a German monument

'In a few years I will come to know what some of these books mean to me; in some instances it may take a very long time. First they will be deposited, as it were, in the wine cellar, buried in the library.' These sentences come from a letter that Benjamin wrote on 31 July 1918 to Ernst Schoen. In reply to Schoen's birthday greetings, the passionate book collector takes the opportunity to talk about the many presents he has just received. At the end of a long list of the fond offerings from his wife comes 'a small book of reminiscences about Baudelaire', richly illustrated and containing anecdotes from his life.[20] As his letter to Schoen suggests, this book, deposited in his intellectual 'wine-cellar', was to be of capital importance for Benjamin. The fact that he had been familiar with Baudelaire for a long time is shown not only in some of his earliest studies,[21] but also in the regular bulletins that he sent to his friends and acquaintances on his current reading matter and the latest acquisitions to his library.[22] Despite this, the physiognomies of both Baudelaire and his times (of which the small book that Benjamin mentions here may well have given him his first impressions) had yet to emerge for Benjamin with the clarity which they were to gain in his later writings, above all in the work surrounding the 'Arcades' project. In this work, in which Baudelaire is portrayed as the writer *par excellence* of literary modernism, Benjamin took the person and work of the French poet as the background for an attempted interpretation of the nineteenth century, which allowed outlined insights into the understanding of the social conditions of the twentieth century.

Such focused images only emerged after long years of evaluation which consisted of a number of intermediary stages, including university seminars,[23] lectures[24] and a number of shorter works, above all reviews.[25] Consequently, the contexts in which Benjamin worked on his Baudelaire translations, on the one hand, and his 'Arcades' project on the other, exhibited different accents. Instead of reflections of a socio-theoretical nature, reflections on philosophy and linguistic theory formed a background for Benjamin's initial appraisal of Baudelaire. Yet he was convinced that there was 'a bridge to the way dialectical materialism looks at things from the perspective of [one's] specific stance to the philosophy of language, strained and problematic as that bridge may be'.[26]

By the time Benjamin was commencing his Baudelaire translations, the French city-poet had long since become better known in the German-speaking world. The first extensive edition of his works, translated by Max Bruns, had already appeared between 1901 and 1910. This edition was preceded and accompanied by numerous translations of individual poems and prose texts, of which the first, Stefan George's poetic rendering of *Les fleurs du mal,* surpasses all those which came after it. George's versions had already circulated amongst writers and scholars as a private publication in the early 1890s, before a much larger edition, published by Bondi of Berlin in 1901, made the work available to a wider audience in 1901. By 1922 – a year before the appearance of Benjamin's translations – George's *Blumen des Bösen* had already reached its sixth edition. Subsequently, a number of writers and translators of repute tried their hand at Baudelaire's works, including Paul Wiegler (1900), Camill Hoffmann and Stefan Zweig (1902), Graf Wolf von Kalckreuth (1907), Fritz Grundlach (1909) and Mario Spiro (1913). So Benjamin was not setting foot on virgin soil when he started his translation of *Les fleurs du mal* shortly after the beginning of the war. And he knew some, if not all of his predecessors. The translations of Baudelaire's *Poems in Verse and Prose* by Hoffmann and Zweig had long since had a place in the bookshelves of his library – admittedly 'relegated to a corner'[27] as the 'third worst'[28]; and George's version, anything but a poor example, took its place in his library in January 1918.[29]

Not only was George's translation the very first attempt of its kind,[30] it also set the standards for every subsequent attempt to establish Baudelaire in the German-speaking world. Naturally this applied equally to Benjamin's translations, a point that he reflected on in his foreword, 'Die Aufgabe des Übersetzers' [The Task of the Translator]. At the same time it is clear that his version of the 'Tableaux parisiens' was determined far more by his efforts to overcome the weaknesses of a great model than by any attempt to emanate its strengths. In addition, Benjamin's Baudelaire translations are primarily the aesthetic evocation and revocation of a man whom, for the whole of his life, he not only considered a great poet and translator, but in addition to whom he remained highly indebted for a long time on numerous accounts: in questions of literary taste and aesthetic judgement, indeed in his entire bearing as a writer. As such, these translations were a move to free himself from a man whose influence on his thought and creative output cannot be overestimated.

Most critics today would accept that Benjamin's Baudelaire translations do not bear formal comparison with those of George. Even if he did not fully realize this himself at the time, his friends and acquaintances must have made it clear to him. He was quite aware that his 'translation [was] metrically naïve', as he wrote in January 1924 to Hugo von Hofmannsthal, simply repeating what he had already admitted to Rang.[31] This remark related less to 'the verse form of the translations' and more to 'the fact that metre had not posed itself as a problem' to the same extent that his 'foreword mentions this with regard to literalness'.[32] These formal weaknesses in his translations were more than compensated for, however, by their strengths. At the points where the modernity of Baudelaire's poems was most tangible, Benjamin gave a far more faithful rendering than George. This becomes clear when their versions of the poem 'Paysage' [Landscape] are compared.[33] In a certain respect George transfigures and naturalizes the typical features of the modern age – technology, social unrest, the city – and even allows them on occasion to disappear completely. The city, which is the focal point of the 'Tableaux parisiens' cycle, does not appear in George's translations, or is not recognizable as such. He archaizes 'Les tuyaux, les clochers, ces mâts de la cité' to become 'Den rauchfang den turm und die wolken weit' [The chimney, the tower and the clouds afar]: the city is simply avoided, so that its specific profile melts into the physiognomy of a rural centre in this German version. How differently this reads in Benjamin's 'Auf Turm und Schlot, die Masten von

Stefan George (charcoal sketch by Melchior Lechter, 1900).

Paris' [To the tower and smokestack, the masts of Paris]!
Similarly transfigured is George's translation 'Rauchende säule
zum himmel schiesst' [Smoking pillar shoots into the sky] of
Baudelaire's 'Les fleuves de charbon monter au firmament';
Benjamin's 'Der Kohlenströme Flößen übers Firmament' [The
floating of rivers of coal over the firmament] does more justice
to the literal meaning; and the fact that Baudelaire's 'L'Émeute
tempêtant' is not some 'bestürmendes toben' [assailing turmoil]
of nature, but more an 'Orkan' [hurricane] as the social uproar
sweeps through the streets, once more underlines these
differences forcibly.

Judgements about the success of translations, so long as they
are not simply concerned with linguistic or easily recognizable
stylistic mistakes, are not merely a question of taste, but rather
of the way in which the author or his work is approached. How
is it read and received? In which historical context? What
considerations and problems regarding theories of linguistics
and art play a role in its reception? Benjamin poses these
and similar questions right from the start in his preface on 'The
Task of the Translator', which presents nothing less than a
thinly veiled reception theory. Nowadays some of his central
tenets are more likely to prompt rejection than endorsement of
his plan. But it should be remembered upon reading them that
they were written against the background of a form of aesthetic
reception that was principally ahistorical. Bearing this in mind,
the immediately apparent contradiction within the opening
lines may be viewed somewhat differently:

*In the appreciation of a work of art or an art form, consideration
of the receiver never proves fruitful. Not only is any reference to a
certain public or its representatives misleading, but even the
concept of an 'ideal' receiver is detrimental in the theoretical
consideration of art, since all it posits is the existence and nature
of man as such. Art, in the same way, posits man's physical and
spiritual existence, but in none of its works is it concerned with
his response. No poem is intended for the reader, no picture for the
beholder, no symphony for the listener.*[34]

These sentences seem to betoken a thoroughly elitist view of art
and literature. But had not the autonomy of art already become
highly questionable? And had not the opinion long since been
established that art and literature are created primarily for the
recipient? By answering these questions, the various features that
distinguish the quality of a translation become finally visible.

112

The beginning of modern poetry is commonly dated at Baudelaire. As stated in a document from the second half of the 1930s, Baudelaire's special role and significance for Benjamin consisted in the fact that in his poems, the city had for the 'first time' become

a subject of poetry. This poetry is not folk art; rather, the gaze of the allegorist that encounters the city is the gaze of alienated man. It is the gaze of the 'flâneur', whose way of life still casts a concili-atory gleam over the approaching desolation of the inhabitant of the city. The 'flâneur' is still on the threshold, of the city as of the bourgeois class. Neither has yet overwhelmed him; in neither is he at home. He seeks asylum in the crowd.[35]

Naturally Benjamin's first attempts at translation, which we are discussing here, were not modelled on the socio-theoretical observations that underlie this perception, and which were the foundations of his many years of deep involvement with modern French literature as well as of the changes in his political views. Nevertheless – and this is perhaps the justification for this jump in the 'chronology of events' – it gives an incomparably clear picture of the major differences between George's and Benjamin's translations of Baudelaire. George phrased his opinions on Baudelaire in slightly broader terms: 'It needs scarcely to be mentioned these days', he wrote in his foreword to the first edition of his translation of *Les fleurs du mal*,

that it is not the repugnant and repellent images which for a while enticed the master which have won him the great admiration of the entire younger generation, but rather the zeal with which he conquered new territory for poetry and the keen intellectuality with which he penetrated even the most unyielding matter.[36]

Benjamin would have agreed with this with little reservation. It is no accident that in his own preface he wrote that one of the decisive functions of translation is to extend the linguistic 'boundaries of the German language'.[37]

The common background to their translations was formed by the aesthetic debates during the late nineteenth and early twentieth centuries on the crisis of language or rather of the linguistic signifier. The 'decline of language' (or the 'ruin of language'[38] as the barely 19-year-old Benjamin once called it) was the key expression in the discussions that revolved primarily around a discontent with the traditional forms of (nature) poetry represented by classicism, Heine and naturalism. (Hugo von Hofmannsthal's famous story 'A Letter' – better known as the 'Chandos Letter'[39] – written in 1902 can be seen as just *one* example of this.) The core of these debates was the view that language failed as a vehicle for the representation of social reality in all its breadth and diversity – or did so just as long as writers were forced to resort to traditional poetic forms. And this failure was also largely due to the fact that there was no formal system available that met the needs of the altered social conditions. It was evident that nature poetry, regardless of which genre, could not provide this: and city poetry, in which society's changes were conveyed in a vivid manner, was simply non-existent at the time in German literature, or had not yet been able to establish itself.

A response to this problem can already be discerned in George's motives behind his poetic renderings of Baudelaire. It was not his intention to introduce the reader to a virtually unknown foreign-language writer and his work. Rather he was driven by the desire to provide an exemplary model. Consequently he viewed his attempts 'less [as] a faithful replica' of Baudelaire's poetry, and more as the erection of a 'German monument',[40] with the emphasis on the adjective.

In some respects Benjamin's life-work also embraces this aspect: it is the attempt to liberate himself from a mental attitude whose fascination he was never able completely to escape, but whose danger was to become increasingly evident to him with the advancement of historical events. The fact that his Baudelaire translations were not a complete success was quite clear to Benjamin. But it seemed justifiable to him to present them before the public, because he viewed a translation's task not so much as providing examples, but rather as an indispensable and strict schooling for developing language itself'.[41] And for Benjamin, at least, his work completely fulfilled its purpose in this sense.

When in October 1923 Benjamin at last held the printed copy of his translations in his hands, there was no more talk of the 'foolish paper-conjuring trick' he had originally feared.[42] Rather, he found the dual-language edition with its easily legible, semi-bold roman type and its marbled pasteboard cover (also available in linen, half-linen and even half-vellum) had 'turned out well and [looked] impressive, after all'.[43] He had managed to assert himself against Weißbach, his publisher, at least in the matter of the book's external design. To his disapproval, though, it was only printed in an edition of 500. But the publisher's far-sightedness in this decision is demonstrated in the fact that this collectors' edition was still far from sold out ten years after publication.[44] Consequently the wish that Benjamin expressed to Weißbach for a 'popular edition' fell on deaf ears.[45]

The book's sales corresponded with its reception by the critics. Basically, they did not take any notice of it, and they were in any case somewhat overtaxed by the rapid succession of Baudelaire editions that had appeared in those few years. A total of just two reviews are recorded. The first, written by Stefan Zweig, who himself was part of the phalanx of renowned Baudelaire translators, appeared in early June 1924 in the Sunday review supplement of the *Frankfurter Zeitung*. The critique sent Benjamin into a rage. This was firstly because the scathing verdict that was pronounced on him by a seemingly competent

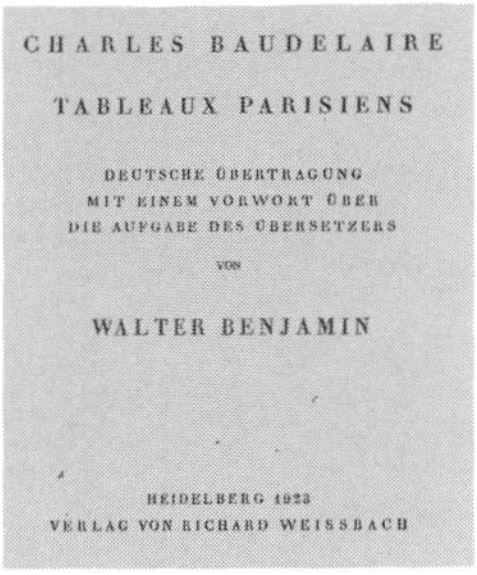

CHARLES BAUDELAIRE

TABLEAUX PARISIENS

DEUTSCHE ÜBERTRAGUNG
MIT EINEM VORWORT ÜBER
DIE AUFGABE DES ÜBERSETZERS
VON

WALTER BENJAMIN

HEIDELBERG 1923
VERLAG VON RICHARD WEISSBACH

'This translation will be ensured its appropriate place by the fact that it not only conscientiously obeys the dictate of faithfulness, which the translator established irrefutably in his foreword, but also because the work's poetry has been convincingly captured.'[39] (Benjamin's Baudelaire translation)

Musset und Baudelaire
in deutscher Uebertragung.
Von Stefan Zweig.

ß man im Jahre 1924, beinahe also ein Jahrhundert
ver Entstehung, noch Alfred de Mussets Dichtungen
ersspiele ins Deutsche übertragen würde, war eigentlich
u erwarten, denn Musset gilt heute selbst in Frankreich
ehr viel. Ein paar Gedichte, das von der Andalusierin
Madrid und die „Oktobernacht" vor allem sind in die
ogien, selbst in die Schullesebücher übergegangen, hie
gibt die Comédie Française noch als Hors d'oeuvre
er entzückenden Proverbes. Aber die Epen und epischen
e, die sich am Weltschmerz Lord Byrons berauschten
ie pathetische Melancholie des großen Engländers gra-
romantischer und weibischer einer gerührten Frauen-
arboten, sind verblüht und verblaßt, er ist im Grunde,
ne Alfred de Musset, heute längst ein Vergessener in
und in Frankreich: umso sonderbarer nun, daß sich
Deutschland ein Dichter seiner erinnert.
Dichter und ein guter Dichter, Herbert Eulenberg,
: den Propyläenverlag nicht nur die Gedichte, sondern
Rolla", „Mardoche", „Namouna" — ach, wie verklungen,
n und verweht sind doch diese einst so berühmten
! — und dazu noch die kleine Komödie „Die Kastanien
ier" übertragen hat. Man kennt heute Eulenbergs Art,
eiche und einfallreiche, farbige Fähigkeit seiner Darstel-
seinen gleitenden leichten Vers, der ihm vielleicht nur
cht aus den Händen gleitet, mühelos und sorglos die
zusammenklingen läßt, was ja — offen gesagt — oft-
eine Gedichte ein wenig zu wässerig, seine Verse ein
zu zufällig macht. Aber diese sorglose, fließende, strömende
gkeit ist bei Musset gerade an den Rechten geraten, dem
das Dichten um ein paar Grade zu leicht war, der lässig
em wunderbaren, oft kindlichen, oft göttlichen Leichtsinn
erse hinschrieb, wie sie ihm rhythmisch und ungefähr in die
fuhren. Und für die Komödie findet Eulenberg darum
ust den zarten, schwingenden lockeren Ton, das über-
Knabenhafte, Verliebte und Verantwortungslose der
en Stanzen und hingesungenen Chansons. So ist diese
zung, die man ihm ersten Augenblick als etwas Zeit-
s, Unnötiges und zu spät Gekommenes empfindet, durch-
n Glücksfall des Zusammenklingens und wenn eine
e Erweckung der verklungenen Mussetschen Verse über-
noch möglich ist, so müßte diese Ausgabe sie vollbringen.
rtigkeit und Schreibfreudigkeit, die große Gefahr des Dich-
ulenberg, hat sich hier für die Nachdichtung zum glück-
Gewinn entfaltet und man wird auf unabsehbare Zeit

(wenn überhaupt noch einmal der
sollte, was mir reichlich unnötig sch
setzung des französischen Heine lese
mutige und verdienstreiche Herbert
noch von einem geistigen „Schatzenbi
Juwelenkabinett deutscher Uebertrag
Schrein verdient.

*

Bei Musset war das Ungefähre i
laubt: da er selbst das Wort nicht
Reim locker und gelegentlich zusamme
viel zu bedeuten, wenn der Nachdichte
frei und eigenwillig schaltete. Ande
bei einem so verantwortlichen, unge
schen Dichter wie Baudelaire, w
rückbar jedes Attribut auf das kostbar
die in einziger Reinheit des Atems
zur letzten durchschwingt. Hier ist
Uebersetzer eine unendliche, wenn
möglich ist: Stefan George hat
blem einseitig gelöst, durch Verwandl
liche Form, wodurch freilich der ben
Baudelaireschen Gedichtes marmorn
Gebilde kristallen gefror. Das gr
jüngeren, Walther Benjamin (ob
rede zeigt, aller Schwierigkeiten voll
schreckt, eine luxuriöse Ausgabe der
mit dem gegenübergestellten französisc
bei Richard Weißbach herausgegeben.
der gewissenhaften, sorgfältigen und
zeitig die inhaltliche Substanz, die
deutsch dichterische Linie zu bewahren
Sinn finden, um einer Durchsichtun
gelingt unverweigerlich nur bei ein
herrliche, von Blut und melodischem
Blatt um Blatt einer frostigen, un
Reimung gegenüberzustellen, wie e
Man löse sich nur ab und zu eine der
für sich, suche mühsam ihren Sinn, u
beglückt mit dem französischen Orig
lese etwa die vier Zeilen:

Ich denk der Schwarzen, die vo
Im Schlamm sich quält und mi
Die Zauberpalmen Afrikas entb
Wo denen zähe Nebel sich verb

und vergleiche sie, die weder ein Bild
tiefen, hinschwellenden Klang eines n
mit der französischen Meisterstrophe:

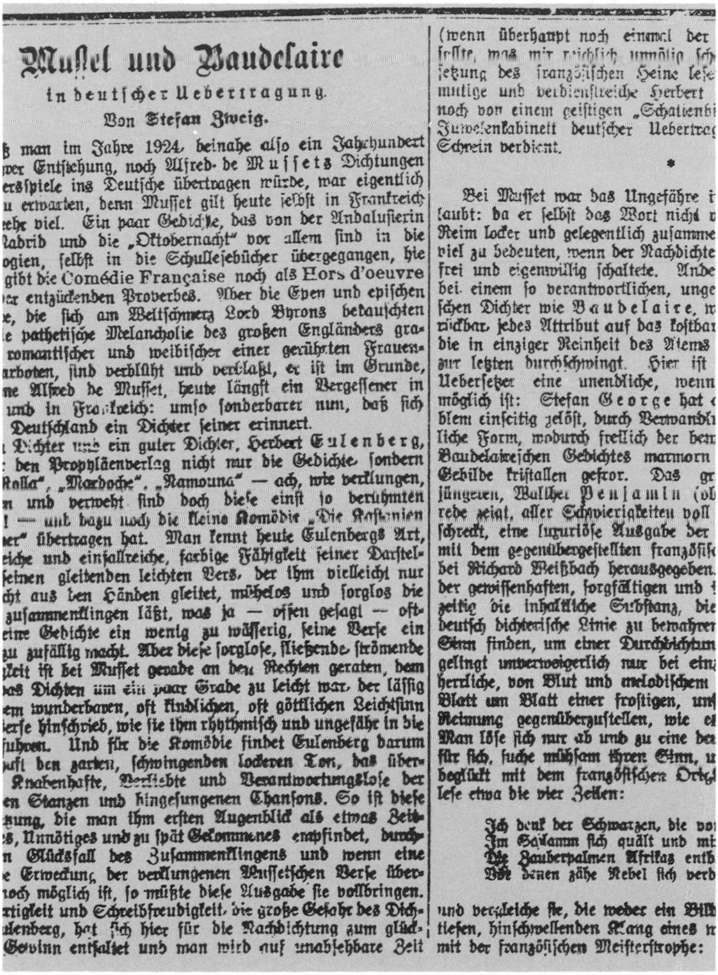

'While fully acknowledging the conscientious, careful and passionate effort to maintain at the same time the substantive content, the external form and the German poetic line, I nevertheless cannot see the sense in [. . .] counterposing to these glorious verses, pulsed with the blood and the singing breath, page after page of frosty, dead, unsensual German rhyme, as is often the case here.'
Zweig's review in the *Frankfurter Zeitung* on 1 June 1924.

judge threatened to compromise his attempts to habilitate in Frankfurt. Secondly he was annoyed by the whole manner in which he was hauled over the coals, a manner which very prudently shielded the *writer* Zweig on the side from which he might expect himself to be threatened. The critic used this shield to be all the more ruthless towards this novice who lacked the protection of any clique, circle or truly influential patron. Indeed, Zweig's critique becomes rather unconvincing when he launches his polemic indiscriminately at virtually any attempt to translate a self-contained cycle of poems: 'faithful renditions, nothing but faithful renditions constantly [create] a feeling of obsessiveness' and 'degenerate into a cold counterpart which [gives] at best' the skeleton of 'the original poem, an X-ray instead of a mirror image or portrait'. It can only 'result in a hybrid' which is of benefit to none, 'neither to German poetry, nor to the French poet – except perhaps in the unintended sense that', as with Benjamin's translations, 'the clumsy German attempt makes the reader feel the indestructible and inimitable glory of the original twice as strongly'.[46] These views of the sense and importance of literary translation are far too simplistic, nor do they really measure Benjamin's attempts against their own demands. (In this respect Benjamin was completely justified complaining about the marring of his foreword by 'shabby parentheses'.)[47] All that remain then are the schoolmasterly reprimands which parade themselves in the guise of well-meaning criticism:

A translation of this kind cannot be accused of carelessness, for it has been performed with tenacity and industry, with honest diligence and the finest use of language, albeit without any inherent genius.[48]

These are the words that first really unmasked the translator, and the victim knew very well why he referred to the review as 'damned clever'.[49]

To add to all this, the review in the *Frankfurter Zeitung* almost put an end to a friendship that had scarcely begun: with Siegfried Kracauer, whom he had come to know around 1922/3. Zweig's scathing critique had, as it turned out, a short prehistory. Originally Kracauer, who had joined the editorial board of the *FZ* in 1921, had told Benjamin that he would support the book by giving it a suitable review. However, the task of writing the review was then passed on to Zweig. Kracauer offered at once to make amends, which he was only to have the opportunity to do years later, when Benjamin's *Origin of German Tragic Drama* was published. But in the intervening years he was to become a staunch advocate of Benjamin in the *Frankfurter Zeitung*.

Benjamin struggled to repair the damage done by Zweig's article with the help of his wife Dora. But all of his attempts to gain a positive review in one of the periodicals published by Ullstein seem to have been in vain. Or at least no reviews of this kind have been discovered as yet, either 'in the *Berliner Zeitung am Mittag*, which is mentioned in a letter from Benjamin to Gottfried Salomon,[50] or in any of the other papers run by the press baron. Only at the end of 1924 did another review appear, this time in the leading Austrian paper *Neue Freie Presse*, which in a certain respect compensated for the humiliation caused him in the *Frankfurter Zeitung*, but only partially, because its rather too well-meaning tone must almost inevitably have raised the suspicion that it was simply a favour done by a friend. Even the very first, emphatic words were unlikely to encourage the expectation of a sober critique that would weigh up the pros and cons: 'The lays of Baudelaire echo like the boom of solemn bells, bells of archaic forms inscribed with mysterious signs and runes, as if cast for all eternity.' This pathos sets the tone for a hymn in praise of the translator:

'One could say that S[iegfried] K[racauer]'s motto was: God protect me from my friends, I can deal with my enemies myself.'[40] (Siegfried Kracauer)

To translate Baudelaire, perhaps the most difficult master of the Parnassus of French poetry, possibly more difficult than Mallarmé, is amongst the most daring of ventures. It was accomplished by Stephan [sic] George, and now once again in most perfect fashion by Walter Benjamin, whose exemplary translation of the 'Tableux parisiens' has at last made them available to German letters.

However, the reviewer fails to provide any criteria whatsoever by which to judge Benjamin's translations. And when in the end he simply talks of a 'translator's hand [which] is simultaneously the hand of an artist and scholar, a person with a profound knowledge of language and the skill of creative reproduction', when even a 'translator-poet' is accoladed as having 'selflessly achieved the noblest artistic work in silence',[51] then even the object of such exultant praise could do no more than to respond with the lapidary remark: 'Appeared in print: a favourable (glowing) review . . . in the *Neue freie Presse*.'[52]

Benjamin had never considered his Baudelaire translations to be entirely finished. His estate contains numerous other versions of poems from *Les fleurs du mal*,[53] but only four more of them ever reached the public eye during his lifetime. They

Dora Benjamin with her son Stefan during the mid-1920s.

117

appeared in 1924 in the short-lived magazine *Vers und Prosa* edited by Benjamin's friend Franz Hessel.[54]

Angelus Novus

The 'eloquent silence' in which Benjamin had cloaked himself when faced with the madness of war was to last until 1920. Only then did he present another text of his, his thesis on 'The Concept of Art Criticism in German Romanticism', for publication.[55] This was followed by the lengthy essay 'Critique of Violence' which appeared in the *Archiv für Sozialwissenschaft und Sozialpolitik*,[56] and which was an attempt to provide a metaphysical foundation for the morality of revolutionary violence in the light of Georges Sorel's *Reflections on Violence*.[57] 1920 also saw the inclusion of the advertisement for his dissertation in

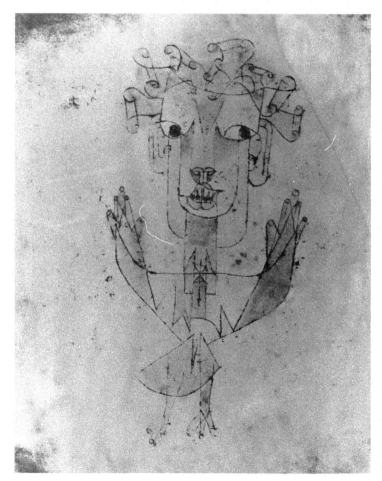

'We are touching now on the ephemerality of this magazine, which it has upheld from the very beginning, for it is the just price to be paid for promulgating genuine topicality. And according to a legend from the Talmud, even the angels are created – new ones at every moment and in countless hosts – simply to sing their hymns before God, then to cease to be and disappear into nothingness. May its very name signify that the magazine will be graced with such topicality, which is the only truth.'[41] (Paul Klee's *Angelus Novus*)

the journal *Kant-Studien*, as well as the publication of two pieces in the expressionist magazine edited by Ernst Blass, *Die Argonauten*: a brief reflection on the concepts 'Fate and Character'[58] and a commentary on Dostoevsky's novel *The Idiot*.[59] These were just a few of the many texts that Benjamin had written during this period, for he had been anything but inactive. A number of the most important essays of his early period of creative production were written in Berlin, Munich and finally Switzerland: apart from those already mentioned, this number includes such major texts as those on 'Trauerspiel und Tragödie' [*Trauerspiel* and Tragedy] and 'Die Bedeutung der Sprache in Trauerspiel und Tragödie' [The Importance of Language in *Trauerspiel* and Tragedy].[60] Only Benjamin's closest friends and acquaintances, such as Alfred Cohn, Ernst Schoen, Gerhard Scholem and Werner Kraft, were given these works to read, which is indicative of the fact that Benjamin had entered a reflective phase. He was trying to find a personal style and was considering what the main aim of his writing should be from then on, for he was aware that the impact of the First World War on world history could only, as he put it to Ernst Schoen, 'end in change',[61] i.e. in a contemplation of the consequences that these events had for personal creative production. Some of this can already be detected in these works. But he only formulated these thoughts in a structured manner in a text that was engendered by his renewed contacts with the literary world in Germany. The text was his 'Announcement of the Periodical: *Angelus Novus*'.

The unexpected prospect of being able to present himself – just a few short years after his return from Switzerland – as the editor of his own journal was the result of his contact with Ernst Blass. Initially he had only approached Blass with the intention of realizing a wish he had long cherished: to see a few examples of his *Les fleurs du mal* translations 'in front of' him, at last 'printed nicely in a journal'.[62] The fact that more was to come of this contact than expected was one of the few happier twists of fate in Benjamin's life. Through Blass he was introduced to the Heidelberg publisher Richard Weißbach, who completely surprised him by making two highly promising proposals at once: the publication of his Baudelaire translations in their entirety, and the opportunity of becoming Blass's successor as editor of *Die Argonauten*. In fact, Benjamin did not take over from Blass because the magazine folded, but Weißbach was willing to establish a new periodical in its place, this time edited by Benjamin. The new editor decided to call his magazine

'I am coming more and more to the realization that I can depend sight unseen, as it were, only on the painting of Klee, Macke and maybe Kandinsky. Everything else has pitfalls that require you to be on guard. Naturally there are also weak pictures by those three – but I see that they are weak.'[42]
(Paul Klee)

Angelus Novus, a title that referred to the eponymous watercolour by Paul Klee whom he so admired, and which he had bought in Munich in spring 1921 for 'one thousand marks'.[63] (It was not the only Klee painting he owned: a year earlier his wife Dora had given him Klee's 'Vorführung des Wunders' [Performance of the Miracle] for his birthday.)

Benjamin had already forged plans for a magazine of his own in 1914. He had been unable to see any further possibility of persuading the editors of *Der Anfang* to adopt his ideas, and so had considered founding his publication with his friend Heinle. Together with Heinle, he wanted to find his way back onto the path of virtue, i.e. to lead the *Magazine of Youth* to its true destiny by shaping it into a periodical that made no allowances for its readers and that, above all, did not permit any specific 'sentiments' to call the tune. But the outbreak of war and Heinle's death had put an end to the project before it could assume any concrete form. Weißbach's completely unexpected offer gave Benjamin the opportunity to dust down the plans he had shelved. And just how keen he was to fashion the new magazine 'entirely and unconditionally' along the lines of the old one is demonstrated by the words that he chose in his 'Announcement'.[64] It was not to evince any political (or other) sentiments, but rather to qualify a specific 'mentality'; one that refrained from 'courting the public's favours in any way' and whose circle of contributors would be restricted to an elite consisting of a 'select few'.[65]

The place of prominence that was to be assigned in the new-old magazine to his departed friend's literary bequest was more than a last, almost self-evident token of friendship from Benjamin: his poems, along with those of his brother, Wolf Heinle, were to be representative of the magazine's poetic configuration. Among the editorial colleagues whom Benjamin chose for his magazine were Scholem, as its specialist for Judaism, and Bloch for philosophical matters, and he reserved questions of linguistic theory and linguistic philosophy for himself and his former teacher in Berlin, Ernst Lewy. Furthermore, Rang was to be responsible for the 'political' section, the Hebrew writer Samuel Joseph Agnon for prose, and the clergyman Ferdinand Cohrs, one-time fellow campaigner in the Berlin Free Students' Union, for theology. In short: a circle of contributors who could not have been more different in their world-views and their literary and academic positions. But uniformity was by no means the editor's intention. The 'Announcement' specified that the 'true assignment' of the magazine was to 'convey the spirit of its times', and that its 'contemporary relevance' was far more important than any 'unity or clarity'. This was not meant to advocate any arbitrariness in its points of view, but to convey the demand for intellectual independence.

But Benjamin left no doubts as to the primary targets of this ostensibly non-binding programme. These were the groupings and schools, societies and sects that had already dominated literary life in Germany for a long time without really filling the moral, political and artistic vacuum which had been created by the collapse of the Wilhelmine Reich, the war and the post-war era, and the ensuing economic deprivation and social distress. Although the 'Announcement of the Periodical: *Angelus Novus*' did not explicitly demand that the 'George School' – a circle of writers, thinkers and public personalities who gathered more or less closely alongside their charismatic leader Stefan George, and who shared (by and large) his views on life, aesthetics and history[66] – be taken to task, it did say that any kind of 'spiritual occultism, political obscurantism' or 'Catholic Expressionism' would be spared none of their criticism.[67]

The announcement amounted to the demand for a clean sweep. New criteria were to be established on every level and in every area – for criticism, poetry, philosophy, theology, and even for translation – which were to hit the literary establishment like a cleansing storm. 'The re-establishment of the power of the critical word, the renewal of dictum and verdict' was given pride of place. 'Only terrorism', wrote Benjamin, could put paid to 'that aping of great artistic creation' which characterized, in his opinion, works of 'literary expressionism'. And while such 'annihilating criticism' required 'the depiction of broader contexts', 'positive criticism' was to 'focus more than previously on individual works of art'. For, contrary to widespread opinion, the task of 'great criticism' is not 'to educate by means of historical representations or to edify by comparisons, but to perceive through absorption'.[68]

Although Benjamin had clear and unequivocal ideas about criticism, the same cannot be said when it came to poetry, a fact that lay essentially in the nature of poetry itself. Here, in his opinion, only experimentation could be of assistance, and all that he could anticipate at this time was that every newer attempt would have to dissociate itself above all from the epigonal tendencies that followed in George's wake. Any further pronouncements on the success of poetic outpourings depended, as Benjamin saw it, on discussions about concrete examples:

Now that the impact of George's final contribution to the riches of the German language has begun to become history, it would seem that nowadays the first work of every younger poet is a new thesaurus of the German poetic language. And as little as it may be hoped that the most enduring effect of a school will soon be seen in its insistence on setting limits on a great master, just as little does the blatantly mechanical nature of its most recent productions instil confidence in the language of its poets. More definitely than in the days of Klopstock – some of whose poems sound as if they were the ones that are being sought today – and more completely than for many centuries, the crisis in German poetry coincides with a decision about the German language itself, one that is determined by neither knowledge, education, nor taste, and in fact whose ascertainment is in one sense only made possible through audacious dictums.

Translation – since time immemorial a healing companion to the 'great crises' in German writing – can, according to the 'Announcement', also help in overcoming this 'crisis in German poetry'. The translation of foreign literature should be 'understood' less as a means of 'providing examples', than as 'an essential and strict schooling for the developing language itself. For where neither this schooling nor original contents are present for language' to build upon, 'its worthy kindred counterpart will present itself' to language 'with the task of abandoning its devitalized linguistic heritage and developing something fresh'. In order to make the 'formal value of genuine translation clearer',[69] he intended placing the German versions opposite the originals. Benjamin reserved all other remarks on the importance of translations for another article, which was finally to become the preface to his own translations.

The magazine would put a strong emphasis on 'universality', although not of a material kind: 'philosophical universality' was 'the form', and it was 'in the interpretation of' this that the new publication was to prove its 'grasp of real contemporary significance. For this, the universal validity of intellectual manifestations of life' must be 'tied to the question of whether' this form is able 'to lay claim to a place in forthcoming religious systems. Not that such systems are foreseeable. But it [is] foreseeable that that which is currently struggling for life as the first of an epoch will be unable to establish itself without them.' And this is the reason why 'it seems to be time to pay less heed to those who think that they have invented the arcanum themselves, than to those who [express] hardship and affliction with the utmost objectivity, and the least feeling and insistence'. Benjamin saw that the fact that a universality of this kind could scarcely any longer be brought into concordance with the customary understanding of academic research was simply a logical consequence. Indeed, contributions to the *Angelus Novus* were supposed to maintain a fitting 'distance' to 'academia because essence and contemporary significance' always diverge 'far more in its manifestations, than in art and philosophy'.[70]

The 'programme' of the *Angelus Novus* was, as the passages quoted here make clear, far more than the mere announcement of a new magazine, for in it Benjamin was permitting a glimpse into his own production workshop. It was not by accident that the pages of the magazine were to be free of 'all that is totally foreign in the form of inconsequential stimuli', to which the editor would be 'feel unable to relate in some way'.[71] The demands of the 'Announcement' for a 'topically relevant' critique of literary works, a philosophy and poetry geared to the present times, or even just for translations that train linguistic ability, were principles that Benjamin had held for a long time. Consequently this short text is an inventory of what he had achieved in his writings, both published and under wraps, to date. From his Hölderlin essay to his reflections on Dostoevsky's *Idiot*, from his expositions 'On Language as Such and on the Language of People' to those on the Kantian concept of experience, and from his 'aphorisms'[72] to his sonnets:[73] there is something of each of these in this 'Announcement'.

However, he only really attempted to put the breadth of his ideas to the test, i.e. to fulfil the promises of this 'programme', in his major works written during the first half of the 1920s. His translations from Baudelaire's *Fleurs du mal*, his essay on 'Goethe's *Elective Affinities*', and his treatise on *The Origin of German Tragic Drama* gave systematic expression to a mental attitude to which Benjamin remained bound in essence until the end of his life.

The first issue of the magazine was to have been in the bookshops by January 1922. But a variety of problems kept delaying the magazine's appearance, long enough for inflation to finally put an end to the whole undertaking. The editor's intellectual purism, the scarcely veiled attacks on the George School (which was, after all, one of the most influential literary cliques at the time) as well as the style and quality of the actual contributions intended for the first issues, must have spoilt the publisher's interest in the project. (The average reader would have been put off Rang's 'Historical Psychology of the Carnival' by its ponderous style alone,[74] and most of the poems by the Heinle brothers would have been better placed in the pages of an adolescents' poetry collection.)

Although none of this was ever mentioned in Benjamin's correspondence with Weißbach, the project was simply overcome by an insoluble conflict of interests: on the one side an editor who thought that he could ignore the expectations of any form of readership, and on the other a publisher who obviously wanted somehow to sell his publications. Or to put it another way: there was a collision between highly antiquated notions of art patronage and commercial interests.

Benjamin's sobering experiences with the *Angelus Novus* project did not prevent him, however, from forging numerous other plans for magazines. But they always met with the same fate: they never outlived the planning stage.

Elective Affinities

Benjamin was unable to shed any more tears when the project for his own periodical finally collapsed. The 'unwritten journal', as he wrote to his friend Rang in October 1922, 'could not be any more important or dear to [him] if it existed'.[75] Relief at being unburdened of the editor's time-consuming task – which could no longer be combined with his academic ambitions,[76] his *Habilitation* – can be sensed in this remark. In addition, Benjamin was experiencing the satisfaction of having at last finished the work that, for him at least, made the magazine itself somewhat superfluous: Weißbach's news that the 'setting up of the Angelus' had had to be discontinued[77] reached Benjamin just as he had completed his long essay on 'Goethe's *Elective Affinities*', which was to assume the role of an 'exemplary piece of criticism' for the programme of the *Angelus Novus*.[78]

'The reestablishment of the power of the critical word, the renewal of dictum and verdict', he had written in his 'Announcement'. And as if the very first sentence of his essay was intended to fulfil this intention of the programme, it begins with a comment which comes across as a sweeping attack on more or less the whole of (academic) literary criticism of the time: 'The existing work on literature suggests that in studies of this kind, thoroughness should be the responsibility of philological rather than critical interests.'[79] This open, or perhaps subliminal attack on 'prosaic' positivism and (Diltheyan) history of ideas[80] is, as becomes clear when Benjamin expands his ideas, merely the backdrop for a polemic addressed to a very particular group: Stefan George's 'circle'. More specifically, Benjamin was throwing down the gauntlet to Friedrich Gundolf (i.e. F. Gundolfinger, 1880–1931). Benjamin classified Gundolf's *Goethe* monograph, which had appeared in 1916, among those 'talented falsifications' in the field of literary criticism[81] which had to be countered without compromise. What Benjamin intended with this 'annihilating criticism' was to be demonstrated in his use of this example of a 'veritable forgery of knowledge':[82] he intended a public execution, by 'passing the final judgement and carrying out the death sentence on Friedrich Gundolf'.[83] And Benjamin's criticism of a book that, for many critics, was the first ever rediscovery of Goethe, was suitably scathing. In his opinion, it was marked by 'empty words' and the 'falsest of judgements', and only the 'blood-thirsty mysticism' of its conceptualization distinguished the 'mentality' that comes to light in it from that 'of a merry caper'.[84]

'Anyone who steps on Gundolf's Goethe gets a case of Georgeian gout.'[43] (Friedrich Gundolf, around 1925)

Thus the essay on the *Elective Affinities* merely continued what Benjamin had begun with his Baudelaire translations. In comparison with these, however, the essay marks a small but not insignificant shift in emphasis in his approach to George and his followers. Whereas previously the 'great master' himself had been the object of Benjamin's criticism in his attempt to counter a questionable world-view in the field of (lyrical) translation, he now changed both arena and opponent. The realization that he might not after all be a match for a person who still constituted a very important model for him, particularly when facing him on his own territory, may have prompted him to shift the controversy to the field of literary criticism. There he would no longer be confronting George himself, but rather his 'friends and disciples'.[85] His antagonists were now George's representatives in academia. The fact that he only devoted his attention to the most talented of them – first to the 'chancellor' of the George empire, Gundolf,[86] and later to Max Kommerell[87] – proves once again just how important it was to him to clarify his relationship with this 'school' with regard to his own intellectual development. For in certain respects he regarded himself as a George pupil – albeit one to whom his demonstrative poses meant little, but to whom the productive appraisal of his 'teacher's' work, his stimuli and 'criticism' meant all the more. A number of Benjamin's basic maxims and reflections on literary and art criticism could equally have appeared in George's *Blätter für deutsche Kunst* [Fascicles of German Art], for they are scarcely anything other than an implicit commentary on the publication's column *Merksprüche*, the 'mnemonic verses'.

A simple truth?

Benjamin's interpretation of *Elective Affinities* is often cited as a typical example of the way in which he introduced, in cryptic form, highly personal and intimate matters into his works. Reference is usually made in this context to the autoritative knowledge of those who were close to him at the time, such as Scholem and Charlotte Wolff (1900–86), a doctor who later gained fame as a sexologist, whom Benjamin met during the early 1920s in Berlin. Her friend Benjamin had only really come to develop his 'great works of literature', as Wolff wrote in her memoirs, 'through his personal involvements and problems'. She had noticed this in particular when Benjamin read from his essay on 'Goethe's *Elective Affinities*'.[88] Scholem goes a step further. He felt, fifty years after the essay was written, that he could at last 'divulge the simple but hidden truth that this work . . . and its insights' were possible only because they were written by Benjamin in a human situation that corresponded uncannily to that of the novel.[89]

Ernst Schoen, drawn by Jula Cohn.

The idea that it is possible to draw conclusions about a work more or less directly from the writer's life (and vice versa) is a seductive one. And all the more so when one is attempting to fill the empty spaces that are left by his autobiographical writings. Generally speaking, it would be right to assume that there are very concrete connections between numerous passages and even entire essays in Benjamin's *œuvre* and his personal biography; and that events and impressions, his reading matter and travels, even his dealings with others, were often both the motive and the inspiration behind his writing. But in the case of his '*Elective Affinities*' essay, this view of things is of little help to interpreters of his work. What, then, were the circumstances that imposed the notion of a precise parallel between Benjamin's life and the constellation of characters in Goethe's famous novel? First and foremost, Benjamin's marriage, which at that time had long since lain in ruins. His wife evidently had a relationship with their mutual friend, Ernst Schoen.[90] And for his part, Benjamin had fallen for the sister of his childhood friend Alfred Cohn, Jula, but was never able to win her love. So on the surface, the constellation of the relationships between these four corresponded very closely to that of the novel's protagonists. Even the way they behaved is supposed to have been highly similar, to the extent that Dora could have been pictured as Charlotte in Goethe's novel, while Jula had assumed the role of Ottilie. Her '"plant-like muteness" and beauty stood . . . at the source' of Benjamin's 'intuitions about the meaning of the beautiful, and about the Luciferian depth of the "appearance"

126

in which the beautiful conceals and reveals itself'.[91] But that was the extent of the similarity. Viewed as a whole, it was too little to provide any cogent reasons for why Benjamin wrote an essay that in any case set about eliminating the illicit commingling of work and life that had become common practice in the philological studies of (not only) Goethe's works. An investigation into Goethe's love life facilitates the understanding of his novel no more – as he elegantly said: there is 'not a touch in it that he had not experienced, and at the same time not a touch as he had experienced it'[92] – than Benjamin's marital crisis can provide the key to understanding his interpretation of the novel.

But perhaps this flight into the biographical aspects of the essay was simply an attempt to clutch at straws. For there is scarcely a work by Benjamin that divided (and continues to divide) opinions to the extent of this one. While one sees it as a unique example of an original Goethe interpretation, the other considers that the interpretation is the victim of complete arbitrariness.[93]

At first sight both evaluations seem to have solid foundations in the essay, even though they view it from completely different angles. While the positive assessment is made mainly with reference to its cultural-historical background, its negative counterpart centres on philological details which are not to be repudiated, but which are of somewhat minor interest when trying to gain a world view or vision from the text and simultaneously to foster one on it. Benjamin was certainly not interested in simply making a further contribution to the existing scholarly literature on *Elective Affinities*. Rather his involvement with the novel was an opportunity for him to express himself fully on certain problems of contemporary (literary) criticism.

In theory, he could have done this with any other work, were it not for the fact that his choice was in a sense preordained in several respects. Since his essay was primarily an attempt to counter the world-view of the George circle, it was important for him to adhere to their representative publications. But at that moment in time, only one of the school's so-called 'books of the spirit' had appeared on a topic of German literature in the closer sense – namely Gundolf's *Goethe*.[94] In addition, this work from Goethe's late period was considered a perfect example of the novel genre – Hermann Cohen called it 'an ideal type of its genre' in his *Ästhetik des reinen Gefühls [Aesthetics of Pure Feeling]*, a work that Benjamin consulted[95]– indeed of classical works of art as such.[96] Finally, the history of this novel's reception could

Jula Cohn 'lived in a studio flat near the Heidelberger castle, where she worked as a sculptor. She was a petite woman of nondescript colouring, who moved gently and cautiously in a literal and symbolic sense. She observed her visitors and everything else through a long ebony handle ... The many freckles on her face and hands made her less different from more ordinary people, and lightened a certain awe she easily aroused.'[44] (Walter Benjamin, bust by Jula Cohn, 1926)

demonstrate the whole dilemma of contemporary literary scholarship with unparalleled clarity.

If the question were raised of what really worthwhile interpretations philological studies of Goethe's *Elective Affinities* had produced until then, one would be left short of an answer. Hardly any of the problems posed by the novel's language, composition and content had really been tackled before, and certainly no attempt had been made to grasp the wealth of interlocking references – 'the presaging and parallel traits in the novel', as Benjamin put it[97]– in all their breadth and depth. All that people claimed was that the novel was Goethe's most modern work. Basically, however, not one of these, in any case none too numerous, essays could give an even moderately satisfying answer to the question of what constituted its modernity. Critics in Benjamin's day remained no less perplexed than Goethe's contemporaries had once been.

For Benjamin, too, the question of its modernity – or perhaps its 'contemporary significance', to borrow a term central to his thought – stands to the fore. His *Elective Affinities* essay attempts to elucidate this modernity and explain how it may be approached methodologically. For Benjamin, this novel, as the first of Goethe's late works, represents a 'turning point' in the author's works as a whole, one that he seems to have been aware of; a turning point inasmuch as Goethe breaks here the pact of his manhood, which had consisted of voluntary submission to the 'mythical orders, wherever they still rule'. In *Elective Affinities*, Goethe raises his protest against the unfathomed and unfathomable mythic world, his 'struggle for release from its grasp', where this 'struggle' and its object – marriage as the social manifestation of the myth – made the subject of his expositions.[98]

Elective Affinities was misunderstood by its early readers as a novel about marriage, for two main reasons. First, the choice of material was due to a somewhat incidental event in Goethe's life: his marriage in 1806, during the French occupation of Weimar, to his companion of many years' standing, Christiane Vulpius, which he regarded as a 'capitulation' to social conventions. Second, Goethe saw emerging from the dissolution of the marriage 'the mythical powers of law' which, once all that is humane has been reduced to appearance, determine its nature. Consequently he felt marriage to be 'a symbol of mythical imprisonment', to be exemplarily 'threatening'.[99] By means of the dualistic polarity of such concepts as passion and the necessity to submit oneself to codified norms, affection and marriage, eroticism and morals – all of which fall into the framework called 'marriage' – Goethe attempts symbolically to portray the inherent conflict in the social relationships that surrounded him. This concludes Benjamin's by no means fully consistent and in places almost cryptic interpretation of the novel, into which he does indeed read a number of original notions, which cannot be inferred directly from Goethe's text.

But for him the interpretation of a work of art presupposes in principle a global interpretation, and that it becomes 'imbued' with personal 'knowledge',[100] because truth, as a metaphysical value, can hardly be distilled from the wording of a work. Consequently Benjamin's critique of *Elective Affinities* is not primarily an attempt to discover some secret or other concerning Goethe's artistic identity, but rather it is mainly an attempt to work out the way in which the protagonists act and react on the basis of their personal circumstances. His interpretation centres on the chaotic elements which he believes he can discern in the social background of Goethe's figures, and which in the end also prove to be a projection of his own perception of reality. 'Recognizing' one's own historical present by 'immersing' one-self in the work of art: that is the maxim of Benjamin's literary criticism. For apart from some theological aspects, there are also certain parallels to the political constellations of the 1920s in Goethe's portrayal of the mythical powers with which there can be no reconciliation, and in the legitimization of the search for the 'semblance of reconciliation', because 'there can only be true reconciliation with God'.[101]

Consequently, the truth that constitutes the essence of the work of art is by no means an ahistorical or timeless one that only resides in the work in question, but one that actually illuminates the interpreter's discoveries and projections. A fitting formulation, which could just as appropriately have appeared in the *Elective Affinities* essay, can be found in the late 'Arcades' project: 'An emphatic refusal of the concept of "timeless truth" is in order. Yet truth is not . . . just a temporal function of knowledge; it is bound to a time-kernel that is planted in both.'[102]

It was in connection with his *Elective Affinities* essay that Benjamin became acquainted with Hugo von Hofmannsthal, who had received a copy of the manuscript from Benjamin via their mutual friend Florens Christian Rang. Rang had already intimated enough about this talented Berlin Jew to Hofmannsthal to raise the Viennese writer's expectations. And, after

A lesson in the politics of literature

'Not allowing oneself to be copied, to be adopted by others, belongs, if not to the very nature of refinement, then most certainly and to a very great degree to that which distinguished Hofmannsthal, from his early days to his maturity, in so many modulations of his being and of as his creations.'[45] (Hugo von Hofmannsthal, sketch by Karl Baner)

an initial look at the essay, he became exceedingly enthusiastic. It was 'simply incomparable', and the 'great beauty of the portrayal, which pierced the mystery in such exemplary fashion', was 'wonderful'; a 'completely confident and clear way of thinking' was expressed in it, which, in his opinion, had become rare in the writing of the day.[103] Hofmannsthal published it almost at once in his periodical, *Neue deutsche Beiträge*. The first two chapters appeared in April, the third and last the following January. So, the essay not only came to the public eye in 'the most exclusive of [the current] periodicals by far' (one, moreover, that represented much of what Benjamin had hoped to achieve with his *Angelus Novus*), but was also published in a place that he considered to be the most fitting, indeed the only possible 'outlet' for his 'attack on the ideology' of the George circle: for here they would be *unable* 'to ignore' the 'invective' that was launched at them.[104]

Nothing was easier, though, for the adepts and epigones of the 'great master' than to do just that. They passed over the essay in silence, with a quite superior air, while simultaneously delivering the author a lesson in the politics of literature; for not another soul commented on the essay, and that was certainly not by chance. Benjamin seems to have had no inkling of what it actually meant to take on an intellectual circle that was not only united in questions of art and literature, but was also able to gain acknowledgement of its views on institutional levels: in the universities, on the editorial boards of periodicals and even the publishing houses. It also required a fair amount of naivety to assume that somebody from the George circle – perhaps even Gundolf himself – would respond openly to such harsh criticism. It would have been almost beneath their dignity to discuss in public the trivial work of an uninitiate, and thus perhaps even enhance its value by the ensuing debate. At the same time they could not and would not let him get away with this 'blasphemy', and so they resorted to a more subtle 'response'. Benjamin had already received, some time previously, an object lesson in the way that this sort of a matter is generally 'dealt with', the mechanisms that are set in motion – less by a physical person than by the presence of apparently occult powers – while he had still tried in vain to get his essay accepted by a publisher or even just by a periodical. But evidently he was quite incapable of making certain connections in his mind. For prior to the appearance of his essay in Hofmannsthal's *Beiträge*, he had received two extremely curious refusals from other sources. One came from the publisher Paul Cassirer in Berlin.

Although he paid 15,000 marks for an option on the work,[105] after allowing himself three months to consider the essay, he declined to print it 'because of technical difficulties'.[106]

Benjamin's other rejection came from the renowned *Deutsche Vierteljahrsschrift für Literaturwissenschaft und Geistesgeschichte [German Quarterly for Literary Studies and the History of Thought]*. By now, the reason for his difficulties should have finally dawned on him. Ostensibly it was the essay's length that stood in the way of its publication; in reality other matters entirely had decided the issue. This emerges fairly unambiguously in a letter by the periodical's co-founder and editor, Erich Rothacker. This unique document in the literature on Benjamin closes with the remark that 'the argumentation concerning Gundolf' is quite unacceptable 'in its present, exceedingly sharp form'. Rothacker advised the author that he should 'preferably formulate' his critique '(perhaps as a separate study) in a way [that might] influence [Gundolf] without his having to compromise himself in any way'.[107] That was almost taking the proverbial 'broad hint' too far, but Benjamin still does not seem to have understood it. So presumably he was the only person to be surprised by the total lack of response to his work – just a few sporadic mentions in the academic literature on the topic, almost in the course of duty, scarcely anything else.

The work received just one real response, very much later in 1938, in distant Moscow. Alfred Kurella, once an active member of the *Wandervogel* and Benjamin's fellow editor on the *Anfang*, published in *Internationale Literatur* a damning review of a special issue of *Cahiers du Sud* on 'German Romanticism', which had included a partial translation of the *Elective Affinities* essay in French.[108] The fact that he featured in this review as a Heidegger supporter – Kurella dismissed the essay as an 'attempt that would have done a great honour to Heidegger'[109] – merely showed Benjamin how much more 'desperate the situation' was in the 'other' camp (among Marxist writers 'that hew', as he put it, 'to the party line').[110]

Benjamin's plans to have the essay published as a book in its own right were by no means shelved after its publication in Hofmannsthal's *Beiträge*. Rather, the author did everything he could to make his work known in this way to a wider readership, but without success. Although by autumn 1925 he had already signed a contract with the publisher Ernst Rowohlt, which included among other things the publication of his *Elective Affinities* essay,[111] the whole undertaking was – for reasons that remain obscure – never to progress beyond proof sheets[112] and

Advertisement for Benjamin's books, from the appendix of *Ursprung des deutschen Trauerspiels*.

Label for the cover of the
limited edition of
'Goethe's *Elective
Affinities*'.

publication announcements, the last of which appeared in
1928. Consequently the limited edition issued by the *Bremer
Presse* (publisher of *Neue deutsche Beiträge*) constituted the only
integral publication of the work during Benjamin's lifetime.
(One of the few copies bearing his handwritten annotations is
still held in the Rowohlt archive.) Only in 1964 did a second
edition of what may be regarded as Benjamin's most important
essay finally appear.[113]

A German tragedy

Looking back on his various efforts to attain admittance to the
profession of university lecturer after receiving his doctorate,
one gains the impression that Benjamin was for a while a kind
of wanderer in the world of *Habilitation*. Berne, Heidelberg and
Gießen, finally Frankfurt am Main: these were the universities
he considered (or which his friends considered for him) during
the three or four years following his doctoral examinations, in
order to make the decisive step towards an academic career. The
fact that he was never to gain a foothold at any university had
little to do with him and the efforts he made. He displayed
more than enough goodwill and dedication, but everyone and
everything seemed to be against him: his parents, the university
professors and the circumstances.

The first prospects of a *Habilitation* had presented themselves
– 'quite contrary to [his] wildest expectations'[114] – as early as
November 1919, in Berne. Benjamin had gone to meet Richard
Herbertz for the last time, and during their conversation the
professor raised hopes in his former model student that he could
receive a lectureship in philosophy. The prospect must have
seemed like a gift from heaven, for he felt that it would mean
peace for once on the 'economic front'. And in his opinion, not
even his parents could object to plans that at least promised
social prestige if they were finally crowned by success. However,
they had absolutely no intention of actually encouraging this
'preposterous idea' by providing for his maintenance. Hence
his first attempt to don the gown of a university lecturer failed
through lack of finances: no money was to be had from his
parents and, despite all efforts, it was impossible to find an
'appropriate' position 'with a suitable salary' for his wife.[115] Thus,
all the notes and thoughts he had prepared for his *Habilitation*
dissertation – a number of more of less extensive schemas and
literature studies[116] for an investigation into 'the large complex
of problems concerning word and concept (language and
logos)'[117] – remained futile labours of love.

Benjamin had little more success in Heidelberg. Private matters (Jula Cohn) and business (discussions with Richard Weißbach about the *Angelus Novus*) brought him there for a number of weeks during 1921 and again in 1922, and gave him the time to make contact with the university teachers there. He attended a course of lectures by Friedrich Gundolf, made the acquaintance of Karl Jaspers, renewed his contact with his former teacher in Freiburg, Heinrich Rickert, and listened to lectures by Hans Ehrenberg and Emil Lederer.[118] But the university courses that he attended proved quite fruitless. He found Gundolf 'terribly feeble' during his lectures 'and harmless in terms of the personal impression' he made, 'quite different' from that 'in his books' (once again Benjamin reveals the fascination that the outpourings of the George circle exerted on him, despite all his reservations). Jaspers was for him likeable 'as a person', but fairly insignificant 'in his thinking',[119] and Rickert struck him as nothing more than 'grey and evil'.[120] At the same time he felt certain in his mind that he had done all that was necessary to pave the way to a *Habilitation* in Heidelberg.

Karl Mannheim.

His disappointment was consequently all the greater when he discovered on his return, in 1922, that the philosophy faculty had come to favour another candidate: Karl Mannheim.[121] With this, his hopes in Heidelberg were also dashed. His only chance now was the university in Frankfurt am Main.[122]

The city of Frankfurt was also the home in the early 1920s of his mother's uncle, Arthur Moritz Schoenflies, so it is reasonable to suppose that this family tie further strengthened Benjamin's decision to seek his fortune (and *Habilitation*) there. Without doubt Schoenflies, as one of the university's founders and a former rector, had the necessary influence and contacts to give his great-nephew's project appropriate support. However, he retired in the very same year that Benjamin put out his first feelers to the philosophy faculty, so Schoenflies was not to be Benjamin's only contact at the university, and was perhaps not even his most important.

This proved to be a person whom Benjamin presumably first met whilst endeavouring to get accepted for his *Habilitation*: Gottfried Salomon-Delatour, who at the time was teaching sociology as a *Privatdozent* in the seminar run by the famous Franz Oppenheimer (who among other achievements was one of the fathers of the 'Settlement Movement' in Germany and Palestine). In all likelihood Benjamin was introduced to Salomon through his circle of friends Lucie and Erich Gutkind in Berlin, perhaps by Adolph Otto, the 'Melech Hagojim' (King of the Gojim) as Benjamin jokingly referred to the founder of the (Grünau-) Falkenberg Colony,[123] and who was often able to help him through his contacts.

A failed *Habilitation*

Benjamin's letters to Salomon during the years 1922–26 have been preserved, and they provide the most detailed account on record of the episodes surrounding his *Habilitation*. In certain respects they are a meticulous record of the academic tragedy which Benjamin's attempt to enter the 'halls of the academic world'[124] turned out to be. Salomon advised his new friend to try his luck among the literary scholars or 'aestheticians' instead of in the philosophy faculty. As Benjamin himself agreed, it would

'I recall the performance of El Cid in Geneva, during which the sight of the king's lop-sided crown produced the first idea that nine years later ended up as the inspiration behind the book on tragic drama.' (Frankfurt University, 1928)

have been 'easiest to subsume' his writings under 'this heading'.[125] However, the heads of the philosophy faculty rejected his application for a *Habilitation* based on his publications, and demanded that he write an original dissertation. Benjamin accepted the suggestion made by the dean, Franz Schultz, to write on the subject of 'German Baroque Literature'. By April 1923 he had already 'established the basic ideas' of this work on Baroque tragedy *in nuce*,[126] and he had collected all the necessary material by spring the following year; the writing was to be done far away from Berlin, in Italy.

To get back to my trip, people in Berlin are agreed that there is a conspicuous change in me. The exaltation with which I prepared for it in the spring by fasting and similar exercises and with which, not without Dora's intensive support, I struggled to achieve this change both externally and internally, was not in vain.[127]

These remarks come from a letter that Benjamin wrote to Scholem on 22 December 1924, and refer to the journey to Capri which he began in April of that year. He spent almost exactly six months on the island. Like many an unemployed or needy intellectual during the crisis-stricken years of the Weimar Republic, he had decided to make this journey to escape the atmosphere of widespread economic and social depression. The French occupation of the Ruhr District, communist uprisings in Saxony and Thuringia, inflation, Hitler's attempted coup in Bavaria, separatist movements in the Rhineland: all these events and more, which had turned 1923 into a fateful year for the fledgling Republic, had happened just a few months ago. But in contrast to Theodor Wiesengrund (later Adorno), with whom he had become acquainted the year before in Frankfurt,[128] Ernst Bloch and Alfred Sohn-Rethel[129] (to name just a few of his friends and acquaintances in those days who had, for similar reasons and at much the same time, fled to the south of Italy), Benjamin's stay on Capri was to mark a turning point in his life that had a lasting influence on his writing.

The trip, which he had planned well in advance, almost came to nothing at the last moment: just a few short months after the government had introduced the monetary reform *(Rentenmark)*, it issued a decree aimed at checking the uncontrolled export of currency. The new restrictions, at once dubbed by the press 'border duties', 'emigration fees' and the like,[130] meant that in future, people travelling abroad would have to deposit a financial security at the border that amounted to several times the sum they were taking with them. Although these directives were already known several days before they came into effect, the date of which was actually after that of Benjamin's intended departure, he made a hurried exit from Berlin. And contrary to his plans, he went alone. He first saw his intended travel companions – his friends Emma and Florens Christian Rang, Lucie and Erich Gutkind and (the latter's Hebrew teacher) Dow Flattau – at his destination. This was on 9 or 10 April, in a pension whose name ('Gaudeamus')[131] gives a good idea of the atmosphere that reigned over this group now that they had finally managed to overcome the obstacles placed before them.

'I think that anyone who has spent a lengthy period of time on Capri qualifies for distant travel, for those who have lived there a long time are deeply convinced that they have everything under control, and that all that that they need will come to them at the right time.'[46] (From Benjamin's postcard collection: Capri)

The province of Campania, with its capital Naples and its off-shore islands Ischia and Capri, as well as historically renowned Positano, Paestum and Pompeii, were favoured destinations for German intellectuals during the 1920s. This northernmost area of southern Italy was at roughly the same time as for Benjamin the place of residence of Marianne and Bertolt Brecht (who at that time was only known to him by name), Caspar Neher, Linda and Ernst Bloch, Melchior Lechter (George's friend and the illustrator of his books), Bernhard Reich (the former artistic director of the Munich Kammerspiele theatre) with his companion Asja Lacis and her daughter Daga, Gott-fried Salomon, Friedrich Gundolf and many other prominent members of contemporary cultural circles. The effect that their time here had on their creative work can be seen in a long list of relevant publications. To name but a few examples: Benjamin himself wrote, together with Asja Lacis, a portrait of Naples for the *Frankfurter Zeitung*; Ernst Bloch wrote a short essay, 'Italy and Porosity' (the concept of the title stems from Benjamin),[132] for the *Weltbühne*; and Alfred Sohn-Rethel's impressions and experiences were contained in the small text 'On Neapolitan Technology'.[133]

Benjamin already knew the majority of these people, and he spent many hours in conversation with some of them on Capri or in Naples. He sat for nights on end with Bloch in a bar by a Capri beach, arguing with him over Tieck's '"Tale of Blond Eckbert" and its contexts'.[134] He acted as Salomon's guide when the latter stopped off in Naples on his return to Germany from Sicily. (Benjamin had regretted being unable to introduce his friend to the subterranean mysteries of the city, the catacombs in which he had gained his most 'important impressions of early-Christian painting'.)[135] And he also accompanied Sohn-Rethel on extensive expeditions through the metropolis at the foot of Vesuvius. Benjamin also made new acquaintances here on Capri: Asja Lacis, for example, to whom he always referred in his letters to Scholem simply as 'a Bolshevist Latvian woman from Riga' or an 'outstanding female communist'[136] instead of by her actual name (soon she was to become far more than a mere acquaintance for Benjamin); and Melchior Lechter, with whom he struck up a conversation in a beerhouse with the enchanting German name 'Zum Kater Hiddigeigei' [The Tom Cat Hiddigeigei].

'I deeply regret that at the time you were staying in Naples, I knew nothing of the city's marvellous catacombs. I have now visited them on two occasions and there I have gained my most important impressions of early Christian painting.'[47]
(The catacombs of S. Gennaro, Naples)

This was not Benjamin's first, nor was it to be his last visit to this part of southern Europe. Yet this trip to Capri in spring 1924 represented much more to him than all his other visits. The remark quoted above, that there had been both an inner and an outer change in him that was intimately linked with this stay, already suggests as much. The actual nature of this 'change', which he described to Scholem as an observation made by his friends and acquaintances (although basically he felt this to be a very appropriate description of his personal experience, as it had manifested itself during the visit), is further elucidated in the course of the letter in question. He mentions hitherto unclear 'communist signals' which, as the first 'indications of a turnabout', had 'awakened in him the will not to mask the current and political elements of [his thoughts] in the old-fashioned way . . . but to develop them by experimenting and taking extreme measures'. That meant first of all that 'the literary

'I began this letter yesterday in the café where I was sitting near Melchior Lechter, whom I met here a few days ago. A friendly, very sophisticated old gentleman with a round, red, child's face. He walks on crutches. In the course of time I have come to know one person after the other in the Scheffel-Café Hidigeigei [sic] (except for its name, there is nothing unpleasant about it). In most cases, with little profit; there are hardly any noteworthy people here.'[48] (The Hiddigeigei café)

exegesis of German literature' would have to take a back seat, because 'this exegesis [was] at best essentially meant to conserve and to restore what is genuine in the face of expressionistic falsifications'.[137] This outline of a 'programme' for his future work raises the question of what could have had such an extra-ordinary effect on Benjamin that it lead to a broad realignment of all of his thinking and creative output.

Benjamin produced a 'Capri Chronicle',[138] which can be pieced together from his extensive correspondence during the months of his stay. His letters and postcards to his wife Dora, to Rothacker, to Salomon and to Scholem all contain detailed information about his work, his reading matter, his discussions with friends and acquaintances, about the living and housing conditions there as well about his various activities (excursions to nearby and more distant parts of the island, where he made 'curious and important observations').[139] What first strikes the present-day reader of these documents is the complexity of what he reports.

The numerous contradictions and conflicting points contained in this 'chronicle' lead to the assumption that the author quite deliberately brought together notions that did not fit the image of his personality held by his friends and acquaintances. He mentions to Scholem, for instance, that he has now taken out a subscription to the reactionary royalist paper *Action Française*. And as if to provoke his friend even further, he follows this by saying that the paper's 'perspective' is the 'only one from which [one can] view the details of German politics without being stupefied'. But in the very same letter he also maintains that a number of the *Studies on Marxist Dialectics* (the subtitle of Georg Lukács's *History and Class Consciousness*) are 'very important, especially for me'.[140] Similarly, he moved in the circles of the non-conformist Italian futurists with the same ease with which he visited the salon of one Count Rocca who resided in Sorrento. These contradictions become even more apparent in the words that Benjamin chooses with regard to his deceased friend Florens Christian Rang, on the one hand, and concerning the communist Asja Lacis, on the other. In a letter to Scholem, he describes Rang's significance with respect to his own thinking by saying that he thanked his paternal friend for 'all the essential elements of German culture' that he had 'internalized'. 'Not only', Benjamin continues in this letter of November 1924, were 'the main objects of [their] steadfast reflection in this area . . . almost always the same', but 'only in' Rang had he also seen 'the life [of] these great subjects humanely manifested, bursting

'I met the famed heads of futurism. Marinetti, whom I visited for tea in very interesting company, Vasari, and the likeable painter Prampolini. Marinetti is certainly quite a lad. He performed a "noise poem" to great effect: neighing, booming guns, rattling carts, machine-gun fire, etc. In addition he told stories of his stay in Fiume during the decisive days of the campaign by d'Annunzio, with whom he fell out on account of the latter's Caesarism.'[49] (Marinetti holding an address from the balcony of the town hall in Capri, probably in 1924)

forth with all the more volcanic force when it lay paralysed under the crust of the rest of Germany'. Their conversations were not so much characterized by 'harmony in [their] thoughts', rather Benjamin, 'weatherproofed and athletic, tested [himself] on the impossible, battered massif of [Rang's] thoughts', often reaching 'a pinnacle that afforded a broad view of [his] own unexplored thoughts'. Rang's 'spirit was shot through with madness, just as a massif with crevices. But, because of his morality, madness

Florens Christian Rang.

'In a love affair most seek
an eternal homeland.
Others, but very few,
eternal voyaging. These
latter are melancholics,
for whom contact with
mother earth is to be
shunned. They seek the
person who will keep far
from them the
homeland's sadness. To
that person they remain
faithful.'[50] (Asja Lacis)

could not gain power over [him].' Benjamin 'was familiar with the wonderfully humane climate of his intellectual landscape: it constantly had the freshness of the sunrise. But [he was] also clear how ossified this landscape [was] after the sun [had] set', and worried 'about the fate of Rang's writings without seeing any prospect of a solution. Who', Benjamin wondered, would be 'up to taking them on?'[141] While Rang satisfied one particular stratum in Benjamin's mental landscape, his love for Asja Lacis was to open up to him a sphere of intellectual production of a very different kind, that of materialistic theory and pratice. 'But that does not prevent the fact', he wrote in a letter dated 16 September, in which for the first time he gives more details about his examination of the 'problem of present-day communism' (which in his opinion would only expose once again 'the foundations [of his] nihilism'), that 'since I have been here, this has not prevented me from seeing the political practice of communism (not as a theoretical problem but, first and foremost, as a binding attitude) in a different light than ever before'.[142]

Without doubt, these and other similar remarks in Benjamin's 'Capri Chronicle' reveal that something had been set in motion in his mind. When a person sways between such extremes, it can only be interpreted as the attempt to give a new direction to their overall activities and production. And it is precisely for this reason that these accounts from Capri are above all the chronicle of a process of learning and of gaining new experiences. The final outcome of this process cannot be gleaned directly from the at times significant, at times curious and at times seemingly banal passages in his epistles. But they do contain figurative descriptions and images, such as in the opening remarks of one of the last letters that Benjamin wrote in Italy:

Dear Gerhard, it is my turn to be at a loss: I do not know why you haven't answered my last letter. Since I now must, as it were, use my last report as a starting point, it is paradoxically twice as hard to pick up the 'narrative thread' again. A few lines from you would have erected a sylphidic bridge over the chasms that are part and parcel of any journey. During which I move along alone but unbound on a golden road.[143]

He talks of abysses and ravines, and a journey through or over them, of a golden road along which he is walking, alone but free of any ties. But where is this journey taking him?

It has long since been acknowledged that Benjamin's style of writing and his mental outlook underwent distinct changes in the mid-1920s, changes whose dimensions cannot really be appreciated if they are simply labelled as a swing towards Marxism (his own references to 'communist signals' tempt one to attach such a label). It is more fitting and felicitous to attribute these changes to his irrevocable break with the esotericism that he had practised until then with respect to truth, fulfilment and fortune.[144] This general renunciation of the metaphysical foundations of his thinking, which Benjamin viewed simultaneously as the attempt to make a fresh start, was prompted by the events and developments that followed in the wake of the First World War. The historical changes compelled him, as he saw it, to adopt a political stance.

He had already given an account of the social conditions of his times in his 'Tour of German Inflation', cited earlier. He gave a preliminary version of this work, which was to become fairly extensive, to Scholem in the form of an untitled scroll to accompany him on his way to Palestine.[145] The dedication alone shows the extent of Benjamin's regret at being unable to emulate his friend in his venture: 'For Gerhard Scholem, on the occasion of your happy departure, Walter Benjamin, September 1923'.[146] For all the ambiguity of this dedication, Benjamin had for a long time considered the political and economic situation, and above all his own personal circumstances, to be so depressing that anyone who managed to escape them seemed to him to be a darling of fortune in the truest sense. The fact that, unlike Scholem, he could not bring himself to turn his back on Germany and Europe once and for all, is not least because of the differences in their initial situations. While Scholem was truly able to discover a new identity for himself in his Jewish origins, one that enabled him to decide on the most natural possible choice, to go to the place where a Jewish state was in the making, Benjamin found, after lengthy reflection, that this route was barred to him, as he eloquently testified in his letters to Rang in 1923.

On the appearance of Benjamin's essays of literary criticism in 1977, Peter von Haselberg justifiably raised the question of the 'German Walter Benjamin'.[147] It has remained unanswered to this day, even though this short article pinpointed the problem that constantly gained the upper hand in all of Benjamin's reflections during this period. 'For me, on the contrary, circumscribed national characteristics were always central: German or French. I will never forget that I am bound to the former and how deep these ties go.' Or, slightly later in the same letter to Rang (18 November 1923): 'Regardless of where I wind up, I will not forget what is German.'[148] And, once again approaching the topic of his German origins, he wrote in a letter to his paternal friend Rang some seven days later:

For me, a love for different peoples, languages and ideas is part and parcel of the same thing. This does not preclude that it may sometimes be necessary to distance myself in order to preserve this love. As far as Germany is concerned, my love for it is of course so ingrained because of all the significant life experiences I have had there, and thus it cannot be lost. Yet I do not want to become a sacrifice to this love.[149]

Although these quotes, seen together, show that Benjamin cannot have been particularly serious when he talked to his friend Scholem about emigrating (voluntarily) to Palestine, they nevertheless provide a decisive indication of the reasons why he sought the distance of Italy in 1924. His journey was the escape which was intended to preserve his love of Germany. That his real destination was not Italy but Germany is made clear by the fact that he had already considered a number of other places for his 'escape': Paris, Holland, Switzerland, and southern Europe as a whole.

So the motivation behind his journey to Capri was basically nothing other than the wish to 'extricate' himself from the whole atmosphere of Berlin and Germany, from its 'pernicious influence' and the 'frustrations'[150] which had weighed down on his activities like lead, and to save himself from 'demoralizing interaction with what is empty, worthless and brutal'.[151] And this defines how one should not attempt to interpret Benjamin's 'Italian Travels' of 1924: no Arcadia, no new (Italian) literary landscapes revealed themselves to him in Italy. Rather, the journey was dominated from the outset by a process of detachment, through which he ultimately distanced himself from his preexisting work and output.

Porosity and interpenetration

His departure from the old physiognomy assumed concrete form in an article he wrote together with Asja Lacis entitled 'Naples', which appeared in the *Frankfurter Zeitung* on 19 August 1925. Individual aspects of his 'Capri Chronicle' appear here in new contexts, which allow free interpretation and association. Moreover, the particular arrangement of the facts takes the discrepancy between theory and reality to the extreme, with the object of making evident the wretched state of theory and academia in the face of the reality with which these claim to be dealing. By digging deeper into this illustration of the city of Naples, indeed, by digging it over, a number of concepts come to light that give a very clear picture of Benjamin's intentions. Two of these concepts in particular convey an impression of how he envisaged finding his way about this labyrinth of the historical present without 'house numbers'[152] (which was consequently a subversive and thus autonomous way of thinking in a controlled society), without at the same time completely renouncing academic research and theory.

The concepts in question are 'porosity' and 'interpenetration', which arise repeatedly until finally they are linked with one another and merge:

As porous as this stone is the architecture. Building and actions interpenetrate in the courtyards, arcades, and stairways. In everything they preserve the scope to become a theatre of new, unforeseen constellations. The stamp of the definitive is avoided. No situation appears intended forever, no figure asserts itself 'thus and not otherwise'. This is how architecture, the most binding part of the communal rhythm, comes into being here. . . . In such corners one can scarcely discern where building is still in progress and where dilapidation has already set in. For nothing is concluded. Porosity results not only from the indolence of the southern artisan, but also, above all, from the passion for improvisation, which demands that space and opportunity be at any price preserved. Buildings are used as a popular stage. They are all divided into innumerable, simultaneously animated theatres. Balcony, courtyard, window, gateway, staircase, roof are at the same time stage and boxes. . . . Porosity is the inexhaustible law of the life of this city, reappearing everywhere. . . . Similarly dispersed, porous, and commingled is private life. What distinguishes Naples from other large cities is something it has in common with the African kraal; each private attitude or act is permeated by streams of communal life. To exist, for the Northern European the most private of affairs, is here, as in the kraal, a collective matter. . . . And thus families interpenetrate in relationships that can resemble adoption.

And finally:

True laboratories of this great process of intermingling are the cafés. Life is unable to sit down and stagnate in them. They are sober, open rooms resembling the People's Café, and are the opposite of everything Viennese, of the confined, bourgeois, literary world. Neapolitan cafés are bluntly to the point. A prolonged stay is scarcely possible.[153]

Concealed behind the concepts of 'porosity' and 'interpenetration' is a complete scheme for an open form of philosophizing or perceiving reality. Grouped around this are methodological aids which are concerned with the procedure and the means of representation, and which ultimately delineate the overall context. The subject of the essay is portrayed as the stage for hitherto unknown, future-oriented constellations. The observer, suspended above this scene, descends from his theatre box. His position interlocks with the observed (the scene). All that is definitive and distinctive in the portrayal, the 'once and for all' and the 'thus and not otherwise', is avoided. Contact with and transition to decay, to decline, is sought in an upright position. The borders of the limited bourgeois literary world are crossed by developing them into political categories and by merging private with public affairs. Openness in methods and architecture (composition), and porosity as a law of the appropriation and alteration of social reality that has constantly to be discovered anew, are ascertained as a programme.

And Benjamin's whole biography vouches for the fact that there is nothing non-committal about these words. Nor had he any doubts that the problem of a more incisive grasp of reality has always to be marked out and encircled anew, in the very same way that he approached a building, a city or a landscape – which can also be understood as the marking out and the encircling of an object, a work, an epoch; in short, of a historical and political present in its entirety, with the aim of recognizing (once again) the outlines of a society more worthy of humankind. He had left Germany to escape a society that was an affront to human dignity, and to look for a way of conceiving a better one. Nothing in his subsequent writing suggests he thought he had found such a society, or saw its coming as a certainty. But the insight he gained on his visit to Capri enabled him to see it as a very real possibility.

Benjamin's attempt to step beyond the limits of his own thinking and creative production left a great and deep impact on his *œuvre*. This becomes most apparent in the comparison of two works which were not only written at almost the same time, but which also appeared in the same year: the books *The Origin of German Tragic Drama* and *One-Way Street*, both published by

Rowohlt in 1928. The first is an academic treatise which presents various facts in scholarly fashion and aims at preserving the baroque allegory for the present age. The second is a collection of aphorisms, or rather of mental images and challenges. It is obvious that the passages in *One-Way Street* are simply the initial attempts to get a proper grasp of new notions. (That is also how they were read by contemporary critics.) With this publication, the author already had a clear outline in his mind of his intended direction: the possibility of giving a political exposition of (the development of) his own thoughts – in a manner that 'experiments with extremes' and 'is not masked in the old-fashioned way'[154] – solely by leaving the 'purely theoretical sphere'.[155]

'I do, however, have one request that is very close to my heart: that you do not see everything striking about the book's internal and external design as a compromise with the "tenor of the age". Precisely in terms of its eccentric aspects, this book is, if not a trophy, nonetheless a document of an internal struggle. Its subject matter may be expressed as follows: to grasp topicality as the reverse of the eternal in history and to make an impression of this hidden side of the medallion. Otherwise the book owes a lot to Paris, being my first attempt to come to terms with this city.'[51] (Cover of *One-Way Street*)

'*The Origin of German Tragic Drama* marks an end for me – I would not have it be a beginning for any money in the world . . . In it [the volume of aphorisms], an earlier aspect of my character intersects with a more recent one. This does not benefit the volume's overall persuasiveness and clarity, but it does make it all the more interesting for [. . .] the quiet and shrewd observer.'[52] (Advertisement from the *Literarische Welt*, 17 February 1928)

This decision to present the political aspects of his thoughts, which he had until then simply cloaked in old-fashioned phrases, in a more open and succinct manner – to present them in new clothes, as it were – is also reflected by the typography and book-covers Benjamin chose for the two publications. While the appearance of the *Trauerspiel* book – the Gothic typeface and uniform design of the cover – indicated a somewhat reserved, profound and considered content, the jacket of *One-Way Street*, designed by Sascha Stone, gave an immediate, forceful impression of modernity, openness, speed, quick-wittedness and simultaneity; in short, the impression of a book that was abreast of the times in every respect. (And this contemporaneity with the present was further underlined by the roman typeface and the 'New Sobriety'-style layout.)

Benjamin left Capri on 10 October, and reached Berlin by about mid November via Positano, Naples, Rome, Orvieto, Assisi, Perugia and Florence. Both 'loneliness' and 'dismal weather' accompanied him on his return journey, and the 'third' in this group was 'Fascism' which, like the bandy-legged competitor in the race between the tortoise and the hare, was always there 'standing at his post'[156] whenever Benjamin reached the next stage in his journey. So, unsuspectingly, he received a slight foretaste of what was to descend on Germany a few years later: mass party rallies, youth processions, and the swearing-in of the fascist militia. All in all, a 'completely hopeless constellation'[157] presented itself to him during his journey.

Back in Berlin, Benjamin finally (in December) finished writing the rough draft of his treatise on Baroque tragic drama – at least those parts which he intended to submit in Frankfurt, where he travelled the following February. Everything there seemed to run according to his wishes, and his only cause for concern was the thought of having to slip into the role of a *Privatdozent*, possibly quite soon. He dreaded 'almost every-thing that would result from a positive' outcome of his efforts to gain his *Habilitation* – 'Frankfurt above all, then lectures, students etc'.[158]

But his fears were to prove unfounded. Hardly any of the professors who were to decide his fate thought seriously of helping an external student on his way to an academic career, particularly since he had not studied under anyone's super-vision and had actually underlined this by demonstrating his intellectual independence; not even the person who had once made concrete promises to him: Franz Schultz. From March of that year, Benjamin sent him his *Habilitation* thesis section by section: first the introduction, which contained 'only the second, tamer half'[159] of the 'Epistemo-Critical Prologue' published in the book version, then the first section headed 'Trauerspiel and Tragedy', and finally the second section with the title 'Allegory and Trauerspiel'. Although he originally planned to conclude with a chapter on methodology, this was never written.

This was followed by a long interval in which Benjamin heard nothing whatsoever from Schultz, although this was presumably not because the work had left him speechless. No, it had simply become clear in the latter's mind that this Berlin Jew might cast a shadow over him, the senior professor of literary history (who, according to the candidate's remarks, distinguished himself more by platitudes than competence in his subject). It was important, therefore, to dispose of Benjamin as elegantly as possible. Schultz believed that he had found the right way of doing so when he referred Benjamin to a faculty whose head was not the slightest bit interested in him. The dean of the philosophy faculty considered a *Habilitation* in literary history out of the question on account of Benjamin's 'preparation' (i.e. background).[160] The only possibility was 'aesthetics'. Benjamin realized all too well that this meant that essentially his project had already foundered; with Schultz's withdrawal, Benjamin was referred back to a person who, although not wishing to stand in the way of his *Habilitation*, stipulated that he would only consent if his own subject was not involved. This man was the positivist philosopher Hans Cornelius,[161] if at all familiar to present-day generations then only as Adorno's doctoral supervisor and the author of an *Introduction to Philosophy* that is mentioned somewhere in Lenin's *Materialism and Empirio-Criticism*. Events now took their foreseeable course. The only item that Benjamin's 'treasury' of practical experiences, which was certainly not short of disappointments, had been lacking until then was an insight into just *how* unwanted candidates are dispensed with by supposedly humanitarian teaching and research institutions: even his powers of imagination were unable to conceive of that much 'chutzpah'.

Although he formally submitted his official application for *Habilitation* 'as a *Privatdozent* in the subject of aesthetics at the University of Frankfurt am Main'[162] on 12 May 1925, the very wording of the *curriculum vitae* that he appended to his application provided the reasons for his rejection. His 'ideas on linguistic theory' had found their 'concrete *literary historical* form in certain sections' of his 'treatise *The Origin of German Tragic Drama*'.[163] How could Benjamin possibly have over-

'The book deploys extremely modern means with an archaic grace to render what are often recondite or forgotten materials. Its form is that of a street, a sequence of houses and shops whose windows are full of bright ideas.'[53] (Advertisement, quoting Hesse, from the *Literarische Welt*, 25 May 1928)

147

ROMA - Anfiteatro Flavio o Colosseo coi nuovi scavi

From Benjamin's
postcard collection:
Rome.

looked this passage in his CV – even assuming that he had
written it at a point in time when he still set his sights on a university career in the subject of literary history? Had he merely
forgotten to revise his CV to match his new situation? Or was
the sentence intended to provoke Schultz? Yet if that was the
case, the result was scarcely more than a nudge which could
have elicited no more than a weary smile from his victim.[164]

But the remark must have been welcomed all the more by
Cornelius, for it seemed to give him a solid argument for rejecting
the work as coming from a candidate who was unworthy of
being a member of the philosophy department. And it is not
surprising that the 'report' that he was asked to write by the
faculty committee referred to this point. His 'historical expositions', he wrote, formed 'by far the largest part of the work';
they were, however, of no significance 'for the philosophy of art,
regardless of how many interesting comments' they actually
contained 'and however important they might be for literary
history', although it was not Cornelius' task to 'judge' this. All
of his further comments focused solely on this clear distinction
between intellectual spheres, subjects and disciplines. So it is
hardly surprising that Cornelius felt unable to recommend that
the faculty accept Benjamin's work as a '*Habilitation* thesis for
philosophy of art'.

On the strength of this 'report', the faculty committee decided to 'suggest' to Benjamin that he withdraw his application for *Habilitation*. The minutes of the committee meeting on 13 July 1925 show just what they meant by this: 'The faculty has decided not to grant Dr B. a *Habilitation* if he fails to follow this advice.'[165] The dean, Franz Schultz, informed Benjamin of the decision two weeks later.[166] Benjamin took the 'advice' so as to avoid jeopardizing in advance any future prospects that he may have had at the university in Frankfurt.

Aside from the power struggles and intrigues within the philosophy faculty, which presumably played a decisive part in the rejection of Benjamin's *Habilitation* thesis, the question remains whether, and if so which, 'objective' arguments were levelled against the work. On the basis of the wording of the report commissioned by the faculty board, Benjamin was only accused of having made one mistake: applying to the wrong address. Benjamin had attempted to gain his teaching qualifications in the subject of 'aesthetics', but Cornelius was unable to discern in *The Origin of German Tragic Drama* any presentation of knowledge within the field of the 'philosophy of art'. The professor of philosophy and lecturer on the philosophy of art was unable to find anything of specific relevance to the subject, in either the questions posed by the thesis, the topic (the 'artistic value of German Baroque *Trauerspiel*' and the investigation of its form), or in the 'analytical *method* as pertaining to art philosophy', and he queried whether the work was indeed even academically rigorous. The author's 'incomprehensible means of expression', his report concluded harshly, 'must be [seen] as betokening a lack of objective clarity'.[167]

Benjamin's treatise was indeed a quite provocatively 'unacademic' work, at least in the customary understanding of the term. Nor did the author try to disguise this – a sign of just how unwilling he was to make any substantial compromises when it came to his creative output. From the work's epigraph to specific aspects of his manner of procedure, to the form in which the material was presented, the book was a complete parody of what German professors understood to be a systematic, methodologically reasoned work. Benjamin's break with these academic 'traditions' was by no means recent; indeed, basically it had always existed. The remoteness of university scholarship had already been the object of his ironically worded protests in Freiburg. They became more explicit with time. In his 'Announcement of the Periodical: *Angelus Novus*' he wrote: 'distance' should be maintained 'from academia because essence

'Unable as I was to determine the author's intentions with regard to art philosophy, I wrote to him with the request that he send me a brief excerpt of his work that will demonstrate to me its relevance to the philosophy of art. Thereupon I received an overview of the sections of his work which he purports to be connected with the philosophy of art, but once again I failed to understand his expositions. In my predicament I turned to Dr Gelb and Dr Horkheimer with the request that they read this extract from Dr Benjamin's work and tell me just how they could interpret his expositions. Both of them answered me by saying that they were unable to understand them.'[54] (Hans Cornelius)

and contemporary significance almost always break apart in its manifestations'.[168] Benjamin's creative production was aimed above all at forging completely new paths in the assimilation of literary topics and in the appraisal of the past. He formulated this retrospectively with reference to his *Trauerspiel* book, which was in fact no more than a continuation of his previous works, as 'paving the way to the work of art by destroying the doctrine of the intrinsic division of art into separate fields', and counter-manding the dissection of academic study into individual disciplines 'by means of an analysis of the work of art' which recognizes its object 'as an integral expression of the religious, metaphysical, political, economic tendencies of its epoch, which is not to be limited in any way to one field'.[169]

These demands shook the foundations of contemporary academic teaching and research, and so it was obvious that he met with no understanding from their traditional custodians. In essence he was touching the pinnacle of their concept of objective science. For him, all knowledge is historically and subjectively determined, and for this reason he wrote, also later, but once again referring to the *Trauerspiel* book, in a letter in 1931: 'there is an index for the condition of historical greatness, on the basis of which every genuine perception of historical greatness becomes historicistic – not psychological – self-perception on the part of the individual who perceives'.[170]

Seven seals

As one contemporary critic complained,[171] the approach to this work is barred by the 'seven seals' of an 'Epistemo-Critical Prologue'. Presumably the author would have advised him to saddle his horse the other way round, as it were, by reading the epistemological prologue last. But instructions for reading his work such as these, with which Benjamin sometimes filled his letters, were not to be taken any more literally than all other instructions which referred to what is doubtlessly the book's most difficult section. Any attempt to gain an idea of the particular way in which he tackled here an epoch of German literary history, whose rediscovery during and directly after the First World War was by no means unrelated to the general breakdown of the existing social order, must obviously begin by struggling through these introductory methodological expo-sitions. This is all the more necessary in that the material section of the examination only partially meets the programmatic demands of its 'Epistemo-Critical Prologue'.

The basic intention of the essay as a whole is already shown vividly by the epigraph at the head of the prologue – a quote from Goethe's *Theory of Colours*:

Neither in knowledge nor in reflection can anything whole be put together, since in the former the internal is missing and in the latter the external; and so we must necessarily think of science as art if we expect to derive any kind of wholeness from it. Nor should we look for this in the general, the excessive, but, since art is always wholly represented in every individual work of art, so science ought to reveal itself completely in every individual object treated.[172]

Benjamin turned this into 'paving the way to the work of art by destroying the doctrine of the intrinsic division of art into separate fields'. It was important here to 'promote' that 'process of integration within science which increasingly' drops 'the rigid divisions between the disciplines that' characterized 'the concept of science during the last century, by means of an analysis of the work of art that [recognizes] it as an integral expression of the religious, metaphysical, political and economic tendencies of its epoch, which is not to be limited in any way to one field'.[173] So Benjamin was concerned with regaining an integrated vision of art which had gradually been lost during the nineteenth century through the departmentalization of science.

If an object is to be illuminated in such a way from all sides, there can be no separation between the methods that are employed and the problems of representation. Consequently, the 'Epistemo-Critical Prologue' begins in a direct manner with the following: 'It is characteristic of philosophical writing that it must continually confront the question of representation'.[174] The difficulties in giving a resumée of this work lie in the fact that the method that Benjamin uses fundamentally resists any concise account. 'Representation' is defined in the prologue

as digression – such is the methodological nature of the treatise. The absence of an uninterrupted purposeful structure is its primary characteristic. Tirelessly the process of thinking makes new beginnings, returning in a roundabout way to its original object. This continual pausing for breath is the mode most proper to the process of contemplation. For by pursuing different levels of meaning in its examination of one single object it receives both the incentive to begin again and the justification for its irregular rhythms.[175]

Nevertheless, it is perhaps possible to summarize a number of the main trains of thought of the 'Epistemo-Critical Prologue'. Its expositions are based on a model consisting of several steps, each leading, within the process of epistemological reflection, from the general to the specific (from the – divine – 'truth' via the – Platonic – 'ideas' to the 'phenomena'), while the thread passing throughout the material section runs in the opposite direction: from individual notions to their representation (configuration) as a complete whole.

In his Goethe essay, Benjamin had already experimented to see how far a complete philosophy can be introduced into the critique of a single work. His treatise on *The Origin of German Tragic Drama* goes a step further. He takes an entire epoch (the seventeenth century) as his object, and as a consequence of objective considerations he does not even remain strictly within these limits. Just how far the essay and the treatise concur can be also be seen by the fact that they mobilize the same 'epistemological theory'. What Benjamin had already once said about the relationship between content and intrinsic truth continues to retain its validity: originally united in the work, the two terms were divided as it was handed down so that, as Benjamin writes in his *Trauerspiel* book, 'the object of knowledge is not identical with the truth . . . knowledge is open to question, but truth is not'.[176] Moreover, at the same time the essay radicalizes the programme for a critique that was formulated in the 'Announcement of the Periodical: *Angelus Novus*', whose underlying ideology must remain recognizable down to the finest details of its conception. Central to the essay is therefore the preservation of the Baroque allegory:

in allegory the observer is confronted with the 'facies hippocratica' of history as petrified, primordial landscape. Everything about history that, from the very beginning, has been untimely, sorrowful, unsuccessful, is expressed in a face – or rather in a death's head.[177]

The original epigraph for the work had been 'Jump over sticks and jump over stones / But take good care not to break your bones'.[178] The lines, taken from a popular nursery rhyme, present an effective image of how daring those schooled in traditional scientific categories must have considered Benjamin's attempt to fulfil the prologue's 'programme' in the material section of the study.

The concept of the allegory that emerged in the *Trauerspiel* book remained one of the central categories in Benjamin's writings. Naturally the emphasis shifted over the years; originally intended as a term for art criticism, its accent became increasingly weighted towards the history of philosophy, and finally Benjamin attempted to give it a materialistic foundation in his works connected with the 'Arcades' project.[179] This reflects the degree to which his creative output continued to develop and change. Moreover, the fact that more than a few of his own writings consist of allegories merely underlines this once more – not to mention the stylistic characteristics (metaphorical language), terminology ('dialectical image') and the methods of research and representation that he used in his essays and articles ('construction of history').

A contemporary critic called *The Origin of German Tragic Drama* a 'document of the times despite itself',[180] which, on deleting the limiting addendum, is a highly apt description of what the work substantially represents: a document above all of the author's times. Just how intentional Benjamin's demonstration was of the striking parallels between the world of the baroque Trauerspiel and his own, is shown vividly in his observations of a German world that was deteriorating in every respect. It is as if the events of the day had guided Benjamin's hand as he wrote:

Like the term 'tragic' in present-day usage – and with greater justification – the word 'Trauerspiel' was applied in the seventeenth century to dramas and to historical events alike. Even the style gives an indication of how close to each other the two things were in the contemporary mind.[181]

The story behind the publication of this book, which Benjamin termed the conclusion of a 'circle of Germanistic production',[182] was as thorny and wearisome as its composition. Almost three years passed after the University of Frankfurt had rejected *The Origin of German Tragic Drama* as a *Habilitation* thesis, before the work became publicly available. All efforts had failed to have it published immediately. A newly established publishing house, which planned to print the book as one of its first titles, went bankrupt before even a line could be set. Likewise, the inclusion of the last chapter in a yearbook published by Ernst Cassirer failed to materialize. So once again it fell to Benjamin's 'staunchest ally',[183] Hugo von Hofmannsthal, to come to the rescue. He felt that the work showed 'absolute mastery in many sections',[184] and published the chapter on melancholy in the August 1927 issue of his *Neue Deutsche Beiträge*. Then, after lengthy delays, the entire work was published the following year by Ernst Rowohlt, after he had received a recommendation from Benjamin's friend, Franz Hessel.

Benjamin was able to exert quite a considerable influence on the typography of the book. Consequently the edition's external form corresponded (to a reasonable extent) to both its subject matter as well as to the particular genre of philosophical reflection that was being presented: a modest cover with a dark blue dustjacket that resembled a school book, and a Gothic type interspersed with spaces between text blocks (the first edition had no cross heads) that not only indicated the structure of the text, but also visually enhanced the intermittent rhythm of his thoughts.

Appreciated by none?

The claim that *The Origin of German Tragic Drama* was scarcely appreciated by the critics and academics in his field, was constantly circulated after being initiated by Benjamin himself. It is a myth. If ever one of Benjamin's books received universal attention during his lifetime, it was this one. The work was reviewed in a number of the most renowned newspapers and periodicals of the time. Willy Haas gave it a detailed review on the front page of his *Literarische Welt*; Siegfried Kracauer wrote a long article in the *Frankfurter Zeitung* on 'The Writings of Walter Benjamin' – his belated appeasement for the damning review Benjamin's Baudelaire translations had received on the same pages,[185] and there was an almost emphatic eulogy in Carl von Ossietzky's *Weltbühne*.[186] However, Werner Milch wrote a very critical review for the *Berliner Tageblatt*, the most important liberal paper in the capital.[187] Benjamin's study even met with a response from abroad. The book's very first review in fact appeared in Hungary;[188] it was reviewed twice in France, together with *One-Way Street*,[189] and there was also a piece in the Cambridge *Modern Language Review* where Roy Pascal criticized Benjamin for not being 'in agreement with the best authorities' in his views on the origin of Greek tragedy and claimed that he had become 'carried away' when calling Shakespeare an allegorical poet. But Pascal found these only 'minor blemishes in a vigorous and comprehensive study'.[190] German academic circles took more than passing note of the treatise. This is shown by the large number of sometimes lengthy reviews that it received in the relevant specialist journals – the *Zeitschrift für Deutschkunde*,[191] the *Zeitschrift für deutsche Bildung* (this review was written by the renowned baroque

'My book *The Origin of German Tragic Drama* was the test case for just how far strict adherence to purely academic research methods leads a person away from the contemporary stance of the bourgeois and idealistic scholarly enterprise. This is borne out by the fact that not a single German academic has deigned to review it.'[55] (A sample of review quotations, in an advertisement in the *Literarische Welt*)

specialist Günther Müller, who recognized the value of the work from the outset),[192] the *Neuere Sprachen*,[193] and even the psychoanalytic journal edited by Sigmund Freud, *Imago*,[194] to name just the best known – as well as numerous philosophical, sociological, art historical and Germanistic monographs.[195] All in all, the work met with a broad resonance, and, if one compares it with the work of Adorno, it was actually accepted very early on. Adorno's writings of the 1930s – from the 'Naturgeschichte des Theaters' [Natural History of the Theatre][196] to his inaugural lecture in Frankfurt on the 'Aktualität der

'By the way, the first review to speak out for the *Trauerspiel* book came from Hungary. A gentleman whom I had not heard of previously gave me an excellent review in a philological journal published with the support of the Academy of Sciences. The editor of this journal informs me that he is already recommending the book in his lectures in Budapest.'[56] (*Vient de paraître*: title and review of Benjamin's works, June 1928)

VIENT de PARAITRE
REVUE MENSUELLE DES LETTRES ET DES ARTS

Philosophie' [Contemporary Significance of Philosophy][197] and his essay 'Kierkegaard' – are scarcely conceivable without *The Origin of German Tragic Drama* (not to mention his later writings, *Negative Dialektik [Negative Dialectics]*[198] and *Ästhetische Theorie [Aesthetic Theory]*).[199] The only voices that failed to join this chorus of largely positive commentaries and critiques were those of the *Deutsche Literaturzeitung* (Benjamin had attached great importance to a review from this paper) and the Warburg Institute in Hamburg. Benjamin was deeply disappointed that he had not received comments from this circle. He was firmly convinced that art historians such as Erwin Panofsky and Fritz Saxl would have been interested readers on account of their own research.[200]

URSPRUNG DES DEUTSCHEN TRAUERSPIELS et EINBAHNSTRASSE par Walter BENJAMIN, (chez Rowohlt — Berlin). Deux livres d'application fort différente et qui rendent pourtant le même son. Dans l'un, Benjamin étudie les origines du drame allemand avec la diligence d'un docteur allemand; dans l'autre, il passe au milieu des signes tangibles de sa journée et les transforme en points de repère du labyrinth... de ses abstractions.

La valeur de ses recherches sur le « drame baroque » du XVIIe siècle, de Gryphius à Hallmann, est éminente. Benjamin, qui est un homme d'avant-garde, saisit l'occasion de ces minutieuses recherches sur l'origine du *Trauerspiel* allemand, mâtiné de tragédie antique, mais qui échappe aux règles d'Aristote, pour montrer ses affinités avec l'expressionisme actuel, par des rapprochements d'époques et des analyses de condition sociale.

En examinant les pièces d'Opitz et d'Haugwitz, Benjamin montre l'évolution des idées de cette époque, les théories de la souveraineté, les concepts théocratiques introduits par la découverte des sources byzantines, du tyran et du martyr, l'importance de la mélancolie, du symbole et de l'allégorie *die Lehre vom Saturn, der Trübsinn des Fürsten*, etc. Il cite une page des Pensées de Pascal : « L'âme ne trouve rien en elle qui la contente, etc. ». Cette œuvre est une thèse de doctorat, savante, érudite, épuisant certainement la question et précieuse aussi par les aperçus généraux sur l'essence du drame, les caractères de la tragédie antique et du drame moderne etc., mais on aimerait que tout cela fût écrit dans un style moins indigeste. Nous n'évoquerons point en parallèle les auteurs philosophiques français. Benjamin, qui est grand connaisseur de notre littérature et excellent traducteur, les connaît ; nous lui ferons seulement remarquer la clarté de style de l'épigraphe qu'il a empruntée à « Contribution à une histoire de la théorie des couleurs » de Gœthe. Ceci dit pour céder à notre faible pour la clarté, nous devons dire que l'œuvre est une manière de monument, elle fait époque.

Einbahnstrasse est un délassement d'intellectuel, recueil d'aphorismes, de rapprochements d'idées aiguisées et subtiles, quelques polémiques enveloppées dans beaucoup d'abstractions, paysages de rêves. Parterre expressionniste tracé suivant les principes de la nouvelle géométrie russe.

I never pass by a wooden fetish, a gilded Buddha, a Mexican idol without reflecting: perhaps it is the true God.[1]

With the failure of his *Habilitation* in Frankfurt, Benjamin had no other choice but to work as a freelance writer. Even though the full weight of misfortune was to descend upon him once again in the summer of 1925,[2] his prospects were certainly not bad. After all, Benjamin had long since made a name for himself in the German literary world through his various publications, and so, having the necessary contacts, he was not short of work or commissions. Through Siegfried Kracauer he was able to gain acceptance in the *Frankfurter Zeitung*, whose review section published its first pieces by him in August: an article that he himself considered trifling, on Karl Wehrhan's *Collection of Frankfurt Children's Rhymes*,[3] and the townscape 'Naples' mentioned earlier. Willy Weigand, whose publishing house, Bremer Presse, also printed the *Neue Deutsche Beiträge*, entrusted him with editing an anthology of Wilhelm von Humboldt's writings.[4] In September he signed a 'general contract' with Rowohlt for the publication of his *Elective Affinities* essay, the *Trauerspiel* book and a 'Plaquette for Friends' (later called *One-Way Street*);[5] and the same Berlin publisher introduced him onto the planning committee of a new cultural magazine (*Die Literarische Welt*). Furthermore, Hofmannsthal asked him to review his drama *The Tower* because the author of *The Origin of German Tragic Drama* seemed to him especially 'competent' to say 'something valid' about this play, which in essence drew 'its power from [the] hidden force field' of seventeenth-century culture.[6] In addition, Benjamin had for a long time been planning a book on fairytales.[7] Finally, he had already made an agreement in July with the Berlin publishing house Die Schmiede, to translate the fourth volume of Proust's *A la recherche du temps perdu (Sodome et Gomorrhe)* 'by 31 March 1926 at the latest'.[8] A further translation was put his way by an acquaintance from his days in Munich, Rainer Maria Rilke, in collaboration with Hofmannsthal: 'Anabase', a prose poem by the French writer Saint-John Perse (Alexis Léger), which, although it struck him as 'of little importance', was at least worth the remuneration.[9]

Between Moscow and Paris

The home of the *Frankfurter Zeitung* in Große Eschenheimer Straße.

Gentleman and artisan

But first he escaped from all his obligations by going on a trip, which he hoped would put physical distance between himself and the disagreeable matter of his *Habilitation*. At the end of August he set off on a journey that was to take him around half of Europe: first by boat from Hamburg to Spain, where he made his way along the Río Guadalquivir to Seville and Cordoba; and then on to Barcelona and across to Italy, where he visited, among other places, Genoa, Rapallo, Lucca, Pisa, Livorno, Capri and Naples. After briefly stopping off in Berlin, he then emerged, in November, in a quite different location: in Riga, where he wished to surprise his friend Asja Lacis with an unexpected visit. The meeting turned out, however, to be a disappointment. Asja was so busy with her work as the director of a political theatre that she had no time for him. 'The police', she wrote in her reminiscences, 'kept interfering with our work, so that we constantly expected to be arrested. The next day was to be the première. I went to the rehearsal, my mind full of problems, and there, standing before me, was Walter Benjamin. At that moment, he seemed to have arrived from another planet.'[10] Benjamin recorded just how deeply the brusque rejection had affected him in an aphorism in *One-Way Street* entitled 'Stereoscope'. While its counterpart, 'Ordnance',[11] had described Riga as a place full of discovery for him, from now on the city revealed a completely different side to him. Everywhere had become cramped, small, low, grey and dirty, and he himself now wandered despondently between the endless rows of 'desolate buildings', because he had been 'scolded by the beloved voice'.[12] This brief episode illustrates just how little understanding he really had of his girlfriend's day-to-day world. Asja Lacis, on the other hand, had far fewer illusions in this respect than Benjamin, as is clear from her sober description of his reaction to the play which she was directing at the time, and which he naturally did not wish to miss seeing performed: 'He did not like anything about it, with the exception of one scene: a gentleman in a top hat who chatted with an artisan under a streetlamp.'[13] A dialogue such as this in a realm that was in principle utterly alien to him, was in fact the only one which he was able to imagine for himself. This notion is very evident in his 'political' writings from the first half of the 1920s.

By the beginning of December Benjamin was back in Berlin. He remained there until the middle of March 1926, when he moved to Paris for over six months. The few works that came into being during this interval would hardly be worth mentioning were it not for the fact that almost all of them already contained elements that were to constitute his particular form of literary criticism. 'The dream as a pivotal point of historical occurrences', he wrote in a sequel to his *Trauerspiel* book (the review of Hugo von Hofmannsthal's *Tower*), that is Hofmannsthal's 'fascinating, strange formula.' Within the bounds of this new 'dream sequence' the blind creature does not rage, but rather the sufferer administers justice to its tormentors. With that the function of the dream has been transformed in its utmost depths. Whereas with Calderón the dream, like a concave mirror, breaks open inwardness to boundless depths, as a transcendental seventh heaven, [Hofmannsthal] presents a more real world, into which the waking world wanders in its entirety.[14]

And the allusions in a gloss headed 'Baedeker Gives His Thanks' already contain all the ingredients for his polemic against 'innermost experience', 'initiation' and 'empathy', in short all the 'German blather'[15] that was a basic part of his debate with the literary or cultural historiography of the day. Central to this debate was the concept of contemporary significance: 'showing things in the aura of their contemporary significance is more valuable, is far more fruitful, even if indirectly, than showing off about what are in the end very petty bourgeois ideas about popular education'.[16]

Benjamin had the opportunity to present his views on the function of critique to a broader public in the *Literarische Welt*, a periodical first published by Rowohlt and later continued independently under the editorship of Willy Haas. The story behind this magazine mirrors the Berlin readers' almost endless thirst for new publications – especially during the years after the inflation, when Berlin gained its reputation as the 'world's greatest newspaper city'. (At the time, well over 2,000 different periodicals – dailies, weeklies, monthlies – could be found in the city's kiosks and bookshops.) 'You virtually had only to think of an idea for a publication and it was already half realized', Haas wrote in his reminiscences in 1960.[17] And the success of his magazine shows the truth of this statement. The *Literarische Welt*, a publication that was, after all, directed at a fairly restricted circle of literary-minded people, soon reached a circulation of 20,000. And at the height of its fame, in 1929, it was bought by nearly 30,000 people and presumably had a great many more readers.

The *Literarische Welt* was Rowohlt's third periodical, following the *Tagebuch*[18] and *Vers und Prosa*.[19] The concept behind it was based on the French *Nouvelles littéraires*, 'but, in keeping with the necessities of literary life in Germany, more uncom-

'Of all the people who have honoured my weekly journal, *Die Literarische Welt*, with regular contributions, I have rated none so highly as Walter Benjamin. Despite his immense knowledge, he was quite the opposite of a mere polyhistor. When he spoke or wrote about a topic he never approached it by means of analogies, metaphors or definitions; rather he seemed always to excavate laboriously from the very heart of the matter itself, like a gnome who hid his treasure in a well that has been filled in.'[57] (Rowohlt and the contributors of the *Literarische Welt*, 1926. Cartoon by B. F. Dolbin)

promising', as Haas's colleague on the editorial staff, Heinrich Fischer, put it, 'and also more lively':[20] a literary weekly in which the weightiness of profound treatises, essays and reviews was counterbalanced by articles on new international trends in art, literature and theatre, as well as by photographs and caricatures. In addition, it also contained stories and poems, some published for the first time, and others as reprints, preprints, or translations. Benjamin's role in the periodical was to produce a 'regular column on new French art theory',[21] although this cannot have been taken too literally, for otherwise very many of his articles would not (even with the broadest interpretation of the term) have reached the magazine's pages.

Some of Benjamin's comments in his letters suggest that his relationship with the *Literarische Welt* was not entirely free of conflict, particularly during the early days. He complains, for example, that the editorial board did not seem interested in 'serious criticism', for really profound observations were hardly ever printed.[22] Indeed, their 'almost panicky fear of every utterance that [did] not simply lose itself in whatever is topical' assumed a quite 'grotesque' form.[23]

Presumably such reservations were largely the after-effect of his all too recent disappointments over the failure of his own periodical project, for they did not prompt any serious doubts about his work on the magazine; on the contrary, the publishing house, the editor and the editorial board hardly ever interfered in their independently minded author's business, for all the consideration they paid to the presumed or even real taste of their readership. The instances in which his articles were abridged or in any other way altered are few and far between.

During his almost eight-year involvement with the periodical (his first article appeared on 16 October 1925,[24] the last in February 1933),[25] the *Literarische Welt* published well over one hundred contributions by Benjamin. Viewed as a whole, his work for the magazine – essays and treatises on literary and art theory, articles and illustrated reports on cultural politics, critiques and reviews, reports, aphorisms, glosses, interviews and, last but not least, stories – cover almost the entire spectrum of the creative production of an *homme de lettres*, which he had become.

Devastating criticism

One of the earliest pieces that he wrote for the *Literarische Welt* was on Fritz von Unruh's novel *Flügel der Nike*, published in 1925. Both French and German critics – from the *Europäische Revue* to *Vient de paraître*, from Kurt Tucholsky to Geneviève Bianquis – were in agreement that this book did not live up to the author's claim to be making a contribution to Franco-German relations. Indeed, its deplorable style and misplaced pathos, not to mention the unintentional humour of several passages[26] positively invited critics to pour ridicule on the work and author. Evidently Benjamin did not wish to let this opportunity pass by, particularly since he intended to use his discussion of the book to outline the critical position that he would assume from now on 'under [his] own name' in the *Literarische Welt*.[27] Given our present knowledge of Unruh's later life,[28] it is hard for us to grasp Benjamin's reasons for compromising a writer who was fairly moderate in political terms, and whose influence as a pacifist was, according to Tucholsky, thoroughly 'decent as well as useful abroad'.[29] And all the more so since there was really no great divide between them politically.[30]

The 'annihilation'[31] of the *Flügel der Nike* was the prelude to a collection of pieces which Benjamin referred to as 'Towards a Critique of the Symptomatic Phenomena of the Times in Literature'.[32] Its programmatic nature prohibited Benjamin from pinning his criticisms to outward appearances: such as to the 'plebeian tone' of the book, which made the Weimar dandy and diarist Harry Graf Kessler so indignant,[33] or the author's indiscretions and lack of tact regarding the better social circles in Paris, which the socialites amongst the German-speaking writers objected to (above all his acquaintances Rilke and Hofmannsthal, who could boast the best connections in the city). Rather, his criticism was directed at something quite different: at the 'seraphic' pacifist Unruh.[34] Benjamin did not wish to give any credence to the public 'reflection'[35] on this former Prussian officer, who, scarcely a decade previously, had entered the literary arena with hair-raising war poems. His intention was not to attack a private individual, but rather to denounce what he saw as a typical kind of literature.[36]

It goes without saying that this review did not just win friends for Benjamin. Heinrich Simon, owner of the *Frankfurter Zeitung*, and Benno Reifenberg, head of its review section, (the former also a personal ally of Unruh), appear to have taken offence at the damning criticism delivered to 'their' author (the *Flügel der Nike* appeared in the *Frankfurter Zeitung*). Hence Benjamin's relationship with his second – after the *Literarische Welt* – major 'mainstay'[37] was at times antagonistic to say the least.

Benjamin and Proust

Benjamin's translations – to which he mainly devoted himself during the months of his first lengthy stay in Paris, in 1926 – have yet to receive their proper place in the minds of his critics. There are still precious few studies in the literature on Benjamin's life and works that look in detail at his Baudelaire and Proust translations. It would appear that few writers can

Benjamin around 1926.

make much of them. And yet they have a very clearly defined position in the overall physiognomy of his thought and creative production. On the one hand they are linked with a number of his reflections on linguistic philosophy – his attempt to translate Baudelaire's poetry provided these with a suitable experimental field; on the other hand they should be seen in the context of his theory of preservation.

Naturally Benjamin's numerous translations also include some that are scarcely worth mentioning: those that were done 'incidentally', as occasional jobs or as favours so as to keep his name circulating among the publishers and editors. These include 'a blague by Tristan Tzara' which he translated in 1924 for Hans Richter's *Zeitschrift für elementare Gestaltung* 'with a verve that commands respect';[38] a German version of Balzac's *Ursule Mirouët*,[39] the first section of which he translated himself 'during weeks of terrible drudgery', only then to pass the second section on to somebody else and merely glance over it when it was finished;[40] and finally a d'Annunzio translation ('Der göttlichen Eleonora Duse'),[41] which is singularly curious in that Benjamin knew, as he himself admitted, scarcely any Italian (but it is possible that he worked from the French version of this homage to the famous actress, instead of from the original).

But the expression 'occasional jobs' should not be taken to mean that these translations were done without due care and attention or in complete abandonment of his principles. The fact that his *Ursula Mirouet* for example, is still in print speaks very much in his favour. But on the whole these were harmonious, unproblematic pieces of work, which he carried out with a certain amount of routine. Only the translation of 'Anabase' mentioned earlier taxed his abilities in linguistic improvisation. Viewed in retrospect, these translations seem to have been useful finger exercises for the task that was to demand the utmost of him, but was also to bring him his renown as a translator: the German version of several parts of Marcel Proust's roman-fleuve *A la recherche du temps perdu [Remembrance of Things Past]*.

'Too many cooks spoil the broth' – this proverb springs to mind when studying the somewhat involved history of the first translation of Proust into German. At one time no fewer than three translators worked simultaneously, but independently, on *A la recherche du temps perdu*: Rudolf Schottlaender (a distant relative of Benjamin, whose first marriage was to Hilde, the daughter of his cousin William Stern), Walther Petry (who worked for Die Schmiede as the editor of a series entitled 'Classics of Erotic Literature'), and Benjamin. Die Schmiede,[42] set up in 1921/2, had acquired its reputation through the (partial) takeover of the small but esteemed Roland-Verlag, as well as through the influx of a number of authors who had left Kurt Wolff's publishing house. It was now regarded as one of the leading publishers of post-expressionist German and contemporary French literature, bringing together some of the best writing produced in Germany during the 1920s, by such names as Johannes R. Becher, Otto Flake, Willy Haas, Franz Kafka, Georg Kaiser, Rudolf Kayser, Egon Erwin Kisch, Klabund, Rudolf Leonhard (who worked for the firm as a reader), Joseph

The publisher's imprint of Die Schmiede.

BERLIN
VERLAG DIE SCHMIEDE
1926

Roth, Kurt Tucholsky, Ernst Weiß and Alfred Wolfenstein. Admittedly, the firm was already surrounded in the mid-1920s by rumours of financial difficulties, oppressive contracts and poor advertising. But this does not seem to have disturbed Benjamin, and at first everything ran more or less according to his wishes.

The Proust translation appeared in one of the publisher's most highly regarded series, the 'Novels of the XXth Century', whose first titles had appeared on the market in the autumn of 1923. The first of this series had been *Auf dem Weg zu Swann [Du côté de chez Swann]* published in two elegant volumes (both available in paperback and hardback versions), and translated by a young man who was by no means lacking in experience: Rudolf Schottlaender, who had already completed a very reasonable translation of the rural novel *La Brière* by Alphonse de Châteaubriant (*Schwarzes Land*, 1925) for Die Schmiede. However, perhaps he had underestimated the task, or perhaps he had thought that he could run it off quickly: either way, his work on *A la recherche du temps perdu* ended before it had really begun; his translation was savaged by the critics. Admittedly, he had particular misfortune in that the reviewers, who were awaiting the Proust translation with a certain degree of expectation after the appearance of Ernst Robert Curtius's ground-breaking essay in 1925,[43] took the rare step of actually comparing the German version with the original French. Curtius himself, no less, was the first to speak his mind; in a survey on the literary event of the year, published in the *Literarische Welt*,[44] he took Schottlaender so severely to task that there was no possibility of his continuing as Proust's translator. And when, in his reply to Curtius, Schottlaender requested that the renowned professor of Romance studies give the work a general assessment over and beyond his criticisms of the details,[45] Curtius responded with unmistakable clarity: 'Herr Schottlaender requests an overall appraisal? Here it is: this sorry piece of work is simply a botched job.'[46]

'I recall a conversation with Benjamin in which we discussed the almost uncanny magnetism that Hessel radiated. "Yes, Helen, didn't you know that Hessel is a magician?" he said. "We come to life in his company, are ourselves once again, this self that fills us with the joys of discovery and with as much interest and pleasure as he finds in us. And then we simply sit there and are caught up in his spell!"'[58] (Franz Hessel)

The directors of Die Schmiede responded to the disastrous first volume of Proust with the necessary action. Schottlaender was relegated from the circle of Proust translators, and so was the firm's own collaborator on the project, Walther Petry, since his translation of *Le côté de Guermantes* was evidently just as incapable of meeting high standards.[47] In their place came Franz Hessel, with whom Benjamin from now on worked on the German Proust project; formally they worked apart, but in practice it was a collective effort.[48] The plan for the work, as set down in contracts during the years 1925–7, was as follows: translating the second, fourth and fifth volumes of *Recherche* (*A l'ombre des jeunes filles en fleurs*, *Sodome et Gomorrhe* and *La prisonnière* respectively), optionally also the last two volumes (*Albertine disparue* and *Le temps retrouvé*), and producing new translations of the first and third volumes (*Du côté de chez Swann* and *Le côté de Guermantes*).[49]

Benjamin did the larger part of work on *Sodome et Gomorrhe* while in Paris, which in his opinion was the perfect location for translating Proust: 'By the way, I am being very diligent', he wrote to his former fiancée Jula Cohn on 8 April 1926, 'at least as far as translating is concerned, and the most amazing thing is that it is becoming very easy.'[50] But he did not always approach the translation with so much verve and enthusiasm. Once 'the whole of Proust in German' had been placed in his and Franz Hessel's hands, he was at times seized by frustration, and at other times his work on Proust made him 'in a certain sense sick', as he confessed to his friend Scholem: 'Unproductive involvement with a writer who so splendidly pursues goals that are similar to my own, at least former goals, occasionally induces something like symptoms of internal poisoning in me.'[51] But he managed to stick to his post, enticed by the prospects the work promised – assuming that it was to be a success: the possibility of being able to 'present [himself] as a Proust translator in France', as well as being able to receive 'proper credentials as a translator' from publishers and editors of periodicals.[52] He achieved both, but at a considerable price. His translation of *Sodome et Gomorrhe*, which he finished ahead of time, was never to appear in public, and the whereabouts of the manuscript are unknown to this day;[53] and Benjamin and Hessel did not even complete their translation of *La prisonnière* on account of the highly quixotic twists and turns that the German Proust translation took.[54] Finally, the only two volumes of *Recherche* to appear on the market in the Benjamin-Hessel version came out three years apart, and were printed by two different publishers. Although

NEUERSCHEINUNG

MARCEL PROUST
IM SCHATTEN DER JUNGEN MAEDCHEN
Übersetzt von Walter Benjamin und Franz Hessel

VERLAG DIE SCHMIEDE BERLIN

'There is not another writer in France whose language is stylized to such a minimal degree as that of Proust, and which has such an organic form, albeit of a cosmic nature; so anyone who translates Proust must not merely recreate the atmosphere, but also transpose the climate of his spiritual zone to another landscape. No one who really knows the original could deny that Benjamin and Hessel have achieved this in a quite outstanding fashion.'[59]
(Advertisement for Die Schmiede)

Benjamin, Paris 1926.

Advertisement from the
Literarische Welt,
5 December 1930.

Im Schatten der jungen Mädchen [A l'ombre des jeunes filles en fleurs] was still published by Die Schmiede in 1927, *Die Herzogin von Guermantes [Le côté de Guermantes]* was only printed in 1930 by the Munich-based publishing house run by Reinhard Piper, under a title that was not authorized by the translators (who had wanted simply to call it *Guermantes).*[55]

There is scarcely a reviewer who will actually examine a translation of several hundred pages in order to check its quality and accuracy. But in the case of Proust this was quite imperative after the debacle that had ensued from Schottlaender's translation. Nor did the critics shy from the task when, in January 1927, the second volume of Proust's *Recherche* at last appeared in German. The work was reviewed in several of the leading periodicals of the day, and particular attention was paid to Benjamin's and Hessel's work as translators: Efraim Frisch reviewed it in the *Frankfurter Zeitung,*[56] Wolf Zucker in *Die Weltbühne,*[57] Erich Franzen for the *Literarische Welt* [58] and Oskar Loerke in the *Berliner Börsen-Courier.*[59] Hermann Hesse also discussed it in the *Berliner Tageblatt,*[60] as did Karl Heinz Ruppel in the *Tagebuch;*[61] and finally Paul Cohen-Portheim presented both the author and the work in the *Neue Bücherschau.*[62] (A similar presentation – for his own ends, so to speak – also appeared in the Stuttgart magazine *Weltstimmen,* written by Franz Hessel.)[63]

The reviews listed here did not necessarily constitute an unbroken song of praise, but the vast majority of them paid great tribute to the work done by Benjamin and Hessel – and not only the reviews written out of friendship, which included the article by Efraim Frisch to some extent. Although Frisch was probably being quite sincere when he referred to the 'outstanding translators who had totally mastered the difficulties of the task', the words had partly been put in his mouth by the editor of the *Frankfurter Zeitung,* Siegfried Kracauer. His letter to Frisch, requesting him to 'quickly write a review of the second volume of Proust with particular emphasis on the technical aspects of the translation', was accompanied by the broad hint that 'one of the two translators, Dr Walter Benjamin, numbers among the finest experts on the French language and is in addition an outstanding stylist in German'.[64]

Frisch's praise was by no means isolated, and a number of other reviews went considerably further. Karl Heinz Ruppel wrote that their work had 'reproduced Marcel Proust's language – which is as fine and intricately shaped as coral – as excellently as this was possible in German'.[65] And Friedrich Burschell wrote a highly effusive letter to the editors of the *Literarische Welt*, which is worth quoting here at some length, for it is not well known:

What makes this new translation so special is the happy fact that it is the successful collaboration of two authors, each of whom is more suited than any other to translating Proust – the most cultivated and demanding of all modern authors – as a result of their linguistic knowledge, education and taste. Yet they have exchanged their ideas, merged together and amalgamated to produce – even where their individual contributions can be clearly distinguished from one another – an astonishing approximation (for even the perfect translation can be no more than an approximation) of not only the original, but also of that which the author had intended to underlie his words. The elements which they each contribute from their individual personalities and scholarly backgrounds seem to have been predestined to blend within the great medium of Proust's ingenuity. Essentially Franz Hessel represents the engaging, affectionate, intuitively acquisitive side of Proust the charmeur, the well-versed, ironic, creatively superior connoisseur; the genius with a mastery of enchanting, beguiling details, of tact and of delicate exposition. Walter Benjamin represents the subtle, exact, unremittingly probing, critically transcending side which is never satisfied with a single solution, and that corresponds with the other aspect of Proust's talent: the passionate compulsion not to leave anything untouched and to retain in the depths of memory and knowledge all that has been experienced. Naturally, Proust cannot be dissected into parts; almost every sentence of this gigantic work is a miracle of modulation and nuance, and nor are the two translators rigid or inflexible: Hessel is sufficiently thoughtful, and Benjamin has shown not only here, but also in his Baudelaire translations, just what strong emotions and powers of expression he can summon to convey poetic virtues and resonances. Consequently this new translation is built on the best of possible foundations. It would have been difficult to entrust this work to more solid, skilfully interlocked hands. The German version of Proust that matches up to the original is at last emerging.[66]

'P.S. I was very pleased with Frisch's Proust review.'[60] (Jacket of the second volume of Proust's novel cycle)

Presumably it was more or less unprecedented for the translation of a novel to receive such a eulogy. Was it a sign that it really was a success? Certainly, there were also a number of quite polemical commentaries on it. For instance the conservative poet Richard von Schaukal, writing in Will Vesper's *Neue Literatur*, dismissed

Benjamin 1926.

the ' "Germanization" of Proust by the firm Franz Hessel and Walter Benjamin' as fashionable 'nonsense'.[67] But such criticism was in fact fairly rare, and was essentially motivated by a dislike of the French original. It does, however, demonstrate that Benjamin even received a certain amount of attention from the political right.

There can be no doubt, though, that Proust had found in Hessel and Benjamin two congenial translators. Their work was particularly successful in the parts where they had to find suitable German versions of the novel's numerous images and metaphors. And precisely in this respect Proust, who declared 'metaphor to be the very essence of style', provided a 'schooling' for Benjamin.

I admire how Proust adapts this practice and, as it were, mobilizes a whole complex of trite, universally known relationships in the service of more profound expression. Thus Proust brings to the most feeble perceptions a beautiful, belligerent laconicism, in that he enlists them in the service of a metaphorical expression.[68]

The first translation of Proust into German was not blessed with infinite luck. The highly praised work by Benjamin and Hessel remained an isolated episode in an undertaking that was evidently doomed to failure from the outset. Although a thoroughly successful theatrical publisher and agency for playwrights, Die Schmiede was unable to establish itself as a book publisher. It was already threatened by bankruptcy in 1926, and only the utmost exertions were able to avert this; then, barely two years later, the company began gradually to be sold off until, in 1931, its inglorious end was sealed when its name was finally removed from the commercial register. As a result of these events Hessel and Benjamin entered into a somewhat unwelcome relationship with another publishing house. In July 1928 Hessel received a letter from his former friend, Reinhard Piper. The Munich-based publisher had acquired the German rights for Proust, and wanted to convert them quickly into liquid assets by publishing 'all the volumes' of *Recherche* in quick succession.[69] The two Proust translators announced that they were willing in principle to complete the work, but during the ensuing negotiations, this was followed by a series of mutual misunderstandings, correspondence that was at times quite undiplomatic, and to end it all a legal skirmish involving both parties. After years of what they considered to be obscure prevarications, Hessel and Benjamin were no longer inclined to return to the drudgery of the translation, particularly because their interests had shifted in the meantime to other fields of literary production. Consequently a good two years were spent haggling over the old publishing liabilities into which the two of them had entered with Die Schmiede, and which Piper considered – quite correctly in formal terms – that he now controlled, in order to settle the fees, the question of corrections, etc. The result was that only one volume of *Recherche* appeared, and until the 1950s, not least on account of the changing political situation, Proust remained virtually unknown in Germany.

Proper credentials as a translator, 'like, for example Stefan Zweig has'[70] – the additional effect that Benjamin had hoped for from his work on Proust – certainly resulted from his translation of the second volume of *Recherche*. He did not wish to resume translating as his main occupation; but he was interested in having a certain reputation: partly for purely material reasons, but also because he viewed translation as an aspect of assimilation with a foreign culture that should not be underrated. This was particularly because he viewed his appraisal of contemporary French literature increasingly as a cultural-political task, performed by a mediator who endeavoured to reflect the historical and political reality of his German readership in the mirror

Adrienne Monnier in her bookshop, the 'Maison des amis des livres', at 7, rue de l'Odéon.

of that which was foreign. Consequently he completed a large number of further translations during the following years for various publications: parts of Louis Aragon's *Paysan de Paris* for the *Literarische Welt*,[71] as well as shorter texts by Proust,[72] Léon Bloy,[73] Marcel Jouhandeau,[74] and Adrienne Monnier, the famous bookseller,[75] whom he had come to know at the beginning of 1930.[76] The value that Benjamin attached to all these works can be judged from the fact that he intended to publish his Jouhandeau translations in one volume (together with the still unpublished 'Das Chateau de la Polie', 'Leda' and 'Prudence Hautechaume oder Die Mannequins der Diebin', the typescripts of which are today kept in the archives of the Kiepenheuer publishing house in Leipzig); this plan was never realized due to the seizure of power by the Nazis.[77] Benjamin also planned an article entitled 'En traduisant Marcel Proust' for the *Cahiers du Sud* published in Marseilles. He knew from the start, however, that this article would be less concerned with translation than with Proust's significance for the modern novel.[78] This essay only came into being many years later.

Preferably for all eternity

It became clear to me that I changed radically every time a great love gained power over me. This is because of the fact that a true love affair makes me similar to the woman I love. This transformation into a similar being was most prominent in my relationship with Asja.[79]

This admission comes from an entry in Benjamin's diary from 1931. Its particular significance lies in the fact that at the time of writing, it had long since been clear in his mind that although his life ran parallel to that of Asja Lacis, there was no hope of the two ever crossing. Yet in the autumn of 1926 Benjamin must still have had a certain amount of confidence that they would converge. When he learnt from her companion, Bernhard Reich, that she was in a sanatorium following a nervous breakdown, he could not conceal his haste as he organized an entry visa for the Soviet Union (which was no easy task at that time). After a strenuous two-day train journey, he arrived in Moscow on 6 December, where he remained for almost exactly two months.

Quite a few of Benjamin's diaries have been preserved, and in part they contain very personal entries. But none of them reveals the intimate details of his life with such absolute candour as that from his time in Moscow, in which he gives a meticulously

detailed record of his relationship with Asja Lacis. This may also
be attributable to his emotional state of mind at the time. He
had entered a serious crisis in his writing and was searching for a
solid 'framework' for his study which would take in the new
political, social and cultural realities. Silently he hoped that a
revolutionary turn in his life might help him to move on, and
he felt that some 'statement of intent' was indispensable for
the framework he sought – a statement of the kind that his
long-considered entry into the Communist Party would have
constituted. The characteristic qualities of the Moscow diary
stem, however, primarily from the uniqueness of his relationship
to his source of inspiration, for not only was Asja his single
greatest passion, but she was also the only woman who had a
double attraction for him. To recount the story of Benjamin's
'turn to Marxism' also entails, perhaps primarily, tracing out the
story of his love affair with Asja; for in a certain respect she was
the irreplaceable medium in his efforts to establish emotional
contact with a social reality that had attracted him ever since
his stay in Capri in 1924. However close Benjamin may have
come to joining the German Communist Party (what had kept
him from joining were 'superficial reservations'), or however
much more agreeable he may have found the 'position of a
left-wing outsider',[80] his reflections on the matter cannot be
separated from the influence and the nature of his relationship
with his communist girlfriend. The Janus character of this
relationship is mirrored in the daily entries in his diary, which,
apart from the vicissitudes of a complicated love affair (jealousy,
and battles with his rather tolerant 'rival', Bernhard Reich), also

First column of the
article on Goethe in the
*Great Soviet
Encyclopaedia.*

173

contains literary plans (the article on Goethe for the Soviet encyclopaedia, which Reich put his way), future plans, descriptions of visits to the theatre (Meyerhold) and encounters with old (Joseph Roth) and new acquaintances. Yet quite contrary to the normal goals and practices of 'revolution tourism' that was so fashionable at the time, Benjamin's journey to Russia ended with a visit to a Tsarist cloister with a rich history, a kind of cold store 'in which an old culture' was being 'preserved under ice during the dog days of the revolution'.[81]

But even if he did not manage to conquer the woman he loved ('preferably for all eternity'),[82] who appears to have kept him at a distance even more than ever during those two months, nor to effect the concrete and conscious transformation from esotericist to 'politician', from mystic to materialist, Benjamin's stay in Moscow did bring him rich rewards in that he gained access to a new cultural sphere and its revolutionary instruments. In keeping with his intentions, he returned to Berlin 'merely manifestly, not theoretically enriched'.[83] He set down the impressions and experiences that he had gained in numerous articles and reports which he managed to sell to the press and radio. The first of these was a short piece on a 'Dispute with Meyerhold'[84] (an article discussing Meyerhold's staging of Gogol's *The Government Inspector*, after which the director, who was present, was sharply attacked). This was followed by further articles in the *Literarische Welt* ('The Political Grouping of Russian Writers' and 'The State of Film in Russia', which was accompanied by a contribution to a discussion on the topic),[85] in the Dutch magazine *i 10. Internationale Revue* ('New Poetry in Russia'),[86] in the journal *Kreatur* (edited, amongst others, by Martin Buber; his townscape 'Moscow' was also published in this journal), as well as a broadcast commissioned by Südwestdeutscher Rundfunk ('Young Russian Writers').[87]

'. . . the excellent portraits and pictures you have done for my little poems. I am so pleased that our joint work has been so successful and I too would be delighted if we could continue to work together from time to time.'[61] (Excerpt from the wall calendar of the *Literarische Welt*, 1926)

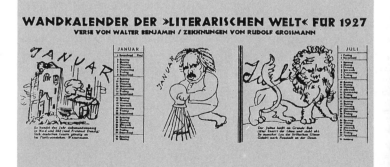

Why should only idealists be permitted to walk a tight-rope, while materialistic tight-rope walking is prohibited?[1]

7
(1929–33)

In the autumn of 1928, Asja Lacis came to Berlin. She was 'detailed'[2] to work in Germany as a film adviser at the Soviet Chamber of Commerce. Her presence promptly led to a further 'turn' in Benjamin's life, for several reasons. He lived with her for a period of time under the same roof[3] (in Düsseldorfer Straße in Berlin-Wilmersdorf) and frequently accompanied her to events organized by the Bund Proletarisch-Revolutionärer Schriftsteller [League of Proletarian-Revolutionary Authors],[4] thus coming into real contact with a literary and political theory and practice to which he now felt allied. And Asja Lacis also presumably gave Benjamin the decisive impulse to file a petition for divorce against his wife Dora.[5] He hoped that the confirmation of their formal separation would provide him with a new start. 'After seven years of procrastination', he felt he had to 'be sure to start a new life before [he was] over 40.'[6] In August 1929, among 'clouds of dust and surrounded by mountains of crates', he put an end to 'ten or twenty years of sedentary life'[7] and left their home in Delbrückstraße. (At first he moved in with his friends Helen and Franz Hessel in the old part of western Berlin.) He had no idea at the time what 'cruel forms'[8] the divorce proceedings would assume: at the conclusion of the bitter legal proceedings, he was left with nothing. The economic obligations that he had taken on through the marriage left him without 'house or home', and above all without the collection of children's books that he had amassed over the last decade and that had grown so dear to him: a collection 'which is growing steadily even today, though no longer in my garden', as he wrote in one of his most charming articles, 'Unpacking My Library',[9] which was originally broadcast on the radio. On 27 May 1930, the couple were legally divorced, and three years later, in December 1933, Benjamin's ex-wife readopted her maiden name. They had no contact with one another for well over two years, but during Benjamin's exile Dora Kellner was one of the few people who really supported him.

In the years 1929/30, Benjamin made two sets of plans to emigrate, but they both foundered as a result of his reluctance to leave the place of his birth. One was connected with Asja, the

Strategist in the literary battle

The beginning of a new life?

'Having begun to loosen the extremely tangled knot of my existence in one place – Dora and I are divorced now – this "Gordian knot" as you once justifiably called my relationship to Hebrew, will also have to be unraveled.'[62] (Benjamin's marriage certificate)

other with Scholem, the two outermost poles of his personal relationships in those years (the 'Latvian communist' and the Zionist). Asja arranged Benjamin's emigration to the Soviet Union before returning to Moscow, where 'they were looking in particular for foreign specialists'.[10] The fact that nothing came of these plans was doubtless not so much because they were looking for 'Marxists' (as Asja Lacis adds reluctantly in her memoirs), but more because it was quite clear to Benjaminin that literary critics were the last thing that was needed by a country that was in the process of catching up with the twentieth century.[11]

At this point in time his renewed preparations for the trip to Palestine he had long since planned had reached an advanced stage. Already by 1928 he seemed to have made up his mind quite definitely to embark on the journey in the foreseeable future. Certainly he was learning Hebrew avidly during this

'Who make all their journeys in bed? – Rivers.' (Benjamin's article on nineteenth-century picture puzzles, *Das illustrierte Blatt*, 1929.)

177

period, and his efforts were suitably encouraged by a generous advance payment from the University of Jerusalem. But subsequently almost all that was to be heard from him was an endless stream of apologies at his non-arrival and new promises that he was preparing to leave almost immediately.[12] Finally the whole matter was shelved because Benjamin began to devote himself to his 'Arcades' project. A final mention can be found in his correspondence with Scholem in 1931, when Benjamin remarked that 'the right moment' had arrived. But whether it was because such moments 'almost always' divided his 'destined path from the outside',[13] or because the reluctance that Benjamin felt to identify visibly with his Jewish origins was too great, he never emigrated to the Promised Land, nor was he to become familiar with it even for the purposes of study.

Away from Berlin, the world becomes beautiful and spacious[14]

In the summer of 1930 he set out on a long journey to the north, in which he travelled 'all the way over the Arctic circle' and reached northern Finland.[15] This journey is yet another clear example of just how close the crossing of borders and escapism were in Benjamin's frenetic love of travel, for this trip was also initially an escape: from his homelessness in Berlin. He refers to this in a passage of a work that makes up part of the literary fruits of this trip. 'Time, even inhabited by the one who has no home', he wrote in a text entitled 'Nordische See' [Nordic Sea], published in the *Frankfurter Zeitung* in August,

becomes a palace for the traveller who leaves no one behind. For three whole weeks its halls, filled with the sound of the waves,

'I have yielded myself to the surrounding, perfect situation for one day before setting my mind to the arctic venture, whose mists at present envelop me.'[63] (From Benjamin's postcard collection: Bergen)

178

stretched out in a row towards the north. Seagulls and towns, flowers, furniture and statues appeared on their walls, and light shone through their windows by day and by night.[16]

The text 'Nordic Sea' reveals a stronger accentuation of Benjamin's political reflections, albeit with that typical form of his that remains incomprehensible to anyone who lacks an inside knowledge of his personality.[17] And perhaps of more importance: here, right in the north of Europe, he found a counterpart to the southern way of life that he had once described together with Asja Lacis in the townscape 'Naples'. Here everything had a great sobriety: 'Wood is wood, bronze is bronze, bricks bricks, [and] nowhere are provisions made for relaxing outdoors; whenever the houses of the middle classes have front gardens, they are so densely packed that no one would be tempted to dally there.' Indeed, even objects used every day had a completely different relationship to the surrounding world, were almost rooted in the soil: 'all the seats of the old chairs', he wrote in his observations on Nordic chairs, 'are closer to the ground than ours. But how insistent they are on this reduced distance, while at the same time these seats take the place of Mother Earth.'

If architecture and furniture already express attitudes to life and images of the world so profoundly, landscape completes the picture, which in its entirety becomes deeply personal:

The boat was sailing southwards. There was still some light to the west. But what happened now to the birds – or to me? – was inspired by the power of this dominating, lonely place, which, out of melancholy, I chose in the middle of the quarter deck. All at once there were two tribes of gulls, one to the east, the other to the west, left and right, so utterly different that the name 'gulls' was no longer appropriate to them. Set against the extinguished sky, the birds to the left retained something of their brightness, flashing with every upward and downward turn, agreeing with or avoiding one another and appearing constantly to weave before me an unbroken, unpredictable sequence of signs, a whole, unspeakably changeable, fleeting – yet legible – network of pinions. But I kept slipping away, each time to find my attention drawn towards the other flock. Here I beheld nothing, nothing spoke to me. I had scarcely begun to watch those in the east, when they, a few sharp, deep black pinions flying towards a final glow of light, vanished in the distance and returned, in a way that I would no longer have been able to describe. I was so transfixed by this that I too, black from suffering, returned to myself from the distance, in a silent flock of wings. The puzzle to the left remained unresolved, and my fate hung on every nod, on the right it had been resolved long ago, and was one sole soundless beckoning. This counterplay continued for a long time, until I myself was no more than the threshold across which the unnameable messengers exchanged black and white in the air.[18]

Benjamin was not being entirely honest here. He had by no means concluded his examination of the 'right'. Not because he was still studying Klages on this journey (he was reading *Der Geist als Widersacher der Seele [The Spirit as the Adversary of the Soul]* – 'regardless of the context in which the author may be and remain suspect', he found that after all, the book was 'without a doubt a great philosophical work'),[19] but rather because his real appraisal of the political right, his critique of George and his circle, was far from reaching any conclusion.

As if this journey to Scandinavia had brought about a similarly lasting change in his view of the world as his trip to Capri had done, shortly after his return to Berlin Benjamin moved into a bright new flat, like an artist's studio, in Prinzregentenstraße. It was 'the first time [in his] life' that he had 'landed in a studio', an abode with the kind of visual and physical coldness that previously he had always loathed. Things were different now. His new home distinguished itself, as he wrote to Scholem, with every 'conceivable advantage' that 'the most profound silence' and 'the remarkable architectural neighbours, both inside and out' could bring. Right outside his house was the new Prinzregentenstraße synagogue (the only one, incidentally, to be built in Berlin after the First World War) which he considered to be a product 'of the protestant theological spirit in church architecture'[20] until it was inaugurated on Rosh Hashanah. In the same house, indeed on the same floor, lived his cousin Egon Wissing with his wife Gert, with whom Benjamin was on very good terms. (Wissing was the son of his maternal aunt, Clara Schoenflies.)[21]

In November 1930, Benjamin's mother died after a lengthy illness (his father had already passed away four years earlier). His circumstances had now 'arrived at the "stretta", during which a decision about the future [had to] be reached'.[22]

Destructive criticism must be rehabilitated. For this, the function   A 'new' critic?
of criticism in general must be entirely reconsidered. What has
happened, gradually, is that criticism has become slackness and
innocuousness itself. In these circumstances corruption itself
has its virtue: that is, a face, a clear physiognomy. . . . Honest,
truthful criticism from a position of neutrality in matters of taste
is uninteresting and basically founded on an objective outline
(a strategic plan), which then has its own logic and its own
truth. Today, this is missing almost everywhere, because political
strategy coincides with the critical only in the most general cases,
though this should ultimately be seen as the aim.[23]

During this process of disentangling and ordering his personal
affairs and living conditions, Benjamin also endeavoured to give
his thinking and creative output a clearer shape. This almost
forced search for a 'new life' corresponded with the search for
himself as a 'new critic' who, as he wrote in a short text in 1931,
has a 'materialist outlook'.[24] This should not be taken to mean
that Benjamin was now aiming to write his critiques and reviews
from a dogmatic *Marxist* standpoint. Although the overall
terminology in his writing of the period might suggest as much,
he lacked the necessary prerequisites for this. His knowledge
of the relevant literature was rudimentary in the extreme. He
only knew the classics of historical and dialectical materialism,
Marx and Engels, from secondary or tertiary sources: from the
writings of Lenin, Lukács and Bloch, from Alfred Kleinberg's
*Die deutsche Dichtung in ihren sozialen Bedingungen [The Social
Conditions of German Literature]* and from conversations and
discussions with his friends and acquaintances. So by 'materialist outlook' he was thinking largely in terms of 'more tangible',
'more concrete', 'closer to reality', 'material' and 'political'.

   In the late 1920s and early 1930s Benjamin wrote numerous
detailed and formative notes on the theory and practice of
literary criticism, which have come down to us in the form of
a manifesto, 'Programm der literarischen Kritik' [Programme
for Literary Criticism], and as observations on 'Die Aufgabe
des Kritikers' [The Task of the Critic].[25] They constitute the
first embodiment of a 'preface' to an anthology of his most
important literary essays,[26] which Benjamin hoped at the time
to have published by Rowohlt. With these reflections he turned
his back once and for all on every kind of programme for
'spiritual renewal',[27] such as were championed in differing ways
by George and his circle, and by Kurt Hiller and his 'logocrats'.
The necessary step for this personal break with a stance that at

times had fascinated him quite considerably was above all his process of reflection on history and the social role of the intellectual in bourgeois society.

Benjamin's ideas on the social position, significance and task of the intellectual are a central motif throughout his works on literary criticism during the 1920s and 1930s. He felt justified in saying that the foundation of the Reich had produced an ideological split within the bourgeoisie and thus among its intellectuals, and their polarization had been manifestly visible by the outbreak of the First World War, when this social stratum split into at least two different groups: those who emphatically welcomed the events of August 1914, and the categorical opponents of the war, the active pacifists, whose protagonists had predominantly fled to Switzerland.

There were also many scientists, critics, writers and academics who, like Benjamin himself, had initially stayed silent. But inevitably they too came to take a public stand regarding the war, and thus to reveal their 'politicization'. Benjamin's own 'politicization' had begun in Switzerland: through his meetings with Hugo Ball and Ernst Bloch. He had already read Ball's *Critique of the German Intelligentsia* whilst in Berne. This was followed by his preoccupation with the question of the position of the intellectual, with the role and significance he is still allotted in society and the tasks he should search out for himself, questions which were largely triggered by Benjamin's reading of Max Weber's *Wissenschaft als Beruf* and the writings of Karl Mannheim, whom he came to know personally in Heidelberg in 1922.

In a number of reviews written between 1929 and 1931, which were quite intentionally directed with equal force against both the conservative and fascist right as well as the radical left, this 'strategist in the literary battle'[28] branded the cultural positions of such writers as Max Kommerell, Ernst Jünger, Erich Kästner and Kurt Tucholsky as attempts to avoid the basic questions surrounding the function of the writer. Kommerell's *Der Dichter als Führer in der deutschen Klassik [The Poet as a Leader in German Classicism]* was for Benjamin primarily an 'esoteric history of German writing', a kind of 'history of the salvation' of the German people, as he wrote in a review of the book, entitled 'Against a Masterpiece'.[29] He realized that there was no denying the quality and style of this work. But what it lacked were the martial components[30] that actually make a critique what it is, and which legitimize the interpretation.

He further corroborated the validity of his thesis in a review

Verlags-Vertrag

Zwischen

Herrn Dr. Walther B e n j a m i n , Berlin W, Meinekestr. 9

einerseits

und

der Firma Ernst R o w o h l t Verlag K.G.a.A.,Berlin W 50,Passauerstr.8/9

andererseits

wurde heute folgender Verlagsvertrag geschlossen und von beiden Teilen zum Zeichen ihres Einverständnisses unterzeichnet.

§ 1

Herr Dr. Walther Benjamin, Berlin. überträgt der Firma Ernst Rowohlt Verlag K.G. a. A. das ausschliessliche Verlagsrecht eines Essaybandes, der etwa folgende Essays enthalten soll:

Aufgabe des Kritikers
Gottfried Keller
Hebel
Hessel
Walser
Kraus
Green
Proust
Gide
Romancier und Erzähler
Ueber den Jugendstil
Surrealism
Aufgabe des Uebersetzers

für alle Auflagen und Ausgaben.

§ 12

Durch diesen Vertrag wurde der zwischen Herrn Dr. Walther Benjamin und der Firma Ernst Rowohlt Verlag K.G.a.A.,Berlin am 31. März 1928 bzw. 2. April 1928 geschlossene Verlagsvertrag über einen Essayband ,enthaltend drei Essays,u.A. über P r o u s t und Franz K a f k a, in allen seinen Teilen aufgehoben.

§ 13

Alle übrigen Fragen regelt das Verlagsgesetz.

§ 14

Erfüllungsort dieses Vertrages ist Berlin W 50.

§ 15

Vorstehender Vertrag wurde in zwei gleichlautenden Exemplaren ausgefertigt, gelesen und von beiden Teilen genehmigt und unterschrieben.

Berlin, den ....1930 Berlin, den 1930

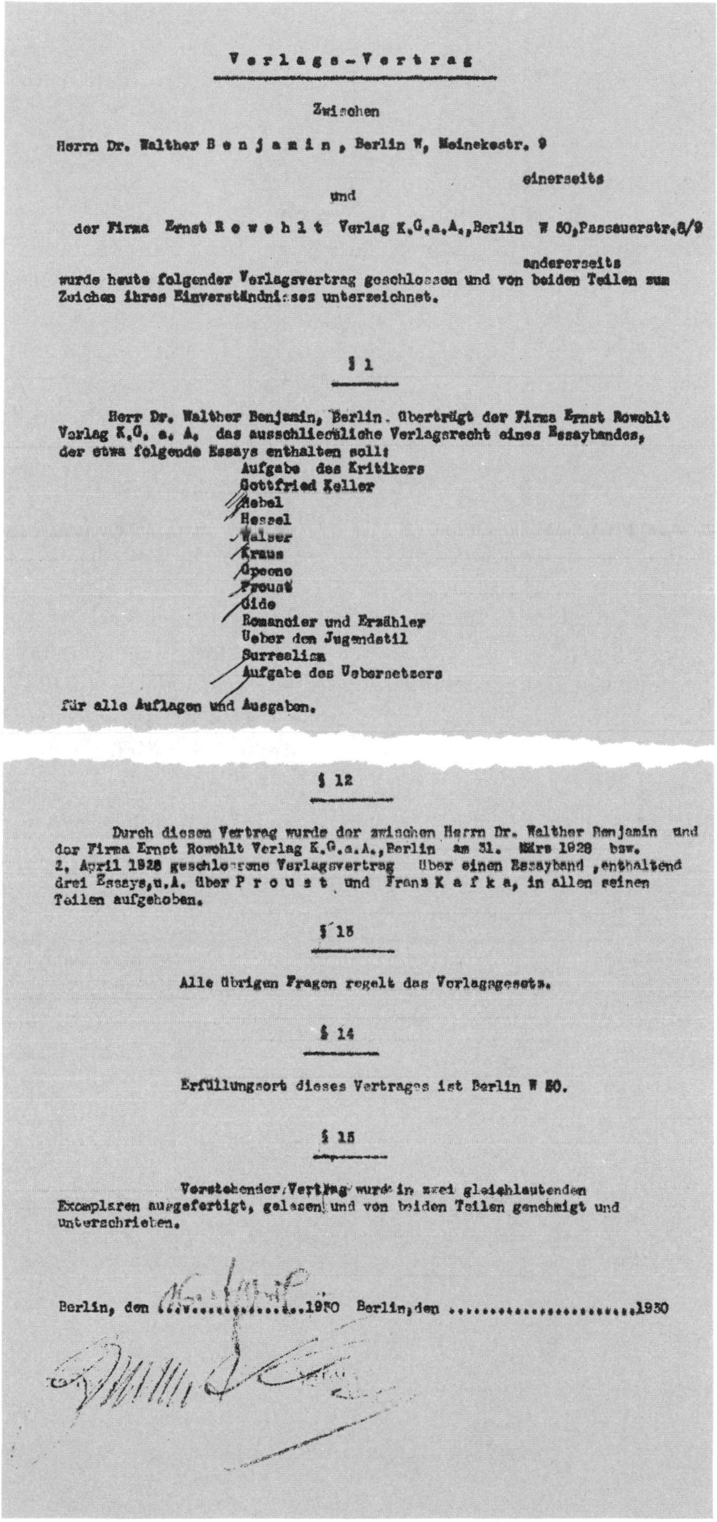

Günther Anders: 'Der Defekt' ['The Defect']

'He lacks something or other,' said the novelist – and he was by no means a poor novelist – 'W.B. lacks something that is required to write novels.'

'Not merely something or other,' said S., 'but a very definite something.'

'What?'

'A defect.'

'A defect?'

'The one people need in order to be able to write novels.'

'You don't say! Have I got one as well?'

'Of course you have, otherwise you wouldn't have been able to write all your books.'

'What he lacks is that small drop of stupidity and illogicality that a novelist must already have if he is to put it into the mouths of his characters and let them talk realistically.'[64]

(Excerpt from a contract concerning a collection of literary essays with the publishers Rowohlt, 16 April 1930)

('Theorien des deutschen Faschismus' [Theories of German Fascism]) of an anthology edited by Ernst Jünger entitled *Krieg und Krieger [War and Warriors]*, in which he maintained that the 'touchstone' of every standpoint is its language.[31] The fascist ideology presented in these pages was, according to Benjamin, both hollow and empty.

Finally, in the famous (or notorious) pamphlet 'Linke Melancholie' [Left-Wing Melancholy], Benjamin denounced so-called left–extremist writing as inappropriate in times when a class struggle was being waged with an open visor. Authors such as Erich Kästner, best known for his children's books, whose collection of poems *Ein Mann gibt Auskunft [A Man Gives Information]* prompted this onslaught, convey an attitude that 'no longer' corresponds 'with any form of political action', for it is not simply 'to the left of this or that direction, but to the left of what is even possible'. Here the concept of what is political, which in substance is a 'compulsion to decide', is debased to an 'object of pleasure'.[32]

Incidentally, 'Linke Melancholie' was the 'sound of the tumult' unleashed by discussions with Bertolt Brecht,[33] whom he came to know personally in early 1929 through Asja Lacis.[34] Through him and those in his circle (Bernhard von Brentano and his wife Margot, Elisabeth Hauptmann, Emil Hesse-Burri, Carola Neher, Helene Weigel et al.), Benjamin's thinking and writing gained a certain amount of stimulus, correction and precision without, however, losing the essential core of his previous intellectual production.

'Aus dem Brecht-Kommentar' [From the Brecht Commentaries] represented merely the 'first product' of his 'very interesting association with Brecht',[35] which was to result in further work and projects. The short text already gives an outline of *what* precisely drew Benjamin to the work of his newly won friend: the experimental gesture that could be discerned in his undertakings (the *Keuner* stories, *Lindbergh's Flight, Fatzer*). For him the Augsburg-born playwright constituted a rarity among politically committed literati. He numbered among those authors who constantly accounted for the contexts of their written work, and who measured their creative production by political yardsticks.

Crisis and critique

Brecht's and Benjamin's common views on a kind of critique that they considered had ceased to fulfil any social function led them 'during long discussions'[36] to plan a periodical, and then to win over Rowohlt as its publisher. The title was to be *Krisis*

New Year's Eve party 1931/2 at Elisabeth Hauptmann's flat in Charlottenburg, Berlin (front row from left to right: Benjamin, Carola Neher, Margaret Mynotti, Elisabeth Hauptmann; back row: Margot von Brentano, ?, Valentina and Alfred Kurella).

und Kritik [Crisis and Critique], which already gives an idea of the manner in which they intended to tackle the current literary and political movements and tendencies: not by showering literary works with preconceived opinions, but rather with a critique that develops an understanding of the general contemporary crisis through questioning itself; as Brecht, who was evidently the initiator of this new forum for the unaligned left, formulated it: a critique that 'reconstrues its whole field as a permanent crisis and so conceives of the present as a "critical period" in both senses'.[37]

There was little difficulty in reaching a consensus among the people working on the project about the basic outline of the programme. The periodical was to become a forum 'in which the bourgeois intelligentsia' gives an 'account of the demands and views which individually and alone permit a radical form of production that brings results amidst the present conditions,

'Bert Brecht is a difficult phenomenon. He refuses to make "free" use of his great literary gifts. And there is not one of the gibes levelled against his literary activity – plagiarist, trouble-maker, saboteur – that he would not claim as a compliment to his unliterary, anonymous, and yet noticeable activity as educator, thinker, organizer, politician and theatrical producer. In any case he is unquestionably the only writer in Germany today who asks himself where he ought to apply his talent, who applies it only where he is convinced of the need to do so, and who abstains on every other occasion.'[65]

as opposed to the usual arbitrary, ineffective kind', as Benjamin wrote in his 'Memorandum zu der Zeitschrift "Krisis und Kritik"' [Memorandum on the Journal *Krisis und Kritik*].[38] These commonplaces allowed even such diverse personalities as Bernhard von Brentano and Herbert Ihering (who were to be the editors), Alfred Kurella (who was evidently intended to supervise editorial coordination) and Franz Hessel (as a Rowohlt editor who had the confidence of the publisher) to become signatories without politically compromising themselves. Indeed, only such general phrases could make the initiators seriously believe that figures like Gottfried Benn, Georg Lukács, Robert Musil, Wilhelm Reich, Theodor Wiesengrund (Adorno), Paul Hindemith and Hanns Eisler (to name but a few of the prospective contributors)[39] could be won over for the periodical simultaneously. The project's eventual failure was not due primarily to the contributors' pot-pourri of ideological positions, but rather to the insurmountable divergences of opinion within the editorial board itself.

Editorial planning for the first issue, which was scheduled for April 1931, included a text entitled 'Der Generalangriff' [Concerted Attack] by Brentano, a report by Kurella on the 'Kharkov Congress' and Plekhanov's 'Idealism and Materialism', but the plan already prompted Benjamin to assume a distance that amounted to a withdrawal from the entire project. He gave his reasons for this in a letter to Brecht, saying that these articles expressed nothing of the 'attitude' which, it had originally been decided, should determine the choice of contributions. 'The magazine should act as propaganda for dialectical materialism by applying it to questions that the bourgeois intelligentsia is compelled to recognize as its very own'.[40] Benjamin's own image of such contributions is given eloquent expression in his notes and records from this period, and more particularly in his numerous works of literary criticism. He attempted to demonstrate this in quite exemplary fashion in an essay on Karl Kraus which not only met with incomprehension from his target, but also from Benjamin's friends.

Benjamin had evidently first come in contact with Kraus's writings whilst in Switzerland, where he fell 'under the influence of Werner Kraft's boundless enthusiasm' for the Viennese writer and became a regular reader of Kraus's periodical *Die Fackel [The Torch]*.[41] Benjamin wrote his first pieces on Kraus in the 1920s: the 'Monument to a Warrior'[42] which was incorporated in *One-Way Street*, and its 'counterpart', 'Karl Kraus',[43] which appeared in the 'international review' *i 10*, edited by Arthur Müller-Lehning in Amsterdam. In addition, Benjamin wrote two articles for the *Literarische Welt*: one on a reading given by Kraus in Berlin,[44] the other on a production of his play *Die Unüberwindlichen* [*The Invincibles*] at the Berlin Volksbühne.[45]

Karl Kraus.

Kraus, who paid close attention to those of Benjamin's texts that concerned him,[46] and who perhaps even knew him quite well through their mutual acquaintances (including Gustav Glück and Ernst Krenek), was nevertheless unable to find much pleasure in them. His harshest judgement was directed at the large, three-part essay in the *Frankfurter Zeitung*, of which he said in passing in an article in *Die Fackel* that 'basically all that [he] understood' was that it was about him. The 'author' appeared 'to know a thing or two' about his person that was not only 'previously unknown' to himself, but also failed to enlighten him in any way. Consequently he could 'merely express the hope

'While talking with [Gustav] Glück I discovered the real reason for Kraus's attitude regarding my series of essays. Admittedly it may have been partly out of consideration towards his supporters. But the real key to his behaviour has at long last been provided by "The Diebold Case" in the last issue of the *Fackel*. The reason is that if my article had contained the name Diebold – even in the most obscure corner – and referred, never mind how vaguely, to his disparagement by Kraus, he would have had no difficulty in praising both the article and the passage.'[66] (Benjamin, cartoon by B. F. Dolbin around 1930)

that other readers [of Benjamin's writings] have understood them better than I. (Perhaps it is psychoanalysis.)'[47] This final pointed remark hurt Benjamin so much that he resolved 'never' to write publicly 'about [Kraus] again';[48] a resolution to which he remained faithful for the rest of his life, however much he continued to occupy himself with Kraus's life and opinions.

'Nothing more desolate than his acolytes, nothing more god-forsaken than his adversaries', as Benjamin wrote in a passus dedicated to Kraus in *One-Way Street*.[49] There is scarcely a remark anywhere in Benjamin's writings on Kraus that expresses more succinctly all that is contained in his long commentary from 1931. It is neither a simple apology, nor a sweeping rejection. Rather, it is the attempt to do justice to both his topic and the task of the critic in general in a *productive* way, so that the interpreter does not conceal his position in either his depiction or his interpretation. Thus in his own words, this essay marks 'the place' where he stood intellectually, from where he was unwilling to participate any further. In 'methodological' terms this meant 'casting one's gaze into the Promised Land of sabotage from the [Mount] Carmel of reason'.[50]

In numerous respects – both in methodological as well as superficial terms – this commentary about Klaus is reminiscent of certain of Benjamin's early works, especially the foreword to his Baudelaire translations and above all the major essay on Goethe's *Elective Affinities*. These works, which were once intended as representative of the *Angelus Novus* programme (and what else is the Kraus essay, basically, than precisely this in relation to the similarly unrealized periodical *Krisis und Kritik* which also never came into being?), testified to a constructive appraisal, which avoided not only being overwhelmed by the products of George and his circle, but also sinking into cheap polemics regarding certain idiosyncrasies demonstrated by the representatives of this 'school'. Instead, they concentrated solely on the essentials: advancing one's personal ideas and standpoint whilst appraising the outstanding products and representatives of a 'school'.

Much the same applies *mutatis mutandis* to Benjamin's Kraus essay. It, too, is concerned primarily with recording his personal world-view through the interpretation of the work of a great man. And as such it is almost impossible to grasp its substance by philologically precisely proving just how admissible certain of these interpretations of Kraus's writings are. The essay does not offer an 'appreciation' of his complete works, nor does it reconstruct the intellectual biography of an important writer.

Rather Benjamin turns an intellectual 'figure's' thinking and standpoint over in his hand, examines it from all sides and dismantles it into its component parts – into the 'Cosmic Man', 'Demon' and 'Monster' (as the essay's three chapters are headed, thus lending its argumentation a seemingly organic character). In the end, he allows the figure to rise anew in an image in which Kraus himself only appears hazily in the background, while his intellectual interpreter's physiognomy becomes all the more defined.

The opening remarks characterize Kraus as a harbinger:

In old engravings there is a messenger who rushes toward us crying aloud, his hair on end, brandishing a sheet of paper in his hands, a sheet full of war and pestilence, of cries of murder and pain, of danger from fire and flood, spreading everywhere the 'latest news'. News in this sense . . . is disseminated by Die Fackel. *Full of betrayal, earthquakes, poison and fire from the* mundus intelligibilis.[51]

Then, after once again allowing the stages in Kraus's life to be recalled – from his attitude to the frenzied enthusiasm at the beginning of the First World War to his struggle with the press, from his aesthetic categories to the ethical convictions in his work – this harbinger finally becomes a soothsayer, a seer, a prophet: 'not a new person', but rather

a monster – a new angel. Perhaps one of those who, according to the Talmud, are at each moment created anew in countless throngs, and who, once they have raised their voices before God, cease and pass into nothingness. Lamenting, chastising, or rejoicing? No matter – on this evanescent voice the ephemeral work of Kraus is modelled. Angelus – that is the messenger in the old engravings.[52]

The fact that these concluding remarks are primarily a self-portrait is made clear in the way that Benjamin defends himself against the harsh words of reproach from Scholem. In a letter to Benjamin in March 1931, Scholem objected to his friend's brash use of dialectical materialism:

It would be clear to any impartial reader of your writing that in the last few years you have been trying – forgive me for saying so, but desperately trying – to present your insights, which are in part far-reaching, in phraseology that is conceptually close to

189

communist phraseology. It also seems clear, however – and to me this is what seems important – that there is a disconcerting alienation and disjuncture between your true and alleged way of thinking. That is, you do not attain your insights through the strict application of a materialistic method, but entirely independent of it (in the best case) or (in the worst case, as in some of the essays of the last two years) by playing with the ambiguities and interference phenomena of this method.[53]

The points that Scholem objected to were certainly not of his own invention. In many instances Benjamin's early views on language, his observations on 'origins' and 'rescue' (as for instance in his *Trauerspiel* book) no longer rang true and seemed strangely isolated from the rest of the argumentation as soon as they were couched in Marxist phraseology. And he even admitted this in part. But he was nevertheless disturbed by Scholem's criticism, above all because in his view he had never done anything else all his life. Basically, his Kraus essay was not, as his friend in Palestine supposed, a betrayal of what he had previously thought and written. As ever, he had tried to bring together disparate elements and link extreme positions. The reason the Zionist Scholem had become so agitated at precisely the moment at which Benjamin was absorbing historical and dialectical materialism was transparently 'political'.

One might wish to argue over whether Kraus really was a Rumpelstiltskin figure ('Glad am I none can proclaim, that Marx and Engels is my name') as Benjamin portrayed him.[54] But by a sleight of hand, and by no means unintentionally, the essay resulted in being an inventory of Benjamin's own creative production, of his own thinking and writing, with which he was trying to find a path from George to Marx, Baudelaire to Kraus. Thus it is no coincidence that he simply varied the wording of the essay's closing image when defending his position in a letter to Max Rychner dated 7 March 1931, which has subsequently received a great deal of attention:

I have never been able to do research and think in any sense other than, if you will, a theological one, namely, in accord with the Talmudic teaching about the forty-nine levels of meaning in every passage of the Torah. In my experience, the most trite Communist platitude possesses more hierarchies of meaning than does contemporary bourgeois profundity, which has only one meaning, that of an apologetic.

'Even the editors are already referring to him as "the best living writer in the German language" – although only those who happen to be Jewish.'[67] (Entry in Kürschners Deutscher Literaturkalender, 1930)

'More reasoned answers' to this problem, Benjamin concluded his letter, could be found 'between the lines' of his Kraus essay.[55]

The year 1923 heralded the wireless era in Germany. The first broadcasts by a company called the Berliner Funk-Stunde AG were begun in October, and the 'provinces' were swift to follow the German capital. From Hamburg to Munich, Frankfurt to Königsberg, Cologne to Breslau, stations sprouted up all over the place, and in no time they had covered almost every corner of the German Reich. The medium opened completely new perspectives for those concerned with the cultural sector, not least in terms of income, for here gratifying work was combined with lucrative returns. These perspectives became even rosier with increasing expertise in the art of hitting two birds with one stone, that is, getting a piece of work accepted by two media – radio and the press. Benjamin perfected this almost to the point of virtuosity: he was able to sell essays, reviews, reports, childhood recollections and much more to both media. More decisive, though, was the fact that radio could make a 'Vienna waltz and a cookery recipe available to the entire world', as Brecht worded it in his lapidary way.[56] Everyone – whether musician, poet, scholar or actor – who stepped up to the microphone stood before an audience numbering hundreds of thousands and comprising every social stratum. The fact that for the first time a technical apparatus was placed between the producer and the recipient meant that artists in this medium had to meet new demands in terms of presentation. A performance on the stage of the Deutsches Theater in Berlin lost part of its effect when it was only heard. The same applied to talks and lectures. The speaker had to manage without any direct response from the auditorium (be it coughs, cat-calls, questions, or any other form of commentary), and could scarcely imagine whom he or she was actually addressing, which had a considerable effect on the content, form and presentation of the talk. It is not by chance that Benjamin's 'theory' of the radio – which exists, jotted down in a number of brief passages, partly as private notes, but also partly made available to the public eye[57] – takes these as its central questions. What function does the apparatus have? And in the light of the answer to this: what are the underlying intentions of that which is spoken into the microphone? At whom is the radio presentation aimed?

Benjamin's first contacts with the new medium were made in 1925 in Frankfurt. The magazine *Radio-Umschau [Radio Review]*

At the microphone: Dr Walter Benjamin

191

was looking for a new editor for its supplement *Die Besprechung [The Critique]*. The editor's task was to 'cast light on the present literary and artistic currents' in general, 'and [to] review works of art and literature in particular'.[58] These requirements could not have suited Benjamin better; and when it came to writing and editing leading articles specifically on radio, which was also part of the task, he would undoubtedly have been able to summon enough powers of improvization to do the job to his prospective employer's complete satisfaction. Unfortunately he was not given the chance to prove his abilities. For all the patronage he received from his friend Ernst Schoen, who was head of programming at the station in Frankfurt, this job was in the end entrusted to someone else (a man named Manfred Heiden).

Although Benjamin made his debut at the microphone of a broadcasting station on 23 May 1927, when he presented a number of his thoughts and observations on 'Young Russian Writers', this guest performance in Frankfurt was to remain an isolated episode for two years. Only in the latter half of 1929 did he begin to work regularly for radio, first for Südwestdeutscher

'I was standing for the first time in a modern broadcasting studio, in which everything is provided to ensure the perfect comfort of the speaker so that he can display his abilities in total relaxation. He can stand before a lectern or sink down into a commodious armchair, he has the choice of a whole variety of light sources, he can even walk back and forth, taking the microphone with him.'[68] (Studio at Südwestdeutscher Rundfunk in Frankfurt)

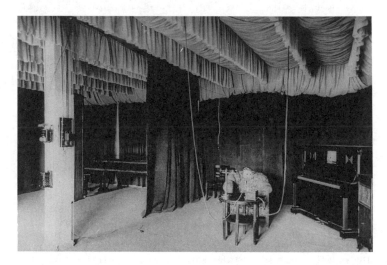

Rundfunk in Frankfurt, and then slightly later for the Berliner Funkstunde as well. Both stations underwent decisive management changes during the summer of 1929. The former director-general in Frankfurt, Hans Flesch (also an acquaintance of Benjamin from his days in the Youth Movement), left to take charge of the station in Berlin. Schoen moved up to assume this position. And it was above all thanks to him that, 'despite all the resistance',[59] Benjamin was now frequently heard on the Südwestdeutscher Rundfunk.

'He wishes to show a series of situations in our social existence in which the individual is still able to achieve something by the use of his skills; at the same time he wishes to "provoke" the strata in question into making opposing statements of their own, so that people from the mass audience who would never have done so of their own accord will step up to the microphone.'[69]
(Recording a radio play in Berlin, 1927/8)

Judging by the scattered remarks that Benjamin made in his letters, he appears at first to have had a somewhat disdainful view of radio and its lack of culture.[60] Nor did he spare his own contributions, for he categorized the larger part of them as insignificant.[61] They more or less exhausted their function by bolstering his housekeeping money and the budget for his travels. However, his self-criticism did allow for certain qualitative distinctions, such that he classed some of his literary talks and above all his radio plays as part of his creative production.

Benjamin based his 'Hörmodelle' [Radio Models] clearly on the tradition of Brecht's epic theatre.[62] But it is of little use to measure them solely in these terms. Even the best of them cannot disguise their improvized character, and nor did Benjamin have any serious intention of competing with his friend as a playwright, that is in the area of radio plays. Rather, by drawing on the theory of epic theatre he was aiming at directing attention towards the central aspect of radio models: their didactic objectives. In this respect, Brecht's theatre experiments contained elements that could well prove fruitful in his own endeavours, Benjamin thought. Brecht characterized the quintessence of this work as the attempt to bring about a change in the audience's receptivity,[63] and Benjamin felt that he could expand on this as follows: the major effects of epic theatre are 'education (knowledge) and training (judgement)'.[64] These are clearly not the words of a playwright, but of a critic who remains constantly faithful to himself during these excursions into 'alien' territory. This is perhaps most easily recognizable in his radio play *Was die Deutschen lasen, während ihre Klassiker schrieben* [What the

'Notable from a technical point of view perhaps is a piece for children, which was broadcast last year in Frankfurt and Cologne; I may be able to secure you a copy at some point. It's called *Radau um Kasperl*.'[70] (From the *Südwestdeutsche Rundfunk-Zeitung*, 28 June 1931 and 13 March 1932)

Germans Read While Their Classic Authors Were Writing] of 1932.[65]

In the three years between 1929 and 1932, Benjamin stood more than eighty times at the microphones of the Frankfurt and Berlin broadcasting stations – this fact underlines the importance of this aspect of his creative work.

Arrival in Ibiza

'Here the Goethe centennial is starting up, and as the only person besides at most two or three others who knows anything about the subject, I of course have no share in it. Plans I cannot make. If I had any money, I would bolt before another day goes by'[66] – Benjamin wrote in a letter from 28 February 1932 to his friend Scholem, who was in the process of preparing for a several-month trip to Europe. This was one of the rare occasions in Benjamin's life when his pessimism was to prove unfounded. So much time and energy was put into the celebrations for the 100th anniversary of Goethe's death that soon even Benjamin had 'towering piles of Goethe books' waiting on his desk to be looked through and reviewed. And in the end even he received some worthwhile income for his labours: 'several hundred marks'[67] for two lengthy contributions to the special Goethe supplement in the *Frankfurter Zeitung*.[68] The unexpected windfall allowed him to fulfil his wish to escape at once from the depressing atmosphere of Berlin and follow his old friend Felix Noeggerath to Ibiza.

On 7 April he boarded the steam freighter *Catania* in Hamburg and travelled for eleven days to Barcelona. The lengthy voyage, which was beset at first by heavy storms, provided him with ample opportunity to befriend the captain and the crew. Their conversations, which Benjamin recorded extremely meticulously in an 'Ibizan diary', covered a wide range of subjects; above all he heard a number of stories from the days of the November Revolution of 1918 – sailors' yarns that Benjamin naturally took at face value.

After landing at Barcelona, he crossed to the shores of Ibiza where he was received by the Noeggeraths (Felix Noeggerath, his wife, his son and daughter-in-law) with bad tidings. As a consequence of 'their impatience' and 'passionate desire to escape the circumstances in which they lived',[69] the Noeggeraths had fallen foul of a 'con man' in Berlin who was 'wanted by the police'.[70] Noeggerath had rented from him a house on Ibiza which was not his property. And Benjamin had in turn rented out his flat in Prinzregentenstraße to the same man for the duration of his trip, so he was never to receive a penny in return. But this was the

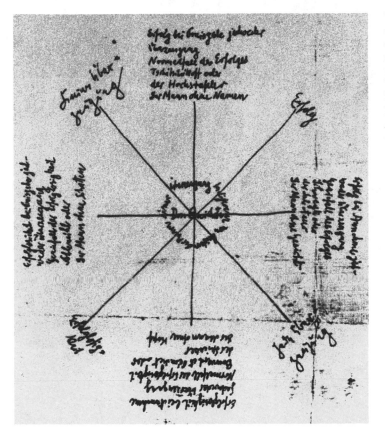

'Success following the abandonment of every conviction. A typical case for success. Tschilihoff or the Confidence-Trickster, The Man With No Name. For Mrs Marietta Noeggerath, San Antonio, 17 May 1932.' (Benjamin's autograph)

only negative side of his stay in Ibiza, which was otherwise unusually relaxing and harmonious. At the time when Benjamin visited the island it was still being spared its fate as a Mecca of mass tourism. The picture that it presented to the visitor in 1932 was that of a completely unspoilt landscape, barren and hopelessly behind the times. 'But already', he noticed, 'in Ibiza and San Antonio there are hotels being built in which the stranger is promised running water. The time until their completion has become precious.'[71] This was his first visit to this island which was 'far removed from international trade and even civilization'.[72]

In its aspirations alone Benjamin's travel diary differed utterly from the only one with which it can really be compared: his diary of his early visit to Italy in 1912. His observations are no longer marred by preconceived opinions, and any temptations merely to rediscover things that he had previously conjured up in his mind were blocked from the outset by appropriate methodological considerations.

'Agriculture has remained quite archaic on this island. The fields are still irrigated in old Arabian fashion using water wheels driven by mules, and the corn is still threshed by the hooves of horses that are led on long reins around the barn floor.'[71] (Benjamin sailing off Ibiza)

Travel writers have the curious habit of adhering to the precedent of 'fulfilment', wishing to retain the haze that distance has spun around each country and the virtue that the idler's imagination lends to every social order. The levelling of the globe by industry and technology [has] made such enormous progress that, by rights, disillusionment [should form] the black backdrop to description, so that the really incommensurable condition of total proximity – of people dealing with others, with the country they are in – will stand out all the more sharply.[73]

Benjamin on Ibiza, 1932.

196

Benjamin stayed on Ibiza until 17 July, slightly longer than originally planned. From there he travelled to Nice, where he had intended to arrive two days earlier, in order to celebrate his fortieth birthday there in the company of 'a pretty strange fellow whose path [he had] often crossed in the course [of his] various travels', and who was to be his guest over 'a glass of white wine'.[74] This contemporary, who appears in his letter to Scholem cloaked in mystery, is none other than Death.

The temptation to 'solve' all his existential problems in one go by suicide had followed Benjamin throughout his life. It seems he finally succumbed to it in 1940 as he fled before the Nazi henchmen. Now, eight years earlier (1932) he found himself in a similarly desperate situation. On top of his personal disappointments – Olga Parem, his friend for four years, had rejected his proposal of marriage during her visit to Ibiza (which Benjamin apparently took very badly)[75] – came problems concerning his profession. The larger projects he had worked on during the last few years were either unfinished or unpublished. The list of his works from this time includes a Goethe book that he had been commissioned to write by Insel (its rejection by Kippenberg a year before had already prompted thoughts of suicide),[76] his 'Arcades' project, a volume of *Collected Essays on Literature*, the anthology of letters entitled *Deutsche Menschen [German Men]* and 'a truly exceptional book about hashish'.[77]

With the exception of the anthology of letters, none of these works was to appear during Benjamin's life: all we have of what was probably his oldest project, which, it is assumed, originated in a book that he planned on the *New Melusine*, is little more than his statements of intent and the descriptions that he gave in his letters (it is also quite feasible, however, that he intended to include in it some of his numerous texts on Goethe – first and foremost his essay on *Elective Affinities*); the essays on literature, which should already have been published by Rowohlt during the mid/late 1920s, only appeared in a posthumous collection in 1969;[78] his notes on hashish were published in 1972;[79] and the fragments of his *magnum opus* on the Paris arcades only appeared in 1982.[80] Finally the utter bleakness of the political situation may well have precipitated him – confronted as he was by his complete lack of means, his general lack of affective ties and the unlikelihood that everything would turn out for the best after all – into such 'profound [spiritual] fatigue'[81] that he felt the time had come to make his final farewells. Just how serious he must have been is demonstrated by the fact that he even wrote his will, in which he placed his

Wilhelm Speyer.

A pretty strange fellow

Es geht.
Aber es ist auch danach!

EIN SCHAUSPIEL
IN DREI AKTEN
VON
WILHELM SPEYER

Drei Masken Verlag / München-Berlin

'The last time you came up with one of your constructive ideas about our society comedy, one of your *bons mots* made me drive suddenly into the railings at the side of the road from St Moritz to Tarasp. That *bon-mot* cost my car insurance three hundred marks.'[72] (*Es geht, aber es ist auch danach*, Speyer's play to which Benjamin made a major contribution)

personal effects in the hands of Scholem.[82] If Benjamin's desire to live did in fact regain the upper hand, this was not primarily because he found 'life' particularly 'worth living', but rather because he felt that 'suicide [was] not worth the trouble',[83] as he wrote in his text on 'fate and character', which was also written at a point in time when he was once again ready to end his life.

From Nice he continued his journey to Italy, in response to a request from his former classmate Wilhelm Speyer to give him some help and advice in writing the play (*Der große Advokat* [*The Great Advocate*]). It was the 'most financially rewarding' job that was available to him at the time – even if the 'term of payment' was quite 'protracted'. He eked out his existence, supporting himself solely 'on credit' and his 'cigarette money', in a place near Pisa whose name was highly appropriate to his humble circumstances:[84] Poveromo [poor man]. Speyer demanded little of his time, so despite (or perhaps precisely because of) his material hardship, he allowed himself the 'great luxury' after such a long time, 'of concentrating' once again 'on a single project': reworking his 'Berlin Chronicle' into the 'Berlin Childhood around 1900'. By September he felt that this work was more or less finished (although he was to claim the same thing on a number of occasions). This fact seemed to him like a shaft of light on the horizon, for despite his severed relation with the *Frankfurter Zeitung*, he hoped that he would shortly be able to have 'Berlin Childhood' published 'in book form, perhaps by Rowohlt'.[85]

Adorno's seminar

If Benjamin had travelled back to Berlin via Frankfurt, he would have been able to witness a seminar discussion whose very occurrence must have granted him some belated satisfaction: an academic exercise on *The Origin of German Tragic Drama* to which Theodor Wiesengrund (Adorno),[86] at that time *Privatdozent* in Frankfurt, had invited a group of select students. Benjamin and Wiesengrund had already become acquainted in the early 1920s in Frankfurt. Their personal relationship only intensified, though, towards the end of the decade. By the time that Benjamin had come into closer contact with the Institut für Sozialforschung during the 1930s, Adorno was already one of his staunch supporters.

The seminar was held within the same institution whose professors had ignominiously rejected Benjamin's study of the baroque as a *Habilitation* thesis barely seven years before.

For two whole semesters the students, together with their lecturer who was scarcely older than them, analysed this book according to all the rules of the art of academia. Several of these students were later to make their names as Germanists (Wilhelm Emrich, Oskar Koplowitz-Seidlin, Wolfgang Pfeiffer-Belli), sociologists (Heinz Maus), art historians (Hermann Usener), journalists (Peter von Haselberg, Kurt Mautz, Richard Plaut) or teachers (Kurt Bergel, who continued to teach at the Jewish School in Frankfurt until the end of the 1930s).[87]

They questioned the work's methodological premises,[88] laid bare its underlying historical-philosophical conception, and compared it with the theories of Wilhelm Dilthey and the 'young' Lukács (from his *Theory of the Novel* to his *History and Class Consciousness*). In addition, they worked their way through the traditions of philosophy, aesthetics and the history of literature in which the work stood. Central to their debates were such questions as the 'The problem of moral insight as a criterion for art critique', and 'How can a theory be developed without presupposing it?' Finally, they clarified such basic categories and concepts as 'the mythical' or 'archaic image', 'the victim', 'the idea', 'immanence', 'guilt', 'melancholy', 'allegory', and many more. In short, they examined the book from every possible angle.

By declining Wiesengrund's invitation to Frankfurt, Benjamin deprived himself of the opportunity to get to know a number of young students who had entirely grasped the novelty and revolutionary nature of his text, as well as its contemporary significance for both German studies and the whole of philosophy and political theory. 'The clear temporal succession of epochs and movements', the minutes of one of the seminars record,

'Furthermore, several restrained remarks I heard you make about Wiesengrund won't deter me from drawing your attention to his newly published *Kierkegaard*. I only know the book in excerpts thus far, but have already found much in it of merit. What's more, the author's case is so complex as to defy treatment in a letter. When I disclose that he is continuing to use my *Trauerspiel* book in his seminar for the second semester running, without indicating this in the course catalogue, then you have a small cameo that should serve for the moment.'[73]
(Theodor Wiesengrund Adorno, early 1930s)

is discarded as being of insufficient relevance, and replaced by a cognitive principle that originates from and depicts the concrete material itself. With that, the material and the interpretation of the material have merged to become one and have achieved objective self-representation, albeit while dispensing with an all-encompassing cognition that grasps the meaning of the totality of events. Since parts of the historical course of events intercept and rescue themselves – in the form of self-examining, fragmentary circular sectors – as moments of their own self, their claim to be the symbolic embodiment of any form of being founders, and, freed then from the emptiness of the universe, they enclasp the plasticity of the hic et nunc.[89]

'If we say that the idea represented in the *Trauerspiel* is fate, this concept will remain without content if we do not realise that implicitly contained within it is the whole field of problems that emerge in the historical material, such as, amongst others: history as natural history in its mythical sense, fate and tragedy, the concept of guilt in fate and tragedy, the earthbound nature of all baroque existence (theory of sovereignty, the capacity to make decisions, the sovereign as creature, the tyrant as martyr, the court as stage, the courtier as saint and schemer), honour, melancholy, properties, the realm of spirits and the haunted hours of night, allegory and symbol, allegorical dismemberment and much else. This means that the greater the differences are in the underlying material, the more extreme and irreconcilable the motives that come to light, the greater then the extremes immanent in the material, that are shown up in the material [. . .]' (From a seminar paper by Wilhelm Emrich, prepared for Adorno's seminar on *The Origin of German Tragic Drama*)

Zur Diskussion der kulturphilosophischen Idee bei Walter Benjamin

Wenn wir das Schicksal als die im Trauerspiel sich darstellende Idee bezeichnen, so bleibt dieser Begriff für uns leer, wenn wir uns nicht darüber im klaren sind, daß darin implicite der ganze Umkreis der Probleme steckt, der sich aus dem historischen Material erschließt wie unter anderen: Geschichte als Naturgeschichte im mythischen Bedeuten, Schicksal und Tragödie, Schuldbegriff im Schicksal und in der Tragödie, Kreatürlichkeit aller barocken Existenz (Theorie der Souveränität, Entschlußunfähigkeit, Souverän als Kreatur, Tyrann als Märtyrer, der Hof als Schau-Platz, der Höfling als Heiliger und Intrigant) die Ehre, Melancholie, das Requisit, Geisterstunde und Geisterwelt, Allegorie und Symbol, allegorische Zerstückelung und viele andere. Das besagt, daß je größer die Differenzen des zugrundeliegenden Materials sind, je extremer und unvereinbarer die zutage tretenden Motive, je größer also die materialimmanenten Extreme, die am Material aufgewiesen werden, um so deutlicher stellen sich in dieser Spannung der Extreme die Probleme selbst dar, d. h. die Extreme sind kontemplär. Sie stehen in einer durch das Kunstwerk festgelegten Beziehung zueinander. Stellt man sich die einzelnen Extreme mit den ihnen entsprechenden Entgegengesetzten ineinem Kreis angeordnet vor, so beschreibt dieser Umkreis den Bereich, in dem sich die Idee des Kunstwerks als Problem in der Konfiguration der Extreme zeigt. Die Idee sind die Extreme in ihrer Synthese.

Mit welchen Methoden arbeitet Benjamin aber, wenn er zu einer solchen Aufweisung geschichtlicher Ideen kommen will? Der Grundsatz von dem er dabei ausgeht ist der, daß die Wirklichkeit der Ratio nicht unmittelbar zugängig ist, daß sie keinen gemeinsamen Sinn haben (wie in der Wissenschaft). Das hat zur Voraussetzung, daß wir uns über die Fremdheit alles geschichtlich Gewordenen, seine Unerschließbarkeit im subjektiven Erleben und seine Unzugänglichkeit in der zweckintendierten Spontaneität des Verstandes klar sind.
Alles Geschichtliche ist als einmal geschaffene und gelebte Wirklichkeit Ausdruck. Ausdruck hat aber doppelte Bedeutung: einmal als zweckintendiertes Ergreifen der Wirklichkeit, das andere Mal als eine jenseits alleer bewußten Äußerung des Subjekts liegende notwendige Zuordnung von Objekten.

Moreover they did not confuse the concepts and the conceptions during their analysis of the work.

By fixing the supertemporal ideas of German idealism to one concrete historical locus, and by reducing the sole eternal idea to the multiplicity of coordinated ideas, yet while simultaneously cloaking it in the eternal light of ruins, Benjamin reveals himself to be an idealist with reservations, and his method as the history of thought in fragments.[90]

These students certainly did not make the mistake of viewing the author of the *The Origin of German Tragic Drama* as some kind of 'materialist'.

Sad Poem
You sit in your chair and write.
You grow more and more and more tired.
You go to bed at the right time,
You eat at the right time.
You have money,
A gift from the Dear Lord.
Life is wonderful!
Your heart beats louder and louder and louder,
The sea grows quieter and quieter and quieter
To the very depths.
San Antonio 11 April 1933[1]

Sad existence: Benjamin in exile

By the spring of 1932, Benjamin could no longer rule out the possibility that the fascists would seize power in Germany. His fears were prompted by the April elections for the Prussian Landtag, when the balance of power in the heart of Germany finally moved into line with the pattern that had already dominated the provinces for some time. The number of National Socialist delegates leapt from a mere 9 to 162, and Prime Minister Otto Braun's left and centre democratic coalition, in power since 1920, lost its majority. Closer analysis of the results shows that in Prussia, the brownshirts – who until then had benefited chiefly from the indecision of the middle classes – had made their first real advance on the front of the Communist and Social Democrat voters.[2] With that, the 'train into the Third Reich' was, as Benjamin saw it, now waiting at the platform, ready to depart. All that it needed was for those to board who, for all their opportunism, still shrank from openly and defiantly going over to the fascist camp.

In view of the events, Benjamin felt that it was the 'dictate of reason' to remain abroad for the time being (he was at that time on Ibiza) and await developments from a safe distance. He felt little inclination to 'honour' the 'inaugural celebrations of the Third Reich' with his presence,[3] for the brown mob that was unleashed during the ensuing months gave him a foretaste of the treatment that the future masters intended to bestow on him and his like, the Jews and nonconformists. In June the central government lifted a scarcely passed ban on 'all paramilitary organizations of the NSDAP, especially the Storm Troops [SA], the Elite Guard [SS] and all their staff and institutions' (this was the wording of the emergency decree issued by President

Hindenburg on 13 April 1932).[4] The devastating result was a hitherto unparalleled wave of political terror which swept across the land in the following weeks. The 'Altona Bloody Sunday' (seventeen people were killed on one day as fascists stormed this working-class district of Hamburg) was just the first of many climaxes to the ensuing escalation of violence. The dead and injured became everyday sights, and the newspapers were neither willing nor able to record all the clashes between the combatting left- and right-wing groups, the brawls at public assemblies, the harassment and persecution, the assaults on the open streets and the manifestations of anti-Semitism.

It is one of the ironies of fate that in the end, Benjamin was spared virtually none of the 'inaugural celebrations' with which the Nazis heralded the beginning of a 'new' – of their – era (torch-light processions after Hitler's appointment as Chancellor, the Reichstag fire, new 'elections', the Act of Enablement, book-burnings, etc.). He returned to Berlin in November 1932, and so became not only an eye-witness to the first systematic acts of persecution of political opponents with which the new lords introduced themselves, but also one of their victims. He scarcely dared to step outside his own four walls, as he informed Noeggerath who was still in Spain, asking him at the same time whether he could take refuge once more in his house on Ibiza.[5]

The fate of his closer friends and acquaintances was a clear warning to him. The majority of them had disappeared in the night of 27 to 28 February 1933, during the Reichstag fire: a few of them (such as Ernst Schoen[6] and Fritz Fraenkel) into the hastily erected concentration camps and torture chambers of the SA, the rest (including Bloch, Brecht, Brentano, Kracauer, Speyer and Wolfskehl), who had read the writing on the wall, by taking immediate flight.

However, it was not this open and direct harassment alone that forced Benjamin into exile. This merely speeded the process. Equally if not more important was the fact that he no longer saw any possibility of continuing his journalistic activities in Germany. 'The air is hardly fit to breathe any more', he wrote to his friend Scholem, adding with a touch of gallows humour that this fact 'of course loses significance as one is being strangled anyway. This above all economically'.[7] The Nazis had assumed control over the radio so quickly and completely that he had no further chance to work in this realm. Even his radio play *Lichtenberg*, which he had completed after an intensive study of the writings of Georg Christoph Lichtenberg,[8] came to

nothing: although he had long since received his fee, it was never broadcast. And his second main source of income, the *Frankfurter Zeitung*, also adopted an initial policy of 'wait and see'. The publication of his works was suspended indefinitely.[9] So it was above all these aspects of a rapidly enforced process of bringing cultural life into line that persuaded Benjamin to 'transform [his] ill-defined wishes to leave Germany into a hard and fast decision'.[10]

Benjamin left the country of his birth once and for all in the middle of March.[11] The last person that he met on German soil was the art historian and contributor to the *Frankfurter Zeitung*, Carl Linfert. He spoke briefly with him while stopping off at Cologne Central Station.[12] From 19 March he lived in Paris, where he met up once again with 'old acquaintances, local ones and quite a few from Berlin'.[13] At first he stayed in the Hotel Istria at 29, rue Campagne-Première.[14] An approximate idea of what this realization of salvation meant to him can be interpreted from the poem at the start of this chapter, which he composed directly after his escape. Naturally the phrase about a wonderful life is purely sarcastic, for he was all too aware of what awaited him in the exile he had now begun.

'The terror against every attitude or manner of expression that does not fully conform to the official one has reached virtually insurpassable heights. Under such conditions, the utmost political reserve, such as I have long and with good reason practised, may protect the person in question from systematic persecution, but not from starvation.'[74] (Jews being expelled from Germany after 1933)

Paris was merely an initial stop-off point for him. By 4 April he was already setting off to Spain, together with Jean Selz and his wife. Benjamin had become more closely acquainted with Selz during his stay on Ibiza the year before, and in 1933 they co-translated a number of sections from 'Berlin Childhood' into French.[15] His destination was once again Ibiza, which he reached with his companions on approximately 10 April, after also spending several days in Barcelona. The events in Germany even followed him to these shores, although less in the form of emigrants residing there, than in that of a 'villa-building petty bourgeois type' who not only slowly 'set the tone and provided the scandal', but who also consisted of a considerable 'percentage of Nazis'.

But such nuisances were restricted to the largest town on the island, San Antonio. On the other side of the island, in the capital Ibiza, 'one [could] live with appreciably more dignity'. But this life was bought at the cost of 'strict isolation'.[16] Possessing just the minimum of means for day-to-day life and roaming around all over the place alone: for Benjamin this kind of existence had almost become the norm at that time. And if one thinks of his years of 'exile' in Switzerland, 1917–20, or his stay of several months on Capri in 1924, it seems that this sort of restriction was quite indispensable for him in order to reflect upon new situations in life. There can be no doubt that he was now in just such a new situation, and he entertained no illusions about his own fate or Germany's political future.

Unlike many others across the whole political spectrum, at no time did Benjamin succumb to the delusion that fascism was just some passing phantasm. On the contrary, he expected to remain in exile for a long time, if not forever. And he organized his affairs accordingly, not so much with regard to his personal circumstances (whose enduringly provisional nature was not least determined by his extremely limited financial means), but rather in the political and literary sense. Whether he was writing a retrospective or a prognosis, or was taking stock of the present, the focal points of his first works during the months directly after leaving Germany were always his new circumstances in life and the consequences that they were having for his literary activities.

When Benjamin wrote later in a *curriculum vitae* that his intellectual development was divided 'quite naturally into the periods before and after 1933',[17] he was not doing this merely for tactical reasons. The statement was justified in that he had made every effort at the beginning of his exile to draw a dividing line between what he had already written and what he was still to write, but it does not in any way suggest a turnaround in his intellectual development. His intellectual make-up was already firmly shaped. Divergences from this intellectual mould, as far as can be discerned from his writings, merely reflected the learning processes engendered by his constantly changing impressions and experiences. Hence the remark should be taken to mean that he had for the last time begun to thoroughly sort through the boxroom of his past experiences.

Consequently the majority of the work he produced during the months after his flight consists of retrospective comment- aries: pieces that accompany him once again through the stages of his childhood and youth (his memories of a 'Berlin Childhood around 1900'), or centre on his relationship with Judaism (the puzzling text 'Agesilaus Santander', dedicated to 'B', the young Dutch painter Toet Blaupot ten Cate, with whom Benjamin fell in love on Ibiza),[18] and a last 'Look Back at Stefan George', an article published under the pseudonym K. A. Stempflinger, which was commissioned by the *Frankfurter Zeitung*.[19]

Toet Blaupot ten Cate.

Benjamin took the opportunity of reviewing a new George monograph to raise personal matters, to reflect on his relation- ship with this author, which had never been free of a certain ambivalence. Just how important it was to him to clarify his stance regarding George can also be seen by the fact that he not only drew the attention of his friends and acquaintances (Scholem, Gretel Karplus and Jula Cohn, among others) expressly (and sometimes repeatedly) to the work on its appearance, but he also requested their opinions on it. (Only Jula Cohn really complied with this wish, by expressing her dis- appointment at this highly personal testimony.)

Benjamin's George retrospective is just one piece in the mosaic of an almost life-long appraisal of the poet which until 1933 had largely taken the form of a polemic against his supporters and 'disciples' (Gundolf, Kommerell).[20] Naturally he knew the 'great master', and had seen and heard him during his stays in Heidelberg in the early 1920s. He could 'not count up the hours' he had spent 'in the castle grounds' of Heidelberg, 'reading on a bench and waiting for the moment when [George] would pass by'. But that was at a time when the 'decisive emotional impact' of George's work had 'long since been reached'.

It would be quite fair to doubt whether this 'retrospective glance' in 1933 gave an exhaustive answer to the question of the influence of George's work on his life. (And it was precisely this that Jula Radt criticized in the short piece: its indecisiveness, Benjamin's 'love–hate' relationship which the work expressed, its inopportune 'pathos'.)[21] But that was not Benjamin's intention. Rather he simply wanted to endow his relationship with George with a new accentuation. With time he 'had gained a new ear for [the] voice [of this] poetry', and without wishing in the least to diminish George's historical and literary importance, from now on he turned his critical attention to the ideological components of his poetry. During the First World War young people had found in it a 'song of consolation' for all the injustice they were suffering. Now he perceived in its seductiveness above all the sounds of catastrophe and a craving for death.

Benjamin had never really been able to break with the roots of his thinking, Hölderlin and George, and for this reason the 'retrospective' states that for him George's influence had always been linked with the 'poem in its most vital sense'.[22] At the same time he was unable to ignore the new constellation in which historical events had placed George's work. The sentence 'If ever God has smitten a prophet by fulfilling his prophecies, then this is the case with George'[23] shows the magnitude of the difference which existed between Benjamin's previous attitude and his present one.

Benjamin's feelings about literary Germany after the fascist seizure of power were very clearly expressed in his review 'Deutsch in Norwegen' [German in Norway], a masterpiece in the art of 'writing between the lines'. A seemingly casual remark on his inability to comprehend how reading material for secondary schools could include such authors as Hermann Sudermann, Gustav Frenssen or Walter Bloem as representatives of 'German prose writers', requires little comment[24] – assuming that one knows what these authors stood for in the history of German literature: reactionary regional art (Sudermann's *Frau Sorge*, published in 1887) and the nationalist-racist novel. The works of Frenssen (especially his novel *Jörn Uhl*) and Bloem (*Volk wider Volk*, published in 1912) were viewed by the new rulers as models of a truly 'national' mentality. (In addition, Frenssen had given public support to the regime from a prominent position: after the expulsion of Alfred Döblin, Ricarda Huch, Georg Kaiser, Franz Werfel and the brothers Heinrich and Thomas Mann from the literary section of the Prussian Academy of Arts, he had become one of its leading members.) Seen in this light, the review's meaning was more than clear, even in its opening remarks: 'It is all too rare that one comes across compelling

(BALEARES) Portal nuevo — Le Portique moderne Foto, V. Ve's
The modern Porch

'Perhaps I can find out something of importance from you about the movements among the emigrants.'[75] (From Benjamin's postcard collection: Ibiza)

evidence of the impression left by one's own people on the minds of another people. This German reader for Norwegian secondary schools is just such a piece of evidence.'[25] Indeed, in linguistic, biographical and political terms, and even in its jargon, the work was modelled completely as dictated by the new circumstances.

Finally, Benjamin's views on the part that writing had now to play can be seen in his short 'Review of 150 years of German Education' which was published in March 1934 in the *Frankfurter Zeitung*. 'To sketch out the fate of the humanist idea of education throughout the changes in its social relativity': this may at first seem to be a rather vague 'programme'. But when it is emphasized that 'the aesthetic idea of life' is subject to 'constrictions', and that the 'task' of current writing is 'to draw attention to these',[26] the programme becomes clear.

Once in Ibiza, Benjamin tried to re-establish his network of contacts. The Balearic Islands, remote from Europe's centres of culture, were not exactly the ideal place for this, and his first results were accordingly disheartening. He failed to establish any new publishing contacts, despite the efforts made by his former wife Dora Kellner. (She wanted to negotiate on his behalf with the publishing house Ullstein,[27] but its Jewish proprietors had already been plunged into a hopeless struggle for survival.)[28] Nor at first did he receive any better news from Paris. *Die Aktion*, an anti-fascist organ founded by Rudolf Leonhard and Maximilian Scheer, had already changed owners even before Benjamin had managed to establish contact. (His friend Alfred Kurella had drawn his attention to the periodical, which would in any case no longer have been an acceptable forum for Benjamin, as its new

Bertolt Brecht: 'To the
Fighters in the Concentration
Camps'

You who can hardly be
   reached
Buried in the
   concentration camps
Cut off from every human
   word
Subjected to brutalities
Beaten down but
Not confuted
Vanished but
Not forgotten!

Little as we hear about you,
   we still hear you are
Incorrigible.
Unteachable, they say, in your
   commitment to the
   proletarian cause
Unshakably persuaded that
   there are still in Germany
Two kinds of people,
   exploiters and exploited
And that the class struggle
   alone
Can liberate the masses in
   cities and countryside from
   their misery.
Not by beatings, we hear, nor
   by hanging can you
Be brought to the point of
   saying that
Nowadays twice two is five.

So you are
Vanished but
Not forgotten
Beaten down but
Never confuted
Along with all those
   incorrigibly fighting
Unteachably set on the truth
Now and forever the true
Leaders of Germany. [76]
(Georg Benjamin during the
mid-1930s)

proprietors had set about turning it into a propaganda magazine for French imperialist policies.)[29] Much the same applied to the magazine *Das blaue Heft*. Benjamin had a 'personal contact' there and so 'offered the editors two pieces', without previously having 'any real knowledge' about the periodical or (more importantly) its editors.[30] The magazine was at that time run by the confidence-trickster Joe Lherman (notorious for his 1929 staging of Musil's *Enthusiasts* and the scandal that ensued) and was also shortly to fold under his aegis.[31] Consequently, Benjamin's contributions remained unpublished (unfortunately his correspondence does not reveal which articles they were). On top of all these difficulties came the fact that Benjamin felt, at the beginning of his exile, that he must exercise the greatest of restraint in his public activities out of consideration for his relatives still living in Germany: his son who was living with his ex-wife, and above all his brother Georg.[32]

Georg Benjamin was taken into 'protective' custody by the Prussian police on 8 April 1933. In contrast to many of his comrades from the Communist Party, who were immediately sent to one of the concentration camps run by the SA or SS, he had the 'fortune' of being imprisoned in the police jail at Alexanderplatz and later in Plötzensee 'prison'.[33] Consequently he was spared the worst forms of maltreatment for the time being.[34] He only became subject to this in the summer, when he was sent to Sonnenburg concentration camp, run under the regime of the infamous SS platoon leader Heinz Adrian (sentenced to death in Schwerin, 1948) and the scarcely less feared SA unit Horst Wessel. Among the thousand or so 'detainees', Georg Benjamin found himself back in the company of the anarchist writer Erich Mühsam, the journalist Carl von Ossietzky and the famous lawyer Hans Litten.[35]

Georg was in certain respects Walter's political alter ego. They had set out together in the Youth Movement, but then their ideological paths had separated. The younger brother's had first led him to support the 'social alliances' which had (religious) socialist leanings, while he was studying at the universities of Marburg and Berlin, then to the Independent German Socialist Party (a left-wing spin-off of the Social Democrats, the SPD), and finally to the Communist Party, which he had already joined in 1922/3. But their personal relationship remained, according to their autobiographical writings, largely unclouded. Georg had doubtlessly encouraged his older brother in his intentions to join the German Communist Party during the latter part of the 1920s, but without being insistent. On the contrary, he 'worked on' his brother in a more discreet manner which seemed to promise more success: by presenting him with books which were fairly unambiguous in their content (in 1925, for example, he gave Walter the 'first German anthology of Lenin's writings' for his birthday).[36]

Georg Benjamin was released from Sonnenburg concentration camp around Christmas time in 1933. The following spring he went on a trip to Switzerland and the lakes of northern Italy, and a year later he visited the village Klein-Aupa on the Czechoslovakian side of the Sudeten. But on neither occasion did he think of fleeing fascist Germany. Instead he at once resumed his illegal work for the Communist regional committee in Berlin, as his brother had foreseen upon his release.[37] He worked for the underground press, translating English, French and Russian articles about the political situation in Germany, about the Popular Front in France and Spain, and about the 7th World Congress of the Communist International in July 1935.[38] In addition, between April and August 1934 he edited and produced the illegal Newsletter of the *Regional Committee of the Communist Party, Berlin–Brandenburg*, and to this end gathered reports on the mood among the workers in the factories and at their meeting places.[39] However, the translation of a lengthy article by Georgi Dimitrov from *Pravda* proved to be his undoing. The manuscript was found in the possession of a Communist student named Margarete Stern. From her the Gestapo traced the text back to Georg Benjamin, who as a result was taken to the notorious Columbia-Haus police station on Potsdamer Platz in May. Five months later he was sentenced to six years in jail. After completing his sentence he was sent to the Wuhlheide Reform Camp in the east of Berlin, and from there to Mauthausen concentration camp, where he died on 26 August 1942. According to official records, he committed 'suicide by touching the power line' connected to the fence surrounding the camp;[40] in reality he was driven to his death by his fascist torturers. His thoughts were with his brother right up to the end of his life,[41] and he had remained in contact with him throughout his years of imprisonment (as far as conditions in the concentration camp had allowed).

His lack of journalistic activity considerably worsened Benjamin's already deficient economic situation. Eventually he had no alternative but to begin to part with the more valuable items of his library. An old acquaintance of his, Thankmar von

Delicate sketches

Münchhausen, assisted him in selling off these bibliophilic rarities. Benjamin used this period of relative inactivity to work on pieces that were either not intended for publication (for example the aforementioned text 'Agesilaus Santander'), or would not be published in the foreseeable future. Among the latter was a crime novel which he only wished to write if he felt more or less certain that it would turn out a success. In addition there were his childhood reminiscences which he had 'in point of fact already' finished.[42] The circumstances which seemed to have made it impossible to find a publisher for his 'Berlin Childhood around 1900' allowed it to ripen in a way that Benjamin found 'not disagreeable'. He translated a number of these reminiscences into French (with the help of Jean Selz on Ibiza), and in doing so he at last got to know the texts 'thoroughly',[43] which was to help him when he later abridged them. (In the subsequent versions he deleted more and more of the purely autobiographical references.)

Benjamin returned to Paris in October of that year, seriously ill. He had caught malaria on Ibiza, and the first heavy bouts of fever had already set in on the day of his departure. This last link in a chain of bleak experiences was finally to rob him of 'what [was] left of [his] no-longer unlimited power of initiative'.[44] Desperation, destitution, and above all uncertainty about his future, drove him into a state of deep resignation. His chances of establishing himself as an author in French were extremely slim, as he fully realized. For despite his extensive

'Benjamin's physical stoutness and the rather German heaviness he presented were in strong contrast to the agility of his mind, which so often made his eyes sparkle behind his glasses. I can see him in a small photograph I saved, with his prematurely grey, closely cropped hair (he was forty years old at the time), his slightly Jewish profile and black moustache, sitting on a deck chair on the front porch of my house, in his usual posture: face leaned forward, chin held in his right hand. I don't think I have ever seen him think without holding his chin, unless he was carrying in his hand the large curved pipe with the wide bowl he was so fond of and which in a way resembled him.'[77] (Walter Benjamin with the Selzs on Ibiza)

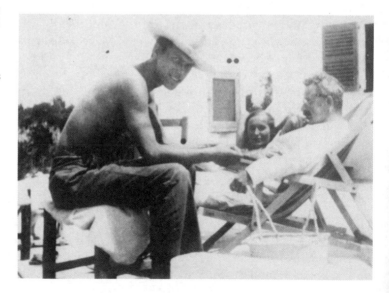

210

education and interests, he evidently felt unable to make effective use of his talents as a writer in this way, although he did manage this in his later works (albeit with the help of French friends).[45] Moreover, he had little desire to 'dance attendance on the gutter press'. He would 'prefer any [other] job', regardless of 'how subaltern', as he wrote to Scholem, as long as it fell within his intellectual field. (He hoped to earn a part of his living by doing 'part-time bibliographical [or] library work'.)[46]

Following his return to Paris, Benjamin made a great effort to find a publisher for his 'Berlin Childhood', and he even turned to Hermann Hesse (among others) for help. This was in January 1934. Hesse had been one of the few people to show any increased interest in Benjamin's literary talent when *One-Way Street* was published.[47] And how well he had predicted Hesse's opinion about his childhood reminiscences was shown in the reply that he received in February:

Dear Mr Benjamin, My wife has read your manuscript to me and as we came to the end, she said, in a tone of regret: 'What a shame, I would have loved to have read a lot more.' I greatly enjoyed these delicate, accomplished, concisely formulated sketches, and I especially liked the Otter and the Little Hunchback.[48]

Sketch of Benjamin by Jean Selz.

It is true that Hesse rarely made negative judgements about the works of others, at least in public, but these remarks, which for Benjamin made up for the complete 'indifference' that the 'literary coterie' had shown towards the short volume,[49] were meant quite sincerely. Almost twenty years later, he discussed 'Berlin Childhood' and its author once again in the Zurich

'Esteemed Mr Benjamin, At the time you wrote & sent your manuscript to me I was undergoing lengthy treatment by my opthalmologist in Bavaria and I have just now returned home. So, at the moment I am only able to write to say that I have received your manuscript, to thank you & to ask for your patience because my impaired vision means that I have difficulty keeping up with all that I must read. But I look forward to reading what you have sent me, & will then write to you again. Best wishes H. Hesse' (Hesse to Benjamin, 28 February 1934)[78]

211

weekly *Weltwoche*, saying that 'a real poet' was revealed in these 'exceedingly graceful, virtuously playful' reminiscences, 'which are all sketched out with the most careful hand and lightly hued as if with watercolours'.[50] (Incidentally, this is one of the few instances in which Benjamin was termed a poet by a man; otherwise it seems that only women – above all Charlotte Wolff, Asja Lacis and Hannah Arendt, each of whom played an important role in his life – recognized this aspect of his work.)

Sadly, Hesse was unable to provide any help for 'Berlin Childhood'. Benjamin did not respond to his proposal about contacting his friend Richard Bermann at the publishers S. Fischer on Benjamin's behalf. He had already turned to Klaus Mann, whom Hesse likewise suggested, without receiving any offers, other than that *Die Sammlung* might conceivably print those parts of the childhood reminiscences that had not yet been published.[51] At the end of their brief correspondence, Benjamin felt able to at last free Hesse from the 'obligations' he had taken on because he had entered into promising negotiations with the publisher Erich Reiss in Berlin. But these too had a disappointing outcome: Reiss also failed to publish the work, and in the end it only appeared in its entirety in 1950.

A look at Benjamin's publications between 1933 and 1940 might create the impression that he had little difficulty in placing his work in the local and foreign press during his years of exile. His articles were published in Germany right up to the mid-1930s (the last, a review of Hermann Schneider's Schiller monograph, appeared in June 1935).[52] Naturally this was only possible in periodicals which had for the time being managed to escape the general standardization of culture under the Nazis (such as the *Vossische Zeitung*, which had the richest tradition of all Berlin's newspapers, and which printed his contributions until September 1933), or on whose editorial staff some of his close friends still occupied influential positions (such as the *Kölnische Zeitung*, on which his friend Max Rychner worked), or which had assumed a special position in the press world, with regard to the new political circumstances (such as the *Jüdische Rundschau [Jewish Review]* or the 'alibi for freedom of expression' in fascist Germany, the *Frankfurter Zeitung*).

The only compromise that Benjamin had to make was to publish the greater part of his articles under pseudonyms (Detlef Holz, K. A. Stempflinger, C. Conrad) or even anonymously. The list of publications where Benjamin's writings appeared is quite considerable, when one adds to it the newspapers and journals that were published by the exile and foreign press.

These range from the *Wort* in Moscow to the *Weltbühne* and the political-cultural bi-monthly *Maß und Wert* edited by Thomas Mann, from the Swiss journal *Der öffentliche Dienst* to the French *Cahiers du Sud*, and from the *Neue Zürcher Zeitung* to the *Prager Tagblatt*, to name just a few.

But if one takes a closer look at the way that these articles came to be published, at the fees he received for them, or indeed at the backgrounds of the periodicals themselves, and moreover at the numerous failures that Benjamin experienced in trying to find new outlets for his work, this produces a very different, and an almost gloomy picture. The majority of the articles – a few cultural-political and theoretical essays, and above all reviews and short prose texts – remained one-off publications which almost never led to regular work.[53] A large number of the periodicals were fairly short-lived and existed constantly on the brink of financial ruin. In many cases, the fees they paid (if they paid any) were scarcely worth the paper the articles were written on. (Benjamin experienced this a number of times, such as with Willy Haas in his attempt to revive his literary review in Prague,[54] and with the *Schweizer Zeitung am Sonntag* edited by his friend Fritz Lieb.)[55]

Finally, if one also considers Benjamin's vain attempts to establish contact with the editors of French periodicals (including the Communist *Monde* for which he was supposed to write an article about Baron Haussmann, and the *Nouvelle revue française*),[56] it can only be concluded that numerous literary strategies which Benjamin associated with writing were dissipated as his exile writings became hopelessly dispersed. The articles he published during these years were written purely in order to survive, and he paid little heed to the cultural or political line of the journals in question. On just one occasion did he feel that he could afford the luxury of attaching certain conditions to the publication of a work – which, with regard to his financial situation, was to have quite dire consequences.

In spring 1934 Benjamin sent a number of manuscripts to Klaus Mann, the editor of the Amsterdam-based magazine *Die Sammlung*. Given Benjamin's many scornful comments about this publication and its editors (behind Klaus Mann was his uncle, Heinrich Mann), this decision might seem rather surprising. Yet, upon consideration of the actual texts he sent and the conditions that he attached to their publication, it seems reasonable to assume that he viewed this simply as an experiment to see how the leading figures of German exile literature would react to a little provocation. Indeed, one of

'Do you know under what sign the literary emigrés are beginning to gather within the framework of an Amsterdam-based periodical? Well, precisely under the sign they deserve the most, namely, with Klaus Mann as editor-in-chief. His uncle opens the first issue with a polemic against the regime, so feeble that it is provocative. I can even see the day approaching when I will attempt to have myself published in these surroundings.'[79] (Letter to Klaus Mann, 9 July 1934)

the pieces he submitted, a talk he had held on the 'Author as Producer',[57] could only have enraged Klaus and Heinrich Mann. The talk openly denounced a standpoint that had been adopted as the programme, as it were, of *Die Sammlung*. In the preface to the first issue, the editor had called, in the most (politically) naive manner, for the 'forces of willpower' to mobilize themselves against fascism. He wanted to counter 'barbarism' with the 'will to the intellect'. The 'will to attain elevated, subtle and binding processes of the mind' was going to halt the goose-step, the 'march of the grand parade', just as the 'will to reason' would put an end to the 'hysterical brutality' and 'a brazenly programmatic "anti-humanism"'.[58] Benjamin responded to this belief in the miraculous power of the written and conceived word – which may have sparked onerous memories of his days with the Youth Movement – with remarks based, partially word for word, on ideas contained in a couple of short works that he had written a number of years before. In his polemic against Kurt Hiller in 1932 he had described the champions of logocracy, of the 'rule of the intellect', as politically blind if not downright dangerous. The potential danger of this modern form of 'quixoticism' had now manifested itself in the fascist seizure of power: what 'today is still agreeable may tomorrow be detrimental', he wrote at the end of his critique of the activist creed.[59]

It appeared detrimental to him in that mere entreaties to humanism and intellectualism were anything but a proven or adequate weapon against political opponents armed with tanks and machine-guns. For any author in these times, a deeper 'comprehension of his dependent social position, of his technical means, and of his political tasks' was now indispensable. An author who felt 'his solidarity with the proletariat only ideologically and not as a producer' could not help but serve counter-revolutionary interests.

'The intellectual attitude which makes itself felt in the name of fascism must disappear': here Benjamin was still in agreement with his antagonists, despite the differences in their ideologies. But this was the full extent of their agreement. 'The intellectual attitude', he believed, that opposes the totalitarian regime 'trusting to its own miraculous power will [also] disappear' – the words 'have to' are absent from this sentence, but the intended appellative character is none the less clear. 'For the revolutionary struggle' will not be 'between capitalism and the intellect, but between capitalism and the proletariat'.[60]

Such dogmatically phrased sentences did little to encourage the reader's or listener's willing reception of his essay, particularly among those at whom it was actually directed. They flatly rejected the piece, and so it remained unprinted. Benjamin's questioning of the autonomy of the writer and artist with respect to the political circumstances was far too vehement.

The only periodical during his years of exile that did offer him certain security in the form of ongoing publication of his articles was the *Zeitschrift für Sozialforschung*. A number of those working at the Institute for Social Research (founded in 1922) had known Benjamin since the early 1920s. He had once met Adorno and Horkheimer at the philosophy department of Frankfurt University when he had attempted to gain his *Habilitation* there, although he only established a 'closer personal relationship'[61] with Horkheimer during his exile. Presumably this was connected with the dubious (or perhaps all too transparent) part that Horkheimer had played in the rejection of his *Habilitation* thesis on *The Origin of German Tragic Drama*. Horkheimer had maintained at the time that he had no better understood the work than the person who wrote the report on it, the Frankfurt Professor Hans Cornelius.[62] Benjamin also first became acquainted with Friedrich Pollock, the 'chief of finance' at the Institute for Social Research, during the 1930s – during their frequent and detailed discussions in Paris, which were mainly concerned with the technical problems of his work on the *Zeitschrift für Sozialforschung*.

While the exiled party-political (Communist) left scarcely gave him any real opportunity to dedicate himself and his creative energies to the movement, Benjamin was equally unsuccessful in making the Institute for Social Research his political home. This is clearly demonstrated by the fact that hardly any of his articles which were published by the institute's journal appeared as they had originally been written. The changes which were made under the guise of suggestions for improvement were already implemented in the first of Benjamin's essays to be published in the *Zeitschrift für Sozialforschung*, 'Zum gegenwärtigen gesell-schaftlichen Standort des französischen Schriftstellers' [On the Current Social Situation of the French Writer], which appeared in March 1934.[63] In a letter written at the time, Benjamin compared the editors' suggested changes with the rising tide of fascism: 'Fascism [was] making great strides outside Germany as well.' He could 'also [tell] how things [stood] in Switzerland' (the Institute was based at the time both in Geneva and New York) 'from certain editorial emendations that the *Zeitschrift für Sozialforschung* proposes for my essay'.[64] The comparison may seem unfair, indeed offensive, in view of the political background of the journal's editors. But it is significant that one of, if not the, most disappointing of Benjamin's experiences with regard to political developments in Germany, consisted of witnessing just how willing intellectuals were to embrace uniformity, and that the programme of cultural standardization could therefore be enforced without recourse to threats of sanctions.

Under Brecht's thatched roof

Thanks to a monthly allowance from the Institute for Social Research, Benjamin was finally able to travel to Denmark in the summer of 1934, to take up the invitation which Brecht had extended to him in December 1933, and which he had constantly been postponing because he did not wish to be financially dependent on his friend.[65] Through mutual experiments and experiences, his relationship with Brecht had become so deep-rooted that, in a letter to Kitty Steinschneider-Marx, a friend of Scholem (who for his part was not favourably disposed towards the playwright), he could boast that his 'approval of Brecht's production' constituted 'one of the most important and most defensible points of [his] entire position'.[66] Thus it was no coincidence that the house in Skovbostrand near Svendborg (where he was also to relocate his library, which he had initially left in Berlin) became one of his points of orientation during the chaos of exile. Benjamin stayed there a total of three times: from June to October 1934, and then during the summers of 1936 and 1938.

His stays on Fyn – the green oasis, as it were, amidst the grey panorama of emigration – always seemed 'tantamount to monastic confinement'.[67] The only diversions offered by the life there were games of chess that he played with Brecht, and a radio which in 1934 gave him an acoustic introduction to Hitler. A 'Reichstag speech'[68] by the *Führer* prompted him to write a short piece which anticipated Chaplin's role as the 'Great Dictator' in the film of the same name in 1940:

Hitler's diminished masculinity – comparable with the feminine touch of the poverty-stricken, as portrayed by Chaplin
so much glitter surrounding so much shabbiness
The poor devil wants to be taken seriously, so he promptly lets all Hell loose
Chaplin's compliancy can be seen by all, Hitler's only by his patron
Chaplin shows the comedy of Hitler's seriousness; when he plays the fine gentleman we know just what is going on in the Führer
Chaplin has become the greatest of comedians because he has incorporated his contemporaries' deepest horrors
The fashionable ideal set by Hitler is not that of the army but rather of the distinguished gentleman, the feudal emblems of dominion are out of vogue; all that remains are gentlemen's fashions. And Chaplin adheres to gentlemen's fashions. He does so in order to take this class of gentlemen at their word. His cane is the staff around which the parasite coils (the tramp is just as good a leech as the gent) and his bowler hat, which no longer has any fixed spot on his head, betrays the fact that the reign of the bourgeoisie is tottering.[69]

But his time in Skovbostrand was not only spent playing chess and listening to the radio, but also in productive polemics. The first manifestation of this was when Benjamin wrote an essay

'Despite the monotony of my daily routine, I am not leading an unsociable life; I spend pleasant hours with Brecht and have great fun with Weigel's two children. Apart from which, the current events in the world provide a substantial distraction. It is easy to follow them here by means of the radio; but we are also not completely cut off from the periodicals, a fact which this evening allowed me to see a copy of *Der Stürmer* for the first time.'[80] (From Benjamin's postcard collection: Svendborg)

Svendborg. Christiansmøllen

on the tenth anniversary of Kafka's death. Brecht read the manuscript and flatly rejected it.

In his opinion, it was not permissible to keep focussing his observations on the question 'of the essence' while overlooking all other contexts, social and personal – in short, to take the work 'as something that has been developed for its own ends'. In political terms, an approach of this kind could – according to Brecht – only 'encourage Jewish fascism'.[70]

Benjamin's essay marks the most intense point of his involvement with Kafka's writing, which had begun with a short,

'Whenever Benjamin and Brecht met up in Denmark, there was immediately an atmosphere of familiarity between them. Brecht had an immense liking for Benjamin, he really loved him. I think they could understand each other even without speaking. They would play chess without saying a word, but when they got up it was as if they had finished a conversation.'[81] (Brecht's house on Fyn)

esoteric text written in 1927 entitled 'Idee eines Mysteriums' [Idea for a Mystery Play].[71] The first of his reflections about Kafka to be published appeared in 1929 under the title 'Kavaliersmoral' [High-handed Morals] in *Die Literarische Welt*.[72] In 1931 he reviewed Kafka's posthumously published novella *The Great Wall of China* on the radio.[73] If one considers that the production of this thoroughly mystical article of 1934 coincided with the writing of his 'Author' essay and the resumption of work on his 'Arcades' project, it becomes clear just how little the intimate-esoteric side of Benjamin's thinking yielded to the political-social side, even during this 'Marxist phase'.

Benjamin's Kafka essay reveals a number of thinly veiled autobiographical traits. In Kafka's world, which is just 'a bad mood of God', hope only seems to be granted to 'the unfinished and the bunglers', those who have escaped 'from the family circle', the socially uprooted.[74] And there can be no doubt that Benjamin viewed himself during these years as a failure in life. In a long, elucidatory letter to Scholem in 1938, in which he distanced himself from the 'apologetic character' of his Kafka essay, he underlined his identification with the writer by stating that it is only possible to grasp the whole beauty of Kafka by considering that he was in fact 'a failure'.[75] But these autobiographical echoes become most clear in his comment that Kafka's work is comparable to 'an ellipse with foci that lie far apart and are determined on the one hand by mystical experience . . . and on the other by the experience of the modern city-dweller'.[76]

219

'I have landed, it seems, for a while in a harbour town which is very quiet, and about which there is little to say.'[82] (From Benjamin's postcard collection: San Remo)

'Even in Nice I managed to avoid German literature.'[83] (From Benjamin's postcard collection: Nice)

In the autumn of 1934 Benjamin travelled to San Remo – after stopping off briefly in Paris – to the boarding house that his divorced wife Dora had purchased. 'I would be terribly pleased if you could come', she had written to him in July.[77] He was to stay at her 'Villa Verde' quite often, before she went into exile in London.[78]

Benjamin was not among the almost one hundred guests who were invited to the First International Writers' Congress that was held in Paris between 21 and 25 June 1935, with the aim of uniting their energies into a popular front in the struggle against the fascist dictatorship and its cultural obscurantism. He did, however, attend the majority of the lectures and discussions, unfortunately with little personal gain. 'Outwardly'

the congress presented 'little to be pleased about', he wrote to Horkheimer, adding, despite the latter's reserved attitude towards the Communist Party: 'but it may [have the] result that its office, which has now been set up permanently and in which the Russians have assumed an important position, will occasionally be able to provide some useful intervention'.[79] The 'most pleasing, almost the only pleasing thing' about it for Benjamin was the fact that he had the renewed opportunity to see his friend Brecht, who attended the congress to considerably more advantage: 'for years' he had been 'carrying around the plan for a long satirical novel about intellectuals', and the congress proved to be a real goldmine of material for him.[80]

Shortly after the Paris congress, and probably stimulated by it, Benjamin devoted himself to an essay that developed several trains of thought contained in his 'Author' essay, but that also progressed beyond them in that he was now attempting to 'advance the direction of a materialistic theory of art'.[81] The essay in question was 'The Work of Art in the Age of Mechanical Reproduction' which first appeared in Pierre Klossowski's French translation in the May 1936 issue of the *Zeitschrift für Sozialforschung*. In this piece of work which was to become the most famous of his essays, Benjamin set himself the task of studying the impact of the technology of modern methods

'We have just saved culture. It took a total of 4 (four) days, during which we decided that it is better to sacrifice everything than to let culture be destroyed. If necessary, we are ready to sacrifice 10–20 million people to this end. Thankfully enough people felt ready to assume the responsibility. Fascism was condemned by all on account of its 'wanton' atrocities.'[84] (International Writers Congress. Seated at the table from left to right: Paul Nizan, Henri Barbusse, Alexei Tolstoy and others)

221

of reproduction – film and photography – on the reception of works of art, a topic that he had already examined in 'A Small History of Photography' published in 1931. In addition his essay 'The Storyteller', published in 1936, had also touched on this issue with respect to the particular matter of literary works of art: 'The art of storytelling is reaching its end because the epic side of truth, wisdom, is dying out.'[82] The direct consequence of advanced capitalism and modern mass media was, according to Benjamin, the 'destruction' or 'decay of the aura'[83] which lends the work of art its seal of authenticity or uniqueness. The concept of the aura, which Benjamin had already used in his 'Photography' essay, was by no means uncommon in contemporary debates about art and literature, but it belonged above all to the terminology of the Stefan George circle. George's friend Wolfskehl termed it the 'breath of life', adding that 'every material form [exudes] it, such that [everything forces] its way out over itself [and surrounds] itself with its own self'.[84] In 1931, Benjamin described the aura as 'a strange weave of time and space: the unique appearance or semblance of distance, no matter how close the object may be':[85] but in 1936 he wrote that it is 'the presence of the original', which 'is the prerequisite to the concept of authenticity'.

Mechanical reproduction of art changes the reaction of the masses toward art. The reactionary attitude toward a Picasso painting changes into the progressive reaction toward a Chaplin movie. The progressive reaction is characterized by the direct, intimate fusion of visual and emotional enjoyment with the orientation of the expert. [. . .] With regard to the screen, the critical and the receptive attitudes of the public coincide.[86]

Benjamin was far too optimistic in his assessment of the new possibilities of perception that were opened up to the masses by mechanical reproduction; but it was an optimism that was more or less enforced by the question he posed: in an attempt to illuminate the utterly unresolved relationship between the work of art and mass reception from a materialist vantage point, he could not help but presuppose the existence of a new mode of perception among the masses.

Just how great his expectations were regarding the response this essay would receive, can be seen from the numerous times he endeavoured to discuss with experts this (in his opinion) first attempt at a truly contemporary materialist theory of art. Two opportunities to do so presented themselves; both were events

Advertisement for
Benjamin's talk, from the
Pariser Tageszeitung, 20
June 1936.

222

organized by the Paris Schutzverband Deutscher Autoren, an association of exiled German authors, in June 1936.[87] At the first meeting he presented his theses, and these were then debated a week later by a large audience. (During this second meeting, Hans Sahl gave a lengthy talk on Benjamin's work, but regrettably the text of this has been lost.)[88] However, Benjamin was disappointed with the response that evening from a circle of people who he had expected would show the greatest interest: the members and sympathizers of the Communist Party. Their conspicuous silence demonstrated their disapproval of the theses, which also met with criticism and rejection from other sides.[89]

The members of the Institute for Social Research, whose journal had only printed 'The Work of Art in the Age of Mechnical Reproduction' after numerous revisions, failed to take it very seriously on account of what they saw as its crass Marxist platitudes. Adorno wrote a long and devastating critique of it in their name, saying that key sections of it were undialectical, unhistorical and showed a romanticization of their topic.[90] The extent of the disappointment of the editors of the *Zeitschrift für Sozialforschung*, after their initially high expectations, is also illustrated by a decision that was reached by the editorial board, and which was communicated to Benjamin in May 1936 in a letter from Friedrich Pollock. After having originally planned 'to use the essay for a small publicity drive for the journal in France', they had now abondoned this idea. The editors found it 'far too impudent' and 'far too problematic with regard to many individual issues.'[91]

Scholem also failed to give any encouragement. Benjamin could discern his friend's distinct reservations from his luke-warm words: 'I found your essay very interesting. This is the first time I have come across something thought-provoking in a philosophical context about film and photography', but 'I am far too lacking in specialized knowledge to be able to pass judgement on your prognoses'.[92]

Finally, Benjamin received an especially harsh rejection from Moscow. He had sent the essay to Bernhard Reich, in the hope that he would be able to get it published in the magazine *Internationale Literatur*. Also speaking on behalf of his silent comrades in Paris, Reich replied that he found the 'method-ology' that Benjamin used quite alien and incomprehensible. Apart from this it was not clear to him what the author actually meant by his concept of the aura, and he felt that Benjamin's evidence in support of his claim, that mechanical reproduction

'Nowadays hailed as "Germany's greatest critic" (I would rather call him the most original philosopher of culture), this important person spent his life in poverty. But it would be wrong to assume that Benjamin always had a pensive or gloomy outlook on life. When I met him in Paris in 1936, he conveyed a strong impression of one with a lot of potential to enjoy life.'[85] (Stephan Lackner in conversation with Thomas Mann)

destroys the aura of the original, was fairly unconvincing, if not in fact absent.[93]

There is scarcely a letter in Benjamin's voluminous exile correspondence in which he does not complain about the precariousness of his financial situation. His worries about his daily bread 'played an ever greater role in the economy of [his] life'.[94] The 'fata morgana of a new emancipation', which had already appeared on the horizon of his new life shortly after his flight from Germany, did not remain a mirage. The 'freedom between the classes' which he had described in his essay 'On the Current Social Situation of the French Writer' as that of the lumpen proletariat,[95] became in some respects a reality for him, and sooner than he can have liked.

These complaints were accompanied by others about his increasing loneliness. Benjamin was not referring simply to having company – he could have had that in any of the Paris cafés.[96] What he missed were the conversations and discussions with close friends and acquaintances that he had been used to in Berlin. The acquaintances he made during his exile that extended beyond superficial encounters could be counted on the fingers of one hand. These included Hans Sahl,[97] Stephan Lackner[98] (whom Benjamin offered 'a helping hand in the first steps of his literary career' in the form of a positive review of his novel *Jan Heimatlos* in the *Neue Weltbühne*, to reciprocate the financial assistance that his father, Ernst Morgenroth, had organized for him),[99] Gisèle Freund and Hannah Arendt.[100] But none of them could really replace the friendships which he had established over the years.

His feelings of personal and intellectual isolation were neither assuaged by his prolific correspondence, which he (in any case an industrious letter-writer) further intensified, nor by his occasional visits to Brecht in Denmark or to his ex-wife in Italy. For most of this period the friends who as individuals meant most to him were effectively out of reach. Scholem had emigrated to distant Palestine a good ten years before; Bloch had gone into exile in Prague; Asja Lacis's 'medieval' calls of longing to be close to her former lover in Moscow and Kislovodsk went, out of necessity, unanswered;[101] his son Stefan Rafael was attending a school in Vienna; Jula Cohn and Fritz Radt stayed in Germany for several more years;[102] Felix Noeggerath and Alfred Cohn had decided to stay in Spain (Noeggerath later returned to Berlin at the outbreak of the Spanish Civil War); Adorno's exile took him to England and then to America.

Hannah Arendt.

A Jewish ark

There are no records of whether Benjamin's works were burnt on the bonfires of 10 May 1933. All that can be ascertained is that initially none of his books figured on the 'Index of Damaging and Undesirable Literature'. Evidently neither he nor his works were sufficiently well known or influential at the time to receive this particular form of public attention. In any case, not many of his works would yet have been present on the shelves of the public and university libraries. And his few book publications had almost completely vanished from the market by then, the last of these being the more important and without doubt more 'political' works. Ernst Rowohlt had had his stock rooms cleared out in 1931/2 in the attempt to reorganize his shaky finances, and he had sold off *One-Way Street*, *The Origin of German Tragic Drama* and other titles at a loss.[103] It is a bitter irony that a publishing ban in Germany was also to affect a work that the publisher and author had taken great pains to save from precisely this fate. This work was *Deutsche Menschen [German Men]*, Benjamin's anthology of annotated letters by the great German minds of the past, including Lichtenberg, Justus Liebig, Goethe and Gottfried Keller, which was printed in 1936 in Lucerne by a publishing house with the hope-inspiring name Vita Nova.

Among the measures that they employed to avoid the book's distribution being halted from the very start were the innocuous title[104] (with the adjective 'German', which enjoyed quite inflated popularity at the time), the typeface for the cover (Gothic type, as propagated by the Nazis in the mistaken belief that it was typically German) and the earthy pseudonym (Detlef Holz, Benjamin's *nom de plume* which had risen like a phoenix from the ashes of the book-burnings, and which he used for the majority of his German publications during his exile until 1935). But despite all their efforts, a keen eye would have noticed just how far this apparent conformity with the reigning style differed from what was customarily seen. The characters of the title were rounded in a way untypical for this style of typeface, the body text used a roman typeface, and the blue (rather than deep black) of the title and the somewhat fine cloth of the binding further emphasized the book's deviation from the norm.

Benjamin collaborated on the artful disguise of the book's outward appearance with Rudolf Roeßler (1897–1958), who was in many ways a specialist in subversion, for not only was he an editor, but also a genuine secret agent. Roeßler, who came from the Bavarian town of Kaufbeuren, was in fact a journalist who belonged to Catholic nationalist circles. During the Weimar era he had worked for a number of periodicals, including the *Augsburger Allgemeine Zeitung* and the magazine *Form und Sinn*, he had edited two stage magazines, the *Deutsche Bühnenblätter*

Book-burnings in 1933.

Wider den undeutſchen Geiſt!

1. Sprache und Schrifttum wurzeln im Volke. Das deutſche Volk trägt die Verantwortung dafür, daß ſeine Sprache und ſein Schrifttum reiner und unverfälſchter Ausdruck ſeines Volkstums ſind.
2. Es klafft heute ein Widerſpruch zwiſchen Schrifttum und deutſchem Volkstum. Dieſer Zuſtand iſt eine Schmach.
3. Reinheit von Sprache und Schrifttum liegt an Dir! Dein Volk hat Dir die Sprache zur treuen Bewahrung übergeben.
4. Unſer gefährlichſter Widerſacher iſt der Jude, und der, der ihm hörig iſt.
5. Der Jude kann nur jüdiſch denken. Schreibt er deutſch, dann lügt er. Der Deutſche, der deutſch ſchreibt, aber undeutſch denkt, iſt ein Verräter! Der Student, der undeutſch ſpricht und ſchreibt, iſt außerdem gedankenlos und wird ſeiner Aufgabe untreu.
6. Wir wollen die Lüge ausmerzen, wir wollen den Verrat brandmarken, wir wollen für den Studenten nicht Stätten der Gedankenloſigkeit, ſondern der Zucht und b̶o̶l̶i̶t̶i̶ſ̶c̶h̶e̶n̶ E̶r̶z̶i̶e̶h̶u̶n̶g̶.
7. W̶i̶r̶ ̶w̶o̶l̶l̶e̶n̶ ̶d̶e̶n̶ ̶J̶u̶d̶e̶n̶ ̶a̶l̶s̶ ̶F̶r̶e̶m̶d̶l̶i̶n̶g̶ ̶a̶c̶h̶t̶e̶n̶, und wir wollen das Volkstum ernſt nehmen. Wir fordern deshalb von der Zenſur: Jüdiſche Werke erſcheinen in hebräiſcher Sprache. Erſcheinen ſie in Deutſch, ſind ſie als Ueberſetzung zu kennzeichnen. Schärfſtes Einſchreiten gegen den Mißbrauch der deutſchen Schrift. Deutſche Schrift ſteht nur Deutſchen zur Verfügung. Der undeutſche Geiſt wird aus öffentlichen Büchereien ausgemerzt.
8. Wir fordern vom deutſchen Studenten Wille und Fähigkeit zur ſelbſtändigen Erkenntnis und Entſcheidung.
9. Wir fordern vom deutſchen Studenten den Willen und die Fähigkeit zur Reinerhaltung der deutſchen Sprache.
10. Wir fordern vom deutſchen Studenten den Willen und die Fähigkeit zur Ueberwindung des jüdiſchen Intellektualismus und der damit verbundenen liberalen Verfallserſcheinungen im deutſchen Geiſtesleben.
11. Wir fordern die Ausleſe von Studenten und Profeſſoren nach der Sicherheit des Denkens, im deutſchen Geiſte.
12. Wir fordern die deutſche Hochſchule als Hort des deutſchen Volkstums und als Kampfſtätte aus der Kraft des deutſchen Geiſtes.

Die Deutſche Studentenſchaft.

'1. Language and writing literature are rooted in the people. It is the responsibility of the German people to ensure that its language and literature are the pure and unfalsified expression of its national character.'
'5. A Jew's thought can only be Jewish. If then he writes in German, he is lying. A German who writes in German but whose thought is un-German is a traitor! A student whose speech and writing are un-German is a thoughtless creature and unfaithful to his duty.'
'6. We want to extirpate these lies and denounce these treasons, and for the German student we want not centres of thoughtlessness but centres of discipline and German education.'
'Against the un-German spirit!'

and *Das Nationaltheater*, and also ran the Bühnenvolksbund [People's Theatre League]. In 1934 he emigrated to Switzerland, where he co-founded the publishing house Vita Nova together with the book dealer Josef Stocker. His early contacts with anti-fascist circles, which operated half legally and half underground, led him in 1939 to work with the Swiss and shortly afterwards the Soviet secret services[105] (although this only became public after two spells of detention in 1944 and 1955). Roeßler's anti-fascist sentiments were also quite evident in his publishing activities, as is vouched for by the inclusion of titles by Paul Claudel, Friedrich Wilhelm Forster and Waldemar

VITA NOVA VERLAG

AKTIENGESELLSCHAFT · LUZERN · VONMATTSTRASSE 36

TELEPHON: Luzern 27.104

POSTSCHECK-KONTO: VII 6183

LUZERN, den 13. 3. 36.

Aktenzeichen:

Herrn Walter Benjamin

Paris XIV, 23 , rue Bénard

Sehr geehrter Herr Benjamin ,

wie Herr Professor Thieme Ihnen sicher schon mitgeteilt hat, würden wir sehr gerne von Ihrem so freundlichen Anerbieten Gebrauch machen und die so ausgezeichnet zusammengestellte und kommentierte Serie von Briefen in Buchform bei uns erscheinen lassen, sofern wir innerhalb möglichst kurzer Frist mit Ihnen eine Einigung erzielen, und das Buch noch bis Ende September 36.erscheinen lassen können. Soviel wir sehen,ergibt der Text ungefähr einen Umfang von 120 bis 130 Druckseiten, doch würden wir es lebhaft begrüssen , wenn da und dort noch die Einleitungen zu den Briefen etwas gekürzt werden könnten. Als Titel möchten wir vorschlagen:

Deutsche Menschen

Von Ehre ohne Ruhm
Von wahrer Menschengrüsse
Von Würde in der Not

Ein neues Vorwort würden Sie uns , wie uns Herr Dr. Thieme sagte, freundlichst zur Verfügung stellen, sofern man nicht die Einleitung wiedergibt, die auch der Frankfurter Zeitung gestanden hat.

Als Honorar würden wir Ihnen eine Tantième von 16% vom Verlagsumsatz, also des Betrages, den der Verlag nach Abzug der Buchhändler-Rabatte vereinnamt, vorschlagen – bei viertel- oder halbjährlicher Abrechnung. Auflegen würden wir die Schrift in 2000 Stück. Wären Sie damit einverstanden? Vertrag würden wir Ihnen, wenn Sie grundsätzlich zustimmen , sogleich zusenden.

Anbei die Abschrift eines Briefes des Freiherrn vom Stein, den ich gerne an den Schluss der ganzen Sammlung gestellt sehen möchte. Würden Sie zustimmen?

Mit der Bitte um freundliche umgehende Antwort begrüsse ich Sie , sehr geehrter Herr Benjamin, als Ihr sehr

ergebener *Roeßler*

Gurian in the house's list of publications. (In addition, the company's recognizably anti-nationalistic programme prompted Goebbels's Ministry for Propaganda and Public Information to place a temporary ban on all of its publications.) To return to Benjamin's anthology: the title *German Men* was originally suggested by Roeßler.[106] This certainly sounded more ambiguous and more subversive than Benjamin's proposal *German Letters*.

After the book's publication, Scholem expressed the fear that it would immediately be placed on the index if the censor actually stopped to read the commentaries, for they were quite 'unmistakably "corrupting"'.[107] The meticulous efforts to camouflage the book were not, however, completely in vain, as was demonstrated by the book's initial success. *German Men* appeared in the second half of October 1936 in an edition of 2,000. At first its distribution was still hindered by the ban on the entire output of Vita Nova. (Roeßler only managed to have the ban lifted in early 1937.) But subsequently it sold so quickly that just one year later, when only '3–400 copies of it were left', the company followed up with a second edition of 2,000.[108] However, in 1938, it was placed on the index after all, and with that the anthology lost its intended audience: the Germans and the Austrians who had by now 'been brought back to the fold'. (The ban pronounced by the Ministry of Propaganda resulted in the publishing house holding on to the remaining copies, a pleasant fact for Benjamin collectors because it meant that the book was still readily available in bookshops right up to the 1980s.)

As Benjamin later wrote, this anthology of letters was triggered by 'little more than a sudden idea, a whim'.[109] It had only assumed its contours gradually, or quite literally piece by piece. *German Men* had first appeared episodically in the literary section of the *Frankfurter Zeitung*. The first text was printed in the edition of 31 March 1931, the twenty-seventh and last on 31 May 1932;[110] but none of these gave any indication of the editor's identity. This anonymity was perfectly fair, however, because the literary documents were intended to speak for themselves – or for the historical and political present – and not to attest to Walter Benjamin the person, to the breadth of his reading, to his experience with libraries and bibliographical matters, or even to his (personal) ability to sense and to extract the relevance to contemporary history of even the oldest documents, and to make a 'text tangibly clear from all perspectives and in all contexts'.[111]

Soon afterwards, and with his almost typical lack of success, the editor tried to get the letters published in their entirety, intending at the same time to extend the collection to twice its original length.[112] Just what pearls Benjamin had earmarked for the anthology can not only be discerned from the allusions he made in his letters,[113] but also from the various articles and publications that drew on this store of planned additions: the 'Unbekannte Anekdoten von Kant' [Unknown Anecdotes about Kant],[114] the article he wrote together with Willy Haas

VORWORT

Die fünfundzwanzig Briefe dieses Bandes umfassen den Zeitraum eines Jahrhunderts. Der erste ist von 1783, der letzte von 1883 datiert. Die Reihenfolge ist chronologisch. Ausserhalb ihrer ist das folgende Schreiben gestellt. Aus der Mitte des hier umspannten Jahrhunderts stammend, gibt es den Blick auf die Anfänge der Epoche — Goethes Jugend — frei, in welcher das Bürgertum seine grossen Positionen bezog; es gibt ihn aber — durch seinen Anlass, Goethes Tod — auch auf das Ende dieser Epoche frei, da das Bürgertum nur noch die Positionen, nicht mehr den Geist bewahrte, in welchem es diese Positionen erobert hatte. Es war die Epoche, in der das Bürgertum sein geprägtes und gewichtiges Wort in die Wagschale der Geschichte zu legen hatte. Freilich schwerlich mehr als eben dieses Wort; darum ging sie unschön mit den Gründerjahren zu Ende. Lange ehe der folgende Brief geschrieben wurde, hatte, im Alter von sechsundsiebzig Jahren, Goethe dieses Ende in einem Gesicht erfasst, das er Zelter in folgenden Worten mitteilte: «Reichthum und Schnelligkeit ist, was die Welt bewundert und wornach jeder strebt. Eisenbahnen, Schnellposten, Dampfschiffe und alle mögliche Facilitäten der Communication sind es, worauf die gebildete Welt ausgeht, sich zu überbilden und dadurch in der Mittelmässigkeit zu verharren ... Eigentlich ist es das Jahrhundert für die fähigen Köpfe, für leichtfassende praktische Menschen, die, mit einer gewissen Gewandtheit ausgestattet, ihre Superiorität über die Menge fühlen, wenn sie gleich selbst nicht zum Höchsten begabt sind. Lasst uns soviel als möglich an der Gesinnung halten, in der wir herankamen; wir werden, mit vielleicht noch Wenigen, die Letzten seyn einer Epoche, die so bald nicht wiederkehrt.»

7

The preface to *Deutsche Menschen* (left).

Benjamin's commentary on the first of the 'letters' to be published in the *Frankfurter Zeitung* (right).

entitled 'Vom Weltbürger zum Großbürger' [From Cosmopolite to Patrician],[115] and the montage 'Allemands de quatre-vingt-neuf'[116] which he assembled in 1939 for the monthly review *Europe* 'in quite the same manner as [his] book of letters'.[117] Finally, Benjamin published one of the letters anonymously in the Moscow periodical *Das Wort*.[118]

Benjamin wrote a new preface for the 1936 edition of the letters because sentences such as those which had introduced the first letter that was published in the *Frankfurter Zeitung* would have quickly called the book to the attention of the Nazi censors. At that time he had written that the letters

bring to mind an attitude that can be defined as humanist in the German sense, and which at present it seems all the more imperative to recall because today people are approaching works of art and literature ever more one-sidedly, while often, quite seriously and fully aware of their responsibility, questioning German humanism.[119]

Despite the fact that such sentences had to be watered down out of tactical considerations, Benjamin remained quite confident that his book would have the desired effect. 'Given the meticulousness with which people over there [i.e. in Germany] read', he wrote in a letter to Horkheimer, his readership would still manage to identify the 'distinguishing marks' in both the introductions and the letters themselves.[120]

And indeed, the letters contained a wealth of such 'distinguishing marks'. Some were of a more personal nature: 'a literary creed' whose maxim 'I write for nothing and no one except for the subject itself' (as Benjamin had written in his commentary on the Romantic Johann Wilhelm Ritter), 'already created difficulties in those days for his confessors'.[121] Could anyone with a close knowledge of Benjamin have failed to read this as a self-portrait? Furthermore, the anthology contained other distinguishing marks of a philosophical-ethical nature: 'Hope warms the heart. I would not sell my hope for a thousand tons of gold', as Samuel Collenbusch had once written to Kant regarding his morality and philosophy, to be followed many years later by Benjamin's commentary: 'neither my reason nor my will could ever mistake this hopeful belief for one completely void of all hope'.[122] No attentive reader could have failed to grasp such lines as a call to rethink his or her attitude towards the 'national movement' that was raging in Germany. Finally a number of more 'political' distinguishing marks can be found:

Title page of the second edition of *Deutsche Menschen.*

At a distance everything appears different from when it is studied close up. It all becomes blind, passionate frenzy, raging faction-alism and hot tempers, which never achieve sensible, calm results. On the one side I find understanding and talent, but without courage or force; on the other a physical energy which, led by ignorance, only does good where the knot really has to be hewn apart.[123]

Who could fail to draw immediate comparisons with their own situation after reading sentences such as these, taken from a letter that Georg Forster wrote to his wife in April 1793?

And yet, was this the full extent of Benjamin's 'message' to the people who had remained in Germany? Had not the changes in the political conditions rendered the anthology's

'Darkness closed in. Just one solitary book was of value to me, one that I carried with me for a year and a day in my meagre baggage during my fugitive existence. It was as important to me at that time as a residence permit or pass. It prevented me from succumbing to lethargy or impotent rage, it helped me to maintain the image of another.'[86] (*Deutsche Menschen:* cover of the first edition, 1936)

231

underlying statement quite obsolete? For its basic analogies related first and foremost to the period at the end of the Weimar Republic. And apart from that, did the anthology not contain a pathos similar to the one whose total impotence had been made so plain to Benjamin just one year before at the Paris Congress? Were all these allusions to and explicit remarks about the existence of a 'real humanity',[124] which were simply there to be read in traditional texts, not just a kind of empty entreaty? Perhaps it is too much to expect that an author, whose lifetime's work belied his dictum that 'convincing others bears no fruit',[125] should also entertain self-doubts such that his very thinking and writing, his political views and their possibilities of exerting any influence, are shaken to the core. For nothing could be taken at face value any more – or perhaps everything was, so revelations of this kind were bound to appear mere anachronisms.

But all in all the publication was received positively. Hugo Marti, reviewer for *Der Bund* in Berne, wrote that these 'letters of German men' were at last something different from the 'carefully tidied and properly aligned propaganda of the New Germany'.[126] Joachim Günther (editor of the *Neue Deutsche Hefte* after the war) called the anthology in the German monthly review *Die Literatur*, the 'work of a literary jeweller', and his one regret was that the collection turned out 'far too short'.[127] Only Rudolf Humm, the review columnist for Thomas Mann's exile periodical *Maß und Wert*, expressed certain reservations. He found the book's 'parabola rather curious', and for all the excellence of its compilation, which made the anthology both a 'work of art' and a 'document of our times', it left its reader with the stale aftertaste of 'melancholy pride'.[128]

Paris arcades

In ancient Greece they pointed out places which led down into the underworld. Our conscious existence too is a country in which secluded places lead into the underworld, full of inconspicuous places where dreams emerge. By day, we pass by them unsuspecting, but as soon as sleep arrives, we feel our way . . . back to them and lose ourselves in dark tunnels. In broad daylight the city's labyrinth of buildings is like consciousness; during the day the arcades . . . open unnoticed onto the streets. But at night, under the dark mass of buildings their more solid darkness leaps out alarmingly; and the late passer-by hurries past them, unless we have encouraged him to journey down the narrow passage.[129]

Benjamin in Pontigny,
1938.

At the beginning of his exile, Benjamin had applied himself
once more to his work on the Paris arcades, which he saw at the
time as 'the actual, if not the only reason not to lose courage
in [his] struggle for existence'.[130] During his stay in San Remo
in 1934/5, he worked systematically through his notes once
more, and on his return to Paris he set about elaborating and
extending the motifs and the material.

His earliest drafts for the 'Arcades' project were written during
the latter half of the 1920s and were intended for a 'dialectical
Fairy Play',[131] inspired by Louis Aragon's *Paysan de Paris*. At that

time Benjamin had planned to write a short essay on the Paris arcades together with Franz Hessel, for the Berlin magazine *Der Querschnitt*. By means of casual observations about the 'spatialized past which manifests itself in these curious mixtures of houses and streets', they intended to present certain insights about the modern state of the world. However, this essay was never to advance beyond a few preliminary formulations.[132]

At that time Benjamin did not yet suspect that the project would grow into a work of several hundred pages and become 'the place where he would stage all [his] ideas and all [the] battles' he had fought during his life, battles with himself and with the world. His longer stay in Paris in 1926 and 1927, the work on the Proust translation and Kracauer's writing provided him with further stimulus. Unlike the latter, who restricted himself to the description of 'the decline of the petty-bourgeois class in a very memorable, "affectionate" account of their legacy',[133] his own work aimed at the representation of the whole bourgeois class and its age. The work only began to assume clearer contours in 1929, after conversations with Wiesengrund-Adorno, and his fiancée Gretel Karplus, Asja Lacis, and Horkheimer.[134] During these discussions, the foundations were laid for a work that was aimed at epistemologically penetrating the nineteenth century from the standpoint of historical materialism.

Benjamin finally sent Adorno a preliminary exposé of the work in the mid-1930s, entitled 'Paris, Capital of the Nineteenth Century'.[135] Adorno was so taken by it that he almost immediately approached Horkheimer, director of the Institute for

'This piece, which is about the Paris Arcades, was begun under a clear sky of cloudless blue, which formed a dome above the foliage but was made dusty by the millions of pages with which the fresh breeze of industriousness, the heavy breath of research, the storm of youthful eagerness and the lazy gust of curiosity had been covered. The painted summer sky which looks down from the arcades into the reading room of the Bibliothèque Nationale in Paris, has cast its dreamy lightless blanket ceiling over the first-born of its sources of understanding.'[87] (Benjamin in the Bibliothèque Nationale, 1937, photograph by Gisèle Freund)

Social Research, and made a resolute plea on behalf of the entire project. Adorno at once considered the 'Arcades' project, whose methods and objectives were conveyed in a preliminary and rather vague manner in this exposé, 'to be Benjamin's real *chef d'œuvre*, a matter of the greatest conceivable theoretical importance', and quite 'ingenious' in its overall conception. In addition, he felt that this work would fit very well in terms of both subject and method into the institute's research activities, for this 'attempt to grasp the nineteenth century as a "style" by means of the category of commodities as a dialectical image contains nothing that is unacceptable from the viewpoint of dialectical materialism'.[136]

It is difficult when reading this exposé to find anything in its wording that would justify such high aspirations, and which in Adorno's letter to Horkheimer wear the mask of certainties. Was this simply exaggeration, employed to make the project seem more appealing to the director of the Institute for Social Research? Or had Adorno's letter been informed by a more intimate knowledge of the project? (He was, after all, one of the few people whom Benjamin had permitted an early glimpse into this enterprise,[137] and so he must have felt more familiar with it than other, more impartial readers of the first draft.)

In principal, Adorno was simply repeating to Horkheimer

what Benjamin had told him and others after he had finally finished his exposé. Adorno's assumption that the 'Arcades' project would develop into Benjamin's second major work after *The Origin of German Tragic Drama* would seem to have been largely suggested by Benjamin's mention of numerous analogies between the two works. Thus 'the main aim' of the 'Arcades' project would, as he wrote to Scholem, also 'be to unfold a handed-down concept. Whereas in the former [the book on German baroque drama] it was the concept of the *Trauerspiel*, here it is likely to be the fetish character of commodities.'[138] And in the lines accompanying the exposé that he sent to Adorno, he added: 'A separate description of the epistemological bases of the baroque book followed only after they had proven their value in the preceding material. This will also be the case here.'[139] Finally, outlining the actual aim of his new work, he wrote to Scholem: 'Just as the baroque book dealt with the seventeenth century from the perspective of Germany, this book will go into the nineteenth century from that of France.[140]

No doubt posing a question in a way that is aimed at giving a completely new philosophical interpretation of the nineteenth century is, and was, a 'matter of the greatest theoretical importance that may be imagined'. But if one were to ask how Benjamin wished to realize this 'research programme', which made a radical break with customary practices in academic circles, and what were to be its central concerns, one would receive greatly diverse and contradictory responses. Consequently it is only possible to distinguish a vague, hypothetical vanishing point towards which all of these almost irreconcilable definitions seem to be heading: Benjamin intended to create a picture of the nineteenth century that showed it, the source of the present, in all of its greatness, but also in all of its frailty. He wanted to show the irreality of the real – or to use one of the central concepts of the 'Arcades' project: the phantasmagoria of past and present times in all of its incidental manifestations and superficial appearances.

It is possible that the concept of 'phantasmagoria' – a term borrowed from Marx's *Capital* – was responsible for leading Adorno to believe that the work would not contain anything that was unacceptable from the viewpoint of dialectical materialism; in addition, Benjamin had instilled this confidence in his young friend with the comment that from now on, he (Benjamin) could 'calmly look at what may be brought to bear against the work's method from the side of orthodox Marxism'. He felt that he was 'on solid footing with it in the Marxist discussion, *à la longue*, if only because the crucial question of the historical image is treated here for the first time in its full breadth'.[141]

It would be idle to speculate on how the orthodox, or even the less orthodox critical Marxists would have received the 'Arcades' project, because the work was never finished. Nevertheless, Benjamin's optimism in this matter is surprising, because the understanding of a materialist approach to history which prevailed in his countless notes, aphorisms, commentaries and only rarely finalized jottings was rather curious, as can be seen in a few examples.

The first remark comes from 'Convolute K' ('Dream city and dreamhouse, future dreams, anthropological nihilism, Jung'), and it alone would have outraged any good Marxist; he writes with regard to the upright economic order of bourgeois society: 'Capitalism was a natural phenomenon which brought a new dream-filled sleep to Europe and with this a reactivation of mythological powers.'[142] When someone appears to begin with such questionable premises, it cannot be too surprising when their methodological creed – in anticipation of one of the central objectives of the theses 'On the Concept of History' – advocates the amalgamation of theology with a materialist approach to history. This assumes the following form in a remark from 'Convolute N' ('Theoretics of Knowledge, Theory of Progress'):

History is not just a science but also a form of memoration. What science has 'established', memoration can modify. Memoration can make the incomplete (happiness) into something complete (suffering) and the complete into something incomplete. That is theology; but in memoration we discover something that forbids us to conceive of history as thoroughly a-theological, even though we barely dare attempt to write it according to literally theological concepts.[143]

It is doubtless unfair to assess an author and his work on the strength of such problematic sentences, which presumably he would never have allowed to be published in this unannotated form. But this already brings us to a basic problem in the question of how one should tackle the 'Arcades' project, which Benjamin worked on for almost a decade and a half (with interruptions). Although a wealth of material relating to this early history of modernism, which itself remained in fragmentary form, has been handed down to us, essentially it is impossible to make more than vague suppositions about its intended content, composition and methodology. Nor are the exposés any real help. Although they provide a rough idea of the topics that were to be broached in the work, they do not permit any definite conclusions as to how the author was to avoid the epistemological antinomies in his grand plan.

Benjamin himself had clearly sensed that his plans were in danger of becoming too unwieldy. And if he was not yet fully aware of this fact, Adorno confirmed his fears in his detailed appraisal of the exposé 'Paris, Capital of the Nineteenth Century' (one that stood in striking contrast to his first, spontaneous evaluation). He delivered an almost devastating critique in a letter he wrote to Benjamin on 2 August 1935. In particular, he deemed the concept of the 'dialectical image' 'undialectical'.[144] As a consequence, Benjamin decided to present for the time being only a 'miniature' version of the 'Arcades' project:[145] a book on Charles Baudelaire, whose life and work was originally intended to form an important chapter of the whole. It ended up a 'mere' essay.

He wrote this essay in 1938 in 'a race with the war'. The Sudeten crisis that summer, as well as all the other events in European politics, gave him every reason for concern. When at the end of September he sent the manuscript entitled 'Paris of the Second Empire in Baudelaire' to New York, he felt 'in spite of all [his] choking fear, a feeling of triumph on the day [he] wrapped up the "flâneur" [the second chapter of the three-part essay], which had been almost fifteen years in the planning, before the end of the world (the fragility of the manuscript!)'.[146] He did not suspect at this point in time how dismissively his American editors would react to this work as well. Benjamin was quite convinced that he had produced a 'lasting [solid] materialist "Baudelaire"'[147] because he had brought to light the revolutionary implications of the poet's work in the context of capitalist developments in the latter half of the nineteenth century, which lay beyond the traditional picture of Baudelaire as a decadent, mystical aesthete. But the very way in which Benjamin achieved this met with incomprehension from the editors of the *Zeitschrift für Sozialforschung*.

The thankless task of sending him an 'extensively argued'[148] account of their reasons for rejecting the essay fell to Adorno. In a long letter, dated 10 November 1938, he attributed his disappointment mainly to the fact that Marxist theory seemed to have been imposed on the work in an extraneous manner and that Benjamin's dialectics lacked 'mediation'. The 'primary tendency was', according to Adorno, 'always to relate the

'benjamin is here. he is working on an essay on baudelaire. there are good things in it, he demonstrates how literature was distorted after '48 by the notion of an immanent, ahistorical epoch. the victory at versailles of the bourgeoisie over the commune was preempted. people became accustomed to evil. it was given the form of a flower. this is useful reading. oddly enough an eccentric idea enabled benjamin to write it. he assumes something that he calls an "aura", which is connected with dreaming (day dreaming). he says: when you feel someone's gaze alight upon you, even on your back, you respond (!). the expectation that whatever you look at is looking at you creates the aura. apparently this has started to disintegrate in recent times, along with rites and rituals. b. discovered this while analysing films, where the aura is destroyed by the capacity of works of art to be reproduced. all very mystical, despite his anti-mystical attitudes. this is the way in which the materialistic approach to history is adapted! it is pretty horrifying.'[88] (Benjamin in front of Brecht's house at Skovbostrand, summer 1938)

pragmatic content of Baudelaire's work directly to proximate characteristics of the social history of his time, and preferably economic characteristics when possible'.[149] In this, Adorno found 'a profoundly romantic element':

The 'mediation' I miss and find obscured by materialistic and historiographic invocation is, however, nothing other than precisely the theory from which your work abstains. Bypassing theory affects the empirical evidence. On the one hand, it gives it a deceptively epic character and, on the other hand, deprives phenomena that are experienced only subjectively of their actual historiosophical importance.[150]

This rejection was to contribute to Benjamin's growing dislike of situations based on unequal dependency. But with the Institute for Social Research there was no alternative: there was nothing he could do other than accept the 'suggested improvements' and revise or in fact rewrite his essay. The result appeared in 1940 under the title 'Über einige Motive bei Baudelaire' [Some Motifs in Baudelaire] in the *Zeitschrift für Sozialforschung*.[151] In this essay, which centres much more on the problems of alienated city life and the shock experienced by the individual amongst the masses and by the worker at the machine, the Marxist tone of his underlying criticism is milder – doubtless under the influence of those who had commissioned the essay. Instead, he returned to his reflections on the fate of the auratic familiar to editors and readers of the *Zeitschrift für Sozialforschung*. Baudelaire, he concluded, 'indicated the price for which the sensation of the modern age may be had: the disintegration of the aura in the experience of shock. He paid dearly for consenting to this disintegration – but it is the law of his poetry, which shines in the sky of the Second Empire as "a star without atmosphere."'[152] This second version was given a far better reception in New York.

Expatriation

The German Embassy in Paris was informed in a letter dated 26 May 1939 of Benjamin's expatriation, which the Gestapo had applied for in February of that year. Benjamin had just one of his publications to thank for this: his (first) 'Paris Letter'[153] in *Das Wort*, 1936. The fact alone that a German, and moreover a Jew, was openly active in the Communist realm may well have sufficed for the Gestapo's henchmen. And a look at his article would have simply confirmed their opinion that Benjamin was a staunch anti-fascist. Pronouncements such as 'culture under the Swastika is nothing but the playground of unqualified minds and subaltern characters', or 'fascist art is one of propaganda', and finally 'fascist ideology is deeply indebted to decadence and aestheticism',[154] were bound to provoke such a response. Benjamin must scarcely have stopped to think about this occurrence, for he had absolutely no illusions about what to expect

Gestapo document
demanding Benjamin's
expatriation.

from Nazism. Nor was there any further need to show consideration towards his relatives who were still in Germany, for they were now beyond outside help. 'The nightmare that oppresses people in his situation', he wrote of his brother, was 'not so much the upcoming day in prison as the concentration camp that threatened after years in imprisonment'[155] (a fate he was not spared in the end).

Benjamin had already returned to Paris (he had been Brecht's guest in Denmark until October 1938) when the synagogues were torched in Germany. The state-organized pogrom, the *Reichskristallnacht* with the ensuing mass arrests (such as the 25,000 or more Jews who were dragged off to concentration camps as security for 'an act of expiation that is to be made by the Jews of German nationality')[156] and the new edicts (including the 'Decree for the Ejection of Jews from German Economic Life'), drove the Germans Jews to a further wave of forced 'emigration'. The 'new arrivals' must have given Benjamin the details of the night from 9 to 10 November. He feared the worst,

Certificate of
expatriation.

'The events in Germany, which are weighing upon us all so terribly – as for my brother, I can only hope that what is now going on in Germany stops before the gates of the prisons. But who can say?'[90] (Jewish men being marched to a concentration camp, Baden-Baden, November 1938)

above all for his brother. And the events were yet another reason for him to press for naturalization in France – an undertaking that did not, however, succeed.

La drôle de guerre

The war arrived without much fuss, it had already been announced too often; it was as if it wanted to say: I'm coming to show you that you can rely on me. The men took their uniforms out of their wardrobes, trimmed their nails and held their hands before their yawning mouths. The sky over Paris darkened, there were battery torches in the night bar. The war was not taken seriously – not as seriously as the war against Hitler's opponents who, on account of the Non-Aggression Pact [the 'Hitler–Stalin

242

Benjamin 1938, photograph by Gisèle Freund.

Pact', of 23 August 1939] had for better or for worse become Hitler's allies. What was to be done with them, there was no time to distinguish between friend and foe, the castles by the Loire were cleared out and encircled with barbed wire, and in Paris a football stadium, the Stade Colombe, was selected as an assembly camp for the refugees from Germany.[157]

'I am unhappy because instead of writing or working, I walk around here on this abandoned farm a hundred steps forth and a hundred steps back; we sleep in a goat shed, eat in the hall of a dilapidated castle some two kilometres from the farm, the days seem to be completely quiet. But a man who is not free is worth nothing. Every day without freedom is a wasted one. And in the middle of this war against Hitler I am not free. I cannot write or act. What an absurd, tragic situation. I do nothing – I write poems. I chat with old and new friends. Sometimes with Benjamin.'[91] (Hermann Kesten)

Hitler's invasion of Poland on the morning of 1 September 1939 and the declaration of war two days later by Britain and France further exacerbated the already precarious situation of the exiles. After losing their homeland, their language and their property, they were now robbed of their last possession: their liberty. *La drôle de guerre* between France and Hitler's Germany, did not begin with fighting on the Maginot Line or in any other location, but internally: against French Communists and socialists as well as against the despised foreigners, above all German-speaking emigrants who, regardless of whether they were anti-fascists or not, were now regarded indiscriminately as Hitler's Fifth Column.

In September, all Germans, Austrians, Czechs, Slovaks and Hungarians aged between 17 and 50, or in some cases 65 (if they were still capable of being 'mobilized'), were interned.[158] Any of the above who were living in Paris or who had chanced to be there at the outbreak of the war had to present themselves at the Stade Colombe – a football stadium that was certainly not designed for accommodating hundreds and thousands of men over a lengthy period of time. The hell they went through – Jewish refugees, opponents of Hitler who had taken flight, tourists caught unawares by the war, veterans of the Spanish Civil War, and perhaps the occasional Nazi agent who was just as unwilling to be there as the rest – lasted ten days and nights. The majority had a completely false idea of what to expect, and turned up in summer clothes and light shoes, with a thin blanket tucked under their arms and provisions for one or two days at the most. Among their number was Walter Benjamin, who unlike most had long since foreseen his fate. In a letter from May 1939 Benjamin expressed his certainty that if war broke out, all that was imminent for the foreigners residing in France were 'concentration camps'.[159] They remained there, lying on the terraces, huddled up on stone benches, strolling along the cinder track, killing time playing cards or chess, racking their brains over how the French government could act in such defiance of international law, and 'drawing up mental petitions to the authorities in which they protested at their treatment and demanded immediate release'.[160] Finally they were bundled into buses like prisoners of war and transported to the Gare d'Austerlitz under military escort, and thence in sealed carriages to hastily improvised internment camps.

The group to which Benjamin belonged arrived at Nevers, a small Loire town roughly half-way between Paris and Lyon. Cleared-out châteaux, vacant factories and farms had been turned into numerous *camps de concentration* for the *ressortissants de l'Empire allemand* (citizens of the German Reich). A total of three camps are listed in an official document dating from October 1939: one in Murgers, in which 40 *ressortissants étrangers* were accommodated, another in Vernuche (288 internees) and the third in Four-de-Vaux (110 prisoners).[161] Together with Hans Sahl, Max Aron and Hermann Kesten, Benjamin was taken to Vernuche, where he soon attempted to restore some normality to his life by editing a camp newspaper.

One day Benjamin took me aside. 'It's about the arm-band,' he whispered. 'No, don't laugh, I have a plan.' He wanted to propose to the commanding office the publication of a literary journal – naturally on the highest niveau – a camp journal for intellectuals that was to show the country exactly who they had locked up as 'the enemies of France'.[162]

Bulletin de Vernuche

The arm-band, which gave access to pass through the camp gates, had been devised by the camp commander. He had been so taken by the idea of two filmmakers to produce a film entitled 'Vive la France', that he had willingly provided them with this 'pass' so that during the day they could attend to preparatory work in the nearest library. And who would begrudge these ingenious souls the fact that their outings were mainly devoted to filling their famished stomachs with wine and French cuisine instead of to academic research? The jealousy and resentment that they inspired amongst their undernourished fellow inmates upon their return to the camp was simply normal. But they set them a useful example by showing that (almost) any expedient was justified if one wished to survive these hard times.

Although the camp newspaper, the *Bulletin de Vernuche. Journal des Travailleurs du 54. Régiment*,[163] planned as a weekly or fortnightly periodical for the prisoners and their relatives, and for both French and German readers, was never actually printed, it did advance beyond the mere planning stage. In Benjamin's

Benjamin's contribution to the *Bulletin de Vernuche.*

estate there are a number of handwritten articles (partly written in pencil on the back of envelopes and by and large left unrevised), which give a vivid picture of life in the camp. And as such, they present the programmatic aim of the magazine to have been a reflection of this life.[164] Roughly 300 men aged between 17 and 50, of the most differing social, 'racial',[165] occupational and intellectual backgrounds arrived one 'September evening' at the empty premises of a former furniture factory. Upon their arrival, each of them had to find his own way of coping with the general chaos. In particular the inmates lacked even the 'most rudimentary comforts': bales of straw for bedding, for instance, only arrived several days later.[166] Gradually a proper camp 'society' developed, perhaps not so multifaceted as a 'real' one, but nevertheless equipped with all of the basic elements. 'Normal' economic aspects were mirrored, for instance, in currency (cigarettes, nails, pencils and buttons), 'entrepreneurship' and the service sector (construction of sanitary installations, water and mains supplies, production of crockery from empty

A letter from Heinrich
Mann to Rudolf Olden,
29 January 1940.

Nice
29 janvier 1940

Cher monsieur,

nous sommes d'accord pour les trois membres nouvellement reçus; je veux dire MM. W. Milch, W. Benjamin et Soma Morgenstern.

Je serais très heureux si nous pouvions avoir l'occasion de nous rencontrer.

Mes salutations les meilleures.

H. Mann

cans, the establishment of a postal service, etc.). And the less respectable side of society was represented by the semi-legal or criminal activities of the camp's speculators, thieves and confidence tricksters. Even culture was not neglected. Lectures ('comparing Freud and Jung, Lenin and Trotsky')[167] and literary matinées (with recitations of Sahl's poems – 'Elegy to the Year 1939'[168] – and talks by Benjamin – 'On the Concept of Guilt'),[169] a choir ('The Voice of the Granary'),[170] and a survey of internees' reading interests and the 'stocks of books'[171] in the camp all bear witness to the hive of activity that developed in this quarter.

After his release from the camp at the end of November 1939 as the result of the concerted efforts of his friend Adrienne Monnier, her aquaintance Henri Hoppenot and the French PEN Club, Benjamin began to warm to the idea of emigrating, if only temporarily, to the United States. He started learning English, he took serious steps to escape the threat Europe posed, and he actually applied for membership to the Exile PEN Club.[172] He had not previously joined any of the influential exile organizations, for with the complete lack of illusion with which he followed political developments, he had not considered this step necessary. His deep distrust of the vigorous activity within such institutions must also have played a part in this. But by now he realized that it would be virtually impossible to leave France without assistance. And the German Exile PEN Club had already demonstrated its effectiveness through the help it had given the Austrian authors after their country had been annexed.

The notion of history

From Vernuche Benjamin returned to a Paris where daily life was dictated by war. Darkened windows, candle-light and battery torches, sirens and the army on every corner: amid this general state of alert he tried as far as possible to regain the traces of 'normality' he required in his life in order to be able to work. As soon as his impaired health permitted (he had been troubled for some time by heart problems), he returned to his manuscripts. Twice at the turn of 1939/40 he met up with his ex-wife Dora, but he did not yield to her entreaties to leave Paris and bring himself into safety.[173] Instead, he had his reader's card for the Bibliothèque Nationale renewed so that he could proceed with his work on the 'Arcades' project, or rather his Baudelaire book.

The first concrete results were the eighteen theses 'On the Concept of History' which he wrote during the winter of 1940. They were connected with the 'Arcades' project in that their task was to act provisionally as the 'theoretical accoutrements' for the 'work on Baudelaire'.[174] But beyond this specific context, the theses represent a political-philosophical testament of Benjamin. Their actual composition was indebted to the 'new war',[175] but as he clearly emphasized, they were concerned with the 'totality' of his 'generation's experiences'. With these theses he was lending form, as he wrote in a letter to Gretel Adorno, to 'ideas' that he had kept to himself, indeed 'kept from' himself, 'for some twenty years'.[176]

Benjamin viewed his reflections as a first approximation of a theory of history 'from which fascism can be examined'.[177] In 1940 fascism appeared to have triumphed all along the line; at first by respecting the rules of the parliamentary democratic

Benjamin's reader's card for the Bibliothèque Nationale.

248

game, then increasingly by means of war and violence, it had conquered Europe piece by piece, country by country. Finally it even appeared to have made peace with its arch-enemy, communism, and sealed this with the Hitler-Stalin Pact. It is with this in mind that the remark from the tenth thesis should be read, which asks that we reflect upon what history really means when 'politicians in whom the opponents of fascism had placed their hopes [are] prostrate and [furthermore confirm] their defeat by betraying their own cause'. The stated aim of the theses was 'to disentangle the political worldlings from [their] snares'. And at their heart is a critique of 'the politicians' stubborn faith in progress'.[178]

The historian schooled in historical materialism can, according to Benjamin, only have some hope of success in this venture if he realizes that the reigning political impotency concurs with that of his conventional theory. So, if he is to escape the snares of a deterministic theory, he must resort to a set of devices whose basic elements are generally attributed to the field of theology. This is already expressed in the first thesis, which was shaped by Benjamin's underlying conviction that 'remembering something' involves an experience that prevents one from 'grasping history essentially as atheological'.[179] This is contrary to a conception of historical progress which, when thought through to its logical end, must in fact perceive the barbarism of fascism as a historical step forward. But what we term 'historical progress' is, according to Benjamin, not at home 'in the continuity of the course of time, but rather in its moments of interference', i.e. it is not embedded within the historical continuum but rather within the structure of history.[180]

Benjamin's concept is a messianic one in that he claims that there is a correspondence between what has occurred in history and messianic redemption. 'The past', he writes in his second thesis, 'carries with it a temporal index by which it is referred to redemption'. For him these interconnecting references link redemption with both the past and the present, although he no longer conceives the fulfilment of the messianic claims as being an act of history itself. Only the Messiah himself completes all historical occurrence in that he 'redeems, completes, creates' their relationship to the messianic.[181]

The theses 'On the Concept of History' are amongst Benjamin's last works. It is fairly obvious that they were not intended for publication, and the curious connection they make between theology and historical materialism (which is in fact a feature of his entire philosophy, although here they are brought

'The story is told of an automaton constructed in such a way that it could play a winning game of chess, answering each move of an opponent with a countermove. A puppet in Turkish attire and with a hookah in its mouth sat before a chessboard placed on a large table. A system of mirrors created the illusion that this table was transparent from all sides. Actually, a little hunchback who was an expert chess player sat inside and guided the puppet's hand by means of strings. One can imagine a philosophical counterpart to this device. The puppet called "historical materialism" is to win all the time. It can easily be a match for anyone if it enlists the services of theology, which today, as we know, is wizened and has to keep out of sight.'[92] (Baron von Kempelen's chess automaton)

into a hitherto unknown harmony) could only lay them open to misunderstanding. Consequently they only appeared posthumously in 1942, in a book published by the Institute for Social Research entitled *Walter Benjamin zum Gedächtnis [In Memory of Walter Benjamin]*, which was only distributed in a small number of duplicates.[182] Four years later a French version, containing a number of deviations from the original, appeared in *Les temps modernes*.[183] Then finally, in 1950, the German text was presented to a wider audience in the *Neue Rundschau*.[184]

Flight and death

In May 1940 Hitler's armies opened the offensive on the western front and swiftly converged on Paris, resulting in a mass exodus from the city. Over two million people fled by car, horse-drawn carriage, or by foot, taking with them their hastily bundled possessions in wheelbarrows, children's carts or simply tied onto their backs. Together with the five to six million Belgians and French from the north and east who were also escaping *les boches* in fear and panic, the refugees formed a never-ending caravan heading for the south of France.

UNE LETTRE DE WALTER BENJAMIN
AU SUJET DE
« LE REGARD » DE GEORGES SALLES

Je vous écris, encore captivé par le livre que vous m'avez fait emporter. Après vous avoir quitté l'autre jour, je suis entré dans un café et j'ai sorti *Le Regard*. Il faut vous dire que le charme a opéré dès la première page. Le plaisir d'y voir bousculé, par la comparaison entre l'art culinaire et l'Art, bon nombre d'idées reçues y fut sûrement pour quelque chose. La frivolité de ce début ne s'attaque pas à ce qu'il y a de sérieux dans l'œuvre d'art mais bien plutôt à ce qu'il y a de convenu dans notre façon d'en parler. Elle fait, en outre, penser à un auteur qui parlerait sensément des choses de la cuisine, et cela ne doit pas vous déplaire.

La particularité essentielle de Georges Salles pourrait bien être une ingénuité souveraine dans la réception de l'œuvre d'art. C'est en tout cas le don qu'il voudrait avant tout communiquer au public. Qui ne l'approuverait parmi ceux qui sont toujours péniblement frappés par le spectacle qu'offre, dans une exposition, en vogue, le grand public — hâtif dans son parcours, impatient d'en venir au jugement et pauvre dans les termes pour l'énoncer. On ne peut donc que tomber d'accord avec Georges Salles quand, résumant certaines expériences dont le champ a été le Louvre, il est amené à écrire : « Un musée réellement *éducatif* aura pour premier but d'affiner nos perceptions, ce qui sans doute n'est pas malaisé chez un peuple qui, si on l'y engage, saura apprécier ses poteries ou ses tableaux aussi bien que ses vins. » Si la prise de conscience et le pouvoir d'articulation dans la joie des sens est une vertu française, on peut penser que c'est un programme essentiellement français qui est ainsi défini par l'auteur.

'Every line we succeed in publishing today – no matter how uncertain the future to which we entrust it – is a victory wrenched from the powers of darkness.'[93] (Benjamin's last publication during his life, in the *Gazette des amis des livres*)

250

GOUVERNEMENT MILITAIRE DE PARIS

DEUXIÈME AVIS

concernant les Ressortissants

Allemands, Sarrois, Dantzickois

ET ÉTRANGERS

DE NATIONALITÉ INDÉTERMINÉE, MAIS D'ORIGINE ALLEMANDE

résidant dans le département de la Seine

Les ressortissants Allemands, Sarrois, Dantzickois, et étrangers de nationalité indéterminée, mais d'origine Allemande, résidant dans le département de la Seine âgés de 56 à 65 ans devront, comme il a été ordonné le 12 Mai pour les Hommes de 17 à 55 ans, y compris les prestataires, rejoindre le centre de Rassemblement du Stade Buffalo, où ils devront se présenter le 25 Mai 1940.

Ceux qui contreviendraient à cet ordre seront mis en état d'arrestation

Les étrangers visés ci-dessus pourront, à leurs frais, prendre le chemin de fer, ou tout autre moyen de transport public, pour rejoindre le Centre de Rassemblement assigné.

Ils devront se munir de vivres pour deux jours et du matériel nécessaire pour leur alimentation (fourchette, cuillère, quart, etc.)

Y compris les vivres, ils ne devront pas avoir plus de 30 kilos de bagages.

Les autorités Civiles et Militaires sont chargées de veiller à l'exécution de ces ordres.

Paris, le 23 Mai 1940.

Le Général d'Armée,
Gouverneur Militaire de Paris,

Signé : HÉRING.

'Cher Ami, je viens d'apprendre que M Hoppenot est intervenu pour vous pour vous dispenser de vous présenter demain au Stade Buffalo. Il a insisté spécialement pour que vous ne vous présentiez pas puisque son intervention auprès des autorités compétentes est close.'[94] (Proclamation from the French authorities, May 1940)

Marching in this desperate procession was Benjamin (along with his sister Dora, who had only just been released from the internment camp at Gurs). Thanks to the intervention of French friends, he had been spared a second internment and thus also renewed ordeals in assembly points, convoys and inhuman camps. But before leaving Paris he had managed to clear out his flat in the rue Dombasle and place his literary bequest in safe keeping.[185] He was able to deposit the greater part of it with friends;[186] the personally more important part – his notes and the material for the 'Arcades' project, as well as the written manuscripts of a number of his works – were hidden in the Bibliothèque Nationale by his friend Georges Bataille. Only a part of the documents that he was forced to leave behind – primarily letters, but also a number of other personal documents as well as numerous pieces for radio – were lost during their subsequent odyssey through various impoundings and transferrals from one store house to the next.

Benjamin's flight first took him to Lourdes, which was by that time swarming with refugees, where he spent the summer months waiting to receive an entry permit for the United States. Then at the end of August, in order to settle the remaining formalities for his emigration from France, he travelled to Marseilles, where Horkheimer had succeeded in obtaining an emergency visa for him from the US consulate. [187] But Benjamin failed to gather all the documents he needed, and thus he decided to slip over the Spanish border illegally. The correctness of this decision was confirmed, shortly before Benjamin's escape attempt, by the historical handshake of Montaire (between Hitler and Pétain) on 24 September 1940. The result of this was that emigrants in the unoccupied parts of the country were also liable to be handed over to the Germans.

I remember waking up in that narrow room under the roof where I had gone to sleep a few hours earlier. Someone was knocking at the door. It had to be the little girl from downstairs; I got out of bed and opened the door. But it wasn't the child. I rubbed my half-closed eyes. It was one of our friends, Walter Benjamin . . . Now how did he get here? – 'Gnädige Frau,' he said, 'please accept my apologies for this inconvenience.' The world was coming apart I thought, but not Benjamin's politesse. 'Ihr Herr Gemahl,' he continued, told me how to find you. He said you could take me across the border into Spain.' He said What? Oh well yes, 'mein Herr Gemahl' – my husband – would say that. He would assume that I could do it, whatever 'it' might be. . . . 'But Mr Benjamin, do you realize that I am not a competent guide in this region?' I don't really know that road, I have never been up that way myself. . . . You want to take the risk?' – 'Yes,' he said without hesitation. 'The real risk would be not to go.'[188]

At dawn on 26 September 1940,[189] a group of three people set out from Banyuls-sur-Mer to cross the Pyrenees to Spain: Lisa Fittko, the guide who had yet to become acquainted with the district, Henny Gurland (née Schoenstedt, who was to become Erich Fromm's second wife in 1944) and her son Joseph. Carrying musettes, small canvass bags typical to the area, the group mixed with the farmers, who always made their way to the vineyards before sunrise, thus managing to escape detection by the police and border guards as they left the village. Further

Hitler in Paris.

on they collected Benjamin, who had used a hiking tour the previous day to cover the first leg of what amounted to almost half a day's ascent and descent. He had let the group return on their own and had spent the night on the open mountainside. The illegal crossing went fairly smoothly. The escape route had already been well tested (just two weeks before a group including Heinrich and Nelly Mann, Alma Mahler, Franz Werfel and Golo Mann had used it to reach Spain).[190] And not even Benjamin's impaired health or his heart condition, which compelled him to take regular breaks (four decades later, Lisa Fittko could recall the exact rhythm that they had been forced to maintain: ten minutes of walking followed by a one-minute break),[191] had proved to be too much of an obstacle. In the

253

afternoon they reached the apparent salvation of Portbou – a small coastal town still bearing the scars of heavy bombardment during the Civil War – on the Spanish side of the border. The journey on to Lisbon was to be made in the comfort of a train. (They had hoped to get from there to the United States without any appreciable difficulties.)

But for 'old Benjamin', as Lisa Fittko referred to him half fondly, half mockingly, Portbou proved to be the end of the road. On announcing themselves to the Spanish police, they discovered that their transit visas for Spain, which had been valid until then, had been made null and void overnight on the orders of the government, and that all refugees from France had to be sent back at once. The possibilities awaiting him on his return – arrest and a return to a French internment camp, which in all likelihood would prove to be the transit point to a concentration camp in Germany – appeared to Benjamin to be an insurmountable obstacle on his road to freedom.

The events that followed have remained unclear until quite recently. The precise circumstances of Benjamin's death, the location of his grave, the fate of his possessions, including the 'manuscript' that he wanted at all costs to prevent from falling into the wrong hands – all these have been shrouded in mystery and become the source of endless speculation, much of it quite fanciful.[192]

The latest research, by Ingrid and Konrad Scheurmann, much of it drawing on recently discovered documents in the Portbou community archive, solves at least some of these puzzles. To give a clear picture of what happened to Benjamin following his arrival in Portbou, it is worth quoting their findings at some length:

After Benjamin's failure to get the official stamp needed for entering Spain, he was allowed . . . to spend a night at Portbou 'sous la garde des gendarmes' – as Grete Freund wrote in a letter dated 9.10.1940[193] *– before being taken back to France. Henny Gurland also mentions . . . that the group was under observation in the hotel, 'and we were introduced to three policemen who were supposed to escort us to the French border in the morning'.*[194]

The hotel ('Fonda de Francia') owner, Sr. Juan Suñer Jonama, was himself obviously on good terms with both the Spanish police and the local representatives of the Gestapo, who came to eat in his restaurant. According to his own statement, Suñer thought it important that all his guests were registered with the police, and those who had crossed the frontier illegally were regularly sent

Benjamin's Spanish death certificate.

back.[195] *Research carried out by Narcisco Alba for* Quimera, *the Spanish journal, confirms the hotel owner's memories. His good connections with the German Nazis were known in the village.*[196]

This ominous situation may perhaps explain why Benjamin (according to Grete Freund) 'était tout à fait désespéré le soir à l'hôtel'. He ate at the hotel on the evening of his arrival . . . , and must have been aware of the nature of the other diners. Nevertheless, despite all this upheaval, he obviously tried to seek help somewhere. Apart from the postcard (mentioned by Hans Mayer) to the Geneva representative of the Institute for Social Research, Juliane Favez,[197] four telephone calls have become known in the meantime — for which the hotel-owner charged

255

'I knew Benjamin, who was an extremely bright man, and received a final letter from him, a cry for help from the border at the Pyrenees in 1940. I did what I could for his emigration (via acquaintances in Spain). Once everything had been arranged, I received by the same post a letter that informed me about this the official news that Benjamin had committed suicide.'[95] (The news article on Benjamin's suicide in the New York weekly *Aufbau*, 11 October 1940)

Scientist Suicide in Spain

Many Refugees Believed Victims of Mountain Gangs

LISBON, Oct. 7 (ONA.) — The suicide of Prof. *Walter Benjamin*, a well-known psychologist, and the mysterious disappearance of many refugees in the mountainous Franco-Spanish frontier zone were reported by reliable sources here today.

The professor, during recent years attached to the faculty of the Sorbonne at Paris and to the Institute for Social Research at N. Y. Columbia University, committed suicide by poison at the Franco-Spanish frontier town of Port Bou after Spanish authorities forbade him to continue his projected journey to Lisbon and the United States, according to four women friends who said they witnessed his death.

At the same time it was reported that many refugees who succeeded in getting into Spain from France had disappeared without trace during recent weeks. It was feared here that they had been killed in the mountainous frontier area by gangs of bandits who had promised to smuggle them across the border.

Prof. Benjamin, who had been granted a visa by the United States but had not been granted an exit permit by the French authorities, succeeded in slipping across the border.

The Spanish police chief at Port Bou, however, took them sternly to task for their getaway over the border and told them he would not permit them to continue their journey. The refugees asked for permission to rest a couple of hours and discuss their next move, a request which was granted. During this period of waiting, the professor, despairing of completing his journey, took a strong dose of poison from a phial he carried and died before the horrified eyes of his four women companions.

The professor was buried in the Catholic cemetery at Port Bou, although he was a Jew, because officials found on his person a note from a prominent French Catholic clergyman to Spanish Catholic church notables urging them to help the professor complete his trip.

8.80 pesetas in the bill. No information is available about possible recipients. Benjamin may have been trying to reach the American consul-general in Barcelona, seeking help there. Grete Freund mentions that on the evening of their arrival the group of refugees intended 'de téléphoner à la première heure au consul Américain de Barcelona pour qu'il avait une récommendation personelle et à qui nous voulions demander pour M. Benjamin aide et assistance'.[198] Whether contact was established remains uncertain. All that is known is that the consulate did nothing to ease the situation of the refugees at Portbou.[199]

According to the Portbou register of deaths, Walter Benjamin died at 10 p.m. on 26 September. It has generally been accepted that he took his own life, in despair at an impossible situation. None of the new evidence contradicts this assumption, although it does not categorically confirm it either. Until now the only 'conclusive' proof was a postcard which Benjamin appears to have written at some point in the night of 25 September to Henny Gurland and Adorno. 'In a situation with no way out, I have no choice but to end it. My life will finish in a little village in the Pyrenees where no one knows me. Please pass on my thoughts to my friend Adorno and explain to him the situation in which I find myself. There is not enough time to write all the letters I had wanted to write.'[200] But the original postcard did not survive. Henny Gurland destroyed it during her flight and only later, in America, reconstructed it from memory, probably at Adorno's request. Inconsistencies in her account of Benjamin's death in the hotel suggest her memory was not infallible. Citing the Scheurmanns' research again, the facts as we now know them are these:

A Spanish doctor, Ramón Vila Moreno, attended Walter Benjamin on the evening of 25 September. However, it still remains unclear who called the doctor and at what time. Grete Freund reports that the group sent for the doctor on the evening of their arrival after it had become clear that Benjamin had taken morphine: 'En dépit de nos efforts il semble avoir pris un stupé-fiant (forte dose de morphium) dans la même nuit et quand nous avons fait venir le médicin tout de suite'. Henny Gurland, on the other hand, maintains that the doctor was only called the following morning. From the doctor's bill and the court files it is apparent that Frau Gurland's account is in all probability wrong. The doctor visited Benjamin four times in all – 'todos los días' (on different days) as the hotel-owner told the judge. . . . The doctor must therefore have paid an initial visit on 25 September.

In his bill Vila Moreno charged for several injections, taking blood pressure, and a blood-letting. . . . Presumably the doctor diagnosed – in a man with a serious heart condition – very high blood pressure after the exertions of crossing the Pyrenees and the afternoon's excitements, and first administered a blood-letting so as to reduce that. If at that time Benjamin had already taken a high dose of morphine – as Grete Freund writes – then it is surprising that the doctor did not notice the signs of that (contracted pupils and changed reactions). . . . However, it may be that Moreno attended and treated Benjamin, already suffering acutely, before morphine was taken, and could not explain to himself the ill man's changed state on the following day. The fact that a large amount of morphine was taken in the night of 25/26 September . . . was at any rate attested to by both Grete Freund and Henny Gurland in their letters. It has been known at least since the publication of Arthur Koestler's Scum of the Earth *that*

'Here rests the extraordinary professor of respectable philosophy.'[96] (View from Columbarien Cemetery, Portbou)

Benjamin carried a supply of morphine. Koestler met Benjamin in Marseilles shortly before the latter set off for Port-Vendres, and thus came to hear of more than the philosopher's plans to flee. 'He possessed fifty morphine tablets, which he intended to take if captured. He told me that was enough to kill a horse, and gave me half of his tablets – "just in case"'.[201]

Nevertheless it remains uncertain whether Benjamin really did take that 'large' dose of morphine on 25 September and then managed to live for a further 24 or so hours despite the poor state of his health.

... According to the now discovered report by the [Portbou] judge, Fernando Pastor Nieto, he heard around 22.35 from the hotel-owner that a 'foreign traveller' had died and went to the hotel. He found Benjamin lying on his bed, fully clothed. All the known documentation indicates that death really did occur at this time – especially as it is completely improbable that Benjamin died considerably earlier and his death was initially kept secret by the women accompanying him.

There is no discernible reason for that. The doctor's regular visits also counter such an assumption.

That once again raises the question of the doctor's competence or motivation. It remains unclear how he could have reached the documented conclusion that his patient died as the result of a "cerebral haemorrhage" – despite having visited Benjamin four times so that he should have diagnosed the drug's impact on the morning of 26 September at the latest. It is also not known whether Vila Moreno was informed about the 'x-ray photograph and the accompanying medical report' ... that – according to

The first memorial plaque to Walter Benjamin in Portbou, erected in 1979.

the judge's account – Benjamin carried with him; and whether the doctor, possibly aware of his patient's poor state, persisted in treating the heart condition with blood-letting, medicaments, and injections. It seems reasonable to ask, along with Joseph Gurland, Henny's son: '. . . how much of the medical situation was really understood by the doctor and the priest and how much was either pity or convenience on their part'.[202] No one at Portbou in 1940 seemed to have doubted that death was from natural causes.

The judge's precise report at no point mentions the existence of morphine. If one assumes that Benjamin probably did not take all 25 tablets that Koestler said he possessed (if he had, he would have died more quickly), then one of the people accompanying him or (less probably) the doctor must have removed what remained of the morphine. Did Moreno perhaps assume that his patient, 'Dr. B. Walter', was a fellow doctor whom he did not want to get into trouble; or might his diagnosis have reflected concealed political sympathy with this German on the run and his women companions, resulting in his covering up a possible suicide? In Franco's Spain suicide was a penal offence, which had to be reported to the Guardia Civil for further investigation. It is not to be excluded either that as a village doctor Vila Moreno was inexperienced and wrongly diagnosed the symptoms of Benjamin's illness.[203]

Much conjecture has also surrounded the fate of the few possessions Benjamin was carrying at the time of his death. The 'manuscript' he was supposedly carrying has acquired almost legendary status. Evidence from his companions confirms his

'Schwerer ist es, das Gedächtnis der Namenlosen zu ehren als das der Berühmten. Dem Gedächtnis der Namenlosen ist die historische Konstruktion geweiht.'
'It is more arduous to honour the memory of the nameless than that of the renowned. Historical construction is devoted to the memory of the nameless.'[97]
(The epitaph on Dani Karavan's 'Passages', his monument to Walter Benjamin in Portbou, inaugurated on 15 May, 1994) [98]

attachment to this manuscript. As Lisa Fittko put it: 'It looks to me as if his life was worth less to him than the manuscript'.[204] It now seems very unlikely that we will ever be sure what it contained. All Benjamin's possessions at the time of his death were handed over to the court in Figueras on 5 October 1940, and were described as follows: 'a leather briefcase like businessmen use, a man's watch, a pipe, six photographs, an x-ray picture, glasses, various letters, magazines, and a few other papers whose content is unknown, and also some money.'[205] Detailed receipts exist. The Figueras archive was moved to another building in 1975; it was there discovered that records 'had been visited by water and rats . . . and had to be thrown away.'[206] Further investigations by the Scheurmanns in 1992 uncovered no trace of Benjamin's belongings, and it must be concluded that they no longer exist. It may well be that the manuscript itself was destroyed immediately after Benjamin's death, perhaps, as Scholem has argued,[207] by Henny Gurland, who may have feared the consequences of it being discovered by the police.[208] In any case, Rolf Tiedemann has argued that the manuscript was probably a copy of one which Benjamin had earlier given to Georges Bataille for safekeeping in the Bibliothèque Nationale: Benjamin's desperate attachment to his copy may have derived from his (incorrect, as it turned out) belief that the other copy would have been found and removed by the Nazis. The most likely text, according to Tiedemann, is *On the Concept of History.*[209]

Finally, confusion long surrounded the circumstances of Benjamin's burial and the precise location of his grave. This has now been carefully unravelled by Manuel Cussó-Ferrer during research for his film about Benjamin's last days, *L'Ultima frontera [The Final Frontier].*[210] Portbou officials assumed that Benjamin was a Catholic, and thus gave him extreme unction, a requiem mass and burial in the town's Catholic cemetery on 28 September. His grave was paid for out of the money in his possession, but this only covered 'rental' for a period of five years. After that time, in December 1945, his remains were transferred, probably to the common grave in the cemetery.

The last, bitter irony in this story is the fact that immediately after Benjamin's death, the Spanish authorities decided to waive the new regulations and allowed his companions to continue their journey through Spain. It has sometimes been claimed that they did this out of compassion, moved by his suicide. This seems highly unlikely: customs officials in war-time are rarely given to displays of generosity, and in any case they would not have known that Benjamin had committed suicide. Perhaps their orders were unclear, or had changed. As with so many aspects of these events, muddle and human error probably played the determining role. It is hard not to ask whether, then, Benjamin's death was 'preventable', 'unnecessary', though these are unanswerable, pointless questions. Hundreds of others were dying, unnecessarily, anonymously, on other borders; millions were to die with no border in sight.

In October 1940, the philosopher Hannah Arendt passed through Portbou and tried, without success, to find the grave of her friend Walter Benjamin. She described her visit to Gershom Scholem in Israel: 'The cemetery looks out over a small bay, directly on the Mediterranean. Its terraces are hewn out of stone, and coffins are also put in these stone walls. This is one of the most fantastic and beautiful places I have ever seen.' Until 1979, when a small plaque was erected in the cemetery, there was no public commemoration of Benjamin in Portbou, although it seems that many in the town remembered the fate of this German refugee, had made him into a kind of local symbol for all the other forgotten victims of fascism. In 1990, commissioned by the Arbeitskreis selbständiger Kultur-Institute (AsKI) in Bonn on behalf of the German government, the Israeli artist Dani Karavan began planning a large-scale monument in Portbou. Karavan was already renowned for his remarkable monumental work in Israel and elsewhere: it included a memorial for victims of the Holocaust at the Weizmann Institute in Rehovot, the 'Kikar Levana – White Square' environment in Tel Aviv, and an installation at the 1976 Venice Biennale dedicated to peace between the Arabs and Israelis, 'Olive Trees Should be Our Borders'.

The Portbou monument, 'Passages', was inaugurated in May 1994. Its centrepiece is a flight of 70 narrow steps cut into the cliff at the seaward side of the cemetery, running down at an angle of 30° through rusty iron walls to a dizzying dead-end overlooking the rocks and sea below. A glass screen terminates the passage; compelled to retrace their steps, visitors turn to face the cemetery and, before emerging from the tunnel, are confronted by a wall of undressed stone, set in the axial extension of the corridor into a rock-face surrounding the cemetery forecourt. The sea, the cemetery: no way out. Engraved into the glass that blocks the passage is a single quotation from Walter Benjamin's theses *On the Concept of History*. 'It is more arduous to honour the memory of the nameless than that of the renowned. Historical construction is devoted to the memory of the nameless.'

263

Notes

Frequently cited English translations of works by Benjamin and anthologies of his writings are referred to by the following abbreviations in the notes:

Illuminations = *Illuminations: Essays and Reflections*, ed. and introduced by Hannah Arendt, trans. Harry Zohn, New York 1968.
The Origin of German Tragic Drama = *The Origin of German Tragic Drama*, introduced by George Steiner, trans. John Osborne, London and New York 1977.
Charles Baudelaire = *Charles Baudelaire: A Lyric Poet in the Era of High Capitalism*, trans. Harry Zohn, London and New York 1968.
One Way Street = *One Way Street and Other Writings*, introduced by Susan Sontag, trans. Edmund Jephcott and Kingsley Shorter, London 1979.
Correspondence = *The Correspondence of Walter Benjamin, 1910–1940*, ed. and annotated by Gershom Scholem and Theodor W. Adorno, trans. Manfred R. Jacobson and Evelyn M. Jacobson, Chicago and London 1994.
Benjamin–Scholem, *Correspondence* = *The Correspondence of Walter Benjamin and Gershom Scholem, 1933–1940*, ed. Gershom Scholem, trans. Gary Smith and André Lefevre, New York 1989.
Scholem, *Friendship* = Gershom Scholem, *Walter Benjamin: The Story of a Friendship*, trans. Harry Zohn, Philadelphia 1977.
Moscow Diary = *Moscow Diary*, ed. Gary Smith, trans. Richard Sieburth, Cambridge, Mass., 1986.

All German references to Benjamin's collected works in German (*Gesammelte Schriften*, eds. Hermann Schweppenhäuser and Rolf Tiedemann, Frankfurt am Main, 1974–89) are indicated by the abbreviation *GS* followed by the volume number.
Further frequently cited works in German are:

Scholem, *Engel* = Gershom Scholem, *Walter Benjamin und sein Engel. Vierzehn Aufsätze und kleine Beiträge*, ed. Rolf Tiedemann, Frankfurt am Main 1983.
Briefe an Kracauer = Walter Benjamin, *Briefe an Siegfried Kracauer. Mit vierzehn Briefen von Siegfried Kracauer an Walter Benjamin*, pub. Theodor W. Adorno Archiv, ed. Rolf Tiedemann and Henri Lonitz, Marbach am Neckar 1987.
Gesammelte Briefe, vol. 1 = Walter Benjamin, *Gesammelte Briefe*, vol. 1: *1910–1918*, eds Christoph Gödde and Henri Lonitz, Frankfurt am Main 1995; vol. 2: *1919–1924*, Frankfurt am Main 1996.

1. Wolf Jobst Siedler, 'Die Tradition der Traditionslosigkeit. Notizen zur Baugeschichte Berlins', in *Preußen. Versuch einer Bilanz*, exhibition catalogue in 5 vols, Reinbek bei Hamburg 1981, vol. 2, p. 311.

Chapter 1

2. Or, more correctly, towns, because these streets also ploughed through the suburbs of Berlin which at that time had still been autonomous: as developments progressed, Charlottenburg, Wilmersdorf, Schöneberg and Grunewald adapted their road networks to those of the capital.

3. 'There was no turning back, from now on the only way was forwards', as Fallada wrote in *Iron Gustav*, trans. Philip Owens, London 1969.

4. *GS* VII, p. 122 ('Die Mietskaserne').

5. 'One-Way Street', in *One-Way Street*, pp. 45–104.

6. Now in *GS* IV, pp. 567–87.

7. The review of Franz Hessel's book *Spazieren in Berlin*, 1929, now in *GS* III, pp. 194–9.

8. Now all in *GS* IV, pp. 307–66. In part in *One-Way Street*, pp. 167–222. ('Naples', 'Moscow', 'Marseilles', 'Hashish in Marseilles'), and in *Illuminations*, pp. 61–9 ('Unpacking my library').

9. 'Moscow', in *One-Way Street*, pp. 177–208.

10. Benjamin's 'Berliner Chronik' has been translated as 'A Berlin Chronicle' in *One Way Street*, pp. 293–346; for 'Berliner Kindheit um Neunzehnhundert' ['A Berlin Childhood Around 1900'] cf. *GS* IV, pp. 235–304 and *GS* VII, pp. 385–433.

11. 'Victory Column', trans. Keith Hamnett, in *German Mosaic: An Album for Today*, ed. Dieter Hildebrandt and Siegfried Unseld, Frankfurt am Main 1972.

12. *GS* V, p. 674.

13. 'A Berlin Chronicle' in *One-Way Street*, p. 317.

14. *GS* IV, p. 253 (*Berliner Kindheit um Neunzehnhundert*).

15. 'A Berlin Chronicle', in *One-Way Street*, p. 293.

16. Hilde Benjamin, *Georg Benjamin. Eine Biographie*, Leipzig 1977, p. 19.

17. Harden bought the house of Lily and Heinrich Braun in nearby Wernerstraße around the turn of the century (cf. B. Uwe Weller, *Maximilian Harden und die 'Zukunft'*, Bremen 1970, p. 58).

18. Werner Hegemann, *Das steinerne Berlin. Geschichte der größten Mietskasernenstadt der Welt*, Brunswick and Wiesbaden 1979, p. 275. Benjamin knew this report on the scandal surrounding the founding of modern Berlin and gave the work a lengthy review in the literary supplement of the *Frankfurter Zeitung*, 1930 (cf. 'Ein Jakobiner von heute'; now in *GS* III, pp. 260–65.).

19. Paul Voigt, quoted in W. Hegemann, *Das steinerne Berlin*, p. 275.

20. 'A Berlin Chronicle', in *One-Way Street*, p. 324.

21. This double 'Benjamin' was presumably a leftover from the times when fathers bequeathed their first names to their sons as family names. However, for legal and administrative reasons a system of unification was introduced by the princely and royal administrations, which put an end to this tradition throughout Germany by the late eighteenth and early nineteenth centuries. From 1812, the year in which they were granted citizenship, the Jews in Prussia mostly selected fixed family names (they only became obligatory on the order of the Prussian Cabinet in 1845). The first among Benjamin's relatives to bear such a name was his great-grandfather Elias (= Emil) Benjamin (1769–1835), who derived it from his father's complete first name Elija ben Bima (cf. Scholem, *Engel*, pp. 133–4; 'Ahnen und Verwandte Walter Benjamins').

22. 'A Berlin Chronicle', in *One-Way Street*, p. 324.

23. Ibid., p. 325 and pp. 326–7.
24. Scholem, *Engel*, p. 130 ('Ahnen und Verwandte Walter Benjamins').
25. 'A Berlin Chronicle', in *One-Way Street*, p. 325.
26. Ibid., p. 327.
27. Ibid., p. 326.
28. Ibid., p. 294.
29. *GS* IV, p. 287 *(Berliner Kindheit um Neunzehnhundert)*.
30. One of many typical examples are the wonderful memoirs of the photographer Erwin Blumenfeld *(Durch tausendjährige Zeit*, Berlin 1988).
31. 'A Berlin Chronicle', in *One-Way Street*, p.299.
32. *GS* IV, pp. 264–5 *(Berliner Kindheit um Neunzehnhundert)*.
33. *GS* VII, p. 404 *(Berliner Kindheit um Neunzehnhundert*, final version).
34. The different spellings of these two names (Benedix instead of Bendix and Schoenflies with 'ö' instead of 'oe' and/or 'ß' instead of 's') that appear in the various documents can be attributed to the mistakes or vagaries of the officials who wrote them. In the documents of the registry office, the names are always given in the manner adhered to here.
35. It is worth recalling in this context the brief autobiographical sketch 'Agesilaus Santander' from 1933, which centres on these two names of Bendix und Schoenflies without actually revealing them. Not even Benjamin's best friend, Gershom Scholem, knew of their existence.
36. 'A Berlin Chronicle', in *One-Way Street*, p. 317.
37. In a letter he once made a direct admission of his scanty knowledge of Heine (*Correspondence*, p. 520, to Werner Kraft, 30 January 1936).
38. *Correspondence*, p. 531 (to W. Kraft, 11 August 1936).
39. Scholem, Engel, p. 133 ('Ahnen und Verwandte Walter Benjamins').
40. *GS* IV, p. 258 (*Berliner Kindheit um Neunzehnhundert*).
41. That was in 1930 when the, by that time, somewhat unworldly and ageing gentleman arrived from Rouen to open a scientific Institute for Graphology at the Lessing college in Berlin (cf. *GS* IV, p. 596, 'Alte und neue Graphologie').
42. The earliest known evidence of Benjamin's interests in this science is to be found in his diary entitled 'Meine Reise in Italien Pfingsten 1912'. Here he mentions in passing: 'Simon is converted to graphology during a conversation' (*GS* VI, p. 262).
43. A fragment of one of these reports is included in the appendix to vol. VI of Benjamin's *GS* (cf. pp. 748–9).
44. Scholem, *Friendship*, p. 112 (Benjamin to Scholem, end of January 1922).
45. It would be interesting to know whether the diary 'Tagebuch für Schreiberhau' that Benjamin wrote at the age of 10 gives any closer insights into his relationship with his aunt. In the custody of the Adorno-Archiv, Frankfurt, it has yet to be made available to interested readers.
46. *GS* VII p. 411 (*Berliner Kindheit um Neunzehnhundert*, final version).
47. 'A Berlin Chronicle', in *One-Way Street*, p. 333.
48. Cf. Scholem, *Engel*, p. 150 ('Ahnen und Verwandte Walter Benjamins').
49. Cf. Paul Kluke, *Die Stiftungsuniversität Frankfurt am Main 1914–1932*, Frankfurt am Main 1972, pp. 167.

50. *GS* VI, p. 414 ('Notizen von einer Reise nach Frankfurt. 30 Mai 1928').
51. For the story of Gertrud Kolmar's life, cf. Gertrud Kolmar, compiled by Johanna Woltmann, 2nd revised ed., Marbach am Neckar 1993 (*Marbacher Magazin*, no. 63). The recollections of Benjamin's sister-in-law, Hilde, of her friend Gertrud Kolmar are contained in the volume of Kolmar's posthumous poems (*Das Wort der Stummen*, Berlin 1978).
52. Cf. Max Rychner, 'Erinnerungen an Walter Benjamin', in *Über Walter Benjamin*, Frankfurt am Main 1968, p. 27, as well as the letter from Gertrud Kolmar to Benjamin, 10 October 1934, quoted below.
53. *GS* IV, pp. 803–4 ('Zwei Gedichte. Von Gertrud Kolmar' [with a preface by Walter Benjamin]).
54. Gertrud Kolmar, 'Zwei Briefe an Walter Benjamin', *Sinn und Form*, vol. 43, 1991, cited on p. 122 (letter dated 10 October 1934).

Chapter 2

1. *Correspondence*, p. 23 (to Herbert Blumenthal, 5 May 1913).
2. In his recollections, Benjamin gave a brief portrait of his two private teachers – a certain Helen Pufahl, and Karl Knoche, the elementary teacher at the school he later attended (cf. 'A Berlin Chronicle', in *One-Way Street*, pp. 331–2.).
3. Adalbert Delbrück was the son of the minister of state; the father of Hans Simmel was the philosopher and sociologist Georg Simmel; the name Ludwig Hecks is linked with the director of the zoological gardens in Berlin; and Edgar Meyer was a scion of the still highly regarded classical historian.
4. Several of Benjamin's most important critiques were published in *Die Gesellschaft* under Salomon's aegis: his 'Politisierung der Intelligenz' (a review of Siegfried Kracauer's study 'Die Angestellten', reprinted in the *GS* under the title originally intended by Benjamin 'Ein Außenseiter macht sich bemerkbar') and 'Krisis des Romans' (a commentary on Alfred Döblin's novel *Berlin Alexanderplatz*), as well as the 'Theorien des deutschen Faschismus' (a review of an anthology edited by Ernst Jünger entitled *Krieg und Krieger*). All of these texts appeared in 1930 (now in *GS* III, pp. 219–25, pp. 230–36 and pp. 238–50).
5. 'Bericht des Direktors der Kaiser-Friedrich-Schule an die vorgesetzte Behörde' [Report of the headmaster of the Kaiser Friedrich School to the school authorities], unpublished, undated document (1905/06), in the Archiv des Pädagogischen Zentrums Berlin, Akten der Kaiser-Friedrich-Schule, p. 23.
6. Cf. *Correspondence*, pp. 5–6. (to H. Blumenthal, 22 July 1910).
7. 'A Berlin Chronicle', in *One-Way Street*, p. 335–6.
8. *Kaiser-Friedrich-Schule, Charlottenburg: 15. Bericht über das Schuljahr 1911*, Charlottenburg 1912, pp. 6, 10 and 16.
9. *GS* VI, p. 801 (sketches for Berliner Chronik).
10. Albert Salomon, 'Im Schatten einer endlosen grossen Zeit. Erinnerungen aus einem langen Leben für meine Kinder, jungen Freunde und Studenten' (unpublished MS, Leo Baeck Institute, New York, estate of A. Salomon), p. 3.
11. *GS* VII, p. 403, p. 406 and p. 404 (*Berliner Kindheit um Neunzehnhundert*, final version).

12. *GS* IV, p. 435 ('Noch einmal').
13. Wyneken already started working for Lietz in October 1900: he taught until 1903 at Ilsenburg im Harz (cf. G. Wyneken, 'Zur Orientierung', unpublished MS, Archiv der deutsche Jugendbewegung, Burg Ludwigstein, estate of G. Wyneken).
14. Cf. *GS* IV, pp. 532–3 ('Der Kampf der Tertia').
15. Thomas Mann, Preface to Erich von Mendelssohn, *Nacht und Tag*, Leipzig 1914, p. XIII.
16. 'A Berlin Chronicle', in *One-Way Street*, p. 304.
17. 'Deutsche Landerziehungsheime'; cited in *GS* II, p. 827.
18. Walter Mjudiß (i.e. Erdmut Wizisla), 'Alles gelernt für später? Kindheit um 1900: Walter Benjamin im Landerziehungsheim Haubinda', in *Die Tageszeitung*, Berlin, 6 August 1987 pp. 11–12.
19. Benjamin describes one of these outings that he made at the age of about 15 with his 'fellow traveller and sufferer' Hellmut Kautel in 'Pfingstreise von Haubinda aus' (cf. *GS* VI, pp. 229–31).
20. *GS* VII, p. 531; this *curriculum vitae* dates from 16 December 1911 and was part of Benjamin's application for admission to his school finals.
21. G. Wyneken, 'Reform des D.L.E.H.' (unpublished MS, Archiv der deutschen Jugendbewegung, Burg Ludwigstein, estate of G. Wyneken), points 4, 16, 32, 9, 33, 3 and 14.
22. *GS* VII, p. 532 ('Lebenslauf', 1911).
23. *GS* II, pp. 37 and 38.
24. *Moscow Diary*, p. 100.
25. *Correspondence*, p. 13, footnote 4 (letter from Franz Sachs).
26. Not only his 'one-year exam', but all of Benjamin's exam papers have been preserved by the Pädagogisches Zentrum in Berlin.
27. Now in *GS* II, pp. 83–4, and pp. 832–4.
28. Ibid., pp. 9 and 12.
29. Here he speaks of the 'fear of having to take the *Abitur* again (under more unfavourable conditions)' adding that his own 'recklessness and folly' had placed him in this position ('A Berlin Chronicle', p. 302). On the other hand, the minutes of the 'conference of the headmaster and the teachers on the examination board' of 13 December 1911 notes that the pupil Walter Benjamin had 'quite clearly' attained the necessary marks (unpublished document; Archiv des Pädagogischen Zentrums Berlin, Akten der Kaiser-Friedrich-Schule, p. 2).
30. Now in *GS* VII, pp. 536–6.
31. *GS* VI, p. 261 ('Meine Reise in Italien Pfingsten 1912').
32. Cf. Scholem, *Engel*, p. 146 ('Ahnen und Verwandte Walter Benjamins'). Emil Benjamin should perhaps be finally freed from the present cloud of incomprehension surrounding his resistance towards his son's *Abitur*. It was anything but the rule at the time, and even the children of the higher strata often only attended school long enough to complete their 'one-year exam'.
33. Cf. *GS* VI, pp. 252–4. ('Meine Reise in Italien Pfingsten 1912').
34. 'A Berlin Chronicle', in *One-Way Street*, p. 327.
35. The 'Tagebuch für Schreiberhau' (Benjamin's earliest notes, written in summer 1902 and still unpublished), his 'Pfingstreise von Haubinda aus', the 'Tagebuch Pfingsten 1911', the 'Tagebuch von Wengen' and 'Von der Sommerreise 1911' (the last four diaries are all now included in *GS* VI, pp. 229–51).
36. *GS* VI, p. 232 ('Tagebuch Pfingsten 1911').
37. Ibid., p. 456 ('Spanien 1932').

38. *Correspondence*, p. 16 (to H. Blumenthal, 21 June 1912).
39. The title of a work by Goethe, whom Benjamin was emulating here.
40. *GS* VI, p. 252 ('Meine Reise in Italien Pfingsten 1912').
41. All allusions and quotes are taken from Benjamin's record 'Meine Reise in Italien Pfingsten 1912' (ibid., pp. 252–92).
42. Ibid., p. 292 ('Meine Reise in Italien Pfingsten 1912').

Chapter 3

1. Cf. Irmtraud and Albrecht Götz von Olenhusen, 'Walter Benjamin, Gustav Wyneken und die Freistudenten vor dem Ersten Weltkrieg. Bemerkungen zu zwei Briefen Benjamins an Wyneken', *Jahrbuch der deutschen Jugendbewegung*, vol. 13, 1981, p. 108.
2. *Correspondence*, pp. 14–15 (to H. Blumenthal, 14 May 1912).
3. Albert Salomon, 'Im Schatten einer endlosen grossen Zeit', p. 3.
4. *Correspondence*, p. 15 (to H. Blumenthal, 21 June 1912).
5. 'Tagebuch', Dr G. Wyneken, April 1912–April 1914, diary entry 5 May 1912 (unpublished MS, Archiv der deutschen Jugendbewegung, Burg Ludwigstein, estate of G. Wyneken).
6. 'Tagebuch', Dr G. Wyneken, April 1912–April 1914, diary entry 13 March 1913.
7. *GS* II, p. 836 (to Ludwig Strauß, 10 October 1912).
8. Cf. Gustav Wyneken, 'Studentenschaft und Schulreform', in *Die freie Schulgemeinde*, vol. 1, no. 1, 1911, pp. 1 ff.
9. Christian Papmeyer, 'Student und Schulreform', in Student und Pädagogik II: *Erste studentisch-pädagogische Tagung zu Breslau am 6. und 7. Oktober 1913*, ed. Alfred Mann (commissioned by the represented groups), Leipzig and Berlin 1914, p. 16.
10. I. and A. Götz von Olenhusen, 'Walter Benjamin, Gustav Wyneken und die Freistudenten vor dem Ersten Weltkrieg', p. 106.
11. Ibid., pp. 106–7.
12. Cf. C. Papmeyer, 'Student und Schulreform', p. 19.
13. *GS* II, pp. 13 and 16 ('Die Schulreform, eine Kulturbewegung').
14. 'A Berlin Chronicle', in *One-Way Street*, p. 300.
15. *Correspondence*, p. 17 (to H. Blumenthal, 12 August 1912).
16. Ibid., p. 18 (footnote 2, letter from Kurt Tuchler).
17. Benjamin cited in Scholem, *Friendship*, p. 35.
18. *GS* II, p. 836 (to L. Strauß, 10 October 1912).
19. 'Bericht des Direktors der Kaiser-Friedrich-Schule an die vorgesetzte Behörde' [Report of the headmaster of the Kaiser Friedrich School to the school authorities], unpublished, undated document (1905/6), in the Archiv des Pädagogischen Zentrums Berlin, Akten Kaiser-Friedrich-Schule, p. 19.
20. 'A Berlin Chronicle', in *One-Way Street*, p. 339.
21. Ibid.
22. Cf. for the following Alex Bein, *Die Judenfrage. Biographie eines Weltproblems*, Stuttgart 1980, as well as Günther Anders, 'Mein Judentum', in *Mein Judentum*, ed. Hans Jürgen Schultz, Stuttgart and Berlin 1979.
23. A. Bein, *Die Judenfrage*, vol. I, p. 259.
24. Walter Benjamin, *Gesammelte Briefe*, vol. 1, pp. 72, 76, 82, 84 and 70 (to L. Strauß, 10 October, 21 November 1912 and 7 January 1913).
25. Cf. *Chronik der Königlichen Friedrich-Wilhelms-Universität zu Berlin für das Rechnungsjahr 1913*, vol. 27, Halle an der Saale 1914, p. 9.

26. Cf. for instance Scholem, *Friendship*, pp. 15 and 92; *GS* VI, p. 215 ('Lebenslauf 1925'); *Correspondence*, p. 599 (to Theodor W. Adorno, 23 February 1939); as well as *Charles Baudelaire*, p. 58; and *GS* V, p. 560.

27. A. Salomon, 'Im Schatten einer endlosen grossen Zeit', p. 3.

28. Cf. *GS* VI, p. 215 ('Lebenslauf 1925'). Where available, Benjamin's university documents have been analysed in Erdmut Wizisla's dissertation, 'Walter Benjamin – Friedrich Heinle – Ernst Joël. Weltanschauung, Literatur und Politik in der Berliner Freien Studentenschaft 1912–1917', Berlin 1987.

29. Cf. Abteilung für Schulreform der Berliner Freien Studentenschaft, 'An die pädagogisch und schulreformatorisch interessierten Studenten-Gruppen (Berlin, 15. Juli 1913)', typewritten circular (a copy of which exists in the Archiv der deutschen Jugendbewegung, Burg Ludwigstein, estate of G. Wyneken), p. 6.

30. Cf. Erdmut Wizisla, 'Die Hochschule ist eben der Ort nicht, zu studieren', in *Wissenschaftliche Zeitschrift der Humboldt-Universität zu Berlin*, vol. 36, 1987, pp. 617–18. A written copy of the list of committee members of the Berlin Free Students' Union [Liste der Präsidialmitglieder der Berliner Freien Studentenschaft] of 29 January 1913 is appended to Wizisla's dissertation 'Walter Benjamin – Friedrich Heinle – Ernst Joël', p. 119.

31. Cf. Bund für Freie Schulgemeinden, 'Verzeichnis der Ein- und Ausgänge vom 23. 10. – 7. 12. 1912' (unpublished document; IISG Amsterdam, estate of Fritz Salomon).

32. Cf. the numerous 'Benjamin' entries in Wyneken's diaries from 1 November 1912 to 7 April 1913.

33. Cf. *Kaiser-Friedrich-Schule zu Charlottenburg, 17. Bericht über das Schuljahr 1914*, Charlottenburg 1914, p. 16. Wyneken had already held the talk on 3 November, but the discussion only took place four weeks later (cf. his 'Tagebuch', April 1912–April 1914, entries for 3 November 1912 and 30 November 1912).

34. Such as on 16 and 17 December (cf. ibid., entries on 16 and 17 December 1912).

35. Siegfried Bernfeld, 'Die Schulgemeinde und ihre Funktion im Klassenkampf', in *Antiautoritäre Erziehung und Psychoanalyse. Ausgewählte Schriften*, Frankfurt am Main 1971, vol. 2, p. 394.

36. Ibid., p. 466, footnote 7.

37. *Gesammelte Briefe*, vol. 1, p. 117 (to G. Wyneken, 19 June 1913).

38. Gustav Wyneken, 'Student und Erziehungsproblem', in *Student und Pädagogik II*, pp. 4–5.

39. *Gesammelte Briefe*, vol. 1, p. 64 (to L. Strauß, 11 September 1912).

40. *GS* II, pp. 13–14 ('Die Schulreform, eine Kulturbewegung').

41. *GS* VII, p. 9 ('Die freie Schulgemeinde').

42. *Correspondence*, p. 20 (to Carla Seligson, 30 April 1913).

43. Ibid., p. 21 (to C. Seligson, 30 April 1913).

44. Ibid., p. 20 (to C. Seligson, 30 April 1913).

45. Ibid., p. 21 (to C. Seligson, 30 April 1913) and p. 37 (to H. Blumenthal, 3 July 1913), as well as I. and A. Götz von Olenhusen, 'Walter Benjamin, Gustav Wyneken und die Freistudenten vor dem Ersten Weltkrieg', pp. 110–12.

46. Presumably he is the friend whose letter prompted Benjamin to go to Freiburg, as described in a letter to C. Seligson dated 30 April 1913 (*Correspondence*, p. 20).

47. *GS* IV, p. 600 ('Für arme Sammler').

48. 'There is a growing revolution here', wrote Benjamin in a letter from this period, 'and I am confidently in control of it. I am Keller's diametric opposite and liberate people from him after having liberated myself from him. . . . Here in Freiburg I have proclaimed the slogan of youth', (*Correspondence*, p. 23, to H. Blumenthal, 5 May 1913).

49. Thus, for instance, he 'deliberately' allowed the School Reform Detachment to be opened 'by a very insipid talk by a lawyer' (presumably Erwin Cuntz), then directly afterwards introduced himself to the audience ('seven people were there with us [!]') as [Wyneken's] pupil and gave a talk that developed [Wyneken's] ideas and those of the *Anfang* from a particular (metaphysical or psychological) corner' (*Gesammelte Briefe*, vol. 1, p. 118; to G. Wyneken, 19 June 1913).

50. *Correspondence*, p. 35 (to H. Blumenthal, 23 June 1913).

51. Cf. in particular Benjamin's letters to Wyneken (19 June 1913) and Blumenthal (23 June 1913 and 3 July 1913) in *Correspondence*.

52. After emigrating, Lehmann founded in 1927 the 'Ben' children's village schemes in Palestine, which assumed a certain importance for the rescue of Jewish children and adolescents during the Nazi era (cf. *Die jüdische Emigration aus Deutschland. Die Geschichte einer Austreibung*, exhibition catalogue, Frankfurt am Main 1985, p. 156).

53. *Correspondence*, p. 21 (to H. Blumenthal, 2 May 1913).

54. Ibid., p. 27 (to C. Seligson, 5 June 1913). Some twenty years later Benjamin described the city in almost the same words. Contrasting it once again with Berlin, he wrote in his 'Paris Diary': 'Against this Paris. How strongly the street here forms an interior for familiar, or even worn-out things' (*GS* IV, p. 568).

55. Now in *GS* IV, pp. 356–9.

56. Translators' note: Pfemfert's publishing house took the same name as the important magazine he founded in 1911, which brought together many of Expressionism's best writers and most radical political minds.

57. Georg Gretor, *Jugendbewegung und Jugendburg*, Zurich 1918, p. 5.

58. Barbizon spent his childhood and early adolescence in France and England (cf. 'Hinweise und Artikel zur Jugendzeitschrift Der Anfang 1913–1914', unpublished MS, Archiv der deutschen Jugendbewegung, Burg Ludwigstein, estate of G. Wyneken, p. 2).

59. *Correspondence*, p. 133 (to Ernst Schoen, 31 July 1918). In 1922, Barbizon married the Dane Esther Kae and moved to Northern Europe. He worked as a journalist in Denmark for the Copenhagen newspaper *Politiken*, and acted for a while as its Hamburg correspondent. Then in 1933, Barbizon broke off all connections with Germany. He remained until 1943 in Copenhagen, where he died on 30 December (cf. 'Hinweise und Artikel', p. 2).

60. G. Gretor, *Jugendbewegung und Jugendburg*, pp. 4–5.

61. The four issues of *Der Anfang*, edited in 1911 by Barbizon and Fritz Schoengarth and published by Jaduczynski's company Niederschönhausener Verlag, constituted an 'interlude' in the magazine's history. Benjamin had three texts published in it: the poem 'Dämmerung' [Twilight] (now in *GS* II, p. 835) as well as the two articles already mentioned, 'Sleeping Beauty' and 'The Free School Community'.

62. Cf. *Der Anfang*, vol. 1, no. 2, June 1913, pp. 34 ff.

63. 'How is it possible', asked Benjamin, 'to allow such a notorious "school reformer" and scribbler to write in our *Anfang*? Now the public has what it wants: the comfortable slogan that will allow it to consign *Der Anfang* to the mass grave of "school reform". People and writers like Oswald are the greatest enemies of our cause, for in the final analysis we do not want just school reform but something else that he can't even imagine' (*Correspondence*, p. 25; to F. Sachs, 4 June 1913).

64. G. Gretor, *Jugendbewegung und Jugendburg*, p. 4.

65. Agathon, a disciple of Socrates, was also the protagonist of a famous novel by Christoph Martin Wieland (*Geschichte des Agathon*, published 1766–7).

66. S. Bernfeld, *Antiautoritäre Erziehung und Psychoanalyse*, p. 393 ('Die Schulgemeinde und ihre Funktion im Klassenkampf').

67. Anonymous, 'Quousque tandem?', in *Neue Preußische Zeitung*, 2 October 1913.

68. The article was originally supposed to be issued by the publishing house Die Hilfe as part of a brochure containing similar sober as well as satirical reflections on such topics as 'Education and Instruction', 'The Communal Life of Pupils', 'Etiquette between Teachers and Pupils', 'Schools and Idealism' and 'Homework' (cf. *Gesammelte Briefe*, vol. 1, p. 65 (to L. Strauß, 11 September 1912).

69. Editorial postface in *Der Anfang*, vol. 1, no. 2, 1913, p. 62.

70. *GS* II, p. 46 ('Romantik. Eine nicht gehaltene Rede an die Schuljugend').

71. *Neue Preußische Zeitung*, 24 June 1913.

72. Cf. Hyperion, Berlin, 'Romantik: die Meinung eines anderen', *Der Anfang*, vol. 1, no. 5, 1913, p. 144, reprinted in *GS* II, pp. 898–9.

73. *GS* II, p. 899.

74. Ibid., p. 47 ('Romantik Walter Benjamin – die Antwort eines "Ungeweihten"').

75. *Correspondence*, p. 53 (to E. Schoen, 30 August 1913).

76. Stern who was unwilling to sacrifice his beliefs at the altar of a career (cf. Martin Tschechne, 'Wie klug sind meine Kinder? Späte Ehrung für William Stern, den Begründer der angewandten Psychologie', *Die Zeit*, 27 June 1986, p. 53), was never to advance beyond a mere associate professorship. Incidentally he was Benjamin's cousin by marriage: the father of Hilde Stern, Eva Michaelis-Stern and Günther Anders was married to Clara Joseephi, daughter of Benjamin's aunt Friederike.

77. Stern spoke on the 'Development of the Differences Between and Sexes', Cohn reported on the experiences in coeducation at senior boys' [!] schools in Baden ('Differences Between the Sexes, as Shown During Joint Instruction'), and Gertrud Bäumer talked on 'Higher Education for Girls'.

78. 'Der Bund für Schulreform', *Frankfurter Zeitung*, 7 October 1913.

79. Now in *GS* II, pp. 60–66.

80. Among the participants were Gertrud Kraker, Hans Reichenbach, Franz Sachs and his brother Walter, Fritz Salomon, Clara Stern and Fritz Sternberg, who at that time was still at secondary school in Breslau (the list of participants is appended to the published minutes of the meeting: cf. *Student und Pädagogik* II, pp. 51–4).

81. Even the way that the promontory, normally called simply the Meißner, was given the name 'High Meißner' sheds light on the sense of mission that this youth possessed. Finer details on the way

it came to be so called can be found in an article by Winfried Mogge, 'Der Freideutsche Jugendtag 1913: Vorgeschichte, Verlauf, Wirkungen', in W. Mogge and Jürgen Reulecke, *Hoher Meißner 1913. Der Erste Freideutsche Jugendtag in Dokumenten, Deutungen und Bildern*, Köln 1988, pp. 390–91, footnote 26).

82. Franz Pfemfert, 'Die Jugend spricht!', *Die Aktion*, no. 41, 11 October 1913, col. 953.

83. Prof. Dr Heinze, 'Jugendkultur', *Casseler Tageblatt*, 2 November 1913.

84. Wyneken replied to Heinze in an article entitled 'Der Anfang' in the same newspaper on 16 November 1913; 'Ein Schlußwort zu den Betrachtungen über den Anfang' by Heinze in the arts section of the *Casseler Tageblatt*, 30 November 1913, concluded this controversy.

85. Translators' note: Ferdinand Avenarius, 1856–1923, writer and champion of drawing-room humour.

86. *GS* II, pp. 66–7 ('Die Jugend schwieg').

87. Ibid., pp. 68–71 ('Studentische Autorenabende'). A foreword signed by the editorial board, which introduced the first issue of the periodical put out by the Central Committee of the Free Students of Greater Berlin, *Der Student. Neue Folge der Berliner Freistudentischen* Blätter, said: 'These words were to be spoken at the students' authors reading on 16 December 1913. The majority of the jury rejected them for reasons of principle' (*GS II*, p. 914).

88. Ibid., pp. 68 and 71 ('Studentische Autorenabende').

89. *Gesammelte Briefe*, vol. 1, p. 204 (open letter to Dr Gustav Wyneken, Munich, 11 April 1914).

90. Cf. *Correspondence*, pp. 69–70 (to E. Schoen, 22–23 June 1914).

91. Ibid., p. 73 (to H. Blumenthal, 17 July 1914).

92. *Correspondence*, p. 73 (to H. Blumenthal, 17 July 1914).

93. Cf. Benjamin's undated letter to David Baumgardt (*c.* March/April 1914), *Gesammelte Briefe*, vol. 1, pp. 214–5).

94. Cf. E. Wizisla, 'Walter Benjamin – Friedrich Heinle – Ernst Joël', p. 20, which refers to an article in the *Vossische Zeitung* of 16 July 1914.

95. *Gesammelte Briefe*, vol. 1, p. 83 (to L. Strauß, 7 January 1913).

96. H., '14. Deutscher Freistudententag', *Göttinger Akademische Wochenschau*, no. 5, 12 June 1914, p. 34.

97. Ibid., pp. 34–5.

98. Cf. [Siegfried] B[ern]f[el]d, 'Bericht über den XIV. Freistudententag in Weimar', *Der Anfang*, vol. 2, no. 4, 1914, p. 121.

99. Walther A. Berendsohn, 'Weimar 1914', *Göttinger Akademische Wochenschau*, no. 7, 25 June 1914, p. 52.

100. H., '14. Deutscher Freistudententag', p. 34.

101. S. Bernfeld, 'Bericht über den XIV. Freistudententag in Weimar', p. 121.

102. H., '14. Deutscher Freistudententag', p. 35.

103. Walther A. Berendsohn, 'Weimar 1914', p. 52.

104. *Gesammelte Briefe*, vol. 1, p. 249 (to Fritz Salomon, *c.* 20 July 1914 [date of receipt]).

105. Cf. the untitled article by Adolf Mandowsky, Breslau, dated 27 July 1914 (unpublished document, IISG Amsterdam, estate of F. Salomon).

106. Cf. Berliner Freie Studentenschaft, circular, 25 July 1914 (IISG, Amsterdam, estate of F. Salomon).

107. Cf. among other texts *GS* III, p. 238 ('Theorien des deutschen Faschismus').
108. 'A Berlin Chronicle', in *One-Way Street*, p. 310.
109. *Correspondence*, p. 72 (to H. Blumenthal, 6 July 1914).
110. Cf. Wieland Herzfelde, *Immergrün. Merkwürdige Erlebnisse und Erfahrungen eines fröhlichen Waisenknaben*, Berlin and Weimar 1975, p. 122.
111. 'A Berlin Chronicle', in *One-Way Street*, p. 310.
112. Bernhard Reichenbach, '"Kriegsfreiwilliger" Benjamin', in *Die Zeit*, 10 March 1967, p. 29.
113. Hilde Benjamin, *Georg Benjamin. Eine Biographie*, Leipzig 1977, p. 32 (Georg Benjamin, diary entry for 5 August 1914).
114. 'A Berlin Chronicle', in *One-Way Street*, p. 310.
115. Wolf Heinle to Erwin Loewenson, 28 August 1914 (unpublished letter; Deutsches Literaturarchiv, Marbach am Neckar, estate of E. Loewenson).
116. Erwin Loewenson, 'Verschiedenes über Wolf und Fritz Heinle' (unpublished MS; Deutsches Literaturarchiv, Marbach am Neckar, estate of E. Loewenson).
117. Cf. F. Wizisla, 'Die Hochschule ist eben der Ort nicht, zu studieren', p. 623; cf. also the copy of the university records appended to 'Walter Benjamin – Friedrich Heinle – Ernst Joël, by the same author, p. 126.
118. Correspondence, pp. 74–5. (to E. Schoen, 25 October 1914).
119. *Urkunden, Briefe: Chronik der Königlichen Friedrich-Wilhelms-Universität zu Berlin für das Rechnungsjahr 1914*, p. 65; cf. also *Bericht für das Jahr 1915*, vol. 29, 1916, p. 53.
120. *GS* VI, p. 174 ('Kritik als Grundwissenschaft der Literaturgeschichte . . . ').
121. 'Gustav Wynekens Rede auf dem "Hohen Meißner" am Morgen des 12. Oktobers', in *Freideutscher Jugendtag 1913. Reden von Bruno Lemke, Gottfried Traub, Knud Ahlhorn, Gustav Wyneken, Ferdinand Avenarius*, 2nd revised edn, ed. Gustav Mittelstraß, Hamburg 1919, p. 34.
122. Cf. Franz Sachs to G. Wyneken, 14 May 1915 (unpublished letter; Archiv der deutschen Jugendbewegung, Burg Ludwigstein, estate of G. Wyneken).
123. A copy was circulated to, among others, Benjamin, Joël, Hermann Kranold, Alexander Schwab, Gustav Landauer, Immanuel Birnbaum and Bernhard Reichenbach. Judging by a letter sent on 14 August 1962 by his brother Bernhard Reichenbach to Friedrich Podszus, the open letter was originally supposed to appear in the magazine *Der Aufbruch*, edited by E. Joël, but fell victim to censorship. Cf. *Walter Benjamin 1892–1940*, edited by Rolf Tiedemann, Christoph Gödde and Henri Lonitz, Marbach am Neckar 1990 (Marbacher Magazin, no. 55), p. 47.
124. These and the following passages originate from the as yet unpublished correspondence between Hans Reichenbach and Wyneken; the quotes, in order of appearance, are from the letters from Reichenbach to Wyneken (18 February 1915), Wyneken to Reichenbach (26 February 1915), Reichenbach to Wyneken (14 March 1915) and Wyneken to Reichenbach (18 March 1915). The documents are contained in Gustav Wyneken's estate, now in the custody of the Archiv der deutschen Jugendbewegung, Burg Ludwigstein.

125. *Gesammelte Briefe*, vol. 1, p. 263 (to G. Wyneken, 14 March 1915).
126. Ibid., p. 263 (to H. Reichenbach), late February/early March 1915.
127. *GS* II, p. 1431 ('Über Stefan George, Lesarten').
128. Ibid., p. 105 ('Zwei Gedichte von Friedrich Hölderlin').
129. The recipients included Alice Heymann (1890–1957), Benjamin's fellow student at Freiburg and Berlin, his friend Herbert Blumenthal and Gershom Scholem, with whom he first became better acquainted in the summer of 1915; Norbert von Hellingrath was also supposed to receive a copy because the work owed its origins to his Prolegomena, 1910, to the first edition of Hölderlin's translations of Pindar (cf. N. v. Hellingrath, *Pindar-Übertragungen von Hölderlin: Prolegomena zu einer Erstausgabe*, Jena 1910). But von Hellingrath was killed in the war before he could see Benjamin's essay.
130. *Correspondence*, p. 365 (to G. Scholem, 25 April 1930).
131. Cf. Wolfram Groddeck, 'Ästhetischer Kommentar. Anmerkungen zu Walter Benjamins Hölderlin-Lektüre', in *Le pauvre Holterling*, vol. 1, 1976, p. 17.
132. *GS* II, p. 105 ('Zwei Gedichte von Friedrich Hölderlin').
133. Friedrich Hölderlin, *Roman Poems and Fragments*, trans. Michael Hamburger, Cambridge 1980, p. 205.
134. A total of three issues appeared, each in a print-run of roughly 450 (cf. Erdmut Wizisla, 'Akademische Freiheit im Kriege? Die Petition Ernst Joël 1916', *Wissenschaftliche Zeitschrift der Humboldt-Universität zu Berlin* (Gesellschaftswissenschaftliche Reihe), vol. 38, 1989, p. 668).
135. For further details, cf. E. Wizisla, 'Walter Benjamin – Friedrich Heinle – Ernst Joël', pp. 67 ff.
136. Scholem, *Friendship*, p. 5.
137. Werner Kraft, *Spiegelung der Jugend*, Frankfurt am Main 1973, p. 72.
138. *GS* II, p. 75.
139. Were not Benjamin's excuses for failing to assemble a circle of Hiller supporters in Munich – which evidently Hiller more or less expected or wished for (cf. Benjamin's as yet unpublished letter to him from 17 November 1915) – the first signs that he was dissociating himself?
140. A remark by Benjamin in a letter to Fritz Radt from December 1915 is revealing in this context: 'One can only first talk about the purity (or "cultural value") of science when one has truly and effectively understood the theory behind it; only in this context does ratio first have its importance, and it is characteristic of the epoch that a science that has become atheoretical, that has lost any awareness of its ideas and has only a vague notion at most of "hypotheses", is faced with activism and aestheticism under their various names in the belief in the purity of a world without theory. That could only be attempted with contortions and violence, and is not even conceivable for the gods' (*Gesammelte Briefe*, vol. 1, p. 299; to F. Radt, 4 December 1915).
141. *GS* III, pp. 351–2 ('Der Irrtum des Aktivismus').
142. Scholem had known Benjamin by sight since 1913. 'One branch of Jung Juda' with which he sympathized 'met in a café at the Tiergarten railway station. There the pupils of Western Berlin secondary schools held their discussions and scheduled lectures . . .' There, as he continues in his memoirs, he 'first saw and heard

Walter Benjamin as the main speaker' in the late autumn of 1913. (Gershom Scholem, *From Berlin to Jerusalem: Memories of My Youth*, trans. Harry Zohn, New York 1980, p. 440.)

143. Scholem, *Friendship*, p. 5.

Chapter 4

1. *GS* III, p. 275 ('Theologische Kritik').
2. Cf. *Correspondence*, p. 77 (to G. Scholem, 27 October 1915).
3. It can be assumed from the entries in the tutorial registers that Benjamin left university at the end of October. Presumably he left Berlin almost at once, for his first letter from Munich was dated 7 November.
4. *Gesammelte Briefe*, vol. 1, p. 302 (to F. Radt, 4 December 1915).
5. Apparently the cream of the expressionists, including Max Brod, Else Lasker-Schüler, Theodor Däubler, Salomo Friedlaender alias Myona, Kasimir Edschmid, Johannes R. Becher, Ferdinand Harde-kopf and Franz Kafka, read from their own works on these evenings. Details of the atmosphere and the response to the readings can be found in the contemporary Munich press. Three such articles are reprinted in the anthology *Franz Kafka. Kritik und Rezeption zu seinen Lebzeiten 1912–1924*, ed. Jürgen Born, Frankfurt am Main 1979 (cf. also the editor's brief outline of the 'Evenings for New Literature').
6. *Gesammelte Briefe*, vol. 1, p. 302–3 (to F. Radt, 4 December 1915).
7. Ibid., p. 286 (to Kurt Hiller, 13 November 1915).
8. Ibid., p. 289 (to F. Radt, 21 November 1915).
9. *Correspondence*, p. 16 (to H. Blumenthal, 12 August 1912).
10. *Gesammelte Briefe*, vol. 1, p. 296–7 (to F. Radt, 4 December 1915).
11. Ibid., p. 290 (to F. Radt, 21 November 1915).
12. *GS* VI, p. 225 ('Curriculum vitae Dr Walter Benjamin 1939/40').
13. In *One-Way Street*, pp. 107–23.
14. *Gesammelte Briefe*, vol. 1, p. 291 (to F. Radt, 21 November 1915).
15. *Correspondence*, p. 50 (to C. Seligson, 4 August 1913).
16. Cf. Rainer Maria Rilke, *Briefe*, Frankfurt am Main 1987, p. 518 (letters of 26 November 1915 and 15 February 1916 to Princess Marie von Thurn und Taxis-Hohenlohe and Anton Kippenberg).
17. *Correspondence*, p. 88 (to G. Scholem, June 1917).
18. *GS* III, pp. 306–7 ('Ein Schwarmgeist auf dem Katheder: Franz von Baader').
19. The fruits of his studies were an anthology of Baader's texts that he edited for the Insel publishing house (cf. Franz von Baader, *Schriften*, ed. Max Pulver, Leipzig 1921 and *GS* III, p. 305.).
20. *Correspondence*, p. 86 (to G. Scholem, 23 May 1917).
21. 'Baader certainly has a lot to do with romanticism', Benjamin wrote in a letter in June 1917 to Gershom Scholem, adding 'and was thus a major influence on Schelling, one that Schelling concealed' (ibid., p. 88).
22. Cf. for instance *GS* I, p. 33, footnote 48 ('Der Begriff der Kunst-kritik in der deutschen Romantik').
23. Cf. *GS* VI, p. 185 ('Zur Graphologie'); *GS* III, pp. 135-39. ('Anja und Georg Mendelssohn: Der Mensch in der Handschrift'); as well as *GS* IV, pp. 596–8 ('Alte und neue Graphologie').
24. Cf. Benjamin's letters of November and December 1915 to Fritz Radt (printed in *Gesammelte Briefe*, vol. 1, pp. 287–306).

25. *Gesammelte Briefe*, vol. 1, p. 315 (to Hans Reichenbach, 3 March 1916).
26. Ibid., p. 301 (to F. Radt, 4 December 1915).
27. Information on Noeggerath's relationship with the George Circle can be found in his hitherto unpublished letters. Noeggerath's estate is now in the keeping of the Deutsches Literaturarchiv in Marbach.
28. *GS II*, p. 623 ('Über Stefan George').
29. *Gesammelte Briefe*, vol. 1, p. 291 (to F. Radt, 21 November 1915).
30. According to the extant university documents, Benjamin, along with Noeggerath, attended Geiger's 'Exercises in Kant's *Critique of Judgement*' and Lehmann's 'Introduction to Ancient Mexican Culture and Language'.
31. *Gesammelte Briefe*, vol. 1, p. 299 (to F. Radt, 4 December 1915).
32. Ibid., p. 298.
33. Now in *GS II*, pp. 91–104.
34. For the following cf. Bernd Witte, *Walter Benjamin*, trans. James Rolleston, Detroit 1991, pp. 22–38.
35. *Correspondence*, p. 83 (to H. Blumenthal, end of 1916).
36. Ibid., p. 81 (to Martin Buber, July 1916); *Gesammelte Briefe*, vol. 1, p. 292 (to F. Radt, 21 November 1915).
37. A third and later example of such flat refusals that is worth mentioning is that to Siegfried Bernfeld. Bernfeld invited Benjamin to contribute to his Zionist magazine *Jerubbaal*, but his invitation was similarly declined (cf. Scholem, *Friendship*, p. 73).
38. Among the more important of Benjamin's publications from this period that have not yet been mentioned are his essay on 'Moralunterricht' [Lessons in Morals] (printed in *Freie Schulgemeinde*, no. 4, 1913, now in *GS II*, pp. 48–54); his 'Gedanken über Gerhard Hauptmanns Festspiel' [Thoughts on Hauptmann's Festspiel] on the occasion of the centenary of Napoleon's defeat at the Battle of the Nations (now in *GS* II, pp. 56–60); and his reflections headed "Erfahrung" [Experience] (*GS* II, pp. 54–6) in which he once again rallied 'all of the rebellious forces of youth against the word "experience"' (*GS* II, p. 902), all of which were printed in *Der Anfang* (vols 4 and 6, 1913). In addition, his essay 'Die religiöse Stellung der neuen Jugend' [The Position of the New Youth on Religion] published in *Die Tat* (vol. 2, 1914; now in *GS* II, pp. 72–4), a *Social-Religious Monthly for German Culture* edited by Eugen Diederichs and Karl Hoffnung.
39. *Correspondence*, p. 81 (to M. Buber, July 1916).
40. *Gesammelte Briefe*, vol. 1, p. 284 (to K. Hiller, 7 November 1915).
41. *Correspondence*, p. 80 (to M. Buber, July 1916).
42. *GS III*, p. 224 ('Ein Außenseiter macht sich bemerkbar').
43. All quotes cited from *Correspondence*, p. 80 (to M. Buber, July 1916).
44. *GS VI*, pp. 48–9 ('Arten des Wissens').
45. Martin Buber, *Briefwechsel aus sieben Jahrzehnten*, Heidelberg 1972, vol. 1, p. 441 (G. Scholem to M. Buber, 25 June 1916).
46. Ibid., p. 81 (to G. Scholem, 11 November 1916).
47. *Correspondence*, p. 108 (to E. Schoen, 28 December 1917).
48. 'On Language as Such and on the Language of Man', in *One-Way Street*, p. 109.
49. *GS II*, p. 142.
50. Cf. Scholem, *Friendship*, p. 34.

51. Now in *GS* VII, pp. 785–90. A number of other notes that are also connected with his early linguistic theory can be found in *GS* VI, pp. 9 ff. The context in which these reflections were made can be seen in a letter from Benjamin to Scholem, 11 November 1916, in which he says that he had not yet managed to 'go into mathematics and language, i.e. mathematics and thought, mathematics and Zion, because [his] thoughts on this infinitely difficult topic are still quite far from having taken final shape' (*Correspondence*, p. 81). A letter from Scholem to Werner Kraft, 3 August 1917, also mentions the 'basic elements' that his friend's early linguistic works still lacked 'regarding the symbolic in language and the theory of signs and writing', (Gershom Scholem, *Briefe an Werner Kraft*, Frankfurt am Main 1986, p. 17).

52. Cf. *The Origin of German Tragic Drama*, trans. John Osborne, London/New York 1977.

53. The notes from 1933, which come to us in two versions (the second version bears the title 'Über das mimetische Vermögen' ['On the Mimetic Faculty', *One-Way Street*, pp. 160–63]), in 'Doctrine of the Similar', trans. Knut Tarnowski, *New German Critique*, no. 17, 1979, pp. 65–9.

54. Now in *GS* III, pp. 452–80.

55. *Gesammelte Briefe*, vol. 1, p. 317 (to F. Radt, 9 March 1916).

56. Untitled Christmas poem by Benjamin, sent to F. Radt (unpublished; Jewish National and University Library, Jerusalem, Walter Benjamin Archives).

57. Cf. Scholem, *Engel*, p. 97 ('Walter Benjamin und Felix Noeggerath'): 'Benjamin came to Berlin during the holidays with the express wish to pave the way to marrying Grete Radt by taking the appropriate steps with her parents. But things turned our differently. While still in Munich, Grete Radt decided to spend the summer alone at a farm (owned by an uncle of Jula Cohn) on the Lüneberg Heath in order to straighten her thoughts. But instead of going to the farm she went to Heidelberg, and shortly after the engagement was broken off.'

58. 'A Berlin Chronicle', in *One-Way Street*, p. 321.

59. Cf. *Correspondence*, p. 85 (to E. Schoen, 27 February 1917).

60. All quotes from Scholem, *Friendship*, p. 35.

61. *Correspondence*, p. 86 (to G. Scholem, 23 May 1917).

62. Ibid., p. 89.

63. Ibid., p. 97.

64. 'On the Program of the Coming Philosophy', in *Benjamin: Philosophy, History, Aesthetics*, ed. Gary Smith, p. 3.

65. *GS* II, p. 56.

66. Ibid., p. 10.

67. Scholem, *Friendship*, p. 39 (Benjamin to G. Scholem, 30 June 1917).

68. *Correspondence*, p. 91 (to E. Schoen, 30 July 1917).

69. Ibid., p. 60 (to H. Blumenthal, 6 May 1914).

70. Ibid, p. 62 (to H. Blumenthal, 15 May 1914).

71. Cf. D. Kellner to Gershom Scholem, 15 July 1941 (unpublished letter; Jewish National and University Library, Jerusalem, Walter Benjamin Archives).

72. This applies for example to his article 'Die Waffen von morgen' [Tomorrow's Weapons] printed in June 1925 in the *Vossische Zeitung* (now in *GS* IV, pp. 473–6); the article is even signed with

Dora Sophie Benjamin's initials ('dsb'), but it was, according to a list of his publications, written in fact by Benjamin.

73. These include the small 'Rätsel' [Puzzles] printed in 1927 in *Die praktische Berlinerin*, now in *GS* VII, pp. 301–2), and a story entitled 'Palais D . . . y' (*Die Dame*, June 1929; now in *GS* IV, pp. 725–8).

74. D. S. Kellner to G. Scholem, 15 July 1941.

75. H[erbert] W[illiam] Belmore, 'Some Recollections of Walter Benjamin', *German Life & Letters*, new series, vol. 28, 1974/5, p. 123.

76. Only in 1939 does he appear to have made a shy attempt at reconciliation by asking Benjamin's wife for his address (cf. H. Belmore to D.S. Kellner, 30 July 1939; unpublished letter, Literaturarchive der Akademie der Künste, Berlin, estate of W. Benjamin). At present there is nothing to confirm that this actually resulted in a renewal of their (written) contact.

77. From H. Blumenthal's notes, 28 December 1917 (unpublished MS; Jewish National and University Library, Jerusalem, Walter Benjamin Archives).

78. Cf. Scholem, *Friendship*, p. 42.

79. *Correspondence*, p. 141 (to E. Schoen, May 1919).

80. *Gesammelte Briefe*, vol. 1, p. 469 (to E. Schoen, 31 July 1918).

81. Cf. G. Scholem, *Briefe an Werner Kraft*, pp. 13–14 (G. Scholem to W. Kraft, 14 July 1917).

82. Ernst Bloch, *Gesamtausgabe*, vol. 16: *Geist der Utopie* (1st version), Frankfurt am Main 1971, p. 9.

83. *Correspondence*, p. 91 (to E. Schoen, 30 July 1917).

84. Hugo Ball (1886–1927), anarchist, playwright, decadent Christian mystic and a founder of Dada in 1916. Cf. Malcolm Green's introduction to *Blago Bung Blago Bung Bosso Fataka!: First texts of German Dada*, London 1995.

85. *Correspondence*, p. 148 (to E. Schoen, 19 September 1919).

86. Ibid., p. 148 (to E. Schoen, 19 September 1919).

87. Benjamin planned a review of his philosophical manifesto of expressionism (cf. ibid., p. 147, to G. Scholem, 15 September 1919) and even appears to have drafted it. Sadly the manuscript, which might have supplied more detailed information on the reasons for his violent dislike of this literary movement, has been lost.

88. Ernst Bloch, 'Recollections of Walter Benjamin', in *On Walter Benjamin, Critical Essays and Recollections*, ed. Gary Smith, Cambridge, Mass., p. 339.

89. Scholem, *Friendship*, p. 47 (D. Benjamin to G. Scholem, 12 November 1917).

90. Scholem, *Friendship*, p. 57.

91. Cf. *Correspondence*, pp. 139–40 (to E. Schoen, 7 April 1919).

92. A complete overview of the courses that Benjamin attended at the University of Berne can now be found in Philippe W. Balsiger, 'Richard Herbertz. Leben und Werk', doctoral thesis, Berne 1990, p. 84.

93. *Correspondence*, p. 111 (to G. Scholem, 13 January 1918).

94. Ibid., p. 113 (to G. Scholem, 31 January 1918).

95. A number of the fragments in *GS* VI, whose dates of origin are mostly vague, are presumably either notes for seminar discussions, or the first drafts of his lectures.

96. *Correspondence*, p. 98 (to G. Scholem, 22 October 1917).
97. Ibid., p. 125 (to E. Schoen, May 1918).
98. Ibid., p. 140 (to E. Schoen, 7 April 1919).
99. Ibid., p. 119 (to G. Scholem, 30 March 1918).
100. Ibid., p. 136 (to E. Schoen, 8 November 1918).
101. Ibid., p. 223 (to Florens Christian Rang, 9 December 1923).
102. Ibid., p. 136 (to E. Schoen, 8 November 1918).
103. Ibid., p. 141 (to E. Schoen, May 1919).
104. Cf. *GS* I, pp. 110–19.
105. Ibid., p. 708 ('Selbstanzeige der Dissertation').
106. Ibid., p. 119 ('Der Begriff der Kunstkritik in der deutschen Romantik').
107. It is evident that Benjamin originally hoped to have the essay published in a journal (cf. Betty Scholem and Gershom Scholem, *Mutter und Sohn im Briefwechsel* 1917–1946, Munich 1989, p. 47, letter from G. to B. Scholem, 26 April 1919). Regrettably our present knowledge does not allow us to say which journal Benjamin was thinking of, or why his plans failed.
108. *Correspondence*, p. 153 (to G. Scholem, 23 November 1919).
109. *Briefe an Kracauer*, p. 9 (to Siegfried Kracauer, 1 March 1924).
110. Cf. Benjamin/Scholem, Correspondence 1932–1940, p. 239 (G. Scholem to Benjamin, 25 January 1939).
111. Not including Benjamin's own advertisement cited here, which appeared in Kant-Studien, vols 1–2, 1921. In a letter to Scholem dated 10 May 1924 (Correspondence, p. 240) Benjamin wrote that his thesis had received a third review, 'this time in great detail, in an essay entitled "New Currents in Literary Studies"'. Reinhard Markner has suggested to me that Benjamin may have confused Rudolf Unger's review essay 'Deutsche Romantik' (*Zeitschrift für Deutschkunde*, vol. 37, 1923, pp. 64–8), where this thesis is briefly summarized (cf. pp. 65–6), with the same author's essay 'Moderne Strömungen in der deutschen Literaturwissenschaft' (*Die Literatur*, vol. 26, 1923/4, pp. 65–73) in which it is not mentioned.
112. Christoph Flaskamp, 'Prophetische Romantik', Literarischer Handweiser, vol. 57, 1921, col. 200.
113. F.C. Rang to Benjamin, 10 October 1920, *Schattenlinien* no. 6–7, 1993, p.71.
114. *Correspondence*, p. 141 (to E. Schoen, May 1919).
115. For the following details cf. Ph. W. Balsiger, Richard Herbertz, pp. 90 ff.
116. Cf. *Correspondence*, p. 145 (to E. Schoen, 24 July 1919).

Chapter 5

1. 'One-Way Street' in *One-Way Street* pp. 54–5.
2. That was on 1 July. His date of departure can be established from a remark by Scholem in a letter to Werner Kraft (cf. G. Scholem, *Briefe an Werner Kraft*, Frankfurt am Main 1986, p. 115; to W. Kraft, 6 July 1919).
3. Or so Scholem then interpreted his express demand to keep to himself for the moment the fact that he had gained his doctorate (Scholem, *Friendship*, p. 84).
4. Cf. *Correspondence*, p. 150 (to Wilhelm Caro, *c.* 20 November 1919).
5. As late as 1922, when their disagreements reached one of their (numerous) climaxes, Emil Benjamin bound any further financial

support to the condition that his son either joined a bank or took up some other job in the business line (cf. ibid., p. 201; to F. C. Rang, 14 October 1922).

6. *GS* VI, p. 45 ('Analogie und Verwandtschaft').
7. *Correspondence*, p. 202 (to F.C. Rang, 14 October 1922).
8. Scholem, *Friendship*, p. 84.
9. *Correspondence*, p. 150 (to W. Caro, *c.* 20 November 1919).
10. Theodor Lessing, *Der jüdische Selbsthaß*, Munich 1984, p. 26.
11. Cf. Werner Fuld, *Walter Benjamin. Zwischen den Stühlen. Eine Biographie*, Munich 1979, p. 102.
12. Cf. *Correspondence*, p. 133 (to E. Schoen, 31 July 1918).
13. Ibid., p. 161 (to G. Scholem, 13 February 1920).
14. Ibid., p. 163 (to G. Scholem, 26 May 1920).
15. Ibid., p. 216 (to F.C. Rang, 18 November 1923).
16. For the following, cf. Scholem, *Friendship*, p. 34; Scholem, *From Berlin to Jerusalem, Memories of my Youth*, trans. Harry Zohn, New York 1980, pp. 80–82; as well as Lorenz Jäger, 'Messianische Kritik. Studien zu Leben und Werk von Florens Christian Rang', doctoral thesis, Frankfurt am Main 1985 pp. 59 ff.
17. *Correspondence*, p. 200 (to G. Scholem, 1 October 1922).
18. Ibid., p. 216 (to F.C. Rang, 18 November 1923).
19. *GS* IV, pp. 918 and 921 ('Gedanken zu einer Analysis des Zustands von Mitteleuropa').
20. *Correspondence*, pp. 132–3 (to E. Schoen, 31 July 1918).
21. In particular an essay on colour and imagination which he worked on from 1914, and for which he found 'some fine things' at that time 'in Baudelaire' (ibid., p. 75, to E. Schoen, January 1915). A large number of shortish notes and even finished texts to this uncompleted work have come down to us (cf. *GS* VI, pp. 109 ff.), of which the longest is 'Der Regenbogen. Gespräch über die Phantasie', ['The Rainbow: A Conversation on the Imagination'], published in *GS* VII, pp. 19–26.
22. Cf. for instance *Correspondence*, pp. 113, 144 ff. and 148 (to G. Scholem, 31 January 1918, as well as to E. Schoen, 24 July and 19 September 1919).
23. It would appear that Benjamin attended a Baudelaire course during the winter term of 1917/18 (cf. Scholem, *Friendship*, p. 47; D.S. Benjamin to G. Scholem, 12 November 1917).
24. In March 1922 Benjamin held a conference during an evening dedicated to Baudelaire at the Berlin bookshop Reuss & Pollack (cf. *GS* IV, pp. 891–2).
25. *GS* III, pp. 303–4 ('Baudelaire unterm Stahlhelm').
26. *Correspondence*, p. 372 (to Max Rychner, 7 March 1931).
27. *Gesammelte Briefe*, vol. 2, p. 459 (to Gottfried Salomon, 10 June 1924).
28. *Correspondence*, p. 245 (to G. Scholem, 7 July 1924).
29. As Benjamin wrote in a letter on 31 January 1918 to Scholem: 'I have recently added some new things to my library, among others Stefan George's translation of *Les fleurs du mal*' (ibid., p. 113).
30. The following commentary draws in several points on the works of Ralph-Rainer Wuthenow (*Das fremde Kunstwerk. Aspekte der literarischen Übersetzung*, Göttingen 1969, pp. 126 ff.), Gerhard R. Kaiser (*Einführung in die vergleichende Literaturwissenschaft*, Darmstadt 1980, pp. 92 ff.) and Willy R. Berger ('Walter Benjamin als Übersetzer Baudelaires', in *Teilnahme und Spiegelung.*

Festschrift für Horst Rüdiger, Berlin and New York 1975, pp. 634–63).

31. Rang's and Hofmannsthal's letters to Benjamin containing their comments on his Baudelaire translations have yet to be published, but their 'reservations' (*Correspondence*, p. 228; Benjamin to F.C. Rang, 10 January 1924) were based primarily on the discrepancy between his ambitions and the reality: 'There are many ways of serving the word', wrote Hofmannsthal to his friend Rang on 26 January 1924. 'The importance of translation in this field has been put quite wonderfully by Benjamin in his preface to his translations of Baudelaire's poems but I find the translations themselves are lacking in beauty' (Hugo von Hofmannsthal and Florens Christian Rang: 'Briefwechsel 1905–1924', in *Neue Rundschau*, vol. 70, 1959, p. 444).
32. *Correspondence*, p. 229-30 (to H. v. Hofmannsthal, 13 January 1924).
33. Cf. Stefan George, *Werke* (edition in 2 vols), Düsseldorf, Munich 1976, vol. 2, p. 302 and *GS* IV, pp. 22–3 (Charles Baudelaire, 'Tableaux parisiens'). A comprehensive study of the history of Baudelaire in German translation can be found in Thomas Keck, *Der deutsche 'Baudelaire'*, 2 vols, Heidelberg 1991.
34. 'The Task of the Translator', in *Illuminations*, p. 70.
35. 'Paris, the Capital of the Nineteenth Century', in *Charles Baudelaire*, p. 170 (revised here).
36. S. George, *Werke*, vol. 2, p. 233.
37. 'The Task of the Translator', in *Illuminations*, p. 81.
38. *GS* VI, p. 232 ('Tagebuch Pfingsten 1911').
39. Hugo von Hofmannstal 'The Letter of Lord Chandos', in *Selected Prose*, trans. Mary Hottinger and Tania and James Stern, New York 1952, pp. 129–41.
40. S. George, *Werke*, vol. 2, p. 233.
41. *GS* II, p. 243 ('Ankündigung der Zeitschrift: Angelus Novus').
42. *Correspondence*, p. 171 (to G. Scholem, 29 December 1920).
43. Ibid., p. 222 (to G. Scholem, 5 December 1923).
44. Cf. *GS* IV, p. 893 (to R. Weißbach, 6 November 1933).
45. Ibid. (to Richard Weißbach, 27 November 1933).
46. Stefan Zweig, 'Musset und Baudelaire in deutscher Uebertragung', in *Frankfurter Zeitung*, 1 June 1924.
47. *Gesammelte Briefe*, vol. 2, p. 459 (to G. Salomon-Delatour, 10 June 1924).
48. Stefan Zweig, 'Musset und Baudelaire in deutscher Uebertragung'.
49. *Gesammelte Briefe*, vol. 2, to G. Salomon-Delatour, 10 June 1924.
50. Ibid., p. 471 (to G. Salomon-Delatour, 1 July 1924).
51. All quotes from Paul Wertheimer, 'Charles Baudelaire "Tableaux parisiens"' in *Neue Freie Presse*, 14 December 1924.
52. *Correspondence*, p. 256 (to G. Scholem, 22 December 1924).
53. Cf. *GS* IV, pp. 65–82 as well as *GS* VII, pp. 824–9.
54. Cf. 'Baudelaire-Übertragungen', *Vers und Prosa*, no. 8, 1924, pp. 269–72.
55. Basically, the sole exception that he allowed himself was no exception: his essay 'The Life of Students', published in 1915/16 in both Efraim Frisch's *Neuer Merkur* and Kurt Hiller's yearbook *Das Ziel*, was based essentially on two talks that he had held in May and June 1914.
56. *One-Way Street*, p. 132–54.

57. Cf. Chryssoula Kambas, 'Walter Benjamin liest Georges Sorel: "Réflexions sur la violence"', in *Aber ein Sturm weht vom Paradiese her. Texte zu Walter Benjamin*, eds Michael Opitz and Erdmut Wizisla, Leipzig 1992, pp. 250–69.

58. Cf. 'Fate and Character', in *One-Way Street*, pp. 124–31. This was one of his numerous attempts to develop his own conceptual thinking. He worked the basic ideas of the essay into his long work 'Goethe's *Elective Affinities*' and in his treatise *The Origin of German Tragic Drama*, but later he was no longer satisfied with the essay as a whole. Although he felt that the small work was still preferable to the smokescreen of a 'lofty demeanour' with which the history of concepts was normally pursued, in retrospect he found that this '"liberation" of two ancient words' from their 'terminological enslavement' by means of forced thinking and the resulting 'unsophisticated pedantry' had proved fairly unconvincing (*Correspondence*, p. 229, to Hugo von Hofmannsthal, 13 January 1924).

59. Cf. '"Der Idiot" von Dostojewskij', now in *GS* II, pp. 237–41.

60. Now in *GS* II, pp. 133–40.

61. *Correspondence*, p. 135 (to E. Schoen, 8 November 1918).

62. Ibid., p. 143 (to E. Schoen, 24 July 1919).

63. Ibid., p. 181 (to G. Scholem, 12 July 1921).

64. Ibid., p. 186 (to G. Scholem, 4 August 1921).

65. *GS* II, pp. 241 and 245 ('Ankündigung der Zeitschrift: Angelus Novus').

66. To take just a few names who figured in some way in Benjamin's life, these included the poet Karl Wolfskehl, the artist Melchior Lechter, the literary scholars Friedrich Gundolf and Max Kommerell, the historian Kurt Breysig and the philosophers Ernst Bertram and Robert Boehringer.

67. All quotes from *GS* II, pp. 241 ff. ('Ankündigung der Zeitschrift: *Angelus Novus*').

68. All quotes from *GS* II, p. 242.

69. All quotes from *GS* II, p. 243.

70. All quotes from *GS* II, pp. 244–5.

71. Ibid., p. 245.

72. Cf. *GS* II, pp. 601–2. ('Aphorismen'); these texts, named so by the editors of the *GS*, date presumably from 1916.

73. The sonnets, which were only discovered a few years ago among the papers that Benjamin left behind him in Paris, were written in the years between 1915 and 1925 (now in *GS* VII, pp. 27–67).

74. The work was first published after Rang's death in *Die Kreatur* (vol. 1, 1926/7).

75. *Correspondence*, p. 203 (to F.C. Rang, 14 October 1922).

76. Cf. *GS* II, p. 993 (to F.C. Rang, end of October/early November 1922).

77. *Correspondence*, p. 200 (to G. Scholem, 1 October 1922).

78. Ibid., p. 194 (to G. Scholem, 8 November 1921).

79. *GS* I, p. 125 ('Goethes Wahlverwandtschaften').

80. The critical remarks on 'criticism and biography' (cf. the schematic outline of his 'Elective Affinities' essay, *GS* I, pp. 835–7) at the beginning of the second chapter (cf. *GS* I, pp. 155–6) are aimed primarily at Dilthey's collection of essays *Das Erlebnis und die Dichtung* (1905/10), and at his phrase 'Poetry is above all the representation and expression of life' (Wilhelm Dilthey, *Das Erlebnis und die Dichtung*, Göttingen 1970, p. 126). Benjamin had already read the

book – although not completely (cf. *Correspondence*, p. 146; to E. Schoen, 24 July 1919) – during his schooldays.

81. *GS* II, p. 242 ('Ankündigung der Zeitschrift: Angelus Novus').

82. *GS* I, p. 828 ('Bemerkung über Gundolf: Goethe').

83. *Correspondence*, p. 196 (to G. Scholem, 27 November 1921).

84. *GS* I, pp. 177, 176 and 163 ('Goethes Wahlverwandtschaften').

85. *GS* III, p. 251 ('Zur Wiederkehr von Hofmannsthals Todestag').

86. Michael Winkler, *George-Kreis*, Stuttgart 1972, p. 67 (Friedrich Gundolf to Stefan George, 10 November 1910). Apart from his *Elective Affinities* essay, Benjamin's article 'Porträt eines Barockpoeten' – a review of Gundolf's 1927 *Andreas Gryphius* monograph – (now in *GS* III, pp. 86–8), constituted a further arena for this dispute.

87. Cf. for instance 'Wider ein Meisterwerk. Zu Max Kommerell, "Der Dichter als Führer in der deutschen Klassik"', from 1930 (now in *GS* III, pp. 252–9) and 'Der eingetunkte Zauberstab. Zu Max Kommerells "Jean Paul"' from 1934 (now in *GS* III, pp. 409–17).

88. Charlotte Wolff, *On the Way to Myself: Communications to a Friend*, London 1969, p. 195.

89. Scholem, 'Walter Benjamin and His Angel' in Smith (ed.) *On Walter Benjamin*, p. 54.

90. Cf. Charlotte Wolff, *Hindsight: An Autobiography*, London 1980, p. 75.

91. Scholem, Walter Benjamin and His Angel, in Smith (ed.), *On Walter Benjamin*, p. 54–5.

92. Johann Wolfgang von Goethe, *Conversations with Eckermann (1823–1832)*, trans. John Oxenford, San Francisco 1984, pp. 284–5 (17 February 1830).

93. Cf. for instance Ulrich Schödlbauer, 'Der Text als Material. Zu Benjamins Interpretation von Goethes "Wahlverwandtschaften"', in Peter Gebhardt et al., *Walter Benjamin: Zeitgenosse der Moderne*, Kronberg/Taunus 1976, p. 106; similarly irreverent, if considerably more subtle in its judgements, is Bernhard Buschendorf's book *Goethes mythische Denkform. Zur Ikonographie der 'Wahlverwandtschaften'*, Frankfurt am Main 1986, passim.

94. The fact that even Benjamin viewed Gundolf's *Goethe* as a programmatic text for the entire George circle is demonstrated by the passing remark on the circle's views, that are 'consolidated by Gundolf's book' (*GS* I, p. 159; 'Goethes Wahlverwandtschaften'). Gundolf's *Habilitation* thesis on Shakespeare, published two years previously, was dismissed – assuming that it was indeed one of the circle's publications that went to shaping their school and 'spirit' – by Benjamin as the object of an exemplary critique simply because his attention was turned at the time primarily to the products of German studies.

95. H. Cohen, *Ästhetik des reinen Gefühls*, vol. 2, Berlin 1912, p. 124.

96. Its purity, the unity of its form, its – in a word – totally artistic character predestined this novel to be the object of a critique that attempted to show, in exemplary fashion, how a literary document is 'to be illuminated from within its own self' (*GS* VI, p. 218; 'Lebenslauf 1928').

97. *GS* I, p. 135 ('Goethes Wahlverwandtschaften').

98. All quotes from *GS* I, p. 164–5 ('Goethes Wahlverwandtschaften').

99. All quotes from *GS* I, p. 165.

100. *Correspondence*, p. 224 (to F. C. Rang, 9 December 1923).

101. *GS* I, pp. 200 and 184 ('Goethes Wahlverwandtschaften').
102. 'N' (Re the Theory of Knowledge, Theory of Progress), trans. L. Hafrey and R. Sieburth, in Benjamin: *Philosophy, History, Aesthetics*, p. 51.
103. Hugo von Hofmannsthal and Florens Christian Rang, 'Briefwechsel 1905–1924', *Die Neue Rundschau*, vol. 70, 1959, p. 440 (Hofmannsthal to Rang, 20 November 1923). Additional material on the correspondence between Hofmannsthal and Rang (with further details relating to Benjamin) can be found in Lorenz Jäger's 'Neue Quellen zur Münchner Rede und zu Hofmannsthals Freundschaft mit Florens Christian Rang', *Hofmannsthal-Blätter*, no. 29, 1984, pp. 3–29.
104. *Correspondence*, p. 237 (to G. Scholem, 5 March 1924).
105. Cf. *GS* I, p. 813 (to F. C. Rang, 3 December 1922).
106. *Correspondence*, p. 208 (to F. C. Rang, 2 April 1923).
107. Erich Rothacker to Walter Benjamin, 26 April 1923 (unpublished letter; Universitätsbibliothek Bonn, estate of E. Rothacker).
108. 'L'Angoisse mythique chez Goethe', trans. Pierre Klossowski, in *Cahiers du Sud*, no. 194, 1937, pp. 342–8; the translation was based on sections of the first and second chapters.
109. Alfred Kurella, 'Deutsche Romantik', on the eponymous special issue of the *Cahiers du Sud, Internationale Literatur* (*Deutsche Blätter*), vol. 8, no. 6, 1938, p. 127.
110. *Correspondence*, p. 571 (to Gretel Adorno, 20 July 1938).
111. Cf. ibid., p. 284 (to G. Scholem, 21 September 1925).
112. Cf. ibid., p. 288 (to G. Scholem, 14 January 1926).
113. Cf. Walter Benjamin, *Goethes Wahlverwandtschaften*, Frankfurt am Main 1964. The essay was first published in its entirety in 1949 in an anthology edited by Hans Mayer, *Spiegelungen Goethes in unserer Zeit* (Wiesbaden).
114. *Correspondence*, p. 154 (to E. Schoen, 5 December 1919).
115. Ibid.
116. Cf. *GS* VI, pp. 21–6 ('Schemata zur Habilitationsschrift'; the text 'Wenn nach der Theorie des Duns Scotus . . . '; 'Sprache und Logik I–III').
117. *Correspondence*, p. 156 (to G. Scholem, 13 January 1920).
118. During a second stay in Heidelberg, Benjamin actually mixed in 'society' after accepting an invitation from Marianne Weber, the widow of Max Weber and an influential figure in academic circles, to hold 'a lecture on poetry' at her home. He spend days and nights conscientiously preparing himself for the event, only to learn afterwards that he had not been comprehended: 'the lecture failed to make an impression' (ibid., p. 204; to G. Scholem, 30 December 1922).
119. Ibid., p. 182 (to G. Scholem, 20 July 1921).
120. Ibid., p. 183 (to G. Scholem, 25 July 1921).
121. Cf. ibid., p. 204 (to G. Scholem, 30 December 1922).
122. Although his friend Rang put out the appropriate feelers for him at the University of Gießen, Benjamin did not shortlist the university and consequently made no efforts to establish any contacts there (cf. *GS* I, p. 871; to F. C. Rang, *c.* November 1922).
123. Scholem, *Friendship*, p. 90.
124. *Correspondence*, p. 295 ('Vorrede zum Trauerspielbuch').
125. *Gesammelte Briefe*, vol. 2, p. 294 (to G. Salomon-Delatour, 8 December 1922).

126. Benjamin to G. Salomon-Delatour, 14 April 1923 (unpublished letter; IISG Amsterdam, estate of G. Salomon-Delatour).
127. *Correspondence*, p. 257 (to G. Scholem, 22 December 1924).
128. Cf. Adorno's reminiscences in his book *Über Walter Benjamin*, Frankfurt am Main, 2nd edition 1990, p. 78.
129. A. Sohn-Rethel (born 1899), a close friend of Siegfried Kracauer, Bloch and Adorno, studied at Heidelberg, among other places, where he met Benjamin in 1921 (cf. his conversation with Uwe Herms in *L'invitation au voyage. Zu Alfred Sohn-Rethel*, eds Bettina Wassner, Joachim Müller, Bremen 1979, p. 8). From 1931 to 1936 he worked for the Mitteleuropäischer Wirtschaftstag, a 'central contact-point between high finance and Nazism' (Sohn-Rethel). He was forced to flee in 1936 as a result of his contacts with the anti-fascist resistance. He emigrated first to Switzerland, and then to England, where he lived for many years as a 'private tutor' in Birmingham. His major publications: *Geistige und körperliche Arbeit*, Frankfurt am Main 1970 (2nd rev. and augmented edn 1972); *Warenform und Denkform*, Frankfurt am Main 1971 (inc. the essay on which Benjamin was commissioned to give a report by the Institut für Sozialforschung in 1937: 'Zur kritischen Liquidierung des Apriorismus'); *Ökonomie und Klassenstruktur des deutschen Faschismus*, Frankfurt am Main 1973; Theodor W. Adorno and A. Sohn-Rethel, *Briefwechsel 1936–1969*, Munich 1991.
130. Cf. Morus (i.e. Richard Lewinsohn), 'Abrechnung', *Die Weltbühne*, no. 15, 10 April 1924, pp. 485–6.
131. Cf. L. Jäger, 'Messianische Kritik', p. 213.
132. In *Die Weltbühne*, no. 26, 29 June 1926, pp. 995 ff. (reprinted in the *Gesamtausgabe*, vol. 9: *Literarische Aufsätze*, Frankfurt am Main 1965, pp. 508–15).
133. Cf. 'Das Ideal des Kaputten. Über neapolitanische Technik' (reprinted in the anthology *L'invitation au voyage*, op. cit.).
134. E. Bloch, *Gesamtausgabe*, vol. 9, p. 240 ('Bilder des déjà vu').
135. *Gesammelte Briefe*, vol. 2, p. 461 (to G. Salomon-Delatour, 10 June 1924).
136. *Correspondence*, p. 242 (to G. Scholem, 13 June 1924).
137. All quotes from *Correspondence*, pp. 257–88 (to G. Scholem, 22 December 1924).
138. Ibid., p. 242 (to G. Scholem, 13 June 1924).
139. Ibid., p. 250 (to G. Scholem, 16 July 1924).
140. All quotes from *Correspondence*, p. 244 (to G. Scholem, 13 June 1924).
141. All quotes from *Correspondence*, pp. 252–3 (to G. Scholem, 12 October–5 November 1924).
142. Ibid., p. 247–8 (to G. Scholem, 16 September 1924).
143. Ibid., p. 252 (to G. Scholem, 12 October–5 November 1924). Throughout his life, Benjamin only ever addressed his friend by the German form of his first name.
144. Cf. Jürgen Habermas, 'Walter Benjamin: Consciousness-Raising or Redemptive Criticism' in *Philosophical-Political Profiles*, trans. Fred Lawrence, Cambridge, Mass. 1983, pp. 129–63.
145. Cf. *GS* IV, pp. 928–35.
146. Ibid., p. 914.
147. Cf. Peter von Haselberg, 'Der Deutsche Walter Benjamin', *Merkur*, vol. 32, 1978, pp. 592–600.

148. *Correspondence*, pp. 214–5 (to F. C. Rang, 18 November 1923).
149. Ibid., p. 220 (to F. C. Rang, 26 November 1923).
150. Ibid., p. 236 (to F. C. Rang, 5 March 1924).
151. Ibid., p. 212 (to F. C. Rang, 24 October 1923).
152. 'Naples', in *One-Way Street*, p. 170.
153. Ibid., pp. 169 ff.
154. *Correspondence*, p. 257 (to G. Scholem, 22 December 1924).
155. Ibid., p. 300 (to G. Scholem, 29 May 1926).
156. *Gesammelte Briefe*, vol. 2, p. 507 (to G. Salomon-Delatour, 5 November 1924).
157. *Correspondence*, pp. 255 (to G. Scholem, 12 October–5 November 1924).
158. Ibid., p. 261 (to G. Scholem, 19 February 1925).
159. Ibid., p. 264 (to G. Scholem, 6 April 1925). The typewritten copy handed in to Frankfurt University appears to have been lost, so that it is impossible to say for sure which parts of the 'Epistemo-Critical Prologue' Benjamin kept back from the professors of the philosophy faculty.
160. Ibid., p. 266 (to G. Scholem, 20–25 May 1925).
161. Benjamin already knew in summer 1923 that Cornelius would not accept him as a *Habilitation* candidate (cf. his letter of 1 August 1923 to G. Salomon-Delatour, in *Gesammelte Briefe*, vol. 2, p. 345).
162. Burkhardt Lindner, 'Habilitationsakte Benjamin. Über ein "akademisches Trauerspiel" und über ein Vorkapitel der "Frankfurter Schule" (Horkheimer, Adorno)', *Literaturwissenschaft und Linguistik* nos. 53–4, 1984, p. 152 (Benjamin to the Honourable Faculty for Philosophy of the University of Frankfurt am Main, 12 May 1925).
163. *GS* VI, pp. 215–16 ('Lebenslauf 1925'); my emphasis.
164. All quotes from B. Lindner, 'Habilitationsakte Benjamin', p. 155 (Hans Cornelius,'Erstes Referat über die Habilitationsschrift von Dr. Benjamin' [Initial Report on the *Habilitation* thesis by Dr Benjamin]).
165. Ibid., p. 156 (Minutes of the Philosophy Faculty, 202nd meeting).
166. Cf. Ibid., p. 157 (Franz Schultz to Benjamin, 27 July 1925).
167. All quotes from B. Lindner, 'Habilitationsakte Benjamin', p. 155 (Hans Cornelius, Erstes Referat über die Habilitationsschrift von Dr. Benjamin).
168. *GS* II, p. 245.
169. *GS* VI, pp. 218–19 ('Lebenslauf 1928').
170. *Correspondence*, p. 372 (to M. Rychner, 7 March 1931).
171. J.M. Lange, 'Der Ursprung des deutschen Trauerspiels', *Die Weltbühne*, no. 43, 23 October 1928, p. 649.
172. *The Origin of German Tragic Drama*, p. 27.
173. *GS* VI, pp. 218–19 ('Lebenslauf III')
174. *The Origin of German Tragic Drama*, p. 27.
175. Ibid., p. 28.
176. Ibid., p. 30.
177. Ibid., p. 166.
178. Cf. *Correspondence*, p. 261 (to G. Scholem, 19 February 1925). The lines are from the famous nursery rhyme 'Hopp, hopp, hopp' (text Carl Hahn, tune Carl Gottlieb Hering), which Benjamin, if he did not already know it from his childhood, presumably found somewhere in his extensive collection of children's books.
179. Cf. Harald Steinhagen, 'Zu Walter Benjamins Begriff der

Allegorie', in *Formen und Funktionen der Allegorie*, ed. Walter Haug, Stuttgart 1979, p. 667.

180. Cf. Willy Haas, 'Zwei Zeitdokumente wider Willen', *Die Literarische Welt*, no. 16, 20 April 1928, pp. 1–2. Beside Benjamin's book, Haas also reviewed Rudolf Borchardt's *Handlungen und Abhandlungen*.

181. *The Origin of German Tragic Drama*, p. 63.

182. *Correspondence*, p. 322 (to G. Scholem, 30 January 1928).

183. *Briefe an Kracauer*, p. 31 (to S. Kracauer, 20 October 1926).

184. H. v. Hofmannsthal, cited by Benjamin in his *Correspondence*, p. 276 (to G. Scholem, 21 July 1925).

185. Cf. Siegfried Kracauer, 'Zu den Schriften Walter Benjamins', in *Literaturblatt der Frankfurter Zeitung*, no. 29, 15 July 1928, p. 8. Now in *Schriften*, vol. 5.2, *Aufsätze 1927–1931*, ed. Inka Mülder-Bach, Frankfurt am Main 1990, pp. 119–24.

186. Cf. J. M. Lange, 'Der Ursprung des deutschen Trauerspiels', p. 649.

187. Cf. Werner Milch, 'Walter Benjamin', in *Berliner Tageblatt*, 11 November 1928.

188. Cf. S[ándor] [Vutkovi]ch, 'Walter Benjamin: Ursprung des deutschen Trauerspiels', *Egyetemes philologiai közlöny*, vol. 52, 1928, p 43.

189. Cf. Marcel Brion, 'L'actualité littéraire à l'étranger', *Les nouvelles littéraires* no. 283, 17 March 1928, p. 8; Paul Dubray, 'Les lettres allemandes', *Vient de paraître* vol. 8, 1928, pp. 293–94.

190. R[oy] P[ascal], 'Ursprung des deutschen Trauerspieles [sic], by Dr Walter Benjamin', *The Modern Language Review*, vol. 25, 1930, p. 124.

191. Cf. Walther Linden, 'Walter Benjamin, Ursprung des deutschen Trauerspiels', *Zeitschrift für Deutschkunde*, no. 43, 1929, p. 341.

192. Cf. Günther Müller, 'Neue Arbeiten zur deutschen Barockliteratur', *Zeitschrift für deutsche Bildung*, vol. 6, 1930, pp. 325–33.

193. Cf. Franz Heinrich Mautner, 'Walter Benjamin, Ursprung des deutschen Trauerspiels', *Die Neueren Sprachen*, vol. 38, 1930, pp. 681–3.

194. Cf. Alexander Mette, 'Walter Benjamin: Ursprung des deutschen Trauerspiels', in *Imago*, vol. 17, 1931, pp. 536–8. Benjamin returned the compliment for Mette's friendly critique by reviewing his work *Über Beziehungen zwischen Spracheigentümlichkeiten schizophrener und dichterischer Produktion* for the *Frankfurter Zeitung* in 1929 (now in *GS* III, pp. 164–6).

195. Admittedly the majority of these specialist studies first appeared in the 1930s: cf. for example Theodor Wiesengrund-Adorno, *Kierkegaard. Konstruktion des Ästhetischen*, Tübingen 1933; Karl Thieme, *Das alte Wahre. Eine Bildungsgeschichte des Abendlandes*, Leipzig 1934; Hans Gerth, 'Die sozialgeschichtliche Lage der bürgerlichen Intelligenz um die Wende des 18. Jahrhunderts' (unpublished doctoral thesis, Frankfurt am Main 1935); Heinz Maus, 'Kritik am Justemilieu. Eine sozialphilosophische Studie über Schopenhauer', in *Die Traumhölle des Justemilieu und Erinnerung an die Aufgaben der Kritischen Theorie*, eds Michael Th. Greven and Gerd van de Moetter, Frankfurt am Main 1981, pp. 42–242 (Maus's doctoral thesis, submitted in 1940; cf. pp. 49–50); Carl Linfert, 'Die Grundlagen der Architekturzeichnung. Mit einem Versuch über französische Architekturzeichnungen des 18. Jahrhunderts', in *Kunstwissenschaftliche Forschungen*, vol. 1,

1931, pp. 133–246. (Benjamin reviewed the entire issue in 1933 for the *Frankfurter Zeitung:* cf. 'Strenge Kunstwissenschaft', now in *GS* III, pp. 369–74); G. Müller, 'Höfische Kultur der Barockzeit', in Hans Naumann and Günther Müller, Höfische Kultur, Halle an der Saale 1929, pp. 79–154 (esp. 89–90); Leo Spitzer, *Die Literarisierung des Lebens in Lope's Dorotea*, Bonn and Cologne 1932 (esp. pp. 61–2); Helmut Kappler, *Der barocke Geschichtsbegriff bei Andreas Gryphius*, Frankfurt am Main 1936.

196. The individual items contained in 'Naturgeschichte des Theaters' appeared in various periodicals at the beginning of the 1930s; they have been reprinted, in extended form, in Theodor W. Adorno, *Gesammelte Schriften*, ed. Rolf Tiedemann, vol. 16: *Musikalische Schriften I–III*, Frankfurt am Main 1978, pp. 309-20. 'The Natural History of the Theatre' in Theodor W. Adorno, *Quasi una Fantasia: Essays on Modern Music*, trans. Rodney Livingstone, London 1992, pp. 65–80.

197. Cf. Theodor W. Adorno, *Gesammelte Schriften*, vol. 1: *Philosophische Frühschriften*, Frankfurt am Main 1973, pp. 325–44 (Adorno's inaugural lecture from 1931).

198. First published in 1966. *Negative Dialectics*, trans. E. B. Ashton, London 1973.

199. Cf. Theodor W. Adorno, *Aesthetic Theory*, trans. C. Lenhardt, London 1984.

200. Hofmannsthal had turned to Panofsky with the request that he should consider doing a review of the *Trauerspiel* book (cf. his letter of 12 December 1927, printed in Wolfgang Kemp's essay 'Walter Benjamin und die Kunstwissenschaft, Teil 1: Benjamins Beziehungen zur Wiener Schule', *Kritische Berichte*, vol. 1, no. 3, 1973, pp. 30–50). An answer to Hofmannsthal's letter from Panofsky is unknown, so that it is unclear just what resistances he felt to writing such a review. Saxl must also have known Benjamin's *Trauerspiel* book – Aby Warburg had it sent to him – but any reactions on his part are equally unknown (for the overall context, cf. Momme Brodersen, ' "Wenn Ihnen die Arbeit des Interesses wert erscheint . . . " Walter Benjamin und das Warburg-Institut: einige Dokumente', in *Aby Warburg. Akten des internationalen Symposions*, Hamburg 1990, eds Horst Bredekamp, Michael Diers and Charlotte Schoell-Glass, Weinheim 1991, pp. 87–94).

Chapter 6

1. 'One-Way Street' in *One-Way Street*, p. 51.
2. Littauer, his publisher from whom he first managed in late 1924 to wrest a two-year blanket contract after dogged but successful negotiations, went bankrupt before there was a word in the press about the forthcoming inauguration of his publishing house (cf. Benjamin's letters dated 29 December 1924 and 24 April 1925 to G. Salomon-Delatour, *Gesammelte Briefe*, vol. 2, p. 518 IISG Amsterdam, estate of G. Salomon-Delatour); his wife Dora, who appears to have at times earned the entire family budget with her activities as secretary, translator and journalist, had lost a lucrative side-line; and Benjamin's plans for *Habilitation* in Frankfurt had also miscarried.
3. This, his very first work for the *Frankfurter Zeitung*, appeared on 16 August 1925 (now in *GS* IV, pp. 792–6).
4. Cf. *Correspondence*, p. 278 (to G. Scholem, 21 July 1925).

5. Ibid., p. 284 (to G. Scholem, 21 September 1925) as well as his letter on the same day to Salomon (IISG Amsterdam, estate of G. Salomon).
6. Hugo von Hofmannsthal–Willy Haas, *Ein Briefwechsel*, Berlin 1968, p. 55 (H. v. Hofmannsthal to W. Haas, 19 January 1926).
7. Cf. *Correspondence*, pp. 273 and 303 (to H. v. Hofmannsthal, 11 June 1925 and to G. Scholem, 29 May 1926).
8. Die Schmiede to W. Benjamin, 20 July 1925 (unpublished letter, Piper Verlag Archive, Munich).
9. *Correspondence*, p. 267 (to G. Scholem, *c.* 20–25 May 1925).
10. Asja Lacis, 'Städte und Menschen. Erinnerungen', *Sinn und Form*, vol. 21, 1969, pp. 1347–8.
11. 'One-Way-Street' in *One-Way Street*, pp. 68–9 and 86–7.
12. Ibid., pp. 86–7.
13. A. Lacis, 'Städte und Menschen', p. 1348.
14. *GS* III, p. 31.
15. *GS* IV, p. 450.
16. Ibid., p. 449 ('Nichts gegen die Illustrierte').
17. Willy Haas, *Die Literarische Welt. Erinnerungen*, München 1960, p. 164.
18. The *Tagebuch*, founded by Stefan Großmann, was published until issue 17 of year 4 (1923) by Rowohlt.
19. This monthly, edited by Franz Hessel, only appeared for one year (twelve issues all in 1924) before folding.
20. Heinrich Fischer to Wilhelm Lehmann, 12 May 1925, in *Kurt Wolff – Ernst Rowohlt*, ed. Friedrich Pfäfflin, Marbach am Neckar 1987 (*Marbacher Magazin*, no. 43), p. 117.
21. *Correspondence*, p. 277 (to G. Scholem, 21 July 1925).
22. *GS* III, p. 616 (to H. v. Hofmannsthal, 25 January 1926).
23. *Correspondence*, p. 291 (to H. v. Hofmannsthal, 23 February 1926).
24. Cf. 'Büchereinlauf' (now in *GS* IV, pp. 1017–8).
25. Cf. 'Memoiren aus unserer Zeit' (now in *GS* III, pp. 377–80).
26. For instance: '"Why", asks Jacques, "do your fellow countrymen speak so badly of you?" "Where?" I stammered, felled by this direct question. "Here in Paris! Almost every writer who visits me has a bad opinion of you!" I am lost for an answer' (Fritz von Unruh, *Flügel der Nike. Buch einer Reise*, Frankfurt am Main 1925, p. 19).
27. *Correspondence*, p. 284 (to G. Scholem, 21 September 1925).
28. Unruh, the founder of the Eiserne Front, a federation of the Social Democrats, the unions, Workers' Sports Associations and the Reichsbanner Schwarz-Rot-Gold that was set up in defense of the Republic after Royalists and Nazis had joined the Harzburg Front, was driven into exile in Italy and France in 1932, after his home in the Frankfurt *Rententurm* was sacked by the brownshirts.
29. Peter Panter (i.e. Kurt Tucholsky), 'Der neue Morand', *Die Weltbühne*, no. 34, 25 August 1925, p. 295.
30. Only rarely did Benjamin give anyone such a 'thrashing' during his career as a critic. Apart from Unruh, his victims included Walter Mehring for his *Gedichte, Lieder und Chansons* that appeared in 1929 ('Gebrauchslyrik? Aber nicht so!', now in *GS* III, pp. 183–4); Erich Kästner, whom Benjamin attacked in his (in)famous pamphlet 'Linke Melancholie' (this text appeared in 1931 in *Die Gesellschaft* after it was refused by the *Frankfurter Zeitung* on the insistence of the art editor Friedrich T. Gubler; now in *GS* III, pp. 279–83); and Kurt Hiller (a review of his collection of essays,

Der Sprung ins Helle, entitled 'Der Irrtum des Aktivismus', now in *GS* III, pp. 350–52, which brought him the undying animosity of his former advocate).

31. *GS* III, p. 611 (to H. v. Hofmannsthal, 15 June 1926).
32. Ibid., p. 644 (to Bernard von Brentano, 11 October 1930).
33. Harry Graf Kessler, *Tagebücher 1918–1937*, ed. Wolfgang Pfeiffer-Belli, Frankfurt am Main 1961, p. 434.
34. *GS* III, p. 27 ('Friedensware').
35. *Briefe an Kracauer*, p. 22 (to S. Kracauer, 3 June 1926).
36. Ibid., p. 23 (to S. Kracauer, 3 June 1926).
37. Benjamin appeared in the *Frankfurter Zeitung* from 1925 to 1935. Roughly 120 contributions of his were published in this paper during these ten years.
38. *Correspondence*, p. 249 (to G. Scholem, 16 September 1924). The Tristan Tzara text mentioned here, 'Die Photographie von der Kehrseite', appeared in no. 3 (1924) of *G. Zeitschrift für elementare Gestaltung*.
39. Honoré de Balzac, *Ursula Mirouet*, Berlin 1925.
40. *Correspondence*, p. 249 (to G. Scholem, 16 September 1924). He claimed that the remuneration was too small for the work that it involved (ibid., p. 278; to G. Scholem, 21 July 1925), but the real reason, which he only confided to Salomon, was that he felt that he should no longer let himself be distracted by anything because he had begun to write *The Origin of German Tragic Drama* (to G. Salomon, 10 June 1924). For an excellent study of this translation and Benjamin's problems with Balzac, cf. Barbara Kleiner, 'Mißverstandene Tugend – verworfene Leidenschaft. Benjamins Übersetzung von Balzacs *Ursule Mirouet*', in *Namen, Texte, Stimmen. Walter Benjamins Sprachphilosophi*e, ed. Thomas Regehly, Stuttgart 1993, pp. 91–107.
41. Published in the magazine *Der Querschnitt*, vol. 6, 1926, pp. 23–4.
42. More details on the firm's history can be found in Joachim Unseld's book *Franz Kafka. Ein Schriftstellerleben*, Munich and Vienna 1982, pp. 209 ff.
43. Cf. 'Marcel Proust', in *Französischer Geist im neuen Europa*, Stuttgart 1925, pp. 9–145.
44. Cf. E[rnst] R[obert] Curtius, 'Die deutsche Marcel-Proust-Ausgabe, Eine Umfrage', *Die Literarische Welt*, no. 2, 8 January 1926, p. 4. Apart from Curtius, the survey was also answered by Friedrich Burschell and Hans Jacob (cf. 'Die deutsche Marcel-Proust-Ausgabe. Eine Umfrage (Schluß)', *Die Literarische Welt*, no. 4, 22 January 1926, p. 4).
45. Cf. 'Die deutsche Marcel-Proust-Ausgabe. Eine Umfrage. Erwiderung des Übersetzers an Prof. E. R. Curtius', *Die Literarische Welt*, no. 3, 15 January 1926, p. 4.
46. Ernst Robert Curtius, 'Zum Streit über die Proust-Übersetzung' (reply), Die Literarische Welt, no. 5, 29 January 1926, p. 7.
47. Cf. *Correspondence*, p. 306 (to G. Scholem, 18 September 1926).
48. Cf. the two letters written by Die Schmiede to Franz Hessel (and Benjamin) dated 27 February 1926 and 24 September 1926 (unpublished, Piper Verlag Archive, Munich).
49. Besides the two letters already cited from the unpublished correspondence between Die Schmiede and Benjamin and Hessel, cf. also the two from 19 October 1926 and Franz Hessel's letter to Fritz Wurm (Piper Verlag Archive, Munich).

50. *Correspondence*, pp. 296–7 (to Jula Radt, 8 April 1926).
51. Ibid., p. 305 (to G. Scholem, 18 September 1926).
52. Ibid., p. 278 (to G. Scholem, 18 September 1926) and p. 395 (to G. Scholem, 21 July 1925).
53. The MS of the translation had already been lying around at the publisher's 'for a long time', as Benjamin wrote on 18 September 1926 to Scholem (ibid., p. 305). After the German Proust rights were bought by Piper, it proceeded to wander back and forth between Berlin and Munich. Precisely when the MS got lost cannot be said with certainty, but by all appearances it would seem to have been lost in Benjamin's hands.
54. Benjamin and Hessel 'stopped' work 'in despair' (Reinhard Piper, *Briefwechsel mit Autoren und Künstlern 1903–1953*, Munich and Zurich 1979, pp. 214–15; F. Hessel to R. Piper, 14 July 1928) when once again the translation project reached a deadlock. They never resumed their work, not even when Piper demanded that they honour their contractual agreements. What became of these fragments is as little known today as the whereabouts of the manuscript of *Sodome et Gomorrh*.
55. Not even a sharply worded letter, in which Hessel threatened the company that he would refuse to allow it to go to press, was able to prevent this (cf. R. Piper, *Briefwechsel mit Autoren und Künstlern*, p. 220; F. Hessel to R. Piper, 25 September 1930).
56. Efraim Frisch, 'Der zweite Band der Proust-Ausgabe', *Literaturblatt der Frankfurter Zeitung*, no. 14, 4 April 1927, pp. 12–13.
57. Cf. Wolf Zucker, 'Marcel Proust', *Die Weltbühne*, no. 14, 5 April 1927, pp. 556–8.
58. Cf. Erich Franzen, 'Marcel Proust: Im Schatten der jungen Mädchen', *Die Literarische Welt*, nos. 15–16, 15 April 1927, pp. 5–6.
59. Cf. Oskar Loerke, 'Vorläufiges zum Thema Marcel Proust', *Berliner Börsen-Courier*, 6 May 1927.
60. Cf. Hermann Hesse, 'Mai im Kastanienwald', *Berliner Tageblatt*, 12 May 1927.
61. Cf. K. H. Ruppel, 'Marcel Proust: Im Schatten der jungen Mädchen', *Das Tage-Buch*, vol. 8, 1927, pp. 959–61.
62. Cf. Paul Cohen-Portheim, 'Marcel Proust', *Die Neue Bücherschau*, vol. 4, 1926/27, pp. 219–22.
63. Cf. Franz Hessel, 'Im Schatten der jungen Mädchen. Von Marcel Proust', *Weltstimmen*, vol. 2 1928, pp. 204–8.
64. S. Kracauer to E. Frisch, 11 March 1927 (unpublished letter, Archive of the Leo Baeck Institute, New York, estate of E. Frisch).
65. K.H. Ruppel, 'Marcel Proust: Im Schatten der jungen Mädchen', p. 959.
66. Friedrich Burschell, 'Zur neuen Proustübertragung', *Die Literarische Welt*, no. 17, 29 April 1927, p. 8.
67. Richard von Schaukal, 'Erbe und Besitz. Ein Umblick und Rückblick im "Goethejahr"', *Die Neue Literatur*, vol. 33, 1932, p. 557.
68. *Correspondence*, p. 286 (To H. v. Hofmannsthal, 28 December 1925).
69. R. Piper to F. Hessel, 20 July 1928 (unpublished letter, Piper Verlag Archive, Munich).
70. *Correspondence*, p. 278 (to G. Scholem, 21 July 1925).
71. Cf. Louis Aragon, 'Don Juan und der Schuhputzer. Briefmarken. Damentoilette-Café Certâ', trans. W. Benjamin, *Die Literarische*

Welt, no. 23, 8 June 1928, pp. 3–4 and no. 24, 15 June 1928, pp. 7–8.

72. Cf. Marcel Proust, 'Über das Lesen. Zu John Ruskins 30. Todestag', trans. W. Benjamin, *Die Literarische Welt*, no. 9, 28 February 1930, pp. 3–4.

73. Cf. Leon Bloy, 'Auslegung der Gemeinplätze', trans. W. Benjamin, in *Die Literarische Welt*, no. 12, 18 March 1932, pp. 3–4.

74. Cf. Marcel Jouhandeau, 'Die Schäferin Nanou', in *Die Literarische Welt*, nos. 15–16, 8 April 1932, pp. 9–11; 'Fräulein Zéline oder Gottes Glück zum Gebrauch eines alten Fräuleins' in Félix Bertaux and Hermann Kesten, eds, *Neue französische Erzähler*, Berlin 1930, pp. 168–86; 'Der Dorfbräutigam', in Europäische Revue, vol. 7, no. 2, 1931, pp. 105–31.

75. Cf. J. M. Sollier (i.e. Adrienne Monnier), 'Kluge Jungfrau', authorized trans. by W. Benjamin, *Kölnische Zeitung*, no. 613, 8 November 1932.

76. Cf. *GS* IV, p. 580 ('Pariser Tagebuch').

77. Benjamin had already finalized the contract 'for a volume of selected novellas by Marcel Jouhandeau' with Kiepenheuer in 1930 (Scholem, *Friendship*, p. 163; Benjamin to G. Scholem, 14 June 1930); it was to be about 250–80 pages in length (cf. the unpublished letter from the firm Kiepenheuer to Robert Aron, the representative of Librairie Gallimard, 5 May 1930; Literaturarchive der Akademie der Künste, Berlin, estate of W. Benjamin).

78. Cf. *Correspondence*, p. 305 (to G. Scholem, 18 September 1925).

79. *GS* VI, p. 427 ('Tagebuch', May–June 1931).

80. All quotes from *Moscow Diary*, p. 72.

81. *Correspondence*, p. 314 (to H. v. Hofmannsthal, 5 June 1927).

82. *Moscow Diary*, p. 28.

83. *Briefe an Kracauer*, p. 38 (to S. Kracauer, 23 February 1927).

84. The article appeared on 11 February 1927 in *Die Literarische Welt* under the somewhat sensationalistic title 'Regisseur Meyerhold – in Moskau erledigt? Ein literarisches Gericht wegen der Inszenierung von Gogol's "Revisor"' ['Meyerhold the Director – Finished in Moscow? A Literary Trial Prompted by his Production of Gogol's The Government Inspector'] (now in *GS* IV, pp. 481–3).

85. All published in *Die Literarische Welt*, 11 March 1927 (now in *GS* II, pp. 743–55). Another article in the same periodical, in 1930 ('Wie ein russischer Theatererfolg aussieht'; now in *GS* IV, pp. 561–3) is based in essence on his 'Moscow experiences' during 1926/7.

86. Appeared in no. 7, 1927 (now in *GS* II, pp. 755–62).

87. Benjamin held his lecture on 23 March 1927. A typescript of it has not come down to us, but presumably the wording was largely identical to that of his article in the periodical. A further, by no means final echo of his Moscow trip can be found in an article 'Russische Spielsachen', first published on 10 January 1930 in the *Südwestdeutsche Rundfunkzeitung* (now in *GS* IV, pp. 623–5).

Chapter 7

1. Scholem, *Friendship*, p. 153 (utterance from Benjamin).

2. A. Lacis, 'Städte und Menschen. Erinnerungen', *Sinn und Form*, vol. 21, 1969, p. 1351.

3. That was in December 1928 and January 1929 (cf. Scholem, *Friendship*, p. 157).

4. Cf. A. Lacis, 'Städte und Menschen', p. 1352.

5. For details of the story of their divorce, cf. also Hans Puttnies and Gary Smith, *Benjaminiana*, Gießen 1991, pp. 135–66.
6. *Correspondence*, p. 365 (to G. Scholem, 25 April 1930).
7. Ibid., p. 355 (to G. Scholem, 4 August 1929).
8. Scholem, *Friendship*, p. 158 (Benjamin to G. Scholem, 1 November 1929).
9. *Illuminations*, p. 69 ('Unpacking My Library'). Benjamin broadcast his 'Talk about Book Collecting' (the subtitle) on 27 April 1931 on the Südwestdeutscher Rundfunk; it then appeared three months later in *Die Literarische Welt*. The collection of children's books that is mentioned is now in the possession of the Institut für Kinderbuchforschung at the University of Frankfurt am Main.
10. A. Lacis, 'Städte und Menschen', p. 1355.
11. Benjamin remained in (written) contact with Asja Lacis right into the 1930s. (The meagre remains of their once extensive correspondence are now in the keeping of the Akademie der Künste; individual letters were published in 1968 and 1987: cf. Benjamin's 'Brief an Asja Lacis', *Alternative*, nos 59–60, 1968, pp. 62–3, as well as Asja Lacis's 'Briefe an Walter Benjamin' in Fritz Micrau, ed., *Russen in Berlin. Literatur, Malerei, Theater, Film 1918–1933*, Leipzig 1987, pp. 573–6). Asja Lacis strove constantly in Moscow to achieve something for her friend. Even if her efforts were not crowned with success, Benjamin truly valued her selfless solidarity. Her help did not awaken, as he put it in one of his letters, any 'cheap hopes' – something that he was exceedingly wary of during his time in exile as a consequence of his numerous disappointments.
12. He announced at the end of June 1929 that he would be travelling in September (cf. *Correspondence*, p. 353, to H. v. Hofmannsthal, 26 June 1929), and then in mid-September that his trip would be in November (cf. ibid., p. 356, to G. Scholem, 17 September 1929).
13. Ibid., p. 381 (to G. Scholem, 20 July 1931).
14. Cf. *GS* VI, p. 791 (to Gretel Karplus, 25 July 1930).
15. *Correspondence*, p. 366 (to G. Scholem, 15 August 1930).
16. *GS* IV, p. 383.
17. Not without reason did Ernst Bloch call the short essay 'strange' and 'slightly too subjective' for his taste (Ernst Bloch, *Briefe 1903–1975*, Frankfurt am Main 1985, p. 347; Bloch to S. Kracauer, 18 September 1930).
18. All quotes from *GS* IV, pp. 383–7 ('Nordische See').
19. *Correspondence*, p. 366 (to G. Scholem, 15 August 1930).
20. All quotes from *Correspondence*, pp. 367–8 (to G. Scholem, 4 October 1930).
21. For more details on Egon Wissing, cf. Scholem, *Engel*, p. 149 ('Ahnen und Verwandte Walter Benjamins').
22. *Correspondence*, p. 369 (to G. Scholem, 3 November 1930).
23. *GS* VI, p. 161 ('Programm der literarischen Kritik').
24. *GS* III, p. 295 ('Wie erklären sich große Bucherfolge?').
25. Cf. *GS* VI, pp. 169–75.
26. Scholem, *Friendship*, p. 167 (Benjamin to G. Scholem, 5 February 1931).
27. Cf. Burkhardt Lindner, 'Links hatte noch alles sich zu enträtseln . . .' in *Links hatte noch alles sich zu enträtseln . . . Walter Benjamin im Kontext*, ed. B. Lindner, Frankfurt am Main 1978, p. 8.

28. 'One-Way Street', in *One-Way Street*, , p. 66.
29. *GS* III, p. 254 ('Wider ein Meisterwerk').
30. Cf. ibid., p. 259 ('Wider ein Meisterwerk').
31. 'Theories of German Fascism', trans. Jerolf Wikoff, in *New German Critique*, no. 17, 1979, p. 124.
32. 'Left-Wing Melancholy (on Erich Kästner's New Book of Poems)', trans. Ben Brewster, in *Screen*, no. 2, 1974, p. 30.
33. Theodor W. Adorno and Walter Benjamin, *Briefwechsel 1928–1940*, ed. Henri Lonitz, Frankfurt am Main 1994, p. 15 (to T. Wiesengrund-Adorno, 10 November 1930).
34. For a highly detailed portrait of the intellectual and personal relationship between Benjamin and Brecht, cf. Erdmut Wizisla, 'Walter Benjamin und Bertolt Brecht. Eine Bestandsaufnahme. Mit einer Chronik der Beziehung' (unpublished doctoral thesis, Berlin 1993).
35. *Correspondence*, p. 365 (to G. Scholem, 25 April 1930).
36. Ibid., p. 368 (to G. Scholem, 4 October 1930).
37. Bertolt Brecht, *Gesammelte Werke*, vol. 18, Frankfurt am Main 1967, pp. 85–6 ('Entwurf zu einer Zeitschrift "Kritische Blätter"').
38. *GS* VI, p. 619.
39. Further collaborators who were considered (above all by Benjamin) during the project stage included Hans Borchardt, Erich Franzen, Sigfried Giedion, Willy Haas, Siegfried Kracauer, Karl Korsch, Ludwig Marcuse, Walter Mehring, Erwin Piscator, Arthur Rosenberg, Hans Sahl, Fritz Sternberg, Peter Suhrkamp and Kurt Weill (cf. *GS* VI, pp. 619–20, 'Memorandum zu der Zeitschrift Krisis und Kritik"' and p. 827, 'Lesarten').
40. *GS* VI, p. 826 (to B. Brecht, end of February 1931).
41. Scholem, *Friendship*, p. 82.
42. 'One-Way Street', in *One-Way Street*, pp. 79–80.
43. *Correspondence*, p. 343 (to G. Scholem, 30 October 1928; the short text is now printed in *GS* II, pp. 624–5.
44. Cf. 'Karl Kraus liest Offenbach' (now in *GS* IV, pp. 515–7).
45. Cf. 'Wedekind und Kraus in der Volksbühne' (now in *GS* IV, pp. 551–4).
46. Cf. *Die Fackel*, no. 781–6, 1928, p. 74 ('Notizen') and p. 83 ('Vorlesungen im Ausland'), as well as *Die Fackel*, nos. 800–805, 1929, p. 72 ('Notizen').
47. Karl Kraus, 'Um Perichole', *Die Fackel*, nos. 852–6, 1931, p. 27.
48. Scholem, *Friendship*, p. 175 (Benjamin to G. Scholem, 8 June 1931).
49. *One-Way Street*, pp. 79–80.
50. *GS* II, p. 1092 ('Paralipomena zum Kraus').
51. *One-Way Street*, 'Karl Kraus', p. 258.
52. Ibid., p. 290.
53. *Correspondence*, p. 374 (G. Scholem to Benjamin, 30 March 1931).
54. *GS* II, p. 1092 ('Paralipomena zum Kraus'). Translators' note: 'Gott sei Dank, daß niemand weiß, daß ich Rumpelstilzchen heiß.' Benjamin is playing on this famous line from the Brothers Grimm tale, a line which he also quoted in his note on Kraus, in *One-Way Street*. In the tale, Rumpelstiltskin, who can spin gold from flax, destroys himself when his name is discovered.
55. *Correspondence*, pp. 372–3 (to Max Rychner, 7 July 1931).
56. B. Brecht, *Gesammelte Werke*, vol. 18, p. 119 ('Radio: eine vorsintflutliche Erfindung').

57. These include an interview ('Gespräch mit Ernst Schoen', now in
    GS IV, pp. 548–51), an exchange of letters concerning radio-
    related matters with Schoen (GS II, pp. 1497–1505), the fragments
    'Situation im Rundfunk' (GS II, p. 1505) and 'Reflexionen zum
    Rundfunk' (GS II, pp. 1506–7) as well as the texts 'Hörmodelle'
    (GS IV, p. 628), 'Theater und Rundfunk' (GS II, pp. 773–6) and
    'Zweierlei Volkstümlichkeit' (GS IV, pp. 671–3).
58. Quoted from the 'Introduction' to the first issue (cited in Sabine
    Schiller-Lerg, *Walter Benjamin und der Rundfunk*, Munich 1984,
    p. 40).
59. Paul Laven, 'Aus dem Erinnerungsbrevier eines Rundfunkpioniers',
    in *Literatur und Rundfunk*, ed. Gerhard Hay, Hildesheim 1975,
    p. 9.
60. The relevant notes range from an early 'All the university lecturers
    blather away on the radio etc.' (*Correspondence*, p. 262; to
    G. Scholem, 19 February 1925) to a later 'in Frankfurt [he had] to
    take care of some piddling radio matters' (Scholem, *Friendship*,
    p. 167; Benjamin to G. Scholem, 19 February 1931).
61. Cf. *Correspondence*, p. 356 (to G. Scholem, 18 September 1929).
62. Cf. *GS* II, pp. 773–6 ('Theater und Rundfunk').
63. Instead of sharing an experience the spectator must come to grips
    with things, as Brecht wrote in an article entitled 'Betrachtungen
    über die Schwierigkeiten des epischen Theaters' written in 1927.
    ('The Epic Theatre and its Difficulties', in *Brecht on Theatre*, trans.
    John Willett, New York 1977, p. 23).
64. *GS* II, p. 776 ('Theater und Rundfunk').
65. Now in *GS* IV, pp. 641–70.
66. Scholem, *Friendship*, p. 181 (Benjamin to G. Scholem, 28 February
    1932).
67. Benjamin to Albert Salomon, 5 April 1932 (unpublished letter; Leo
    Baeck Institute, New York, estate of A. Salomon).
68. These were an annotated bibliography ('Hundert Jahre Schrifttum
    um Goethe') and a review essay entitled 'Faust im Musterkoffer'
    (now in *GS* III, pp. 326–46).
69. *GS* VI, p. 455 ('Spanien 1932').
70. *Correspondence*, p. 390 (to G. Scholem, 22 April 1932).
71. *GS* VI, p. 448 ('Spanien 1932').
72. *Correspondence*, p. 390 (to G. Scholem, 22 April 1932).
73. *GS* VI, p. 453 ('Spanien 1932').
74. Benjamin–Scholem, *Correspondence*, p. 10 (to G. Scholem, 25 June
    1932).
75. Cf. Scholem, *Friendship*, pp. 188–9.
76. 'This diary does not promise to grow very long. Today I received a
    refusal from Kippenberg, and so my plan assumes all the relevance
    that only hopelessness can give it'; so Benjamin opened at that time
    a 'Diary from the seventeenth of August nineteen hundred and
    thirty-one until the day I die' (*GS* VI, p. 441).
77. Benjamin–Scholem, *Correspondence*, p. 15 (to G. Scholem, 26 July
    1932).
78. Cf. *Über Literatur*, Frankfurt am Main 1969.
79. Cf. *Über Haschisch. Novellistisches, Berichte, Materialien*, Frankfurt
    am Main 1972.
80. Cf. *GS* V.
81. Benjamin–Scholem, *Correspondence*, p. 14 (to G. Scholem, 26 July
    1932).

82. Cf. Scholem, *Friendship*, pp. 187–8 (Benjamin to Egon Wissing, 27 July 1932).
83. 'The Destructive Character', in *One-Way Street*, p. 159.
84. Benjamin–Scholem, *Correspondence*, p. 16 (to G. Scholem, 7 August 1932). In a written agreement, Speyer promised his colleague '10% (ten)' of the 'box-office takings' or max. 'RM. 5,000 (five thousand) as payment' for his 'advice' (*Walter Benjamin 1892–1940*, p. 178; Wilhelm Speyer to Benjamin, 12 November 1932). Benjamin collaborated on a number of Speyer's productions, such as the play *Es geht, aber es ist auch danach* and the novel *Gaby, weshalb denn nicht?* The extent of this collaboration can be seen from the percentage that Speyer gave his co-author or adviser: 15 per cent of the gross royalties for the play, and 5 per cent of all earnings' on the novel (cf. Speyer's written declarations to Benjamin of 1 September 1928 and 15 May 1929, unpublished letters, Literaturarchive der Akademie der Künste, Berlin, estate of W. Benjamin).
85. Benjamin–Scholem, *Correspondence*, p.19 (to G. Scholem, 26 September 1932).
86. The testimony to their extremely productive, if not completely conflict-free intellectual relationship is the lengthy correspondence that was published in 1994 (cf. Theodor W. Adorno and Walter Benjamin, *Briefwechsel 1928–1940*, ed. Henri Lonitz, Frankfurt am Main; cf. *Aesthetics and Politics*, London 1980, for some of the most important letters; cf. also Adorno's collected essays on Benjamin, *Über Walter Benjamin*, ed. Rolf Tiedemann, Frankfurt am Main, second, enlarged edn 1990).
87. Further details on this seminar can be found in my article '"Ein Idealist mit Einschränkung". Ein Seminar zu Walter Benjamins Ursprung des deutschen Trauerspiels' in *Die Tageszeitung*, 4 March 1986, pp. 12–13.
88. Cf. the individual records of this seminar, which have recently been published in *Frankfurter Adorno-Blätter*, vol. 4, 1995, pp. 52–77.
89. Wilhelm Emrich, 'Zum Ergänzungsprotokoll vom 13. 6. 1932', in *Frankfurter Adorno-Blätter*, vol. 4, 1995, p. 71.
90. Wilhelm Emrich, 'Ergänzung zum Protokoll vom 13. 6. 1932', in *Frankfurter Adorno-Blätter*, vol. 4, 1995, p. 69.

Chapter 8

1. *GS* VI, p. 520.
2. Cf. Hellmut v. Gerlach, 'Gefesselte Regierung', *Die Weltbühne*, no. 27, 5 July 1932, p. 2.
3. Scholem, *Friendship*, p. 173 (Benjamin to G. Scholem, early May 1932).
4. Cited in Carl von Ossietzky's 'Das Verbot der SA', *Die Weltbühne*, no. 16, 19 April 1932, p. 579.
5. Benjamin's letter to Noeggerath has evidently been lost. Its content can be concluded, though, from an unpublished letter from Noeggerath, 24 March 1933, to Jean Selz (now in the keeping of Dr Marga Noeggerath, Munich).
6. Benjamin was informed about the arrest of his former promoter at Südwestdeutscher Rundfunk in early March (cf. Benjamin–Scholem, *Correspondence*, p. 34, to G. Scholem, 20 March 1933). His arrest led to Schoen's dismissal as artistic director of the Frankfurt radio station. After being briefly imprisoned once again in mid April, he finally managed to flee to London (cf. Ansgar

Diller, 'Der Frankfurter Rundfunk 1923–1945 unter besonderer Berücksichtigung der Zeit des Nationalsozialismus', unpublished thesis, Frankfurt am Main 1975, p. 66).

7. Benjamin–Scholem, *Correspondence*, p. 27 (to G. Scholem, 28 February 1933).

8. Benjamin was commissioned from 1931 to 1932 to work on an extensive Lichtenberg bibliography by the Berlin lawyer (and friend of Brecht) Martin Domke. (For the story of how this work came about, cf. my essay '"Addestramento del giudizio in luogo di formazione delle conoscenze". Sulla costellazione della bibliografia lichtenberghiana di Walter Benjamin', *Quaderno* [Palermo], no. 19, 1984, pp. 55–75.) The card index for the bibliography has survived. It is now in the possession of the Justus Liebig University, Gießen.

9. Cf. Benjamin–Scholem, *Correspondence*, p. 27 (to G. Scholem, 28 February 1933). In his justifiable anger at the ambiguous, not to say opportunist behaviour of numerous editorial boards, Benjamin did not always adhere strictly to the facts. Thus it should be noted in all fairness that this suspension cannot have lasted too long. Even if one allows for the fact that one or two articles would have already been received before the decisive events of February and March, so that the editorial board of the *Frankfurter Zeitung* had a small stock of received and paid-for pieces that they could draw on, Benjamin's reviews and prose texts nevertheless appeared throughout the whole of 1933, and no less regularly than beforehand. The only difference was that they now had to be published anonymously as a result of the political conditions.

10. Ibid., p. 34 (to G. Scholem, 20 March 1933).

11. The exact date of his flight was in all probability 17 March, as evinced by a letter from Benjamin to Jean Selz postmarked the 16th of the month. In it, Benjamin announces that he is about to leave straight away: 'I shall depart from Berlin tomorrow evening in the direction of Paris' ('Carteggio W. Benjamin e J. Selz 1932–1934,' *Aut aut*, new series, nos. 189/90, 1982, p. 52).

12. Personal letter from Carl Linfert to the author (8 November 1979).

13. Benjamin to Thankmar von Münchhausen, 31 March 1933 (unpublished letter, in the possession of Countess M. von Hatzfeld, Cologne).

14. Benjamin listed his domiciles during his exile in a personal record (which is, however, unreliable in this respect) written in 1938 while trying, unsuccessfully, to gain French citizenship (cf. *GS* VI, p. 223).

15. These co-translations were first published in 1954 in *Lettres nouvelles* (no. 11, pp. 1–10) (cf. now *GS* IV, 979–86). For Selz's reminiscences of his relationship with Benjamin, cf. his articles 'Benjamin in Ibiza' in *On Walter Benjamin*, ed. Gary Smith, pp. 352–66, and 'Une expérience de Walter Benjamin' in the French Benjamin anthology *Écrits français*, Paris 1991, pp. 380–86. Their correspondence appeared in 1982 in the Italian journal *Aut aut*, vol. 189/90, pp. 48–64. (Cf. note 11.)

16. All quotes from Benjamin to Alfred Kurella, 2 June 1933 (unpublished letter; Literaturarchiv der Akademie der Künste, Berlin, estate of A. Kurella). That Benjamin was not completely able to avoid contact with Nazis can be seen from his lengthy correspondence with one Maximilian Verspohl from Hamburg – SS company leader by trade! He came to know him on Ibiza, but how or through whom cannot be discerned from Verspohl's letters (at present the only

documents that are known from their correspondence; these hitherto unpublished letters are in the keeping of the Benjamin-Archiv der Akademie der Künste in Berlin).

17. *GS* VI, p. 227 ('curriculum vitae Dr Walter Benjamin'). This *Curriculum vitae*, written at the turn of the year 1939/40, is presumably one of the documents that Benjamin had to submit in order to obtain his visitor's visa for the United States.

18. Now in *GS* VI, pp. 520–3. For more on Benjamin's life circumstances and production at the time that he wrote this short (autobiographical) text on Ibiza, cf. Wil van Gerwen's posthumous book *Walter Benjamin op Ibiza* (Groningen, Historische Uitgeverij, forthcoming).

19. Benjamin–Scholem, *Correspondence*, p. 58 (to G. Scholem, 16 June 1933).

20. An exception is Benjamin's short article on George's sixtieth birthday ('Über Stefan George') from 1928 (cf. *GS* II, pp. 622–4).

21. Jula Cohn-Radt to Benjamin, 17 August 1933 (unpublished letter; Literaturarchive der Akademie der Künste, Berlin, estate of W. Benjamin).

22. All quotes from *GS* II, pp. 622–3 ('Über Stefan George').

23. Benjamin–Scholem, *Correspondence*, p. 59 (to G. Scholem, 16 June 1933).

24. *GS* III, pp. 404 and 406.

25. Ibid., p. 404.

26. Ibid., pp. 408–9.

27. Cf. D. S. Kellner to Benjamin, 7 December 1933 (unpublished letter; Literaturarchive der Akademie der Künste, Berlin, estate of W. Benjamin).

28. Cf. Peter de Mendelssohn, *Zeitungsstadt Berlin. Menschen und Mächte in der Geschichte der deutschen Presse*, Berlin 1959, pp. 301 ff.

29. Cf. Benjamin to A. Kurella, 2 June 1933; Dieter Schiller and Regine Herrmann, 'Kulturelle Tätigkeit deutscher Künstler und Publizisten im französischen Exil 1933 bis 1939', in *Kunst und Literatur im antifaschistischen Exil 1933–1945*, Frankfurt 1981, vol. 7: *Exil in Frankreich*, p. 136).

30. Benjamin to A. Kurella, 2 June 1933.

31. Cf. Murray G. Hall, 'Der Schwärmerskandal 1929. Zur Rezeption von Robert Musils *Die Schwärmer*', *Maske und Kothurn* vol. 21, 1975, pp. 153–86. More details on Lherman can be found in Will Schaber's essay 'Der Fall Ullmann – Lherman – Oulmàn', *Exilforschung*, vol. 7, 1989, pp. 107–18).

32. Cf. Benjamin to A. Kurella, 2 June 1933.

33. Cf. Hilde Benjamin, *Georg Benjamin: Eine Biographie*, Leipzig 1977, p. 210.

34. Such as are mentioned in Benjamin's letter 7 May 1933 to Scholem (cf. Benjamin–Scholem, *Correspondence*, pp. 46–7). A few weeks later he was informed about his brother's true condition in a letter from his ex-wife (cf. D. S. Kellner to Benjamin, 30 May 1933; unpublished letter; Literaturarchive der Akademie der Künste, Berlin, estate of W. Benjamin).

35. Among other things, Litten came to fame because he managed to drag Hitler before an ordinary court as a witness in the sensational 'Felsenecke Trial' in 1931, in which the latter made himself ridiculous during a two-hour examination.

36. *Correspondence*, p. 279 (to G. Scholem, 21 July 1925).

37. 'Anyway, I consider it practically certain that he [Georg Benjamin] will resume illegal work in one way or another', Benjamin confided to Scholem on 18 January 1934 under the pledge of secrecy (Benjamin–Scholem, *Correspondence*, p. 96).
38. Cf. H. Benjamin, *Georg Benjamin*, pp. 237–38.
39. Cf. Jürgen Stroech, *Die illegale Presse. Eine Waffe im Kampf gegen den deutschen Faschismus. Ein Beitrag zur Geschichte und Bibliographie der illegalen antifaschistischen Presse 1933 bis 1939*, Frankfurt am Main 1979, p. 241.
40. H. Benjamin, *Georg Benjamin*, p. 291.
41. Even in 1941, almost a year after Walter's death, Georg Benjamin implored his wife not to conceal anything of Walter's fate from him, even 'unfavourable things' (H. Benjamin, *Georg Benjamin*, p. 305; G. Benjamin to H. Benjamin, 19–20 July 1941).
42. Benjamin to T. v. Münchhausen, 14 May 1933 (unpublished letter, in the possession of Countess M. von Hatzfeld, Cologne).
43. Benjamin to T. v. Münchhausen, 31 May 1933 (unpublished letter, in the possession of Countess M. von Hatzfeld, Cologne).
44. Benjamin–Scholem, *Correspondence*, p. 106 (to G. Scholem, 16 October 1933).
45. The first of his texts 'written directly in French' (*GS* II, p. 966; to Max Horkheimer, 4 February 1935) was his essay, written 1934/35, on 'Johann Jakob Bachofen' (published posthumously in 1954; now in *GS* II, pp. 219–33). For all his declarations of his intention to write, from then on, his articles directly in French (such as in the undated and hitherto unpublished letter he wrote to Gisèle Freund, c. 1938–39, Literaturarchive der Akademie der Künste, Berlin, estate of W. Benjamin), his subsequent publications in this language can be counted on one hand. These include two articles published 1938–39 in the magazine Europe ('Peintures chinoises à la Bibliothèque Nationale' and 'Allemands de quatre-vingt-neuf'; now in *GS* IV, pp. 601–5 and 863–80) as well as 'Une lettre de Walter Benjamin au sujet de "Le regard" de George de Salles', printed in 1940 in the *Gazette des amis des livres* (now in *GS* III, pp. 592–5).
46. Benjamin–Scholem, *Correspondence*, p. 82 (to G. Scholem, 16 October 1933).
47. 'Walter Benjamin/Hermann Hesse, Briefwechsel 1934', *Suhrkamp Information*, no. 1, 1974, p. 83 (to Hermann Hesse, 13 January 1934).
48. Ibid. (H. Hesse to Benjamin, late February [recte: early March] 1934).
49. Ibid., p. 85 (to H. Hesse, 7 March 1934).
50. Hermann Hesse, 'Welche Bücher begleiten Sie', *Die Weltwoche*, 20 July 1951.
51. The negotiations over this failed because they were unable to agree on several basic questions regarding Benjamin's collaboration on *Die Sammlung*. This discussion was primarily concerned with his talk on the 'Author as Producer', which Klaus Mann did not wish to publish pseudonymously, as Benjamin wished. The pseudonym that Benjamin wanted to use for this article was the palindrome of the Latin word *lateo* (being unknown, remaining concealed): O. E. Tal (cf. unpublished letter to K. Mann, 2 May 1934, Literaturarchive der Akademie der Künste, Berlin, estate of W. Benjamin).
52. The review entitled 'Volkstümlichkeit als Problem' appeared on

30 June 1935 in the literary supplement of the *Frankfurter Zeitung* (now in *GS* III, pp. 450–52).

53. To name one example among many: Benjamin managed in 1934 to get a short prose text published in the supplement of the Copenhagen daily *Politiken* – but it was to remain his only publication there.

54. In 1933 Benjamin had given Haas's *Welt im Wort* two shorter texts. But the magazine folded so quickly that evidently the publisher had not even the time to pay the author his outstanding royalties. Benjamin refers to this in a letter to Gretel Karplus in February 1934: 'The magazine run by Haas has indeed folded, so obviously there is no hope of the royalties for my work' (*GS* V, p. 1099). The articles in question were 'Erfahrung und Armut' and his answer to a survey on 'J. P. Hebels Schatzkästlein des rheinländischen Hausfreundes' (published in nos. 10 and 11, 7/14 December 1933 in *Die Welt im Wort*; now in *GS* II, pp. 213–19 and 628).

55. This newspaper published in 1939 Benjamin's commentary to Brecht's poem on 'Die Legende von der Entstehung des Buches Taoteking auf dem Weg des Laotse in die Emigration' [The Legend of the Origin of the Book of Tao Te Ching during Lao-tzu's Path to Emigration] (now in *GS* II, pp. 568–72, in English in *Understanding Brecht*, pp. 70–73). In some ways the *Prager Tagblatt*, a newspaper with a rich tradition, also belongs here, for in 1934 it published Benjamin's 'Vier Geschichten' [Four Stories] (now in *GS* IV, pp. 757–61). When this paper also failed to send the author his fee, he felt compelled to ask Max Brod to intervene for him (cf. Benjamin's unpublished letter to M. Brod, 28 August [1934], Literaturarchive der Akademie der Künste, Berlin, estate of W. Benjamin).

56. Benjamin wrote the previously mentioned 'Bachofen' essay for this periodical; it first appeared, though, posthumously in another place (1954 in *Les Lettres nouvelles*).

57. Benjamin appears to have held this talk before the close circle of the direct associates of the Institute for the Study of Fascism that was founded by, among others, Kurt Kläber and Bertolt Brecht (cf. Chryssoula Kambas, *Walter Benjamin im Exil*, Tübingen 1983, pp. 16 ff.).

58. 'Die Sammlung', in *Die Sammlung*, vol. 1, 1933, p. 2; the programmatic introduction to the first issue in its first year is signed 'The Editors', but was written by Klaus Mann.

59. *GS* III, p. 352 ('Der Irrtum des Aktivismus').

60. All quotes from 'The Author as Producer', trans. John Heckman, *New Left Review*, no. 62, 1970, pp. 83–96.

61. *GS* V, p. 1174 ('Meine Beziehungen zum Institut [für Sozialforschung]').

62. Cf. B. Lindner, Habilitationsakte Benjamin, p. 155; H. Cornelius, "Erstes Referat über die Habilitationsschrift von Dr. Benjamin"'.

63. Now in *GS* II, pp. 776–803.

64. Benjamin–Scholem, *Correspondence*, p. 62 (to G. Scholem, 29 June 1933).

65. In a letter to Scholem, 18 January 1934, Benjamin wrote: 'As close as I am to Brecht, I do have my reservations about having to rely solely on him once I am there. Moreover, it is good to be able to seek the anonymity that a large city has to offer' (Benjamin–Scholem, *Correspondence*, p. 96).

66. *Correspondence*, p. 430 (to Kitty Steinschneider-Marx, 20 October 1933).
67. Benjamin–Scholem, *Correspondence*, p. 230 (to G. Scholem, 8 July 1938).
68. Ibid., p. 130 (to G. Scholem, 20 July 1934).
69. *GS* VI, pp. 103–4 (untitled).
70. Ibid., pp. 527–8 ('Notizen Svendborg Sommer 1934').
71. Now in *GS* II, pp. 1153–54.
72. Now in *GS* IV, pp. 466–8.
73. That was on 3 July 1931; the talk is printed in *GS* II, pp. 676–83.
74. 'Franz Kafka', in *Illuminations*, p. 113.
75. Benjamin–Scholem, *Correspondence*, p. 226 (to G. Scholem, 12 June 1938). At this point Benjamin had resumed his work on Kafka following the appearance of Max Brod's Kafka biography.
76. Ibid., p. 223 (to G. Scholem, 12 June 1938).
77. D. S. Kellner to Benjamin, 25 July 1934; unpublished letter, Literaturarchive der Akademie der Künste, Berlin, estate of W. Benjamin.
78. She left Italy for England after the *Anschluß* of Austria, the Munich Conference and above all after the introduction of state anti-Semitism decreed by Mussolini following his visit to Hitler.
79. Max Horkheimer, *Gesammelte Schriften*, vol. 15: *Briefwechsel 1913–1936*, ed. Gunzelin Schmid Noerr, Frankfurt am Main 1995, p. 370 (Benjamin to M. Horkheimer, 10 July 1935).
80. *Correspondence*, p. 493 (to A. Cohn, 18 July 1935). Brecht made a similar comment in a letter from June/July 1935 to Karl Korsch: 'I was personally at the writers congress and was able to make quite a few catches for my "Tui-Novel"' (Bertolt Brecht, *Briefe*, Frankfurt am Main 1981, p. 254).
81. *Correspondence*, p. 509 (to M. Horkheimer, 16 October 1935).
82. 'The Storyteller', in *Illuminations*, p. 86.
83. 'The Work of Art in the Age of Mechanical Reproduction', in *Illuminations*, pp. 216–17.
84. Karl Wolfskehl, *Gesammelte Werke*, Hamburg 1960, p. 419 ('Lebensluft'). The short text appeared on 19 April 1929 in the *Frankfurter Zeitung*. For Benjamin's usage of the concept, cf. Heinz Brüggemann, *Das andere Fenster: Einblicke in Häuser und Menschen. Zur Literaturgeschichte einer urbanen Wahrnehmungs-form*, Frankfurt am Main 1989, pp. 252 ff.
85. 'A Small History of Photography', in *One-Way Street*, p. 250.
86. 'The Work of Art in the Age of Mechanical Reproduction', in *Illuminations*, pp. 214 and 247.
87. According to announcements on 20 and 28 of June 1936 in the *Pariser Tageszeitung*, they took place on 22 and 29 June; for more detail cf. C. Kambas, *Walter Benjamin im Exil*, pp. 171 ff.).
88. Letter from H. Sahl to the author (7 April 1986). During the period of the Weimar Republic, the poet, novelist and journalist Hans Sahl (1902–93) mainly worked as a literature and film critic for such periodicals as *Das Tagebuch*, the Berlin *Montag Morgen* and the *Berliner Börsen-Courier*. Presumably Benjamin and he already knew one another from this time. They met again in the mid 1930s in Paris (Sahl had first fled to Prague in 1933, and finally arrived in France via Switzerland). After the outbreak of war in 1939, they spent several months together in the French internment camp at Vernuche.

89. Benjamin viewed this as a boycott (cf. *Correspondence*, pp. 529–30, to Alfred Cohn, 4 July 1936).

90. Cf. the complete wording of the letter of 18 March 1936 in T. W. Adorno and W. Benjamin, *Briefwechsel 1928–1940*, ed. Henri Lonitz, Frankfurt am Main 1994, pp. 168–77.

91. Friedrich Pollock to Benjamin, 12 May 1936 (unpublished letter; Literaturarchive der Akademie der Künste, Berlin, estate of W. Benjamin).

92. Benjamin–Scholem, *Correspondence*, p. 185 (G. Scholem to Benjamin, 26 August 1936).

93. Bernhard Reich to Benjamin, 19 February 1936 (unpublished letter; Literaturarchive der Akademie der Künste, Berlin, estate of W. Benjamin). The final stone in the Communist wall of rejection was placed by Willi Bredel: he was not prepared to have the article published (in *Das Wort*) because of its length (cf. Willi Bredel to Benjamin, 28 March 1937; unpublished letter; Literaturarchive der Akademie der Künste, Berlin, estate of W. Benjamin), although that was merely the ostensible reason.

94. *Correspondence*, p. 508 (to M. Horkheimer, 16 October 1935).

95. *GS* II, p. 789 ('Zum gegenwärtigen gesellschaftlichen Standort des französischen Schriftstellers').

96. Cf. for instance Benjamin–Scholem, *Correspondence*, p. 96 (to G. Scholem, 18 January 1934).

97. Cf. Sahl's reminiscences of Benjamin: Hans Sahl, 'Walter Benjamin in the Internment Camp', in *On Walter Benjamin*, ed. Gary Smith, pp. 346–52; H. Sahl, 'Fluchtpunkt Marseille', *Die Zeit*, 28 March 1986, pp. 61–4; Wolfgang Nagel, 'Fliehen – wie geht das überhaupt? Ein Gespräch mit Hans Sahl', *Die Zeit*, 22 May 1987, p. 24; H. Sahl, *Gesammelte Werke*, ed. Klaus Schöffling, vol. 5: *Memoiren eines Moralisten. Erinnerungen I*, Zurich 1982, pp. 25–6.

98. The playwright, novelist and critic Stephan Lackner (i.e. Ernest Gustave Morgenroth, born 1910) is chiefly known for his numerous works on Max Beckmann. For his relationship with Benjamin cf. his autobiography *Selbstbildnis mit Feder. Erinnerungen*, Berlin 1988 (esp. pp. 90 ff. and 135 ff.).

99. *GS* V, p. 1176 (to M. Horkheimer, 18 April 1939). Benjamin's review is now in *GS* III, pp. 546–8.

100. Isolated letters from Benjamin's correspondence with Freund and Arendt are in the keeping of the Akademie der Künste in Berlin (in the case of Arendt, also in the Washington Library of Congress) and have yet to be published. (The sole exception is a letter from Benjamin dated 8 July 1940 to H. Arendt which is included in the *Correspondence*, pp. 637–8.)

101. Cf. her letters from 2 July and 30 August 1936 to Benjamin (in Fritz Mierau, ed., *Russen in Berlin: Literatur, Malerei, Theater, Film 1918–1933*, Leipzig 1987, pp. 573–4.

102. Benjamin seems to have first met up with Radt once more in autumn 1936 in Paris (cf. Benjamin to Fritz Radt, *c.* September–October 1936; unpublished letter; Jewish National and University Library, Jerusalem, Walter Benjamin Archives).

103. What nowadays number among the great rarities of the antiquarian book trade were almost thrown away at the time: Benjamin's translation of Balzac's *Ursule Mirouët* could be had for 1,35 marks, *One-Way Street* for 3 marks, and the cloth-wrapped edition of his *Trauerspiel* book went for a mere 6 marks (cf. *Die schönsten Rowohlt*

Bücher zu bedeutend ermäßigten Preisen, Berlin 1932, p. 2).

104. In the following I have drawn on Michael Diers's excellent article 'Einbandlektüre: Zu Walter Benjamins Briefsammlung "Deutsche Menschen" von 1936', in *Idea* vol. 7, 1988, pp. 109–20.

105. Further details on the life and career of the master spy 'Lucy' (Roeßler's cover name) can be found for instance in David J. Dallin's *Soviet Espionage*, New Haven 1955.

106. Cf. Rudolf Roeßler to Benjamin, 13 August 1936 (unpublished letter; Literaturarchive der Akademie der Künste, Berlin, estate of W. Benjamin).

107. Benjamin–Scholem, *Correspondence*, p. 192 (to Benjamin, 1 March 1937).

108. As told by the proprietor of the company, Josef Stocker, in 1983 (cf. Albrecht Schöne, '"Diese nach jüdischem Vorbild erbaute Arche": Walter Benjamin "Deutsche Menschen"', in *Juden in der deutschen Literatur. Ein deutsch-israelisches Symposion*, eds Stéphane Mosès and Albrecht Schöne, Frankfurt am Main 1986, p. 363), and also partly confirmed by a letter from Roeßler to Benjamin, August 1936, which mentions an initial print run of 2,000 (cf. Vita Nova Verlag Rudolf Roeßler to Benjamin, 13 August 1936).

109. *GS* IV, p. 942 ('Auf der Spur alter Briefe').

110. The sole missing article in the book edition of 1936 was Friedrich Schlegel's letter to Schleiermacher, which was later included in the posthumous edition of the book.

111. *GS* IV, p. 942 ('Auf der Spur alter Briefe').

112. Cf. for instance the 'Memorandum zu den "Sechzig Briefen"' (in *GS* IV, pp. 949–50).

113. Thus, to name just one example, a letter from Rahel Varnhagen to Leopold Ranke (15 June 1832) should have been included in the anthology: Benjamin was especially sad about the exclusion of his unwritten commentary on 'the incomparable letter written by Rahel on Gentz's death' (Benjamin–Scholem, *Correspondence*, p. 193; to G. Scholem, 4 April 1937).

114. First published in the *Literarische Welt*, 11 December 1931, under the title 'Allerhand Menschliches vom großen Kant' (now in *GS* IV, pp. 808–15).

115. First published with the subtitle 'From German Writings of the Past' in *Literarische Welt*, 6 May 1932 (now in *GS* IV, pp. 815–62).

116. Now in *GS* IV, pp. 863–80.

117. *Correspondence*, p. 608 (to Margarete Steffin, presumably July 1939).

118. Cf. 'Brief von Seume an Karl Böttiger', *Das Wort*, no. 4, 1936, pp. 86–7. It is clear from the hitherto unpublished letters of Willi Bredel to Benjamin, which are in the keeping of the Akademie der Künste in Berlin, that Benjamin had letters from Seume, Hölderlin and Georg Forster sent to the editors. Only Seume's letter appeared – in the section headed 'Cultural Heritage' and without Benjamin's commentary. Finally, further details on the possible enlargement can also be found in a list headed 'Second Series of Letters' printed in *GS* VII, pp. 829–30.

119. Now *GS* IV, pp. 954–5.

120. Ibid., p. 948 (to M. Horkheimer, 17 December 1936).

121. Ibid., p. 177 ('*Deutsche Menschen*').

122. Ibid., pp. 163–4 ('*Deutsche Menschen*').

123. Ibid., p. 161 ('*Deutsche Menschen*').

124. Ibid., p. 156 ('*Deutsche Menschen*').
125. Cf. *One-Way Street*, p. 47. Translators' note: The original German aphorism contains a wordplay which has been rendered nicely in this translation as 'To convince is to conquer without conception'. The present alternative translation has been given in order to underline the aphorism's literal meaning.
126. [Hugo] M[arti], 'Briefe deutscher Menschen', *Der Bund*, 3 December 1936, p. 7.
127. Joachim Günther, 'Deutsche Menschen', *Die Literatur*, vol. 39, 1936/7, p. 314.
128. R[udolf] J[akob] Humm, 'Deutsche Menschen', *Maß und Wert*, vol. 1, 1937/8, pp. 157–8.
129. *GS* V, p. 1046 ['Pariser Passagen II'].
130. *Correspondence*, p. 322 (to G. Scholem, 30 January 1928).
131. *GS* V, p. 1041 ('Passagen').
132. Cf. now *GS* V, pp. 1041–3.
133. Cf. *Correspondence*, p. 489 (to T.W. Adorno, 31 May 1935).
134. Briefe an Kracauer, p. 17, (to Kracauer, 20 April 1926).
135. This project description was also sent shortly afterwards, in a very slightly altered form, to the Institute for Social Research. Details on the versions of the first exposé of the 'Arcades' project can now be found in *GS* V, pp. 1206–54.
136. Max Horkheimer, *Gesammelte Schriften*, vol. 15, p. 361 (T. Wiesengrund-Adorno to M. Horkheimer, 8 June 1935).
137. Otherwise Benjamin kept a jealous watch over his idea and ensured that no one learned any details of it for fear that it might get stolen. Whenever works concerning similar questions appeared, he suspected them to be more or less successful plagiarisms. This applied to Bloch's 'Hieroglyphen des XIX. Jahrhunderts' (published in 1935 in his *Erbschaft dieser Zeit*), Kracauer's 1937 monograph on *Jacques Offenbach und das Paris seiner Zeit*, and Dolf Sternberger's book, published in 1938 in Hamburg, *Panorama oder Ansichten vom 19. Jahrhundert*, which Benjamin described as an accomplished synthesis 'of a new world of ideas which links [the author] with Adolf Hitler, and an older one which' once linked him with Benjamin (*GS* III, p. 701; draft of letter to D. Sternberger, *c.* spring 1938; Benjamin also reviewed the book – cf. *GS* III, pp. 572–9 – but his slating review was not printed in the *Zeitschrift für Sozialforschung*).
138. Benjamin–Scholem, *Correspondence*, p. 159 (to G. Scholem, 20 May 1935).
139. *Correspondence*, p. 489 (to T.W. Adorno, 31 May 1935).
140. Benjamin–Scholem, *Correspondence*, p. 159 (to G. Scholem, 20 May 1935).
141. *Correspondence*, p. 489 (to T.W. Adorno, 31 May 1935).
142. *GS* V, p. 494 ('Das Passagen-Werk').
143. 'N (Theoretics of Knowledge, Theory of Progress)' in *Benjamin: Philosophy, History, Aesthetics*, ed. Gary Smith, Chicago 1989, p. 61.
144. Cf. *Aesthetics and Politics*, p. 110–20.
145. *Correspondence*, p. 556 (to M. Horkheimer, 16 April 1938).
146. All quotes from *Correspondence*, p. 576 (to T. W. Adorno, 4 October 1938).
147. Chryssoula Kambas, '"Und aus welchem Fenster wir immer blicken, es geht ins Trübe." Briefwechsel aus der Emigration: Walter Benjamin – Fritz Lieb – Dora Benjamin (1936–1944)',

Cahiers d'études germaniques, no. 13, 1987, p. 266 (Benjamin to Fritz Lieb, 20 October 1938).

148. Benjamin–Scholem, *Correspondence*, p. 240 (to G. Scholem, 4 February 1939).

149. *Correspondence*, p. 581 (T. W. Adorno to Benjamin, 10 November 1938).

150. Ibid., p. 582.

151. In issue 1–2, 1939, which was however first distributed in 1940 (in English in *Charles Baudelaire*, pp. 109–54).

152. A second text entitled 'Painting and Photography' did not appear in *Das Wort*, even though it had also been commissioned. It remained unpublished throughout his life. (Now in *GS* III, pp. 495–507.)

153. 'Some Motifs in Baudelaire', in *Charles Baudelaire*, p. 154.

154. *GS* III, pp. 485, 488 and 487 ('Pariser Brief' [I]).

155. *Correspondence*, p. 578 (to G. Adorno, 1 November 1938).

156. As it was phrased in the 'decree' from 14 November, which named the incredible sum of '1,000,000,000 Reichsmark, payable [by the] German national Jews as a whole to the German Reich' as 'expiation' for their 'hostile attitude to the German people and Reich' (*Reichsgesetzblatt*, part I, Berlin, 14 November 1938, p. 1579)

157. H. Sahl, *Fluchtpunkt Marseille*, p. 61.

158. Cf. 'Circulaire du Ministère de l'Intérieur du 17 septembre 1939 sur les étrangers et les apatrides suspects, dangereaux ou indésirables, et sur les mesures d'internement les concernant', in *Ex*, no. 3, 1984, p. 97. Reprinted in *Zone d'ombres 1933–1944. Exil et internment d'Allemands et d'Autrichiens dans le sud-est de la France*, eds. J. Grandjonc and T. Grundtner, Aix-en-Provence, 1990.

159. Benjamin to M. Horkheimer, 16 May 1939; (unpublished letter, Max-Horkheimer-Archiv, Frankfurt am Main).

160. H. Sahl, *Fluchtpunkt Marseille*, p. 61.

161. Cf. Petra Lingerat and Sybille Narbutt, 'L'Allemagne et les Allemands.dans les "Cahiers du Sud" de 1933 à 1942. A propos d'une correspondence inédite de Jean Ballard avec Walter Benjamin et Rudolf Leonhard', in *Ex*, no. 3, 1984, p. 60 (footnote 36; Lettre du Préfet au Ministre de l'Intérieur du 5 octobre 1939, A. D. Nièvre, série M. Etragers); reprinted in *Zone d'ombres 1933–1944*.

162. H. Sahl, 'Benjamin in the Internment Camp', in *On Walter Benjamin*, ed. Gary Smith, p. 350–51.

163. My thanks to Ms Chryssoula Kambas for drawing my attention to the existence of the *Bulletin de Vernuche*, as well as for details that go beyond Hans Sahl's reports; cf. her article 'Bulletin de Vernuche. Neue Quellen zur Internierung Walter Benjamins', in *Exil*, no. 2, 1990, pp. 5–30.

164. Cf. 'Bulletin de Vernuche', now in C. Kambas, 'Bulletin de Vernuche', pp. 28–9.

165. 'Vernuche, miroir de l'émigration allemande', now in C. Kambas, 'Bulletin de Vernuche', p. 29.

166. 'Trois cents gîtes', now in C. Kambas, 'Bulletin de Vernuche', p. 29.

167. H. Sahl, 'Benjamin in the Internment Camp', p. 349.

168. Cf. Hans Sahl, 'Elegie auf das Jahr 39', *Das Neue Tagebuch*, no. 36, 2 September 1939, p. 861.

169. Cf. Hans Sahl, *Gesammelte Werke*, vol. 5, p. 25.

170. Cf. 'La Voix du Granier', now in C. Kambas, 'Bulletin de Vernuche', p. 30.

171. Cf. 'Enquête sur les livres dans le Camp de Vernuche', now in C. Kambas, 'Bulletin de Vernuche', p. 29.
172. Cf. *Der deutsche PEN-Club im Exil 1933–1948. Eine Ausstellung der Deutschen Bibliothek Frankfurt am Main*, Frankfurt am Main 1980, pp. 386–7 (Benjamin to Rudolf Olden, 30 November 1939). The application was finally accepted (cf. Heinrich Mann's letters confirming this on 29 January 1940 and 10 February 1940 to Rudolf Olden and Herman Ould [unpublished documents; Archiv der Arbeitsstelle Exilliteratur in the Deutschen Bibliothek, Frankfurt am Main] as well as Rudolf Olden's letter of notification, 21 January 1940, to Benjamin [unpublished; Literaturarchive der Akademie der Künste, Berlin, estate of W. Benjamin]).
173. Benjamin–Scholem, *Correspondence*, p. 263 (to G. Scholem, 11 January 1940).
174. *GS* V, p. 1181 (to M. Horkheimer, 22 February 1940).
175. S. Lackner, '"Von einer langen, schwierigen Irrfahrt." Aus unveröffentlichten Briefen Walter Benjamins', *Neue Deutsche Hefte*, vol. 26, 1979, p. 66.
176. *GS* I, p. 1226 (to G. Adorno, April 1940).
177. Ibid., p. 1244 ('Notizen und Vorarbeiten zu den Thesen "Über den Begriff der Geschichte"').
178. 'Theses on the Philosophy of History', in *Illuminations*, p. 250.
179. 'N (Theoretics of Knowledge, Theory of Progress), in Benjamin: *Philosophy, History, Aesthetics*, ed. Gary Smith, Chicago 1989, p. 61.
180. Ibid., p. 65.
181. 'Theses on the Philosophy of History', in *Illuminations*, p. 250.
182. Cf. *Walter Benjamin zum Gedächtnis*, published by the Institut für Sozialforschung, Los Angeles 1942.
183. 'Sur le concept d'histoire', trans. Pierre Missac, in *Les Temps modernes*, vol. 2, 1946/7, pp. 623–34.
184. 'Über den Begriff der Geschichte', *Die Neue Rundschau*, vol. 61, 1950, pp. 560–70.
185. Cf. the letter from his sister, Dora, to Fritz Lieb dated 26 January 1943, in which she mentions that Benjamin had 'fortunately' been able to 'remove everything from his flat' (C. Kambas, 'Und aus welchem Fenster wir immer blicken, es geht ins Trübe', p. 272).
186. This constituted that part of his literary estate which, with the manuscripts he bequeathed to his friend and his friend's wife during his life and a number of documents that Hannah Arendt brought with her to the United States, made up the basis of Adorno's archive of Benjamin's writings. The papers fell into the hands of Benjamin's sister Dora in 1941 (she was at that time in the south of France). Following her brother's instructions, she had them taken to Adorno by Martin Domke. A detailed reconstruction of the fate of numerous of Benjamin's writings – their whereabouts, their loss or their destruction – would be enough for a cultural history of the German intelligentsia during the years 1914 to 1940.
187. Cf. *GS* V, p. 1071 (Dora Benjamin to T.W. Adorno, 13 February 1946).
188. *GS* V, pp. 1185–6 [Lisa Fittko, 'The Story of Old Benjamin'].
189. The literature on the last weeks and days of Benjamin's life would nowadays fill a whole bookshelf. Among the articles and documents containing more detailed information that have yet to be mentioned are those by Juan-Ramón Capella ('Sobre la "muerte" de Walter

Benjamin', *El Ciervo*, no. 252, 1975, pp. 16–18.), Pierre Klossowski ('Lettre sur Walter Benjamin', *Mercure de France*, no. 1067, 1 July 1952, pp. 456–7 and 'Between Marx and Fourier', in *On Walter Benjamin*, ed. Gary Smith, pp. 367–70), Arthur Koestler (*The Invisible Writing: An Autobiography*, London 1954.) and Adrienne Monnier ('Note sur Walter Benjamin' in *Mercure de France*, no. 1067, 1 July 1952, p. 451 ff.).

190. Cf., for example, Varian Fry, *Surrender on Demand*, New York 1945; Alma Mahler-Werfel, *And the Bridge is Love*, London 1959, pp. 223–48.

191. Cf. *GS* V, p. 1189 (L. Fittko, 'The Story of Old Benjamin').

192. One of the first examples of such speculations came from Arnold Zweig. According to him, Benjamin had killed himself following a mix-up by the authorities, who were instructed to prevent 'another' Benjamin from entering Spain (cf. Arnold Zweig, 'Todesnachrichten', unpublished manuscript; Literaturarchive der Akademie der Künste, Berlin, estate of A. Zweig). The most recent comes from the Spanish writer Juan Goytisolo: Benjamin, he claims, was murdered by the Gestapo with the collusion of the Spanish (cf. 'El crimen fue en Port Bou', *El País*, 5 August 1984, p. 9).

193. Grete Freund to unknown recipient, Lisbon, 9 October 1940, in *GS* V p.1194.

194. Ibid, p. 1195.

195. Cf. Carles S. Costa, 'Zwischen Nazis und Franquisten. Walter Benjamin in der Falle', in *Walter Benjamin 1892–1940*, p. 351.

196. Narciso Alba, 'El demonio no, la Gestapo. Precisiones a un libro de Lisa Fittko sobre muerte de Walter Benjamin', *Quimera*, no. 81, 1980, pp. 52–7.

197. Benjamin to Juliane Farez, postcard dated 25 September 1940, in Hans Mayer, *Ein Deutscher auf Widerruf, Erinnerungen I*, Frankfurt am Main 1982, p. 257.

198. Grete Freund in *GS* V, p. 1195.

199. Extracts taken from Ingrid Scheurmann, 'New Documents on Benjamin's Death' in *For Walter Benjamin*, eds Ingrid and Konrad Scheurmann, trans. Timothy Nevill, Bonn 1993, pp. 268–9.

200. *GS* V, p. 1202 (Benjamin to H. Gurland and T.W. Adorno, Portbou 25 September 1940).

201. In A. Koestler *Abschaum der Erde. Gesammelte autobiographische Schriften*, vol. 2, Vienna, Munich, Zurich 1971, p. 529–30. But as Ingrid Scheurmann has pointed out, there are significant differences between this 1971 German translation and the original 1941 American edition of Koestler's *Scum of the Earth*. The German translation is incomplete and the passage quoted is in a new chapter only included in the German edition. In the original edition, Koestler describes his encounter with Benjamin in Marseilles as follows:

'And more suicides: . . . Walter Benjamin, author and critic, my neighbour in 10, rue Dombasle in Paris, fourth at our Saturday poker parties, and one of the most bizarre and witty persons I have known. Last time I met him was in Marseilles, together with H., the day before my departure, and he asked me: 'If something goes wrong, have you got anything to take?' For in those days we all carried some 'stuff' in our pockets like conspirators in a penny dreadful. I had none, and he shared what he had with me, sixty-two tablets of a sedative, procured in Berlin during the week which followed the burning of the Reichstag. He did it reluctantly, for he did not know whether the thirty-one remaining tablets left him would be enough. It was enough. A week after my departure he made his way over the Pyrenees to Spain, a man of fifty-five, with heart disease. At Port Bou the Guardia Civil arrested him. He was told that the next morning they would send him back to France. When they came to fetch him for the train, he was dead'. (*Scum of the Earth*, New York 1941, p. 278)

'Sedatives' changes to 'morphine' in the later German version. And whether these were 'enough to kill a horse' is contradicted later in the German edition (p.530) when Koestler adds a kind of post-script to the Marseille encounter: 'On the following morning the Spanish gendarmes changed their mind, but Benjamin had already taken the tablets he still had and was dead. I viewed that as a sign and tried to follow his example. However, Benjamin obviously had a better stomach since I vomitted the stuff.'

202. J. Gurland to R. Tiedemann, 25 June 1981 in The Jewish National and University Library, Jerusalem, Arc 4° 1598/173-377 quoted in *For Walter Benjamin*, p. 270.
203. From I. Scheurmann, 'New Documents on Walter Benjamin's Death' in *For Walter Benjamin*, pp. 270–71.
204. In 'Lisa Fittko on Walter Benjamin's Flight', interview by Richard Heinemann, in *For Walter Benjamin*, p. 145.
205. In Dirección General de Seguridad, Comisaria de Investigacíon y Vigilancia de la Frontera Oriental, Figueras (Gerona) to Max Horkheimer, 30 October 1940, printed in *GS* V, p. 1197.
206. Cf. R. Tiedemann in *GS* V, p. 1200.
207. G. Scholem, 'Vorbemerkung zu Lisa Fittko. Der alte Benjamin' in *Merkur*, vol. 34, 1982, pp. 35–49.
208. For a fuller discussion of the research into the fate of Benjamin's possessions cf. I. Scheurmann, 'New Documents on Walter Benjamin's Death', pp. 265–76.
209. Cf. R. Tiedemann in *GS* V, p.1204–5.
210. Cf. Manuel Cussó-Ferrer, 'Walter Benjamin's Last Frontier. Sequences of an Approach' in *For Walter Benjamin*, pp. 154–60.

Caption notes

1. Julius Meyer, *Die Pariser Kunstausstellung von 1861 und die bildende Kunst des 19. Jahrhunderts* (1861); cited in *GS* V, p. 185 ('Das Passagen-Werk').
2. *GS* V, p. 1007 ('Pariser Passagen [I]').
3. *GS* VII, p. 120 ('Die Mietskaserne').
4. 'One-Way Street', in *One-Way Street*, p. 317.
5. Franz Hessel, *Ein Flaneur in Berlin*, Berlin 1984, p. 154. This publication is a new edition of Hessel's *Spazieren in Berlin* [*Walking in Berlin*], 1929, which Benjamin reviewed in *Die Literarische Welt* (cf. 'Die Wiederkehr des Flaneur', now in *GS* III, pp. 194 9).
6. *GS* IV, p. 261 ('Berliner Kindheit um Neunzehnhundert').
7. Scholem, *Friendship*, p. 64.
8. Ibid., p. 61–2.
9. *One-Way Street*, pp. 48-9.
10. *Correspondence*, p. 336 (to G. Scholem, 2 June 1928).
11. 'A Berlin Chronicle', in *One-Way Street*, p. 335.
12. *GS* VI, p. 195 ('Die Landschaft von Haubinda').
13. *GS* VII, p. 86 ('Das dämonische Berlin').
14. *GS* VI, p. 232 ('Tagebuch Pfingsten 1911').
15. *Correspondence*, p. 14 (to H. Blumenthal, 14 May 1912).
16. Friedrich Seyfarth, *Unser Freiburg and seine Umgebung*, Freiburg im Breisgau 1913, p. 282.
17. *Gesammelte Briefe*, vol. 1, p. 71–2 (to L. Strauß, 10 October 1912).
18. *GS* VI, p. 215 ('Lebenslauf 1925').
19. *Correspondence*, p. 18 (to H. Blumenthal, 29 April 1913).
20. Ibid., p. 30 (to H. Blumenthal, 7 June 1913).
21. Ibid., p. 49 (to C. Seligson, 4 August 1913).
22. Walther A. Berendsohn, 'Weimar 1914', *Göttinger Akademische Wochenschau*, 25 June 1914, p. 52.
23. *GS* III, p. 282 ('Linke Melancholie').
24. 'A Berlin Chronicle', in *One-Way Street*, p. 311.
25. Ibid., p. 310.
26. Erwin Loewenson, 'Verschiedenes über Wolf and Fritz Heinle', c. September 1914 (unpublished notes; Deutsches Literaturarchiv, Marbach am Neckar estate of E. Loewenson).
27. *Correspondence*, p. 69 (to E. Schoen, 22[23] June 1914).
28. Ibid., p. 71 (to H. Blumenthal, 6/7 July 1914).
29. *GS* II, p. 916 (Kurt Hiller to Theodor W. Adorno, 6 February 1965).
30. *Gesammelte Briefe*, vol. 1, pp. 289–90 (to F. Radt, 21 November 1915).
31. 'One-Way Street', in *One-Way Street*, p. 71.
32. *Correspondence*, p. 90 (to G. Scholem, 17 July 1917).
33. Werner Kraft, *Spiegelung der Jugend*, Frankfurt am Main 1973, p. 71; Charlotte Wolff, *Hindsight: An Autobiography*, London 1980, p. 66.
34. Dora Sophie Pollak to Herbert Blumenthal and Carla Seligson, 29 June 1915 (unpublished letter; Jewish National and University Library, Jerusalem, Walter Benjamin Archives).

35. *Correspondence*, p. 144 (to E. Schoen, 24 July 1919).
36. Ernst Bloch, 'Die Welt bis zur Kenntlichkeit verändern' (1974, interview with José Marchand), in *Tagträume vom aufrechten Gang. Sechs Interviews mit Ernst Bloch*, ed. Arno Münster, Frankfurt am Main 1977, p. 48.
37. *Correspondence*, p. 238 (to G. Scholem, 5 March 1924).
38. Ibid., p. 212 (to F.C. Rang, 24 October 1923).
39. *Gesammelte Briefe*, vol. II, p. 358 (to Richard Weißbach, 12 October 1923).
40. Ibid., p. 461 (to G. Salomon-Delatour, 10 June 1924).
41. *GS* II, p. 246 ('Ankündigung der Zeitschrift: Angelus Novus').
42. *Correspondence*, p. 178 (to G. Scholem, 26 March 1921).
43. *Amtliches Lehrgedicht der Philosophischen Fakultät der Haupt- and Staats-Universität Muri*, by Gerhard Scholem, janitor to the religious philosophy seminars; second revised edn, in accordance with the latest certified achievements of philosophy, Berlin 1927 (private publication, unpag.). Scholem on Benjamin's mocking of academia.
44. C. Wolff, *Hindsight*, p. 80.
45. *GS* III, p. 250 ('Zur Wiederkehr von Hofmannsthals Todestag').
46. *GS* VI, p. 424 ('Tagebuch Juan les Pins Mai–Juni 1931').
47. *Gesammelte Briefe*, vol. II, pp. 461–2 (to G. Salomon-Delatour, 10 June 1924).
48. *Correspondence*, p. 242 (to G. Scholem, 13 June 1924).
49. *Gesammelte Briefe*, vol. II, p. 493 (to G. Salomon, 16 September 1924).
50. 'One-Way Street', in *One-Way Street*, p. 75.
51. *Correspondence*, p. 325 (to H. v. Hofmannsthal, 8 February 1928).
52. Ibid., pp. 261 and 293 (to G. Scholem, 19 February 1925 and 5 April 1926).
53. Ernst Bloch, 'Philosophy as Cabaret', *New Left Review*, no. 116, 1979, p. 94.
54. B. Lindner, 'Habilitationsakte Benjamin', p. 155 (Hans Cornelius, initial report on the *Habilitation* dissertation submitted by Dr Benjamin).
55. *Correspondence*, pp. 371–2 (to Max Rychner, 7 March 1931).
56. Ibid., p. 332 (to G. Scholem, 23 April 1928).
57. Willy Haas, 'Hinweis auf Walter Benjamin', *Die Welt*, 9 October 1955.
58. Helen Hessel, 'C'était un brave. Eine Rede zum 10. Todestag Franz Hessels', in *Letzte Heimkehr nach Paris. Franz Hessel and die Seinen im Exil*, Berlin 1989, p. 74.
59. K.H. Ruppel, 'Marcel Proust: Im Schatten der jungen Mädchen', *Das Tage-Buch*, vol. 8, 1927, p. 959.
60. *Briefe an Kracauer*, p. 42 (to S. Kracauer, 13 April 1927).
61. Benjamin to Rudolf Grossmann, 13 January 1927 (unpublished letter, Leo Baeck Institute, New York, estate of R. Grossmann).
62. *Correspondence*, p. 364 (to G. Scholem, 25 April 1930).
63. *Briefe an Kracauer*, p. 69 (to S. Kracauer, 26 July 1930).
64. Günther Anders, 'Der Defekt' (1935), in Anders, *Der Blick vom Turm*, Munich 1968, p. 90.
65. 'From the Brecht Commentary', in *Understanding Brecht*, p. 27.
66. *GS* VI, p. 443 ('Tagebuch vom siebenten August neunzehnhunderteinunddreißig bis zum Todestag').
67. Benjamin–Scholem, *Correspondence*, p. 89 (Dora Kellner to G. Scholem, 29 November 1933).

68. *GS* IV, p. 762 ('Auf die Minute').
69. 'Gehalterhöhung, wo denken Sie hin?', *Frankfurter Zeitung*, 1 April 1931.
70. Benjamin–Scholem, *Correspondence*, p. 29 (to G. Scholem, 28 February 1933).
71. *GS* VI, p. 448 ('Spanien 1932').
72. *GS* VII, p. 611 (Speyer, quoted in 'Rezepte für Komödienschreiber. Gespräch zwischen Wilhelm Speyer and Walter Benjamin').
73. Benjamin–Scholem, *Correspondence*, p. 26 (to G. Scholem, 15 January 1933).
74. Ibid., p. 34 (to G. Scholem, 20 March 1933).
75. *Briefe an Kracauer*, p. 73 (to S. Kracauer, 23 April 1933).
76. B. Brecht, *Poems*, trans. John Willett, London 1976, p. 218.
77. Jean Selz, 'Benjamin in Ibiza', trans. M. Martin Guiney, in *On Walter Benjamin*, ed. Gary Smith, Cambridge, Mass. 1991, p. 355.
78. Unpublished (Literararchive der Akademie der Künste, Berlin, estate of W. Benjamin).
79. Benjamin–Scholem, *Correspondence*, p. 77 (to G. Scholem, c. 10/12 September 1933).
80. *Briefe an Kracauer*, p. 74 (to S. Kracauer, August 1934).
81. Ruth Berlau, *Brechts Lai-tu. Erinnerungen and Notate*, Darmstadt and Neuwied 1985, p. 105.
82. *Briefe an Kracauer*, p. 75 (to S. Kracauer, 24 November 1934).
83. Ibid., p. 78 (to S. Kracauer, 10 December 1934).
84. Bertolt Brecht, *Briefe*, ed. and annotated by Günter Glaeser, Frankfurt am Main 1981, p. 258 (Brecht to George Grosz, c. July 1935).
85. Stephan Lackner, 'Von einer langen, schwierigen Irrfahrt', extracts from unpublished letters from Walter Benjamin, in *Neue Deutsche Hefte*, no. 1, 1979, 161, p. 48.
86. Elisabeth Freundlich, 'Verfehlte Begegnung mit Walter Benjamin. Ein achtzigster Geburtstag als Anlaß eines Symposions, einiger Richtigstellungen and Erinnerungen', *Die Presse*, Vienna, 29–30 July 1972.
87. *GS* V, p. 1058/9 ('Das Passagen-Werk').
88. Bertolt Brecht, *Arbeitsjournal*, ed. Werner Hecht, Frankfurt am Main 1973, vol. 1, p. 15 (entry on 25 July 1938).
89. Unpublished letter; Literaturarchive der Akademie der Künste, Berlin, estate of W. Benjamin.
90. Benjamin to Max Horkheimer, 17 November 1938 (unpublished letter, Max-Horkheimer-Archiv, Frankfurt am Main).
91. *Deutsche Literatur im Exil. Briefe europäischer Autoren 1933–1949*, Vienna, Munich, Basle 1964, p. 112 (H. Kesten to Toni Kesten, 20 September 1939).
92. 'Theses on the Philosophy of History', in *Illuminations*, p. 245.
93. Benjamin–Scholem, *Correspondence*, p. 262 (to G. Scholem, 11 January 1940).
94. *Briefe an Kracauer*, p. 87 (to S. Kracauer, 14 May 1940).
95. Carl J. Burckhardt/Max Rychner, *Briefe 1926–1965*, Frankfurt am Main 1970, p. 137 (Burckhardt to Rychner, 4 June 1951).
96. E. Bloch, *Briefe 1903–1975* vol. 2, p. 442 (Bloch to Theodor W. Adorno, 16 October 1940).
97. *GS* I, p. 1241.
98. 'It was only during my first visit my first visit to Portbou . . . that I understood that his final resting place – and no one knows exactly

where this is – was the only possible place for commemorating the tragedy experienced by Walter Benjamin and a generation of European intellectuals, anti-fascists, and Jews who attempted to flee from darkness to light. . . . I knew that the place of homage had to be close to Portbou's little cemetery. And suddenly nature granted me an astonishing, moving drama – a turbulence in the sea breaking between the rocks. The water swirled around, fell wildly back again, once more leapt up ferociously, and then was calm, quiet, tranquil. This astonishing drama was repeated all over again, like the beating of a wounded heart. And the waves beat against the rocks as one beats one's own breast.

I climbed further up the steep, stony path, and saw the olive tree that struggles for survival against the salt-laden sea-wind and arid dry ground. Searching for additional elements I went behind the cemetery, above the rock, from where I regarded the sea, the horizon, freedom – blocked by a barrier. The barrier of the cemetery. And there is no way out. From there you return by way of the cemetery to the starting-point – to the turbulent sea. The vicious circle of fate.'

Dani Karavan, '1 Corridor, 1 Stairs, 1 Seat = Passages' in *Dani Karavan, Homage to Walter Benjamin*, eds Ingrid and Konrad Scheurmann, trans. Timothy Nevill, Mainz 1995, pp. 100–106.

Select bibliography

Lamentably, there is still no collected edition of Benjamin's writings in English translation. The following checklist will help the reader to assemble those miscellaneous publications that complement the well-known selections *Illuminations* and *One-Way Street*. For a full account, cf. Gary Smith and Reinhard Markner, 'Englisch/Amerikanisch', in Momme Brodersen [et al.], *Walter Benjamin. Eine kommentierte Bibliographie*, Morsum 1996, pp. 141–8.

Benjamin in English Translation

(1) '8 Notes on Brecht's Epic Theatre', *The Western Review*, no. 12, 1948, pp. 167–73. Trans. Edward Landberg.

(2) 'The Work of Art in the Epoch of Mechanical Reproduction' *Studies on the Left*, no. 2, 1960, pp. 28–46. Trans. from the German typescript by H. H. Gerth and Don Martindale.

(3) 'The Story-Teller: Reflections on the Works of Nicolai Leskov', *The Chicago Review*, no. 50, 1962, pp. 80–101. Trans. Harry Zohn.

(4) 'From "A Berlin Childhood"', *Art and Literature*, no. 4, 1965, pp. 37–45. Trans. Mary-Jo Leibowitz.

(5) *Illuminations: Essays and Reflections*, ed. Hannah Arendt. New York: Harcourt, Brace & World, 1968; London: Jonathan Cape 1970, Fontana 1992. Trans. Harry Zohn.
Preceded only by the four early translations listed above, this variously reprinted selection from *Schriften* (1955) remains the most important collection of Benjamin's essays in English to this day.

(6) *Charles Baudelaire: A Lyric Poet in the Era of High Capitalism*. London: NLB/Verso, 1973. Trans. Harry Zohn and Quintin Hoare. Translation of *Charles Baudelaire. Ein Lyriker im Zeitalter des Hochkapitalismus* (1969), supplemented by 'Paris, Capital of the Nineteenth Century'.

(7) 'Program for a Proletarian Children's Theatre', *Performance*, no. 5, 1973, pp. 28–32. Trans. Susan Buck-Morss.

(8) *Understanding Brecht*, London: NLB/Verso, 1973. Trans. Anya Bostock.

(9) 'Left Wing Melancholy (On Erich Kastner's New Book of Poems)', *Screen*, no. 2, 1974, pp. 28–32. Trans. Ben Brewster.

(10) 'Agesilaus Santander', in Gershom Scholem, *On Jews and Judaism in Crisis*. New York: Schocken, 1976. Trans. Werner Dannhäuser.
Presented and commented upon in the essay 'Walter Benjamin and His Angel'.

(11) *The Origin of German Tragic Drama*, introd. George Steiner, London: NLB/Verso; New York: Schocken, 1977. Trans. John Osborne.

(12) 'Rastelli narrates', in Carol Jacobs, *The Dissimulating Harmony: The Image of Interpretation in Nietzsche, Rilke, Artaud, and Benjamin*, Baltimore and London: Johns Hopkins University Press, 1978, pp. 117–19. Trans. Carol Jacobs.

(13) *Reflections: Essays, Aphorisms, Autobiographical Writings*, ed. Peter Demetz, New York and London: Harcourt Brace Jovanovich, 1978. Trans. Edmund Jephcott.
The original selection was again made by Hannah Arendt (†1975).

(14) *One-Way Street and Other Writings*, introd. Susan Sontag, London: NLB/Verso, 1979. Trans. Edmund Jephcott and Kingsley Shorter. British equivalent of Reflections, containing the first unabridged translation of Einbahnstraße and two additional essays, 'A Small History of Photography' and 'Eduard Fuchs, Collector and Historian', but none of the texts already included in (6) and (8).

(15) 'Doctrine of the Similar (1933)', *New German Critique*, no. 17, 1979, pp. 65–9. Trans. Knut Tarnowski.

(16) 'Theories of German Fascism: On the Collection of Essays "War and Warrior", edited by Ernst Jünger', *New German Critique*, no. 17, 1979, pp. 120–28. Trans. Jerolf Wikoff.

(17) 'A Radio Talk on Brecht', *NLR*, no. 123, 1980, pp. 92–6. Trans. David Fernbach.

(18) 'Goethe: The Reluctant Bourgeois', *NLR*, no. 133, 1982, pp. 69–93. Trans. Rodney Livingstone.

(19) 'N (Theoretics of Knowledge; Theory of Progress)', *The Philosophical Forum*, vol. 15, 1983/84, pp. 1–40. Trans. Leigh Hafrey and Richard Sieburth. The central section of 'Das Passagen-Werk'.

(20) 'Program of the Coming Philosophy', *The Philosophical Forum*, vol. 15, 1983/84, pp. 41 – 51. Trans. Mark Ritter.
Revised versions of (19) and (20) are included in *Benjamin: Philosophy, History, Aesthetics*, ed. Gary Smith, Chicago and London: University of Chicago Press, 1989.

(21) 'Socrates', *The Philosophical Forum*, vol. 15, 1983/84, pp. 52–4. Trans. Thomas Y. Levin.

(22) 'The Life of the Students', *A Jewish Journal at Yale*, no. 1, 1984, pp. 46–55. Trans. Ken Frieden.

(23) 'Central Park', *New German Critique*, no. 34, 1985, pp. 32–58. Trans. Lloyd Spencer, in collaboration with Mark Harrington.

(24) *Moscow Diary*, ed. Gary Smith, Cambridge, Mass. and London: Harvard University Press, 1986. Trans. Richard Sieburth.
Translation of *Moskauer Tagebuch*, with appendices slightly differing from those of the German edition. First published as a special issue of *October* (no. 35, 1985).

(25) 'Robert Walser', in *Robert Walser Rediscovered*, ed. Mark Harman, Amherst: University of Massachusetts Press, 1985, pp. 144–7. Trans. Mark Harman.

(26) 'Rigorous Study of Art', *October*, no. 47, 1988, pp. 84–90. Trans. Thomas Y. Levin.

(27) *The Correspondence of Walter Benjamin and Gershom Scholem, 1932–1940*, New York: Schocken, 1989. Cambridge, Mass. and London: Harvard University Press, 1992. Trans. Gary Smith and André Lefevre.

(28) 'Literary History and Literary Scholarship'; 'Traveling with Crime Novels'; 'Crisis of the Novel: On Döblin's "Berlin Alexanderplatz"', *Critical Texts*, no. 1, 1990, pp. 3–17. Trans. Delphine Bechtel.

(29) 'Lichtenberg: A Cross-Section', *Performing Arts Journal*, no. 42, 1992, pp. 37–56. Trans. Gerhard Schulte.

(30) *The Correspondence of Walter Benjamin, 1910–1940*, ed. Gershom Scholem and Theodor W. Adorno, Chicago and London:

University of Chicago Press, 1994. Trans. Manfred R. Jacobsen and Evelyn M. Jacobsen.

Translation of Briefe, the dated and rather ill-reputed German collection of 1966, supplemented by all of Benjamin's letters to Scholem from (27). Cf. also Theodor Adorno: 'Correspondence with Benjamin', *NLR*, no. 81, 1973, pp. 55–80. Trans. by Harry Zohn. Reprinted in Theodor Adorno, Walter Benjamin et al., *Aesthetics and Politics*, ed. Rodney Livingstone, Perry Anderson and Francis Mulhern, London: NLB/Verso, 1977, pp. 110–41.

Secondary Literature in English

Over the last two decades, a vast amount has been written on Walter Benjamin. What follows, therefore, is only a very limited choice of easily available books and essay collections in English. For more detail, see (a) Momme Brodersen, *Walter Benjamin: Bibliografia critica generale (1913–1983)*, Palermo: Centro internazionale studi di estetica, 1984; (b) *Literatur über Walter Benjamin. Kommentierte Bibliographie 1983–1992*, ed. Reinhard Markner and Thomas Weber, Hamburg: Argument, 1993.

(1) 'The Actuality of Walter Benjamin', *New Formations*, no. 20, 1993. Edited by Laura Marcus and Lynda Nead. Contains essays by Zygmunt Bauman, Andrew Benjamin, Susan Buck-Morss, Victor Burgin, Axel Honneth, Martin Jay, Julian Roberts, Gillian Rose, Sigrid Weigel, Irving Wohlfarth and Janet Wolff.

(2) Agamben, Giorgio, *Infancy and History: Essays on the Destruction of Experience*, London and New York: Verso, 1993. Trans. Liz Heron. Contains two essays on Benjamin.

(3) Alter, Robert, *Necessary Angels: Tradition and Modernity in Kafka, Benjamin and Scholem*, Cambridge, Mass.: Harvard University Press, 1991.

(4) Benjamin, Andrew (ed.), *The Problems of Modernity: Adorno and Benjamin*, London and New York: Routledge, 1989, 2nd edn 1991. Contains essays on Benjamin by Andrew Benjamin, John Rignall, Irving Wohlfarth and Janet Wolff.

(5) Benjamin, Andrew, and Peter Osborne (eds), *Walter Benjamin's Philosophy: Destruction and Experience*, London and New York: Routledge, 1994. Contains essays by Andrew Benjamin, Howard Caygill, Rebecca Comay, Alexander García Düttmann, Rodolphe Gasché, Werner Hamacher, Gertrud Koch, John Kraniauskas, Peter Osborne, and Irving Wohlfarth.

(6) Buck-Morss, Susan, *The Dialectics of Seeing: Walter Benjamin and the Arcades Project*, Cambridge, Mass. and London: MIT Press, 1989.

(7) Cohen, Margaret, *Profane Illumination: Walter Benjamin and the Paris of Surrealist Revolution*, Berkeley and London: University of California Press, 1993.

(8) 'Commemorating Walter Benjamin', *Diacritics*, nos. 3 – 4, 1992. Introduction by Ian Balfour. Contains essays by Eduardo Cadava, Christopher Fynsk, Fritz Gutbrodt, Anselm Haverkamp, Fredric Jameson, Elissa Marder, Rainer Nägele, Samuel Weber, and Irving Wohlfarth.

(9) Eagleton, Terry, *Walter Benjamin, or Towards a Revolutionary Criticism*, London: NLB/Verso, 1981, 2nd edn 1985.

(10) Geyer-Ryan, Helga, *Fables of Desire: Studies in the Ethics of Art and Gender*, Cambridge: Polity Press, 1994.
Contains three essays on Benjamin.

(11) Jennings, Michael W., *Dialectical Images: Walter Benjamin's Theory of Literary Criticism*, Ithaca and London: Cornell University Press, 1987.

(12) Löwy, Michael, *On Changing the World: Essays in Political Philosophy from Karl Marx to Walter Benjamin*, Atlantic Highlands, NJ: Humanities Press, 1992.
Contains four essays on Benjamin.

(13) McCole, John, *Walter Benjamin and the Antinomies of Tradition*, Ithaca and London: Cornell University Press, 1993.

(14) Mehlman, Jeffrey, *Walter Benjamin for Children: An Essay on his Radio Years*, Chicago and London: University of Chicago Press, 1993.

(15) Missac, Pierre, *Walter Benjamin's Passage*, Cambridge, Mass. and London: MIT Press, 1995. Trans. Shierry W. Nicholsen.

(16) *Modern Language Notes*, vol. 106, 1991, no. 3.
Contains in a special section on Benjamin essays by Ian Balfour, Alexander García Düttmann, Fritz Gutbrodt, Rainer Nägele, Thomas Schestag and Samuel Weber, and a review essay by Henry Pickford.

(17) 'Walter Benjamin (1892–1940)', *Modern Language Notes*, vol. 107, 1992, no. 3.
Contains essays by Carrie-Lee Asman, Eva Geulen, Helga Geyer-Ryan, Philippe Lacoue-Labarthe, Arne Melberg, Beryl Schlossman, Hent de Vries and Heiner Weidmann.

(18) Nägele, Rainer, ed., *Benjamin's Ground: New Readings of Walter Benjamin*, Detroit: Wayne State University Press, 1988.
Contains essays by Timothy Bahti, Rodolphe Gasché, Werner Hamacher, Rainer Nägele, Avital Ronell, Beryl Schlossman and David E. Wellbery.

(19) Nägele, Rainer, *Theater, Theory, Speculation: Walter Benjamin and the Scenes of Modernity*, Baltimore and London: Johns Hopkins University Press, 1991.

(20) 'Special Walter Benjamin Issue', *New German Critique*, no. 17, 1979.
Contains essays by Philip Brewster, Carl Howard Buchner, R.G. Davis, Jürgen Habermas, Ansgar Hillach, Anson Rabinbach and Irving Wohlfarth, and a bibliography by Gary Smith.

(21) 'Second Special Walter Benjamin Issue', *New German Critique*, no. 39, 1986.
Contains essays by Susan Buck-Morss, Marcus Bullock, Wolfgang Fietkau, Philippe Ivernel, Chryssoula Kambas, Heinz Dieter Kittsteiner, Burkhardt Lindner, Bernd Witte and Irving Wohlfarth.

(22) Scheurmann, Ingrid and Konrad, eds: *On Walter Benjamin*, Bonn: Arbeitskreis selbständiger Kultur-Institute e.V. and Inter Nationes. Trans. Timothy Nevill.

(23) Scholem, Gershom, *Walter Benjamin: The Story of a Friendship*, Philadelphia: Jewish Publications Society of America, 1981; London: Faber and Faber, 1982. Trans. Harry Zohn.

(24) Smith, Gary, ed., *On Walter Benjamin: Critical Essays and Recollections*, Cambridge, Mass. and London: MIT Press, 1988.
Contains texts by Theodor W. Adorno, Ernst Bloch, Hans Robert Jauß, Jürgen Habermas, Pierre Klossowski, Hans Mayer, Pierre

Missac, Charles Rosen, Hans Sahl, Gershom Scholem, Hermann Schweppenhäuser, Jean Selz, Peter Szondi, Rolf Tiedemann and Irving Wohlfarth, and a bibliography by Gary Smith.

(25) Smith, Gary, ed., *Benjamin: Philosophy, History, Aesthetics*, Chicago and London: University of Chicago Press, 1989.
Contains essays by Theodor W. Adorno, Leo Löwenthal, Stéphane Mosès, Sándor Radnóti, Richard Sieburth, Gary Smith, Joey Snyder, Rolf Tiedemann, Jennifer Todd and Richard Wolin.

(26) 'Walter Benjamin on Romanticism', *Studies in Romanticism*, vol. 31, 1992, no. 4. Ed. David Ferris.
Contains essays by David Ferris, Rodolphe Gasché, Carol Jacobs, Philippe Lacoue-Labarthe and Tom McCall.

(27) Wiggershaus, Rolf, *The Frankfurt School: Its History, Theories, and Political Significance*, Cambridge, Mass. and London: MIT Press, 1994. Trans. Michael Robertson.
Contains a chapter on Benjamin.

(28) Witte, Bernd, *Walter Benjamin: An Intellectual Biography*, Detroit: Wayne State University Press, 1991. Trans. James Rolleston.

(29) Wolin, Richard, *Walter Benjamin: An Aesthetic of Redemption*, 2nd edn with a new preface, Berkeley and London: University of California Press, 1994.

319

Index

Picture acknowledgements

Michael Neumann, Berlin: 2, 3, 6
Ullstein Bilderdienst: 77, 165, 197, 249, 253
Momme Brodersen: 7, 27
Hilde Benjamin, 'Georg Benjamin': 11, 70, 178, 196, 208
Günther Anders: 12
Eva Michaelis: 16
'Hundert Jahre Deutschland 1870–1970, Bilder, Texte,
    Dokumente', Munich 1969: 17
Universitäts-Archiv Frankfurt: 18
Bettina Schulz: 31
Archiv der deutschen Jugendbewegung: 24, 35, 40, 59, 60
Walter Benjamin, 'Gesammelte Schriften': 34
Albert-Ludwigs-Universität: 38
Stadtarchiv Freiburg: 39
Deutsche Presse-Agentur: 47
Deutsche Akademie der Wissenschaften: 47
Deutsches Literaturarchiv Marbach: 53, 70, 82, 117, 130,
    137, 173, 207, 218
Bernfeld-Archiv, Ulrich Herrmann: 55
Freideutscher Jugendverlag: 61
Stadtbibliothek Vienna: 187
Gertrud Breysig: 'Kurt Breysig. Ein Bild des Menschen': 71
Gershom Scholem: 'Von Berlin nach Jerusalem': 77
Marga Noeggerath: 85, 195, 210
Netty Kellner: 96, 117
Karola Bloch: 100
Carola Giedion-Welcker, Paul Klee, Stuttgart 1954: 118
Bundesbildstelle: 120
Stadtarchiv Frankfurt: 133, 157
Universität Frankfurt: 134
Universitätsbibliothek Bonn: 148
Touring Club Italiano: 136
Centro Capresse Ignazio Cerio: 137
Archivo Teodoro Pagano, Capri: 138
Archiv Asja Lacis: 140
Zeitschrift 'alternative', 1968: 163
Gisèle Freund: 171, 221, 233, 234, 235, 243

Das Illustrierte Blatt, 1929: 177
Akademie der Kunst der DDR, Benjamin-Archiv: 183, 185, 211, 246
Hessischer Rundfunk, Dokumentation und Archiv, Historisches Archiv: 192
Landesbildstelle Berlin: 193
Horkheimer-Archiv: 199
Wilhelm Emrich: 200
Archiv Jean Selz: 210, 211
Stadtbibliothek Munich: 214
Mogens Voltelen: 219
Edita Koch: 224
S. Fischer Bildarchiv: 225
Jewish National Library Jerusalem: 97, 126, 127, 169, 239
Leo Baeck Institute: 242
Deutsche Bibliothek Frankfurt: 244, 247
Revue de la Bibliothèque Nationale, 1983: 248
Deutsches Allgemeines Sonntagsblatt: 255
Helga Niemeyer: 258, 259
Paul Raabe: 'Die Autoren und Bücher des literarischen Expressionismus', Stuttgart 1985: 59, 69, 74, 77, 99
Bertolt-Brecht-Archiv Berlin: 186
R. Mensing, courtesy of Dr Konrad Scheurmann: 260, 263
Bildarchiv Preußischer Kulturbesitz, Berlin: Frontispiece, 15, 67, 90, 203, 226
Germaine Krull/Fotografische Sammlung, Museum Folkwang, Essen: 167
International Benjamin Foundation, Amsterdam: 205